East Asi

M000303288

Series editors
Yasue Kuwahara
Department of Communication
Northern Kentucky University
Highland Heights, KY, USA

John A. Lent
Temple University
School of Communication and Theater
Philadelphia, PA, USA

This series focuses on the study of popular culture in East Asia (referring to China, Hong Kong, Japan, Mongolia, North Korea, South Korea, and Taiwan) in order to meet a growing interest in the subject among students as well as scholars of various disciplines. The series examines cultural production in East Asian countries, both individually and collectively, as its popularity extends beyond the region. It continues the scholarly discourse on the recent prominence of East Asian popular culture as well as the give and take between Eastern and Western cultures.

More information about this series at
http://www.palgrave.com/gp/series/14958

Steven T. Brown

Japanese Horror and the Transnational Cinema of Sensations

palgrave
macmillan

Steven T. Brown
Department of Comparative Literature
University of Oregon
Eugene, OR, USA

East Asian Popular Culture
ISBN 978-3-319-88969-6   ISBN 978-3-319-70629-0   (eBook)
https://doi.org/10.1007/978-3-319-70629-0

Cover illustration: © GarryKillian/Shutterstock.com

Printed on acid-free paper

This Palgrave Macmillan imprint is published by Springer Nature
The registered company is Springer International Publishing AG
The registered company address is: Gewerbestrasse 11, 6330 Cham, Switzerland

For my dog Guinness, who never complains when I watch
yet another horror movie

Acknowledgments

I wish to thank my colleagues in Comparative Literature for their generous support and feedback during the writing of this study, especially Katya Hokanson, Jenifer Presto, Ken Calhoon, Lisa Freinkel, Leah Middlebroook, Michael Allan, and Tze-Yin Teo. University of Oregon's Department of Comparative Literature prides itself on not simply tolerating but actively embracing nomads of every stripe, and I couldn't be happier to be among my fellow "nomadologists." Special thanks to Cynthia Stockwell for providing logistical support that enabled me to conduct research in Japan in 2015 during an especially critical juncture.

A huge "thank you" to Akira Lippit and Tom Mes for their very generous endorsements of this study. It is difficult to put into words how much I appreciate their supportive remarks, especially since I have learned so much from these two luminaries of Japanese film scholarship over the years.

Very special thanks to Gordon Stainforth for answering my questions about the complex multilayering techniques he applied to the editing of the soundtrack for *The Shining*, as well as making available a high-resolution image of a working music chart from the film, which has been reproduced in Chap. 2 in the context of my discussion of sonic palimpsests. Mr. Stainforth is one of the most innovative and influential music editors in the history of cinema, and his work deserves a monograph of its own!

I would also like to thank organizers Dan O'Neill and Miri Nakamura and fellow participants of the "Asian Horror Cinema and Beyond" symposium held at Berkeley in 2011 for their enthusiastic responses and constructive feedback to my research on J-horror sound design. Sincere thanks are also due to Daisuke Miyao, Colleen Laird, Michael Stern, David Browne, Trace Cabot, Nick Hoffman, and Eugene Seock for responding to my (sometimes) unexpected queries and nascent brainstorming about Japanese and Asian horror cinema at various stages of this study's errant genealogy. I am also indebted to the hundreds of students who have taken my seminars on Japanese and Asian horror cinema over the years, who never cease to amaze me with their critical insights and fearless questions.

I also owe a debt of gratitude to the Oregon Humanities Center for awarding me with a Vice President for Research and Innovation Completion Award that provided essential release time from teaching and administrative responsibilities so that I could focus my attention on completing and revising the entire manuscript. I cannot thank the Humanities Center enough for all its support. In an era when critical thinking is increasingly under siege by the ideologues of alternative facts, the Oregon Humanities Center offers a much-needed oasis.

Portions of Chap. 2 appeared previously in a special issue of *Horror Studies* devoted to "sonic horror" in an article titled "Ambient Horror: From Sonic Palimpsests to Haptic Sonority in the Cinema of Kurosawa Kiyoshi," *Horror Studies* vol. 7, no. 2 (Autumn 2016): 253–273. I am grateful to Steven Bruhm and Intellect Ltd. for permission to incorporate and expand upon this earlier research.

I am grateful to the two external reviewers of my book manuscript for their perspicacious criticism and constructive advice. I also wish to thank my editor at Palgrave, Shaun Vigil, for helping shepherd the manuscript through the publication process, along with his assistant, Glenn Ramirez. It is always a pleasure to work with Palgrave's very professional and conscientious staff.

Finally, I want to thank my family for all their support over the years, especially Verlin and Maryanne Brown, Carrie and Ken Wallyn (and family), William and Kay Hokanson, and Jon Hokanson and Jocelyn Worrall (and family). Time spent with family at Lake Kegonsa

(Stoughton, Wisconsin) and Corey Lake (Three Rivers, Michigan), as well as in far-flung places around the world, has been more precious than words can describe, providing much-needed breaks from the daily routine and allowing me to collect my thoughts (and "convalesce" in a Nietzschean sense) when I most needed to do so.

Most of all, I wish to thank my wife Katya and son Gabe, who have indulged my fascination with Japanese horror cinema for decades and with whom I have had numerous thought-provoking discussions late into the night about its subtleties. No matter how scary the world may seem at times, Katya and Gabe provide the bedrock that gives me hope for the future.

Note on Japanese Names and Words. In the text, Japanese names are typically given in Japanese word order (unless they have been Anglicized)—that is, surname first and given name second. All Japanese words have been transliterated according to the modified Hepburn system of romanization used in *Kenkyūsha's New Japanese-English Dictionary*, except in cases in which there are already accepted English spellings.

Contents

List of Figures

1

Introduction

Ah, yes, "J-Horror"; everyone knows its tropes by now: vengeful
ghosts, long stringy black hair, impossible physical gymnastics,
meowing little ghost boys, cursed videos (or cell phones or computers),
old rotted buildings and corpses, moldy books and newspapers,
elliptical storylines (or a total abandonment of logic),
creepy sound design, and creepy cinematography.

—Nicholas Rucka[1]

What Was J-Horror?

J-horror is dead, long live J-horror! In an article titled "The Death of
J-Horror?" that was published in 2005 on the once highly acclaimed but
now (sadly) retired *Midnight Eye* website, Nicholas Rucka surveyed the
state of the art with respect to Japanese horror cinema and concluded that
the spate of J-horror film and video releases that had flooded the market in
recent years lacked the creative spark of earlier, more groundbreaking films.
In response, Rucka made a strong appeal to Japanese filmmakers and producers "to work in a creative manner and put an end to the obsessive

© The Author(s) 2018   **1**
S. T. Brown, *Japanese Horror and the Transnational Cinema of Sensations*,
East Asian Popular Culture, https://doi.org/10.1007/978-3-319-70629-0_1

sequel-making and regurgitation of the *shinrei-mono eiga* ('ghost film') that is dragging down Japanese film (and Hollywood horror for that matter)."[2] If J-horror was already running out of steam at the time that Rucka penned his essay in 2005, the intervening years have shown few signs of revival. Indeed, few would disagree that by the time the crossover experiments started to appear—such as in the critically panned *Sadako vs. Kayako* (dir. Shiraishi Kôji, 2016), a mashup of the *Ringu-Ju-on* franchises—it was a clear sign that the "J-horror" brand was not simply in its final death throes—it was already dead, if not yet buried. However, rather than pounding the final nail into its coffin, I would contend that it is precisely when the J-horror boom has finally run out of box office steam that the time is ripe for a critical reassessment.

Just over 25 years have passed since the origins of modern J-horror first emerged—coinciding not with Nakata Hideo's *Don't Look Up* (*Joyūrei*, 1996) or *Ring* (*Ringu*, 1998), as is often claimed, but rather with Director Tsuruta Norio's straight-to-video anthology, *Scary True Stories* (*Hontō ni atta kowai hanashi*, 1991–1992).[3] That V-Cinema anthologies such as *Scary True Stories* mark the true beginnings of the J-horror movement is the opinion of no less an authority than Takahashi Hiroshi, the screenwriter responsible for numerous J-horror classics—most notably the original *Ringu* trilogy that garnered so much attention around the turn of the millennium.[4] In a fascinating and sometimes contentious interview, Takahashi challenged accepted wisdom about the genealogy of J-horror and reaffirmed the movement's transnational hybridity. Conducted in connection with Takahashi's role as the series supervisor for the "Horror Banchō" (2004) series of which *Marebito* (dir. Shimizu Takashi, 2004) was a part,[5] Takahashi reflected on the early beginnings of the "J-horror" genre before it became a globally recognized brand at a time when directors such as Tsuruta Norio and screenwriters such as Konaka Chiaki were just starting to make "true ghost stories" (*shinrei jitsuwa*) for the straight-to-video V-Cinema market. "True ghost stories" (*shinrei jitsuwa*), or "real ghost stories" (*jitsuwa kaidan*) as they are sometimes called, are a particular subgenre of the *kaidan* ghost storytelling tradition set in everyday settings that exemplify many of the narrative traits associated with legends, whether urban or rural: e.g., like legends, true ghost stories purport "to relate something that actually happened, an event which occurred in the same world in which the teller and listener live, but which took place in front of others (often the friend of a friend, in the case of modern 'urban' legends, or a deceased relative in the older ones)."[6] Indeed, the connection between the two is made even stronger by the fact that, as Takahashi has acknowledged, many true ghost stories were actually inspired by urban legends circulating around Japan in the 1980s and 1990s that were collected and popularized in a range of successful publications and television dramatizations that fueled pop cultural interest in the paranormal.[7] Moreover, "unlike the folktale, which is clearly fiction," the legendary narratival form of true ghost stories uses "details and a convincing style to create a lifelike account," so that, as folklorists Iwasaka Michiko and Barre Toelken point out, "even when the teller is not entirely convinced of the 'facts,' the story will be narrated as if it could be true, as if it were being held up for verification—or at least serious scrutiny."[8] In a wide-ranging interview on the genealogy of J-horror, Takahashi acknowledged that

> The nature of this Original Video cinema movement was that it was extremely low-budget. How to make movies without spending money was the question. The other question was: "What is really scary?" "What is a truly scary movie?" We used to discuss that amongst ourselves. As expected, it was ghosts. For example, we could make it as an urban legend and make it feel like a "true ghost story" [*shinrei jitsuwa*]. We gathered many details of true ghost stories and pursued making them visually realistic as a method. In horror movies prior to that, for example, a ghost appears. But for many people, what is scary about a ghost is that it attacks you. They are scary because they attack people. That's how it's depicted. However, we didn't show the attack. We didn't think that way. The presence of a ghost is what is scary. It's scary just standing there. That shot was the challenge. That was our way of thinking. The taste for "true ghost stories" is what we called it amongst ourselves. That's how we approached making movies.
>
> In my movies—those that I wrote, such as *Don't Look Up* [*Joyūrei*] and *Ring* [*Ringu*]—this [taste for true ghost stories] was well received in America and Europe. For Mr. Kurosawa [Kiyoshi], it was *Séance* [*Kōrei*, 1999] and *Pulse* [*Kairo*, 2001b]. That kind of expression became popular overseas. I think it was interpreted as the "Japanese taste" and spread as "J-horror," but we don't think of it as "Japanese" by any means. On the contrary, this type of "true ghost story" was first done in British ghost movies and

American ghost movies, such as Robert Wise's *The Haunting* [1963]. So the "J" for "Japanese" makes me a little uneasy. In fact, this type of expression is the result of pursuing the reality of what is really scary. That's basically it.[9]

Regardless of its putative origins in Japanese folklore and performing arts traditions, it is noteworthy that Takahashi pointedly resists positioning J-horror as authentically "Japanese." Here Takahashi's uneasiness is one that is shared by Donald Kirihira, who has openly questioned the Orientalist traps that Western scholars of Japanese film have sometimes fallen prey to when they assume that "Japanese film is different because of its isolation," or "Japanese cinema is different because the creators (and to a lesser extent, the viewers) have a different aesthetic sense."[10] Rather than insisting on the cultural authenticity of J-horror, Takahashi questions its "Japaneseness" by underscoring the connections it has to world horror cinema, especially American and British horror movies from the 1960s and 1970s. Moreover, as Jasper Sharp has noted, it is precisely because J-horror does not limit itself to "Japanese-specific fears" that the films have appealed to international audiences and J-horror producers such as Ichise Takashige have been "so successful at specifically targeting" such audiences.[11] Likewise, other scholars, such as Steffen Hantke and Andrew Dorman, have suggested that J-horror's "lack of distinctive cultural features" and "generic blandness" have contributed significantly to its international success.[12] In short, it is the transnational hybridity of J-horror that has enabled the films to travel so well for so long.

Somewhat surprised by Takahashi's questioning of the "Japaneseness" of J-horror, the interviewer pressed him further, asking if it is not also the case that J-horror is "a reflection of Japanese society, of Japanese reality?" To this Takahashi responds in a way that both acknowledges the cultural specificity of Japanese horror while continuing to insist upon its transnational hybridity:

> We create fiction in the environment in which we live. So I think Japanese society is reflected. So let's say, for example, a "well" appears. This is Japanese. I don't think it's the case that for an American or European the well will trigger scary thoughts. And with ghosts, when a woman wearing white with long black hair appears, I hear that people point their fingers

and yell "*Ju-on!*" But I don't think female ghosts clothed in white are exclusive to Japan. It's a scary image that frequently appears in American ghost stories. I think I'm doing something commonplace. I don't think it means that anything typically Japanese is being received [*Nihontekina mono o uketeiru to iu wake de wa nai to omou desu ne*]. It's just that the Japanese incorporated and developed this direction in the '90s.... The "J-horror" moniker stuck. It started to sell to a large market. Those of us who'd been doing it do feel uneasy about it. But as I said earlier, in the beginning, it was to make it really scary, truly scary [*shinko ni kowai*].

After seeing the movie and going home—being alone in one's room and becoming scared—there's a sensation of dread that stays with one [*ato ni tsuzukeru kyōfukan*]. To create an encroaching sensation of dread through a movie—that was the objective. But after all, to have the masses understand and receive scariness as something that does not leave an aftertaste—to surprise—I do feel that a paradigm shift is occurring toward shock value. In other words, there are often scenes that shock and surprise. Everybody goes, "Yahh!" The audience says, "That was scary!" and goes home. If you ask us, that was just surprising people. I feel people consume a certain level of entertainment, go home, and forget about it. I think the horror boom is leaning towards the "surprise" kind of entertainment as a product. This makes me feel a little uneasy. I do want to return the paradigm toward the truly scary [*shinko ni kowai*]."[13]

Without denying the importance of Japanese practices of ghost storytelling, Takahashi resists the nativist foundation myth of J-horror by resituating it as a hybrid form of cinema that combines a particular subgenre of the *kaidan* tradition known as "true ghost stories" with elements drawn from non-Japanese cinematic traditions. Although Takahashi singles out Robert Wise's *The Haunting* (1963), many other films could easily be added to the list of influences he has in mind, including *The Uninvited* (dir. Lewis Allen, 1944), *House on Haunted Hill* (dir. William Castle, 1959), *The Innocents* (dir. Jack Clayton, 1961), *Don't Look Now* (dir. Nicolas Roeg, 1973), *The Legend of Hell House* (dir. John Hough, 1973), *The Changeling* (dir. Peter Medak, 1980), and *The Shining* (dir. Stanley Kubrick, 1980). Indeed, as I hope to show in this study, the transcultural interchange between Japanese horror and world horror is hardly limited to Anglophone ghost movies.[14]

In previous studies of Japanese horror cinema, the transnational has often been construed in terms of remakes and adaptations. This is the approach taken in notable studies by Wee, Honisch, Herbert, Balmain, Kalat, and Dorman in relation to the numerous Hollywood remakes of J-horror classics that have sought to capitalize on their popularity for Anglophone audiences, including such films as *The Ring* (dir. Gore Verbinski, 2002), *The Grudge* (dir. Shimizu Takashi, 2004), *Dark Water* (dir. Walter Salles, 2005), *Pulse* (dir. Jim Sonzero, 2006), and *One Missed Call* (dir. Eric Valette, 2008).[15] However, another way to approach the transnational is in the sense suggested by Takahashi in relation to the global microflows that have cross-fertilized Japanese horror and greatly complexified how one situates the "J" in "J-horror." First and foremost, this means recontextualizing Japanese horror in terms of world horror cinema as a strategy that avoids the isolationist traps and shortcomings outlined by Kirihira. Here I have also benefited from Lúcia Nagib's redefinition of world cinema away from a center-periphery model towards a conception of cinema as "a global process" without center: "World cinema, as the world itself, is circulation. World cinema is not a discipline, but a method, a way of cutting across film history according to waves of relevant films and movements, thus creating flexible geographies."[16]

Jay McRoy has attempted something similar in relation to Shimizu Takashi's *Ju-on: The Grudge* (*Ju-on*; 2002), but stops short of extending such an approach to Japanese horror, more generally. In an otherwise perceptive interpretation of *Ju-on: The Grudge*, McRoy underscores the film's "transcultural hybridity": "*Ju-on: The Grudge* is a curious filmic hybrid, combining carefully chosen aesthetic trappings of western— particularly US—horror films with visual and narrative tropes long familiar to fans of Japanese horror cinema....By combining, in his own words, 'an American and Japanese style' of horror cinema, Shimizu creates a hybrid of the US slasher film and the Japanese *kaidan*."[17] I agree with McRoy's analysis of *Ju-on*'s hybridity, but disagree with his conclusion that such hybridity is "what sets *Ju-on: The Grudge* apart from other works of Japanese horror cinema."[18] As I try to show in this study (and this also seems to be Takahashi's point), contemporary J-horror has been characterized by transnational hybridity from its very inception—its origins were already split, already doubled, at the outset. Directors such as Shimizu Takashi did not add hybridity to a cinematic form that previously lacked it, but simply took it in a new direction.

A significant part of the critical reassessment undertaken by this study will be to resituate selected films exemplifying J-horror's transnational hybridity in relation to the larger networks of global cultural flows, including major and minor areas of influence, intermedial intersections, and cross-fertilizations. In this study, I have sought to place Japanese horror in dialogue not only with notable exemplars from world horror cinema, ranging from *The Student of Prague* (*Der Student von Prag*; dirs. Hanns Heinz Ewers and Stellan Rye, 1913) to *The Invisible Man* (dir. James Whale, 1933), from *Suspiria* (dir. Dario Argento, 1977) to *The Shining* (dir. Stanley Kubrick, 1980), from *The Exorcist* (dir. William Friedkin, 1973) to *Oldboy* (dir. Park Chan-wook, 2003), but also in relation to the transnational intermedial flows that connect Japanese horror to non-Japanese works of art, literature, folklore, and music. Previous studies have offered J-horror surveys,[19] but *Japanese Horror and the Transnational Cinema of Sensations* sets out to do something different. Neither a conventional film history nor simply a thematic survey of Japanese horror cinema, what this study offers instead is transnational analysis of selected films from new angles that shed light on previously ignored aspects of the genre that have nevertheless resonated with audiences around the world. In Chaps. 2, 3, and 4, I discuss primarily Japanese films that are contextualized transnationally, whereas in the fifth chapter, I turn to a comparison of Japanese and Korean horror films.

The Subject of "Resonance"

In addition to his repeated calls for a thorough recontextualization of J-horror in terms of its connections to world horror cinema, Takahashi also offers compelling insights into what makes Japanese horror scary. For Takahashi, the scare effects created by Japanese horror are less about shock and surprise and more about the persistence of dread-filled affect. As scholars of horror affect such as Robert Spadoni have suggested, dread relies heavily on atmospherics that are characterized by diffuseness (it is less object-oriented than fear), the ambience of background settings (not only "the indiscriminate off-screen noises that can constitute a sonic backdrop for the shadowy contents of the frame," but also those blurred movements on the periphery of the frame or just barely glimpsed reflections on the surfaces of the mise-en-scène), as well as a sense of anticipatory fear that causes viewers to experience duration as "thick, enveloping, [and] saturating," with a mode of temporality that "swells up and distends."[20] To create a "sensation of dread that stays with one [*ato ni tsuzukeru kyōfukan*]," as Takahashi describes it—a feeling that continues afterward, persisting long after the movie has ended—is to develop an aesthetics of resonance.[21] In addition to resituating how we conceive of Japanese horror by attending to its transnational hybridity in relation to world horror cinema, this study also investigates the techniques by which Japanese horror develops a cinema of sensations that resonates with viewers by filling them with atmospherically enhanced dread along with a range of other moods and intensities that are situated along the continuum of horror affects. Since the concept of "resonance" plays an important role in my analysis, a brief history of the term is probably in order.

In his illuminating essay for Jean-François Augoyard and Henry Torgue's encyclopedic *Sonic Experience: A Guide to Everyday Sounds*, architect Jean Dalmais defines "resonance" as follows:

> The resonance effect refers to the vibration, in air or through solids, of a solid element. The production of resonance requires a relatively high acoustic level and a concordance between the exciting frequency and the object put into vibration. Modal resonance refers to the phenomenon of standing waves in a three-dimensional space. Note in everyday language the term "resonance" includes any acoustically observable sonic effect, particularly reverberation. Resonance is a general physical phenomenon found in all periodic sinusoidal movements, particularly in mechanics, acoustics, optics, and electricity. The identity of the role of certain elements make it possible to perform studies by analogy, referring to a general system that includes the actual case of resonance at the sonic level.... Resonance, perceived as a prolongation and thus interpreted as an amplification, has also been described as being the origin of echo.[22]

The concept of "resonance"—derived etymologically from the Latin verb "*resonare*" (to sound again, resound, ring, re-echo)—is one that straddles numerous fields of study, including not only acoustics, mechanics, medicine, and optics, but also physics, astronomy, chemistry, and electronics. According to the *Oxford English Dictionary*, the primary sense of the term, which derives from Middle French usage that dates back to ca. 1365, involves "the reinforcement or prolongation of sound by reflection or by the synchronous vibration of a surrounding space or a neighbouring object," as well as the sound or "quality of sound" that results from this.[23] It is in this sense that resonance has long been one of the basic principles of musical instrument construction and reception. As Dalmais points out, whether it is the transfer of energy "from the vibrating string to the body" of the instrument, which is "constructed of plates, all of which have characteristic frequencies due to the resonance of the wood and the enclosed air space," or the transfer of energy from the musical instrument to the surrounding air and place in which the instrument is performed, such as a concert hall with its own acoustic characteristics, resonance typically involves "the transformation of mechanical energy into aerial vibrating energy through the intermediary of a 'resonating body,'" whose resonant qualities emphasize particular frequencies.[24] Even in modern electronic instruments, such as analog and digital synthesizers, the concept of "resonance" continues to be used to describe the "emphasized peak of a narrow band of frequencies."[25] By turning up the "resonance" (also known as "emphasis" or "Q") on such electronic instruments, a delimited range of frequencies (called "the resonance peak") near a synthesizer's filter cutoff frequency is thereby boosted, which produces tones "ranging from the song of a humpback whale to a squealing banshee."[26]

Authors of classical Latin texts, such as the architect Vitruvius (c. 80–70 BCE–c. 15 BCE), also employed the noun "*resonantia*" in the sense of "echo," "reverberation," or "a tendency to return sounds," but the modern sense of the term "resonance" does not begin to emerge until the fourteenth century, acquiring additional connotations in subsequent centuries.[27] For example, in the field of mechanical engineering, "resonance" has come to describe "the condition in which an oscillating or periodic force acting on an object or system has a frequency close to that of a natural vibration of the object," which results in the "amplification of the natural vibration."[28] In contrast to musical instrument builders who seek to enhance the acoustic resonance of the instruments they are constructing, one of the primary goals of mechanical engineering is to avoid the amplification of resonance since the vibrations produced by it may eventually lead to structural compromise.

In the field of medicine, doctors began to use the term "resonance" in the nineteenth-century to describe "the intensified sound heard during auscultation or percussion of the lungs or other part of the body that usually contains air or other elements capable of vibration," as well as "the degree of such intensification."[29] In this context, depending upon the quality of the sound heard, such resonance could be a sign of either health or pathology (e.g., if it was symptomatic of an abnormal collection of air or fluid). Likewise, the study of physiology has long recognized that, especially when confronted with low frequency effects, "the body as a whole can be considered as a group of spring-mass-damper subsystems" that is vulnerable to resonance effects such as motion sickness.[30]

In the field of physics since the mid-nineteenth century, "resonance" has designated "a condition in which a particle is subjected to an oscillating influence (such as an electromagnetic field) of such a frequency that a transfer of energy occurs or reaches a maximum," as well as the exchange of energy that may occur under such conditions.[31] In this context, "magnetic resonance" is the spectroscopic technique by means of which a particle transitions "between different quantum states when it is in the presence of a magnetic field and electromagnetic radiation of an appropriate frequency."[32]

However, as Dalmais points out, there is also a parallel history in which the term "resonance" is used by way of analogy. For example, since the late sixteenth century, "resonance" has also been used to suggest a "corresponding or sympathetic response"[33] at the affective level. In this context, it intimates the power or quality of "evoking or suggesting images, memories, and emotions," as well as allusions, connotations, and overtones.[34] Similarly, in Japanese *haikai* poetics of the Edo period, disciples of Matsuo Bashō (1644–1694) used the term "*hibiki*" (echo, reverberation, resonance) to describe the resonant overtones expressed in "hidden or subtle linkages between verses."[35] Such resonant overtones are also invoked in the arts, where the concept of resonance has been used by way of analogy to describe the "richness of colour, esp. that produced by proximity to a contrasting colour or colours."[36] In this sense, a resonant color is one that has been enhanced by means of its juxtaposition with a contrasting color, such as in the paintings of Titian (ca. 1488–1576), whose application of color exerted enormous influence on the Italian Renaissance and beyond and has been praised for the "resonance" that his paintings evoke by means of the juxtaposition of contrasting colors, such as the crimson and blue hues on display in a painting such as *Diana and Actaeon* (1556–1559).[37]

As Veit Erlmann has shown, the concept of resonance performs double duty in the seventeenth-century philosophy of René Descartes (1596–1650): "On the one hand the concept of resonance, having been derived from core epistemological virtues such as intuition, observation, and experiment, names the natural mechanism governing the interaction of vibrating matter, such as strings, nerves, and air. As such resonance is the 'Other' of the self-constituting Cartesian ego as it discovers the truth (of musical harmony, for instance) and reassures itself of its own existence as a thinking entity. On the other hand resonance names the very unity of body and mind that the cogitating ego must unthink before it uncovers the truth (of resonance, for example.)"[38] It is for this reason that, despite Descartes's well-known privileging of mind over body, Erlmann has argued "resonance is eminently suited to dissolve the binary of the materiality of things and the immateriality of signs," compelling us "to call into question the notion that the nature of things resides in their essence and that this essence can be exhausted by a sign, a discourse, or a logos."[39]

In a thought-provoking essay on "Listening" (*À l'écoute*),[40] contemporary philosopher Jean-Luc Nancy draws out this parallel history of "resonance" further in a discussion of the fundamental distinction between "listening" and "hearing." Nancy proposes a turn away from the phenomenological subject towards a "resonant subject" (*sujet résonant*), which would open itself up to "the resonance of being, or to being as resonance."[41] According to Nancy, this resonant subject is "perhaps no subject at all, except as the place of resonance [*le lieu de la résonance*], of its infinite tension and rebound, the amplitude of sonorous deployment and the slightness of its simultaneous redeployment——by which a voice is modulated in which the singular of a cry, a call, or a song vibrates by retreating from it (a 'voice': we have to understand what sounds from a human throat without being language, which emerges from an animal gullet or from any kind of instrument, even from the wind in the branches: the rustling toward which we strain or lend an ear).”[42] In other words, the resonant subject is not only “the subject of the listening or the subject who is listening [*le sujet de l'écoute ou le sujet à l'écoute*],” but also “the one who is ‘subject to listening’ in the sense that one can be ‘subject to’ unease, an ailment, or a crisis).”[43] It is here that the resonant subject—who is subject to listening—is listening “on the edge of meaning [*en bordure du sens*], or in an edgy meaning of extremity [*un sens de bord et d'extrémité*],” as Nancy suggests, “as if the sound were precisely nothing else than this edge, this fringe, this margin … not, however, as an acoustic phenomenon (or not merely as one) but as a resonant meaning [*sens réso-nant*], a meaning whose sense is supposed to be found in resonance, and only in resonance.”[44] Insofar as the resonant subject who is subject to listening may be rendered uneasy by the edgy vibrations received, it is a subject that is obviously ripe for horror. In other words, if the subject of horror is a resonant subject in Nancy's sense, perhaps the “edgy meaning of extremity” that it intimates is one whose sense is found in resonance and “and only in resonance.”[45]

Towards a Cinema of Sensations

Keeping in mind the various connotations of the term “resonance,” it is primarily from the perspective of the term's extended sense that I have approached the genre of Japanese horror and its “resonant subjects,” who are subject to the “edgy meaning of extremity” on the fringes. In this study, I argue that the senses of resonance specific to Japanese horror are produced by a “cinema of sensations.”[46] In their final collaboration together, titled *What is Philosophy?* (*Qu'est-ce que la philosophie?*) and published in 1991, philosophers Gilles Deleuze and Félix Guattari developed an aesthetics of sensation that applies no less to cinema than it does to painting, sculpture, or literature. From this perspective, cinema may be reconceived as the creation and preservation of a bloc of sensations, which consists of percepts and affects. “Percepts are no longer perceptions,” argue Deleuze and Guattari, “they are independent of a state of those who experience them.”[47] Instead of conceiving the percept as an object of perception or a mental representation of an external object, which is how the term has been defined traditionally in psychology and philosophy, Deleuze and Guattari underscore the percept's non-representational status as a perception that has been objectified into a sensation that stands independent of the observer. Likewise, according to Deleuze and Guattari, "Affects are no longer feelings or affections; they go beyond the strength of those who undergo them."[48] Like percepts, affects stand as independent sensations that are ready to act directly upon the nervous system, but have been separated from the subject in the act of their preservation in a work of art. As a compound of percepts and affects, the cinematic work of art is a "being of sensations" (*être de sensation*) that exists independently of not only the director, actors, and crew who created it but also the audiovisual spectators who watch it.[49] For Deleuze and Guattari, "As percepts, sensations are not perceptions referring to an object (reference)," but rather sensations that refer only to their own materiality. If the work of cinematic art is haunted by resemblance, "it is the percept or affect of the material itself," so much so that "it is difficult to say where in fact the material ends and sensation begins."[50]

What distinguishes cinema from other forms of art, such as painting, sculpture, or literature, are the methods and materials employed "to extract a bloc of sensations," "to wrest the percept from perceptions of objects and the states of a perceiving subject, to wrest the affect from affections as the transition from one state to another."[51] This is not to dismiss the affective subjectivity of characters on display in cinema (or the affective states of the audiovisual spectators responding to them)—far from it—but rather to insist that a film's characters can only exist as cinematic "beings of sensation" because they "are themselves part of the compound of sensations"[52] that is produced by cinema's sound-image machine. It is through the invention of new percepts and affects that are "outside of representation, and [are] premised upon the intensity of sensation[s]"[53] that cinema is able to "make us become with them," drawing audiovisual spectators into encounters with the compound of sensations experienced by characters on the screen of cinema's plane of immanence through its "set of movement-images," "collection of lines or figures of light," and "blocs of space-time."[54] As Barbara Kennedy puts it in her study *Deleuze and Cinema: The Aesthetics of Sensation* (2000), it is in this sense that we can think of the cinematic experience "not only as a representation of something with a 'meaning,' but also as an aesthetic assemblage, which moves, modulates and resonates with its audience or spectator through processes of molecularity. It connects. It works through affect, intensity and becoming—and ultimately through sensation, not necessarily through subjectivity, identity and representation."[55] It is here that we encounter "the materialism of a cinematic body that exists as matter," where film functions in Kennedy's words not simply "as an encoder of experience but as a modulator of experience" through an aesthetics of sensation.[56]

If, as Deleuze and Guattari suggest, it is the very definition of the percept itself "to make perceptible the imperceptible forces that populate the world, affect us, and make us become,"[57] then it is the sound-image machine of a film that raises "lived perceptions" to the level of percepts and "lived affections" to the level of affects in the cinematic work of art, thereby rendering invisible forces visible and inaudible forces audible.[58] The difference this makes is that the percepts and affects embodied by the characters and landscapes within a film are able to show dimensions unattainable by lived perceptions or lived affections. For example, as Deleuze and Guattari point out, "Percepts can be telescopic or microscopic, giving characters and landscapes giant dimensions as if they were swollen by a life that no lived perception can attain."[59] And it is not just scale that distinguishes percepts and affects from the phenomenology of lived perceptions and lived affections, but also their intensity, rhythm, and duration, as well as the zones of indetermination from which "nonhuman becomings" and "nonhuman landscapes" emerge.[60] According to Deleuze and Guattari, "art itself lives on these zones of indetermination" with their blocs of sensations that "vibrate, couple, or split apart."[61]

It is here that one encounters the "sensation of dread that stays with one [*ato ni tsuzukeru kyōfukan*]" that Takahashi singled out as one of the defining traits of Japanese horror cinema. In the chapters that follow, in an effort to draw out the percepts and affects that constitute Japanese horror's audiovisual "bloc of sensations," I pay particularly close attention to such zones of indetermination and the materialities of sensation that are produced by a wide range of cinematic techniques, both sonic and visual.[62] In Chap. 2, titled "Ambient Horror: From Sonic Palimpsests to Haptic Sonority in the Cinema of Kurosawa Kiyoshi," I explore how sound flows modulate affect and the noncognitive responses to the ambient horror films of Kurosawa Kiyoshi. Hardly any research has been done on sound design in Japanese horror, yet it remains one of the most productive means by which J-horror distinguishes itself from other forms of horror. Although Kurosawa himself eschews the label of J-horror specialist, there is no question that he has directed some of the most influential and critically esteemed films associated with the J-horror movement. As such, Kurosawa's films warrant an in-depth case study whose insights regarding sound design also apply to varying degrees to notable examples of Japanese horror by other directors ranging from Nakata Hideo to Tsuruta Norio, from Shimizu Takashi to Miike Takashi.

Through advanced spectral and surround field analysis and a careful consideration of elements such as the interrelations between noise and silence, the function of ambient drones and sonic palimpsests, and the status of the acousmatic voice, we gain a better understanding of how soundscapes contribute to the construction of horror as a space for what I call "haptic sonority." Haptic sonority is a liminal space that blurs the boundaries between the sonic and the tactile and compels us to bear witness to the ineluctable molecularity of sound waves vibrating our bodies as if they were resonance chambers. In horror cinema, such haptic sonority opens an intensive space where one does not so much hear sounds as one feels them in one's body in ways that are by turns bone-rattling, gut-wrenching, and hair-raising. It is here that film touches our bodies and invites us to enter into composition with the micropolitics of sound as resonant subjects in a "cinema of sensations."

In Chap. 3, titled "Double Trouble: Doppelgängers in Japanese Horror," drawing upon Deleuze's work in his *Cinema* books, I explore the concept of the frame (that which holds the compound of sensations in place), its distinctive traits, and the forms of framing encountered in J-horror films dealing with the figure of the doppelgänger (or double). Taking into consideration cultural expressions of the double that have appeared in literature, art, folklore, and film from around the world, I focus on the role of Japanese horror as a productive cultural medium for doubles—a topic that has received relatively little attention thus far in J-horror scholarship. As media theorist Friedrich Kittler and others have noted, from its very inception, cinema has been haunted by doubles through the "celluloid ghosts of the actors' bodies."[63] Analyzed both in terms of its evocations of the uncanny and with respect to the ghostly effects of the cinematic apparatus itself (with particular reference to the complex framing techniques employed to help visualize the unstable dynamics between self and double), this chapter investigates the figure of the doppelgänger primarily in relation to the J-horror films *Bilocation* (*Bairokēshon*; dir. Asato Mari, 2013) and *Doppelgänger* (*Dopperugengā*; dir. Kurosawa Kiyoshi, 2003). In a coda to the chapter, I also consider an instructive variation on the double in the form of conjoined twins in Miike Takashi's short film *Box*, which was included in the omnibus *Three … Extremes* (2004). Although conjoined twins are not simply equivalent to the doppelgänger, I argue that they exist along the same continuum as doubles, sharing similar codes, conventions, and problems, while also differing from doppelgänger narratives in some important respects.

For many viewers, one of the creepiest aspects of Nakata Hideo's 1998 J-horror classic *Ringu* is the montage sequence of the cursed videotape itself with its discontinuous imagery, which applies techniques borrowed from surrealist filmmakers to the genre of horror.[64] *Ringu* may be one of the most notable J-horror films to draw inspiration from surrealist cinema, but it is certainly not the only one to do so. In Chap. 4, titled "*Cinema Fou*: Surrealist Horror from *Face of Another* to *Gozu*," I analyze a pair of Japanese surrealist horror films situated in relation to the transnational and intermedial flows of international surrealist artistic production: viz., Teshigahara Hiroshi's *Face of Another* (*Tanin no kao*, 1966) and Miike Takashi's *Gozu* (*Gokudō kyōfu daigekijō: Gozu*, 2003). *Face of Another* is not, strictly speaking, an example of contemporary Japanese horror, but it is included here because it serves as a bridge that connects earlier Japanese surrealist filmmakers to contemporary J-horror directors, who have incorporated experimental surrealist filmmaking techniques and tropes into their films in often underappreciated ways. Although some scholars prefer to restrict surrealist cinema to the films made by members of the original Parisian Surrealist Group, including Luis Buñuel, Salvador Dalí, Antonin Artaud, René Clair, Germaine Dulac, and Man Ray, others have argued that surrealist cinema is not reducible to a single style, genre, movement, or period. As Maurice Blanchot writes in an essay titled "Le demain joueur" (Tomorrow at Stake), which was written shortly after the death of surrealism's founder André Breton in 1966, "One cannot speak of what was neither a system or a school, nor a movement of art or literature, but rather a pure practice of existence [*pure pratique d'existence*]" whose potential has yet to be fully realized. Blanchot's statement is provocative because surrealism has often been described as a school and movement in the past tense, if not a system per se. But what Blanchot tries to get us to see is that, although others may have spoken of surrealism in such terms, for Blanchot the history of surrealism does not tell the whole story, since surrealism is not merely a matter of the past, but is just as much a matter for the present and the future. It is in the sense offered by Blanchot's expanded conception of surrealism that, although not a part of the original Surrealist Group, I argue the two Japanese directors considered in this chapter are also heirs to that practice, albeit reconceived in the context of horror cinema.

In Chap. 5, titled "In the Wake of Artaud: Cinema of Cruelty in *Audition* and *Oldboy*," I tackle thorny debates in horror studies concerning the terms "torture porn" and "Asia Extreme." The term "torture porn" was first coined by film critic David Edelstein in 2006 to designate a subgenre of horror exemplified by films such as *Saw* (2004), *Hostel* (2005), and *The Devil's Rejects* (2005) that emphasize scenes of graphic, visceral violence and gore-filled imagery. Although some film scholars have sought to restrict the designation "torture porn" to a specific cycle of American horror films that they view as expressing anxieties in post-9/11 America involving the fear of terrorism and a profound ambivalence over the application of torture as a technique to secure information that would avoid further acts of terrorism, this does not explain why similar films involving explicit body horror produced outside of the US both before and after 9/11 have also found audiences. In other words, while American torture porn may engage post-9/11 concerns, torture porn may also be construed as a global subgenre of horror that predates 9/11, not just an American response to the "War on Terror" or a cinematic allegory for American historical trauma. However, the term "torture porn" is not without its detractors. An increasing number of film critics and theorists have begun to openly debate the value of the term, pointing out its many shortcomings. More often than not, the formulation "torture porn" functions simply as an expression of moral disapproval of the role of violence in horror rather than signaling anything significant about the genre itself. By attaching the term "porn" to horror films in which sex often plays much less of a role than violence, the term "torture porn" ends up creating more confusion than clarification.

Another term, "Asia Extreme," was first introduced by UK-based distribution company Tartan Films during a marketing campaign to sell violent Asian horror films around the globe between 1999 and 2008. Tartan Films presented "Asia Extreme" as "A New Breed of Extreme. Extreme Action. Extreme Passion. Extreme Horror." The problem with such marketing hype is that it often reduced films by diverse directors operating in different filmmaking contexts to a monolithic conception of Asian cinema that effaced their differences and cultural specificities in favor of an essentializing Orientalist stereotype that construed "extreme" Asian film as representing the inscrutable, violently irrational Orient. This is not to say that films categorized as belonging to the genre of Asian horror featuring stylized violence are unrelated, since such films frequently have transnational links with one another, freely borrowing styles, techniques, conventions, and imagery from one another, as well as from earlier horror films, both those produced across north and southeast Asia and outside of Asia altogether. However, acknowledging the transnational hybridity and linkages between such films, which reach out to one another across their national cinema boundaries, is quite different from reducing them all to the Orientalist marketing hype associated with Tartan Films' "Asia Extreme" series. In response to such debates, I consider two exemplary revenge horror films—the Japanese horror *Audition* (*Ōdishon*; dir. Miike Takashi, 1999) and the Korean horror *Oldboy* (*Oldeuboi*; dir. Park Chan-wook, 2003)—each of which offers engagements with graphic violence but was released before the American cycle of "torture porn" films. Rather than lumping them together with "torture porn" or "Asia Extreme," I develop the concept of "cinema of cruelty" as an alternative way of talking about how these unabashedly visceral horror films resonate with the aesthetics of sensation that Antonin Artaud developed in relation to the Theater of Cruelty.

Finally, in a conclusion titled "Envelopes of Fear—The Temporality of Japanese Horror," I resituate this study's findings in relation to questions of timing and temporality that are evoked by J-horror's cinema of sensations.

Taking into consideration the issue of timing understood not only as the duration of individual images and the durational relationships between and among images but also in terms of the concept of temporal envelopes with individual stages of attack, decay, sustain, and release, I bring this study to a close by reconceiving how the slow attack and long release times of J-horror's slow-burn style impact the affective dynamics of horror spectatorship.

Notes

1. Nicholas Rucka, "The Death of J-Horror?" *Midnight Eye*, December 22, 2005, http://www.midnighteye.com/features/the-death-of-j-horror/ (accessed March 14, 2017).
2. Ibid.
3. Nakata Hideo directed a follow-up anthology in the same series, titled *Scary True Stories: Curse, Death, & Spirit* (*Hontō ni atta kowai hanashi: Jushiryō*, 1992).
4. Takahashi provided screenplays for *Don't Look Up* (*Joyūrei*; dir. Nakata Hideo), *Ring* (*Ringu*; dir. Nakata Hideo, 1998), *Haunted School G* (*Gakkō no kaidan G*; dirs. Kurosawa Kiyoshi, Maeda Tetsu, and Shimizu Takashi, 1998), *Ring 2* (*Ringu 2*; dir. Nakata Hideo, 1999), *Ring 0* (*Ringu 0: Bāsudei*; dir. Tsuruta Norio, 2000), *Requiem from the Darkness* (*Kyōgoku Natsuhiko kōsetsu hyakumonogatari*; dir. Tonokatsu Hideki, 2003), *Kazuo Umezu's Horror Theater: Ambrosia* (*Umezu Kazuo: Kyōfu gekijō—Zesshoku*; dir. Itō Tadafumi, 2005), *Orochi: Blood* (*Orochi*; dir. Tsuruta Norio, 2008), and *The Sylvian Experiments* (*Kyōfu*; dir. Takahashi Hiroshi, 2010).
5. In addition to *Marebito*, other films included in the series were *Fateful* (*Unmei ningen*; dir. Nishiyama Yōichi, 2004), *Sodom the Killer* (*Sodomu no Ichi*; dir. Takahashi Hiroshi, 2004), and *Honey Bullets for Moon Cat* (*Tsukineko ni mitsu no dangan*; dir. Minato Hiroyuki, 2004).
6. Michiko Iwasaka and Barre Toelken, *Ghosts And The Japanese: Cultural Experience in Japanese Death Legends* (Logan: Utah State University Press, 1994), 58.
7. Publications that helped popularize paranormal urban legends (*toshi densetsu*) in Japan during the 1980s and 1990s include Matsutani Miyoko, *Gendai minwa ko*, 5 vols. (Tokyo: Tachikaze Shobō, 1986),

Kihara Hirokatsu and Nakayama Ichirō, *Shin mimibukuro: Anata no tonari no kowai hanashi* (Tokyo: Fusōsha, 1990), and Tōru Tsunemitsu, *Gakkō no kaidan: Kōshō bungei no tenkai to shosō* (Kyoto: Mineruva Shobō, 1993). See also Washitani Hana, *"Ringu* sanbusaku to onnatachi no media kūkan: Kaibutsu kasuru 'onna,' muku no 'chichi,'" in *Kaiki to gensō e no kairo: Kaidan kara J-horā e*, edited by Uchiyama Kazuki (Tokyo: Shinwasha, 2008), 221 n.5; and Joaquín da Silva, "J-Horror and Toshi Densetsu Revisited," January 4, 2016, http://eiga9.altervista.org/articulos/jhorrorandurbanlegendsrevisited.html (accessed May 5, 2017).

8. Ibid., 58. The Brothers Grimm famously defined legend as "a folktale historically grounded, though loosely so." See Hans Sebald, "Review of Norbert Krapf, *Beneath the Cherry Sapling: Legends from Franconia*," *German Studies Review* vol. 13, no. 2 (May 1990): 312–313. See also Donald Ward, ed. and trans., *The German Legends of the Brothers Grimm*, 2 vols. (Philadelphia, Pa.: Institute for the Study of Human Issues, 1981), 1:1.

9. Takahashi Hiroshi, "Interview with Producer Hiroshi Takahashi," *Marebito*, directed by Shimizu Takashi (2004), subtitled DVD (Los Angeles, CA: Tartan Video, 2006) (translation modified). On the usage of "J" as a signifier that not only "stands for 'Japanese' to both Japanese and international audiences" but also "at the same time announces a break from the putative tradition as self-consciously mass-cultural," see Chika Kinoshita, "The Mummy Complex: Kurosawa Kiyoshi's *Loft* and J-horror," in *Horror to the Extreme: Changing Boundaries in Asian Cinema*, edited by Jinhee Choi and Mitsuyo Wada-Marciano (Hong Kong: Hong Kong University Press, 2009), 121–122.

10. Donald Kirihira, "Reconstructing Japanese Film," in *Post-Theory: Reconstructing Film Studies*, edited by David Bordwell (Madison, WI: University of Wisconsin Press, 1996), 501–503.

11. Jasper Sharp, "Review of *Introduction to Japanese Film*," *Midnight Eye*, March 9, 2009. http://www.midnighteye.com/books/introduction-to-japanese-horror-film/ (accessed April 14, 2017).

12. See Andrew Dorman, *Paradoxical Japaneseness: Cultural Representation in 21st Century Japanese Cinema* (London: Palgrave Macmillan, 2016), 108–110; Steffen Hantke, "Japanese Horror under Western Eyes: Social Class and Global Culture in Miike Takashi's *Audition*," in *Japanese Horror Cinema*, edited by Jay McRoy (Honolulu: University of Hawai'i Press, 2005), 54–55.

13. Takahashi, *op. cit.* (translation modified).
14. The importance of non-Japanese cinematic traditions to the development of J-horror is underscored by Kurosawa Kiyoshi in his list of the "50 best horror films," which is included in his study *Eiga wa osoroshii* (2001a). Alongside notable examples of classic Japanese horror cinema, such as *Black Cat Mansion* (*Bōrei kaibyō yashiki*; dir. Nakagawa Nobuo, 1958), *Ghost of Yotsuya* (*Tōkaidō Yotsuya kaidan*; dir. Nakagawa Nobuo, 1959), and *Matango* (Honda Ishirō, 1963), Kurosawa juxtaposes prominent European, American, and British horror films ranging from *Nosferatu* (dir. F. W. Murnau, 1922) to *Vampyr* (dir. Carl Theodor Dreyer, 1932), from *Eyes without a Face* (*Les yeux sans visage*; dir. Georges Franju, 1960) to *The Innocents* (dir. Jack Clayton, 1961), from *Supiria* (dir. Dario Argento, 1977) to *Poltergeist* (dir. Tobe Hooper, 1982). See Kurosawa Kiyoshi, *Eiga wa osoroshii* (Tokyo: Seidosha, 2001a), 28–43. See also J-horror screenwriter Konaka Chiaki's contextualization of J-horror in relation to the history of world horror in Konaka Chiaki, *Horā eiga no miryoku: Fandamentaru horā sengen* (Tokyo: Iwanami Shoten, 2003), 15–48. Konaka singles out for special mention *The Cabinet of Dr. Caligari* (*Das Cabinet des Dr. Caligari*; dir. Robert Wiene, 1920), *The Innocents*, *Kill Baby, Kill* (*Operazione paura*; dir. Mario Bava, 1966), *The Exorcist* (dir. William Friedkin, 1973), *The Legend of Hell House* (dir. John Hough, 1973), *The Texas Chain Saw Massacre* (dir. Tobe Hooper, 1974), *Carrie* (dir. Brian De Palma, 1976), and *Halloween* (dir. John Carpenter, 1978), among others.
15. See Valerie Wee, *Japanese Horror Films and Their American Remakes* (New York: Routledge/Taylor & Francis Group, 2014), 80–203; Stefan Sunandan Honisch, "Music, Sound, and Noise as Bodily Disorders: Disabling the Filmic Diegesis in Hideo Nakata's *Ringu* and Gore Verbinski's *The Ring*," in *Transnational Horror Cinema: Bodies of Excess and the Global Grotesque*, edited by Sophia Siddique and Raphael Raphael (London: Palgrave Macmillan, 2016), 113–131; Daniel Herbert, "Trading Spaces: Transnational Dislocations in *Insomnia/Insomnia* and *Ju-on/The Grudge*," in *Fear, Cultural Anxiety, and Transformation: Horror, Science Fiction, and Fantasy Films Remade*, edited by Scott A. Lukas and John Marmysz (Lanham: Lexington Books, 2009), 143–164; Colette Balmain, "Oriental Nightmares: The 'Demonic' Other in Contemporary American Adaptations of Japanese Horror Film," in *Something Wicked This Way Comes: Essays on Evil and Human Wickedness*, edited by Colette

Balmain and Lois Drawmer (Amsterdam: Editions Rodopi, 2009), 25–38; David Kalat, *J-Horror: The Definitive Guide to The Ring, The Grudge and Beyond* (New York: Vertical, 2007), 239–265; Dorman, 119–123; and Jinhee Choi and Mitsuyo Wada-Marciano, eds. *Horror to the Extreme: Changing Boundaries in Asian Cinema* (Hong Kong: Hong Kong University Press, 2009), passim.

16. Lúcia Nagib, "Towards a Positive Definition of World Cinema," in *Remapping World Cinema: Identity, Culture and Politics in Film*, edited by Stephanie Dennison and Song Hwee Lim (London and New York: Wallflower Press, 2006), 35. As David Deamer puts it, "The Japanese film is not a closed system, nor does it have an internal unity, but rather is a system within the systems of world cinema." See David Deamer, *Deleuze, Japanese Cinema, and the Atom Bomb: The Spectre of Impossibility* (New York: Bloomsbury, 2014), 22.

17. Jay McRoy, "Case Study: Cinematic Hybridity in Shimizu Takashi's *Ju-on: The Grudge*," in *Japanese Horror Cinema*, edited by Jay McRoy (Honolulu: University of Hawai'i Press, 2005a), 176.

18. Ibid., 180.

19. See Uchiyama Kazuki, ed., *Kaiki to gensō e no kairo: Kaidan kara J-horā e* (Tokyo: Shinwasha, 2008); Ōshima Kiyoaki, *J-horā no yūrei kenkyū* (Musashino: Akiyama Shoten, 2010); Jay McRoy, *Nightmare Japan: Contemporary Japanese Horror Cinema* (Amsterdam; New York, NY: Rodopi, 2008); Jay McRoy, ed., *Japanese Horror Cinema* (Honolulu: University of Hawai'i Press, 2005b); Colette Balmain, *Introduction to Japanese Horror Film* (Edinburgh : Edinburgh University Press, 2008); Jim Harper, *Flowers from Hell: The Modern Japanese Horror Film* (Hereford, UK: Noir Publishing, 2008); Salvador Murguia, ed., *The Encyclopedia of Japanese Horror Films* (Lanham, Maryland: Rowman & Littlefield, 2016); and David Kalat, *J-Horror: The Definitive Guide to The Ring, The Grudge and Beyond* (New York: Vertical, 2007).

20. Robert Spadoni, "Carl Dreyer's Corpse: Horror Film Atmosphere and Narrative," in *A Companion to the Horror Film*, edited by Harry M. Benshoff (Chichester, West Sussex, UK; Malden, MA, USA: Wiley Blackwell, 2014), 157–159. The final quotation on the temporality of dread is from Julian Hanich, *Cinematic Emotion in Horror Films and Thrillers: The Aesthetic Paradox of Pleasurable Fear* (New York: Routledge, 2010), 191. On dread in horror cinema, see also Cynthia Freeland, "Horror and Art-Dread," in *The Horror Film*, edited by Stephen Prince

(New Brunswick, N.J.: Rutgers University Press, 2004), 189–205; and Noël Carroll, *The Philosophy of Horror, or, Paradoxes of the Heart* (New York: Routledge, 1990), 42.

21. Here it is worth pointing out that the etymology of the Japanese term "*kyōfukan*," which I have translated as "sensation of dread," has multiple senses and intensities depending upon the context. The "*kyōfu*" of "*kyōfukan*" may be translated not only as "dread" but also "fear," "terror," "horror," "scare," "panic," and "dismay." Based on the overall context in which Takahashi uses the term, "sensation (or feeling) of dread" seems the most apt.

22. Jean Dalmais, "Resonance," in *Sonic Experience: A Guide to Everyday Sounds*, edited by Jean-François Augoyard and Henry Torgue, translated by Andra McCartney and David Paquette (Montreal: McGill-Queen's University Press, 2005), 99–100.

23. "Resonance," *Oxford English Dictionary Online*, Oxford University Press, http://www.oed.com.libproxy.uoregon.edu/view/Entry/163743?redirect edFrom=resonance& (accessed December 12, 2016).

24. Dalmais, 110. See also Mark Vail, *The Synthesizer: A Comprehensive Guide to Understanding, Programming, Playing, and Recording the Ultimate Electronic Music Instrument* (Oxford: Oxford University Press, 2014), 9.

25. Vail, 12.

26. Vail, 63, 150, 161.

27. *Oxford English Dictionary*. Cf. Vitruvius, *De Architectura* 5.3.

28. Ibid.

29. Ibid.

30. Dalmais, 106.

31. *Oxford English Dictionary*.

32. Ibid.

33. Ibid.

34. Ibid.

35. Esperanza Ramirez-Christensen, "Japanese Poetics," in *The Princeton Encyclopedia of Poetry and Poetics*, edited by Roland Greene et al. (Princeton: Princeton University Press, 2012), 759.

36. Ibid.

37. On the resonant color effects in Titian's paintings, see Loren W. Partridge, *Art of Renaissance Venice 1400–1600* (Oakland, California: University of California Press, 2015), 196; Metropolitan Museum of Art, *The*

Renaissance in Italy and Spain (New York: Metropolitan Museum of Art, 1987), 14–15.

38. Veit Erlmann, "Resonance," in *Keywords in Sound*, edited by David Novak and Matt Sakakeeny (Durham; London: Duke University Press, 2015), 177. On resonance in Descartes, see also Veit Erlmann, "Descartes's Resonant Subject," *differences: A Journal of Feminist Cultural Studies* vol. 22, nos. 2–3 (2011): 10–30; and Veit Erlmann, *Reason and Resonance: A History of Modern Aurality* (New York: Zone Books, 2010), 64–68.

39. Erlmann, 181.

40. Jean-Luc Nancy, *À l'écoute* (Paris: Galilée, 2002), 13–84.

41. Jean-Luc Nancy, *Listening*, translated by Charlotte Mandell (New York: Fordham University Press, 2007), 21. On resonance and being, see also Martin Heidegger, *Contributions to Philosophy (Of the Event)*, translated by Richard Rojcewicz and Daniela Vallega-Neu (Bloomington, IN: Indiana University Press, 2012), 85–92, 189–90, 217, 334.

42. Nancy, 21–22.

43. Ibid., 21–22.

44. Ibid., 7.

45. Ibid., 7.

46. On the "cinema of sensations" and its Deleuzean underpinnings, see Barbara M. Kennedy, *Deleuze and Cinema: The Aesthetics of Sensation* (Edinburgh: Edinburgh University Press, 2000) and the insightful contributions to *The Cinema of Sensations*, edited by Ágnes Pethő (Newcastle upon Tyne: Cambridge Scholars Publishing, 2015). See also Thomas Elsaesser and Malte Hagener, *Film Theory: An Introduction through the Senses* (Florence: Taylor and Francis, 2015).

47. Gilles Deleuze and Félix Guattari, *What is Philosophy?*, translated by Hugh Tomlinson and Graham Burchell (New York: Columbia University Press, 1994), 164.

48. Deleuze and Guattari, 164.

49. Ibid., 164. More broadly, Deleuze and Guattari situate percepts as the "nonhuman landscapes of nature" and affects as the "nonhuman becomings of man" (169).

50. Ibid., 166.

51. Ibid., 167.

52. Ibid., 169.

53. Kennedy, 108.

54. Deleuze and Guattari, 175. Gilles Deleuze, *Cinema 1: The Movement-Image*, translated by Hugh Tomlinson and Barbara Habberjam (Minneapolis: University of Minnesota Press, 1986), 61.
55. Kennedy, 114.
56. Ibid., 115.
57. Deleuze and Guattari, 182.
58. Ibid., 170. Deleuze and Guattari underscore the importance of style in going beyond "the perceptual states and affective transitions of the lived" (171).
59. Ibid., 171.
60. Ibid., 173–174, 177.
61. Ibid., 173, 175.
62. Although this study focuses on the aesthetics of sensation in Japanese horror cinema, I am sympathetic to Steven Jay Schneider's general proposal for an "aesthetics of horror cinema" involving "medium-specific and 'middle-level' questions concerning those filmic (including narrative) techniques, principles, devices, conventions, and images that have arguably proven most effective and reliable when it comes to frightening viewers over time, across geographic and cultural borders" (131). See Steven Jay Schneider, "Toward and Aesthetics of Cinematic Horror," in *The Horror Film*, edited by Stephen Prince (New Brunswick, N.J.: Rutgers University Press, 2004b), 131–149.
63. Friedrich Kittler, "Romanticism—Psychoanalysis—Film: A History of the Double," in *Literature, Media, Information Systems*, edited by John Johnston (New York: Routledge, 1997), 96.
64. On the surrealist aspects of *Ringu*, see Adam Lowenstein, *Dreaming of Cinema: Spectatorship, Surrealism, and the Age of Digital Media* (New York : Columbia University Press, 2015), 88–89, 94–99, 114–116.

2

Ambient Horror: From Sonic Palimpsests to Haptic Sonority in the Cinema of Kurosawa Kiyoshi

Over the past ten years, a new wave of film scholarship has emerged that seeks to correct the overemphasis on the visual aspects of narrative film by reclaiming the importance of sound. Following the lead set by earlier groundbreaking work on film sound by scholars such as Michel Chion, Elisabeth Weis, Rick Altman, and Mary Ann Doane, a new generation of film scholars, including Jay Beck, William Whittington, Anahid Kassabian, Lisa Coulthard, Kevin Donnelly, and Andy Birtwistle, are asking important questions about the role of sound in film.[1] For example, in his study *Cinesonica: Sounding Film and Video* (2010), Birtwistle argues that, rather than asking "What does this sound mean?" we should be posing other questions, such as: How are sound-image relations "constituted and understood in terms of materiality"? What is "at stake in the relationship between sound and image"? How might we "come to terms with the materiality of film sound, both beyond and in relation to its semiotic or significatory dimensions"?[2] Without denying that narrative film remains a signifying text, the task set forth by scholars such as Birtwistle and others is to attend to the sonic phenomena constituting cinema's "parallel universe of materiality"[3] and the spectator's affective or noncognitive responses to the sound-image relations of film.

© The Author(s) 2018
S. T. Brown, *Japanese Horror and the Transnational Cinema of Sensations*,
East Asian Popular Culture, https://doi.org/10.1007/978-3-319-70629-0_2

Contemporary Japanese horror cinema offers especially instructive examples of how sound flows modulate affect. Through advanced spectral and surround field analysis and a careful consideration of elements such as the interrelations between noise and silence, the function of ambient drones and sonic palimpsests, and the status of the acousmatic voice, we can better understand how soundscapes contribute to the construction of horror as a space for what I call "haptic sonority." In this endeavor, I have found inspiration in the philosophical work of Gilles Deleuze and Félix Guattari. Deleuze's two *Cinema* books have had an enormous impact on film theory,[4] but there Deleuze is primarily concerned with constructing a taxonomy of cinematic images and signs with sound receiving far less attention. However, in *A Thousand Plateaus* (*Mille plateaux*, 1980),[5] Deleuze and Guattari develop a theory of haptic space and molecular sound that has helped me reconceive the level at which sound design is occurring in Japanese horror, which has more to do with microsounds and nonlinear fluctuations in sound flows that subtly get under one's skin than it does with clangorous musical stingers designed to make the audience jump out of their seats. In this context, I will pay especially close attention to the exemplary horror films of director Kurosawa Kiyoshi.

Kurosawa Kiyoshi (b. 1955), who is no relation to Kurosawa Akira (1910–1998), is one of the most respected contemporary Japanese directors in the world. He has been directing movies since 1975, with over 45 directing credits to his name, a mix of feature-length theatrical release films such as *Cure* (*Kyua*, 1997a), *Charisma* (*Karisuma*, 2000), *Pulse* (*Kairo*, 2001), *Doppelgänger* (*Dopperugengā*, 2003), *Bright Future* (*Akarui mirai*, 2003), *Tokyo Sonata* (2008), *Journey to the Shore* (*Kishibe no tabi*, 2015), *Creepy* (*Kurīpī: Itsuwari no rinjin*, 2016), and *Daguerrotype* (*Le Secret de la chambre noire*, 2016); softcore pink films (*pinku eiga*) such as *Kandagawa Pervert Wars* (*Kandagawa inran sensō*, 1983) and *The Excitement of the Do-Re-Mi-Fa Girl* (*Do-re-mi-fa-musume no chi wa sawagu*, 1985); made-for-TV movies such as *Séance* (*Kōrei*, 1999) and miniseries such as *Penance* (*Shokuzai*, 2012); and low-budget straight-to-video V-Cinema yakuza movies such as *Serpent's Path* (*Hebi no michi*, 1998) and the *Suit Yourself or Shoot Yourself* (*Katte ni shiyagare!*, 1995–1996) series. Many of Kurosawa's theatrical release films have enjoyed successful runs on the festival circuit, receiving special attention at international film festivals held at Cannes, Venice, Toronto, and Rotterdam.

Although often pegged as a J-horror director and included in the group of directors, screenwriters, and producers most often associated with the marketing of the J-horror movement, Kurosawa's films frequently resist such labels by mixing in conventions from other genres, sometimes throwing into question the very meaning of the term "J-horror." The fact is that Kurosawa has made films spanning numerous genres; in addition to horror, he has directed films in the genres of mystery, thriller, yakuza crime drama, family melodrama, social drama, youth crisis movie, spectral romance, science fiction, and softcore pink films. Despite the fact that Kurosawa does not think of himself as a horror specialist per se, he nevertheless freely admits to loving horror films and acknowledges that some of his best-received films belong to the horror genre. In this connection, it is probably also not insignificant that Kurosawa Kiyoshi was not only college friends with Nakata Hideo (director of such J-horror standouts as *Ring* [*Ringu*, 1998], *Ring 2* [*Ringu 2*, 1998], *Dark Water* [*Honogurai mizu no soko kara*], 2002], *Kaidan* [2007], and *The Complex* [*Kuroyuri danchi*, 2013]) and the college roommate of legendary J-horror screenwriter Takahashi Hiroshi (*Don't Look Up* [*Joyūrei*, 1996], *Ring, Ring 2, The Ring* [1998], and *The Ring 2* [2005]) whom he considers one of his closest friends, but also a teacher and mentor to Shimizu Takashi (director of *Ju-on: The Grudge* [*Ju-on*, 2002], *Ju-on: The Grudge 2* [*Ju-on 2*, 2003], *Marebito* [2004], *The Grudge* [2004], *Reincarnation* [*Rinne*, 2005], and *The Grudge 2* [2006]).

As I will argue in this chapter, sound design plays an extremely important role in the horror cinema of Kurosawa Kiyoshi, privileging not only acousmatic voices, ambient noises, and sonic drones, but also the omission of sound and the dynamic manipulation of sound and silence. By subtly adjusting the oscillation between sound and silence, Kurosawa creates a three-dimensional soundscape that is very effective at unnerving the audio spectator. In Kurosawa's films, it often seems as if silence interrupts the noise of modernity itself, making the suspension of sound just as important in the modulation of the horror soundtrack as its presence. In an attempt to show how Kurosawa's horror films push the boundaries of sound design in genre cinema, I will analyze representative examples from some of Kurosawa's most acclaimed J-horror films in the context of transnational horror cinema.

The Sonic Palimpsest

Kurosawa's *Séance* is a loose adaptation of Mark McShane's 1961 novel *Séance on a Wet Afternoon,* which was also adapted by director Bryan Forbes in a 1964 British film of the same name. But whereas McShane's novel and Forbes's adaptation are structured like a crime drama, the Kurosawa adaptation is more horror-melodrama than crime drama. Kurosawa's *Séance* first aired on Japanese television (Kansai TV) in 1999, but then went on for a successful run on the festival circuit. Despite starting out life as a made-for-TV movie, it was even singled out for a special notice of distinction at the Cannes Film Festival in 2001.

Séance deals with a spiritual medium named Satō Junko (played by Fubuki Jun) and her husband, a sound effects technician named Satō Katsuhiko (played by renowned character actor Yakusho Kōji), who get caught up in a difficult situation when a kidnapped girl ends up at the couple's house after trying to escape her assailant. Without the husband realizing it, the girl climbed into his audio equipment chest while he was out collecting wind sounds in a forest near Mt. Fuji. The husband is prepared to call the police, but his wife will not permit him to do so once she starts to get ideas about how she might use her position as a psychic to win favor with the police and take advantage of this strange turn of events to break out of her humdrum life and acquire some measure of distinction. Unfortunately, the girl dies while under the couple's care, and her ghost begins to haunt them both.

On one level, the film is about a spiritual medium who feels marginalized by her psychic gifts who comes into conflict with various agents of modernity (represented by police officers and university professors) in her struggle for social recognition and legitimacy. As is often the case in contemporary Japanese horror cinema, the spiritual medium's struggle is symptomatic of larger issues involving Japanese modernity's repression of the perceived irrationality represented by her premodern belief system and practices. However, on another level, the film deals extensively (and quite self-reflexively) with the important role played by sound effects in the horror film. For example, early on in *Séance*, at about the 24-minute mark, Satō Katsuhiko's boss Tazaki, a fellow sound effects technician, asks him to listen to a strange sound that he has noticed on one of the tapes Satō had taken home the previous evening (Fig. 2.1).

In the history of sound cinema, it is relatively rare for the recording, manipulation, and analysis of sound *itself* to be self-reflexively fore-grounded as part of the diegetic world of a film. However, there are some notable exceptions. For example, Francis Ford Coppola's groundbreaking 1974 film *The Conversation*, starring Gene Hackman as a paranoid sur-veillance expert named Harry Caul, who "has a crisis of conscience when he suspects that a couple he is spying on will be murdered."[6] *The Conversation* is a thought-provoking film that marvelously engages the ambiguities of sound and the ethics of listening. Or take another film that was roughly contemporaneous, William Friedkin's *The Exorcist* (1973), in which Jason Miller plays a Jesuit priest named Father Karras,

Fig. 2.1 Sound effects technician Satō Katsuhiko (Yakusho Kōji) listens intently to a strange recording in *Séance* (1999)

who, although not a sound technician, displays as much care and attention when listening to the sonic phenomena associated with a young girl's possession as Gene Hackman's character does in *The Conversation* when analyzing snippets of conversation captured via surveillance. Another notable example is *Blow Out*, Brian De Palma's 1981 homage to Michelangelo Antonioni's *Blow-Up* (1966), starring John Travolta as a movie sound effects technician, who, while collecting sounds for a low-budget slasher film, inadvertently captures sonic evidence that shows that an automobile accident he witnessed involving a governor was, in fact, a politically motivated assassination.

More recently, the Oscar-winning 2006 film *The Lives of Others* (*Das Leben der Anderen*), directed by Florian Henckel von Donnersmarck, deals with an agent working for the East Berlin secret police, who, while conducting surveillance on a writer and his lover, finds himself becoming emotionally involved in their lives even though his exposure to them is entirely at the level of sound. Although not technically a sound technician, the eavesdropping agent (played by Ulrich Mühe) effectively becomes a sound editor since he must decide what to include and what to leave out of the regular reports that he files about the lives of those he has surveilled. Like Coppola's *The Conversation*, *The Lives of Others* raises profound questions about the ethics of wiretapping in an age of mass surveillance. Both films are also believed to have influenced Edward Snowden's decision to reveal the full extent of the NSA's global surveillance programs.[7]

Then there is *Berberian Sound Studio*, Peter Strickland's 2012 homage to the Italian giallo tradition, starring Toby Jones as a British sound engineer and mixer hired to work on an Italian horror movie whose grasp on reality starts to disintegrate as life begins to imitate art. In all of these films, when the capture, reproduction, editing, and analysis of sonic phenomena become part of the story a film is trying to tell, then it is worth considering what the filmmakers are attempting to convey with such remarkably self-reflexive gestures. On one level, films such as *Berberian Sound Studio* and the others that I mentioned go to the trouble of including such scenes to foreground the constructedness of sound design in cinema by showing us the technologies associated with sonic capture and manipulation. However, on another level, by presenting characters who actively engage with the sound objects and soundscapes that they encounter, we are also invited to consider the different modes of listening that are at work both inside and outside the film.

This is precisely what is accomplished in *Séance* when Satō is called upon to analyze a ghostly vocalization that unexpectedly appears on a reel-to-reel tape that he had handled previously while reviewing sound effects for his job. At the outset of the scene, we see Satō's boss Tazaki in medium shot listening via headphones to the tape in question. However, although we can see and hear Tazaki operate the reel-to-reel tape machine, we do not hear what is on the tape until Tazaki passes the headphones to Satō. At that point, the sound switches to Satō's point of audition and the visual sequence cuts to a medium close-up of Satō's face so that we can see his reaction to the strange audio. Tazaki asks Satō what the sound is, but Satō is uncertain, noting simply that there is something strange on the recording. Satō then passes the headphones back to Tazaki, and Tazaki cues it up again *without* the point of audition switching to Tazaki. Then Tazaki asks Satō to listen once more. Although remarking that it sounds like a person's voice, Tazaki notes that it is difficult to make out what is said since it is mixed in with the sound of the wind. Even for the audio spectator, it is difficult to detect a voice, much less make out what is said, despite the fact that the audio has already been replayed twice from Satō's point of audition.

At the level of the diegetic world in *Séance*, this scene offers an example of electronic voice phenomenon, which is referenced at the very outset of the movie in a discussion between a university professor and one of his graduate students, who is seeking advice about whether to publish an essay he has written on paranormal phenomena and the "expansion of the subconscious self." In particular, the student mentions a 1956 electronic voice phenomenon experiment conducted by parapsychology researcher Attila von Szalay using a reel-to-reel tape recorder to capture the voices of dead spirits and communicate with them. In the context of the story, it is implied that the tape being analyzed by Satō and Tazaki became imprinted by an electronic voice phenomenon during the séance performed by Satō's wife Junko at their house the previous evening. Tazaki is clearly disturbed by the spectral voice, but Satō dismisses it as a stray transmission from some trucker's CB radio and promises to clean it up.

The scene ends with a whip pan to Tazaki after Satō has left the room and we hear the strange audio again, but this time from Tazaki's point of audition. Although ghosts appear throughout the movie, this is the only ghost who actually speaks, yet the message remains unintelligible.

However, if one analyzes the audio by means of a spectrogram, which displays the frequency content of the audio over time, with the x-axis showing time in seconds, the y-axis showing frequency measured in hertz, and color showing the intensity of the frequency with brighter colors indicating louder volumes at a given frequency, then it becomes more obvious that *there is* a sonic signature of an apparently male voice submerged in the sound spectra of the wind. What is distinctive about the spectral voice (which is highlighted on the stereo spectrogram in Fig. 2.2 by means of rectangles) is that its fundamental frequency and harmonics have been pitch-shifted down well below the normal range of the male voice (with the fundamental frequency appearing in the 20 to 70 Hz range), and its tempo has also been slowed down. In effect, the spectral voice in *Séance* functions as a kind of *sonic palimpsest* within the film, a non-signifying sound flow that not only resists the hermeneutic

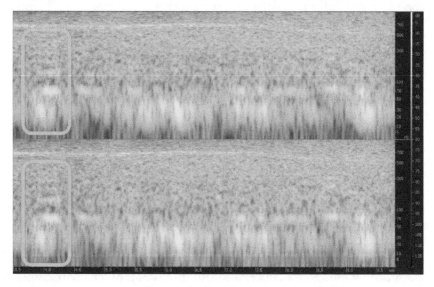

Fig. 2.2   A spectrogram of the spectral voice in *Séance* (1999)

desire to decipher its meaning but also modulates the affective states of both characters and spectators in resonant fashion.[8]

In the history of horror cinema, two films greatly admired by the director of *Séance* stand out for the ways in which they helped establish the sonic palimpsest as an effective technique for horror sound design: William Friedkin's *The Exorcist* (1973) and Stanley Kubrick's *The Shining* (1980).[9] In both films, it is noteworthy that the sonic palimpsest is animated by excerpting the avant-garde compositions of Polish composer Krzysztof Penderecki. Given the role of Penderecki's music in two of the scariest and most acclaimed horror movies ever made, it is worth pausing to consider how Penderecki figures into the application of the sonic palimpsest.

A few years ago, the Chief Classical Music Critic for *The Guardian*, Tom Service, proclaimed what everyone familiar with the genre of horror already knew: that Penderecki was the "favourite composer" of some of horror's leading directors.[10] Although it was never Penderecki's intention to become the patron composer of horror cinema, his inclusion in film soundtracks ranging from *The Exorcist* to *The Shining*, from *The People Under the Stairs* (dir. Wes Craven, 1991) to *Inland Empire* (dir. David Lynch, 2006), from *Shutter Island* (dir. Martin Scorsese, 2010) to *Demon* (dir. Marcin Wrona, 2015), has ensured that he remains one of the most imitated composers for the genre of horror, especially if the soundtrack calls for terrifyingly atonal string cues. One need only listen to the soundtracks of some of the most successful recent horror films, such as Joseph Bishara's deeply disturbing scores for the James Wan-directed films *Insidious* (2010) and *The Conjuring* (2013), to realize just how pervasive Penderecki's influence on horror cinema remains even to this day.

In the case of *The Exorcist*, although Friedkin and his music editor Eugene Marks excerpted fragments of atonal music from a number of modernist composers, including Hans Werner Henze, Anton Webern, and George Crumb, it was the work of Penderecki that was featured most of all. Friedkin typically makes use of Penderecki's music to create unsettling textures and dissonant atmospheres during transitional moments and montage sequences while largely avoiding the use of music as an underscore for scenes of dialogue or intense drama. For example, it is notable that there is hardly any musical underscoring for even the most dramatic scenes of exorcism within the film. Indeed, in some instances, one may not even be aware that one is listening to music, such as is the case in one scene when an excerpt from one of Penderecki's most famous compositions is spliced into the soundtrack as a sonic palimpsest.

The scene in question takes place in a doctor's office as the possessed girl Regan (played by Linda Blair) undergoes the first in a series of increasingly disturbing diagnostic tests. Throughout much of the scene, we hear the exotica instrumental "Quiet Village" (1952) by Les Baxter playing as background music over the speakers of the waiting room and inside the doctor's office, but towards the end of the sequence, just before Regan collapses, an excerpt from Penderecki is inserted quite subtly. The shift from easy listening to avant-garde modernism could have been quite jarring, but the Penderecki piece is barely audible—more sonic palimpsest than musical underscoring. As Regan hums to herself in the doctor's office, the string swarms and microtonal clusters of composer Penderecki's avant-garde piece for 48 strings titled *Polymorphia* (1961) bleeds through like a sonic palimpsest from underneath Regan's humming, so subtle that it is almost subliminal, making it difficult to ascertain whether it is diegetic or nondiegetic. This sonic palimpsest complements the visual palimpsest of the demon Pazuzu that occurs earlier in the scene whose face momentarily flashes to show us the otherness that resides just beneath the surface.

When considering the role of music within a film's soundtrack, the most obvious distinction typically made is between diegetic and nondiegetic music. Film music is considered "diegetic" if it is part of the fictional world of the film and is something that might conceivably be heard by one or more characters within the film. For example, if the music is being transmitted by a source situated within the fictional world of the film, such as an orchestra, radio, television, or MP3 player, then it is diegetic. However, if the music is not part of the film's fictional world per se and is not audible to any of its characters, then it is "nondiegetic." However, as scholars such as Robynn Stillwell and others have reminded us,[11] the boundaries between diegetic and nondiegetic are not fixed in stone and can become fluid in certain situations, especially when the diegetic or nondiegetic status of a particular sound or musical cue changes during the same scene or across scenes, or if it veers off into "metadiegetic" territory.

The concept of the "metadiegetic" (sometimes referred to as "subjective diegetic"), which was introduced by Claudia Gorbman in her ground-breaking study *Unheard Melodies: Narrative Film Music* (1987), refers to sounds that are only perceived inside the head or mind of a character.[12] In the scene under consideration from *The Exorcist*, if the character of Regan is, indeed, humming along with the barely audible musical excerpt from Penderecki's *Polymorphia* and there is no obvious diegetic source for that music, then that would suggest that Regan is, in some sense, responding to *Polymorphia* as a sort of sonic palimpsest that she hears inside her head, which would make it an example of "metadiegetic" music.

However, in addition to the metadiegetic status of the music itself, it is worth pointing out that the circumstances surrounding Penderecki's composition of *Polymorphia* make the choice of this particular piece especially suitable in its role as a sonic palimpsest. The title *Polymorphia*, which is derived from the Greek for "many shapes or forms," gestures towards the composer's fundamental principle in his early work of exploring "noise as sound as music" in an effort to "liberat[e] sound beyond all tradition," as he put it.[13] Penderecki composed the piece during a period when he was especially interested in the exchange and interpenetration of music and noise. For Penderecki, whose approach to musical composition in the early 1960s arose out of the sonorist movement of avant-garde Polish music that emphasized timbre and texture over melody, rhythm, and harmony, what is most important about *Polymorphia*'s composition is that the "many forms" implied by its title refer not simply to "musical forms" but rather to "sound effects."[14] For Penderecki, *Polymorphia* is composed not of melody, but rather of expressive "sound events."[15] In other words, in boundary-pushing early works such as *Polymorphia*, *Threnody to the Victims of Hiroshima* (1960), and *Fluorescences* (1961–62), Penderecki effectively transformed himself from a musical composer into a sound designer. What Penderecki's sonorist avant-garde compositions have offered most of all to horror cinema is a "zone of indiscernibility" between music and noise.

When writing *Polymorphia*, Penderecki was inspired by human electroencephalograms, which translate the electrical activity of the brain into graphic marks that are interpreted according to wave type and frequency. For this purpose, Penderecki solicited the assistance of patients at the Kraków Medical Center, whose actual electroencephalograms were recorded while they listened to the recording of *Threnody for the Victims of Hiroshima* (1960), one of Penderecki's most acclaimed and disturbing compositions. To translate the resultant EEGs into music, Penderecki dispensed with conventional musical notation and developed an innovative visual language of graphic notation that attempted to translate the unbroken sliding wave forms of electroencephalograms into sustained microtonal clusters of multiple adjacent notes played simultaneously, which sound quite dissonant, as well as into the eerie, often uncoordinated, sliding pitches known as glissandi.

By transcribing the electroencephalograms of patients who were listening to his music, the composition that provided musical stimuli for this experiment, *Threnody for the Victims of Hiroshima*, itself functioned as a sonic palimpsest that was then refigured and transfigured via multiple layers of translation, modulated via multiple translation machines—not only the translation machine of the EEG device itself, but also the translation machines that were the bodies of the patients who were hooked up to an array of EEG devices. Indeed, the sonic palimpsest is at work here on multiple levels. In this connection, it is noteworthy that Penderecki does not claim that *Polymorphia* "traces" the electroencephalograms of the patients who were subjected to his listening experiment; rather he says that *Polymorphia* "diagrams" them: "When working on *Polymorphia*, I went to a Cracow nerve clinic and played a tape of *Threnody* for the patients. Their brain waves, reactions to the music, were transcribed visually by means of an encephalograph; I simply took that graph as the diagrammatic curve for *Polymorphia*."[16]

According to Penderecki, whereas the electroencephalograph "transcribes," *Polymorphia* "diagrams." To unpack what the difference is, it helps to think of Gilles Deleuze and Félix Guattari's work on the concept of the "diagram" and what they call the "diagrammatic." Deleuze and Guattari define the diagrammatic as a transformation that positively deterritorializes a semiotic system or regime of signs, carrying it off in a non-representational direction. For Deleuze and Guattari, diagrams must be distinguished not only "from indexes, which are territorial signs, but also from icons, which pertain to reterritorialization, and from symbols, which pertain to relative or negative deterritorialization."[17] In their view, the diagrammatic functions as an abstract machine that "produces continuums of intensity, effects conjunctions of deterritorialization, and extracts expressions and contents."[18]

From a Deleuzoguattarian perspective, the "diagrammatic curve" of Penderecki's *Polymorphia* does not simply "represent," "resemble," "symbolize," or "stand in for" the electroencephalograms of patients listening to *Threnody for the Victims of Hiroshima*. On the contrary, what the abstract machine of *Polymorphia* enacts with its "diagrammatic curve" is a deterritorialization of the electroencephalograms in a transsemiotic sense. In a transsemiotic register, the diagrammatic translation performed by *Polymorphia* not only includes the "untransformable residues," as Deleuze and Guattari call them, that are left behind in the diagrammatic act of translation, but also the creative transformations that form new assemblages, new conjunctions of matter and function, that had not existed before the abstract machine called *Polymorphia* constructed its diagram.[19]

It is probably no accident that one of the diagnostic tests undergone by Regan in *The Exorcist* in the scene that incorporates *Polymorphia* as a sonic palimpsest is an electrocardiogram, which we are shown in close-up. Although electrocardiograms are obviously different from electroencephalograms—electrocardiograms transcribe the electrical activity of the heart, whereas electroencephalograms transcribe the electrical activity of the brain—nevertheless, the choice of Penderecki's *Polymorphia* for this particular scene and the insertion of a close-up of the electrocardiograph transcribing Regan's heart activity suggests that Friedkin was well aware of the strong associations between *Polymorphia*'s unique style of graphic notation for its score and the electroencephalograms of patients listening to Penderecki's music.[20]

The other film that I mentioned that makes effective use of Penderecki's *Polymorphia* as a sonic palimpsest is Stanley Kubrick's *The Shining*. Fig. 2.3 shows a single sheet from the rough, working music dubbing charts for *The Shining*, which were created by music editor Gordon Stainforth (with additional annotations by Kubrick) and "used for a first run-through in the dubbing theatre."[21] The music chart for reel 14, which Stainforth told me he literally had beside him while he was layering the tracks on a Steenbeck flatbed film editor,[22] shows the complexity and technical sophistication of the soundtrack in the last 25 minutes of the film—from the time that the character of young Danny writes "Redrum" (the mirror image of "murder") on the door to warn his mother of his father Jack's evil intentions until Jack breaks through the bathroom door, murders the African-American chef, Dick Halloran, and begins hunting Danny in the labyrinthine outdoor maze. What makes the soundtrack for *The Shining* so interesting is that, although it is well known that Kubrick incorporated musical snippets from mostly preexisting modernist compositions by Penderecki, Ligeti, and others, what most viewers do not realize is that in some cases, what we hear are excerpts of one musical cue layered with others, taken either from the same or different compositions, which are played simultaneously. For example, on the music dubbing chart that appears in Fig. 2.3, the first column on the far left describes the action taking place while the columns to the right of the action indicate what musical cues were to be layered—in some cases, excerpts from as many as three musical cues were layered simultaneously.[23] In addition to being filled from top to bottom with excerpts from Penderecki's avant-garde compositions, the chart also includes Kubrick's annotation in blue ink to "play [them] together," which underscores the importance of simultaneity to Stainforth's multilayering technique. During the mixing of the music for *The Shining*, Stainforth has recounted that Kubrick pushed him to increase the complexity of the soundtrack in the movie's climax by layering multiple pieces of music "on top of each other":

> There was very little discussion, but he [Stanley] was very positive and would make snap decisions in every case when I played him my choices. And by what he chose, he was nudging me always in a particular direction, of a kind of manic madness. And the more I went that way the more he liked it. But when it came to the climax of the movie (Jack axing the doors onwards) I'd got all the most dramatic stuff laid up in a kind of complex mosaic, and still it wasn't enough for him.
> "You've got to beef it up, Gordon!"
> "How, Stanley, I've got the most dramatic stuff I can find in the whole of Penderecki!"
> "Just lay two pieces on top of each other!"
> "But we can't do that—what will the musicologists say?"

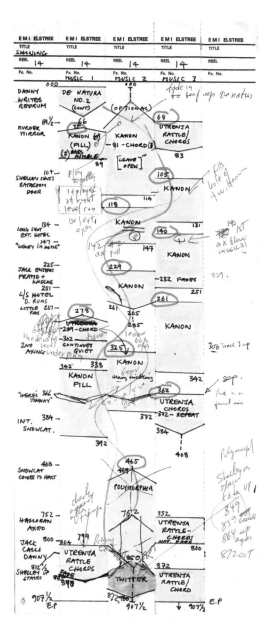

Fig. 2.3 Rough working music chart for reel 14 of *The Shining* (1980)

"Oh, they'll never notice!"
And amazingly, he was right…well, certainly I never heard or read any comments about that liberty we took.[24]

It was as if Kubrick and Stainforth were applying the techniques of music sampling that were becoming all the rage in the world of hip hop around the time that *The Shining* was being made in the late 1970s, in which a DJ takes a portion (or sample) of one sound recording and reuses it in an entirely different context, often overlaying it with other samples. When two or more sources are sampled and layered in this way, not only is there a palimpsestic relationship between the musical excerpts that have been multilayered, but a new piece of music is thereby created, often making it difficult to ascertain the identity of the source material. Although such sampling techniques are commonplace today, they were considered quite innovative in the late 1970s and early 1980s and almost unheard of in a mainstream film from this period when the integrity and boundaries of individual musical cues were typically respected within cinema.

One question that is sometimes posed in relation to *Psycho* (1960) concerning whether Bernard Herrmann's so-called stabbing strings cue for the shower scene functions as music or sound effects is just as applicable to the avant-garde pieces by Penderecki that were spliced into the soundtracks of *The Exorcist* and *The Shining*, since Penderecki deliberately set out to blur the boundaries between music and sound effects even if his sonorist compositions were not originally intended for the cinema. That blurring of boundaries continues to be felt in the films that sample Penderecki's work. In the case of *The Shining*, Kubrick was especially interested in how such boundary-blurring sounds, which he termed "low fly-bys," could modulate affect without one noticing, since they were "sounds that would sneak into you, subconsciously," as Kubrick explained to composer Wendy Carlos,[25] whose electronic reorchestration via Moog modular synthesizer of the medieval Roman Catholic requiem for the dead known as "Dies Irae" (Day of Wrath) during the opening titles of *The Shining* remains one of the most haunting title scores ever, offering a clear foreshadowing of the dark things to come. In short, Kubrick's "low fly-bys" are what I have been referring to as "sonic palimpsests." The sonic palimpsest is a sound or sounds that are hidden beneath layers of other sounds, which one may not be aware of consciously but which are felt subconsciously at the level of affect.

We have taken a long detour through *The Exorcist* and *The Shining* by way of Penderecki's *Polymorphia* to elucidate how a sonic palimpsest functions within a horror film. Although Penderecki's music plays no role in Kurosawa's film *Séance*, if we return to the scene from *Séance* that prompted this detour, we are now in a better position to understand how the sonic palimpsest in that scene of two sound men trying to make sense of a strange spectral voice produces new continuums of intensity within the world of that film by both showing us different modes of listening and engaging the problem of the "acousmatic voice."

Renowned theorist of film sound Michel Chion (following *musique concrète* pioneer Pierre Schaeffer [1910–1995]) distinguishes between three modes of listening: (1) causal listening, which is "[l]istening for the clues in sounds that point to the sound's cause," so that "the auditor asks what object, phenomenon, or creature is making the noise, where it is located, or how it's behaving and moving";[26] (2) semantic listening, which is "[l]istening for 'meaning'…in contexts involving coded audio signals (most usually spoken language, but think also of Morse code or a code between prisoners), where the listener focuses on decoding that signal to arrive at the message";[27] and (3) reduced listening, which is "[l]istening in a mode that intentionally and artificially ignores causes and meaning … in order to concentrate on the sound in itself, in terms of its sensory properties including pitch, rhythm, texture, form, mass, and volume."[28] In Kurosawa's *Séance*, Satō and Tazaki engage in all three modes of listening to varying degrees. In the mode of semantic listening, they attempt to decipher what the strange audio signal "means," but the diagrammatic force of the sonic palimpsest frustrates their attempts to decipher it. In the mode of causal listening, they speculate about what might have caused the sound (whether it was a trucker's CB radio or something else) without being able to pin it down (if Satō suspects that it was imprinted the night before during his wife's séance, he keeps it to himself). Finally, by focusing their attention on the sensory properties of the sonic palimpsest, Satō and Tazaki also engage in the reduced mode of listening, and it is in this mode, perhaps more than any other, that they open themselves up to being deterritorialized by the diagrammatic force of the sonic palimpsest.

However, it should also be pointed out that, by analyzing a spectrogram of the spectral voice, as I did earlier, I am also placing myself in the mode of reduced listening in an effort to attend to the sensory properties of the sonic sequence. Taking Michel Chion and Pierre Schaeffer's lead, Andy Birtwistle argues that "if [film] sound can be listened to and conceptualised as a concrete sonic event, dissociated from its representational functions, then its materiality can be registered in terms of complexity, amplitude, tonal qualities, timbre, duration, development over time, and so on."[29] In so doing, we begin to approach "a new domain of sound, referred to by Schaeffer as…sonorous objects."[30] By inviting an engagement with the sounds (and sonorous objects) of his films through different modes of listening, Kurosawa self-reflexively foregrounds the importance of sound design in his filmmaking. However, there is something else that is accomplished by listening to the sonic palimpsest in this scene from *Séance*: viz., the creation of an opening for the acousmatic voice.

The Acousmatic Voice

According to Michel Chion, the acousmatic describes "the auditory situation in which we hear sounds without seeing their cause or source."[31] In everyday life, we are frequently confronted with the acousmatic voice, such as when we use the telephone or listen to the radio. In such contexts, the acousmatic voice is not disturbing because it often carries with it "a mental visual representation" of the presumed cause or source. However, when neither cause nor source can be seen or clearly imagined, such as in the auditioning of the electronic voice phenomenon in *Séance*, then the acousmatic voice becomes something of an enigma.

It is at such moments that the acousmatic voice approaches what Chion describes as the "*acousmêtre*," a French neologism meaning "acousmatic being." The *acousmêtre* arises, according to Chion, "when the acousmatic presence is a voice" that we cannot connect to a face, thereby creating "a kind of talking and acting shadow."[32] In its extreme form, the complete *acousmêtre* creates the impression that it is everywhere, all-seeing, all-knowing, and all-powerful. The acousmatic voice of the computer HAL 9000 (played by Douglas Rain) in *2001: A Space Odyssey* (1968), the Great

Oz (Frank Morgan) in *The Wizard of Oz* (1939), or Yahweh (Charlton Heston) in *The Ten Commandments* (1956) all exemplify Chion's notion of the complete *acousmêtre*. However, even when the *acousmêtre* is merely partial and does not exemplify or create the impression of ubiquity, panopticism, omniscience, or omnipotence, it can still function as an enigma, as it does in the case of the electronic voice phenomenon in *Séance*, evoking feelings of unease, confusion, dread, or terror. Satō and his colleague try to dismiss the voice heard on the tape as simply a bad recording, but the affective impact that it has on both characters is undeniable, especially Tazaki, who becomes so disturbed by the recording that he stays home sick the next day, effectively removing himself from the narrative altogether. Moreover, by offering an example of the acousmatic voice, whose intelligibility cannot be deciphered even by the sound technicians within the film, *Séance* underscores the importance of listening more closely to the non-signifying sound flows that are interwoven into a movie's soundscapes.

The acousmatic voice is used to good effect in other Kurosawa Kiyoshi films as well, such as in a scene from the critically acclaimed Internet horror *Kairo* (aka *Pulse*) with sound design by Ika Makio, in which a character named Michi (played by Asō Kumiko) receives a strange phone call from her coworker Yabe asking for help. In his study *Film, A Sound Art*, Michel Chion offers a typology of telephemes in film that is relevant here. "Telepheme" is the term given to "a unit of telephone conversation."[33] According to Chion, cinematic telephemes can be classified into seven types according to their audiovisual relations. The first type of telepheme is "typical of silent films," which shows "two interlocutors in alternation, but we don't hear what they're saying."[34] In the second type, "we alternately see each interlocutor, and as we see each person, we hear what he or she is saying."[35] In the third type, "we see (and hear) only one of the interlocutors and stay with him or her for the duration of the telepheme, without hearing what the other says."[36] In the fourth type, "we see and hear one of the two speakers, but we hear the filtered voice of the other speaker, whom we don't see."[37] In the fifth type, "we see first one then the other of the two characters, and the voice of one is either paired with his or her own image or with the image of the other person listening over the receiver."[38] The sixth type of telepheme is "filmed in split screen, allowing us to see and hear both speakers, without having either voice sound filtered."³⁹ Finally, Chion reserves the seventh type for "various cases that are deliberately aberrant or paradoxical to one degree or another, often resulting from combinations of the preceding types."⁴⁰

The scene from *Kairo* offers an example of the fourth type of telepheme discussed by Chion, in which we see and hear one of the two speakers (viz., Michi), but we only hear the filtered voice of the other speaker (Yabe), whom we do not see. Signal processing in the form of filter effects, equalization, and reverb has been applied to the voice of the unseen interlocutor Yabe to make it sound even more electronic than it normally would.⁴¹ More importantly, what distinguishes this particular telepheme is that the voice on the other end is acousmatic in an uncanny way. Typically, Chion explains, the *acousmêtre* is only effective so long as it has not been visualized, since as soon as it enters the visual field—as soon as the voice shows itself and "the person speaking…inscribe[s] his or her body inside the frame"—then the *acousmêtre* becomes "de-acousmatized" and "loses its power, omniscience, and (obviously) ubiquity."⁴² However, in the case of Yabe in *Kairo*, his *acousmêtre* momentarily "de-acousmatizes" only to re-acousmatize again: just as we think we will be able to attach a body to the voice of Yabe after the phone call ends when Michi goes to the location where Yabe placed his call to speak directly to him, the body of Yabe disappears—turning into a black stain on the wall—and Michi is confronted with the enigma of Yabe's acousmatic voice yet again (Fig. 2.4). To underscore the effect, ambient noise drops out completely in the mix and only the repeated sound of Yabe's disembodied, whispered pleas for help can be heard.

Although distribution prints of *Kairo* were originally released in Dolby SR (Spectral Recording), a noise reduction format that provided four channels of audio (left, center, right, and mono surround), on the standard optical soundtrack for exhibition venues that could accommodate it, the initial 2001 DVD release of *Kairo* in Japan, as well as the 2006 DVD release in North America, included only a Dolby Digital two-channel stereo audio track. However, the 2007 DVD re-release in Japan added 5.1 surround audio as an option. When listened to in multichannel surround, the effect of Yabe's acousmatic voice becomes even more pronounced. As William Whittington notes, in the surround sound version

Fig. 2.4   The Hiroshima-like shadow left by Yabe in *Kairo* (2001b)

of the film, Yabe's voice "moves hauntingly from the surrounds, to left and right channels, and finally to the front channel, affirming the sense of disembodiment."[43]

Kairo's use of the acousmatic telepheme also links up with other issues engaged by the film, which I explore at greater length in my study of Japanese posthumanism titled *Tokyo Cyberpunk: Posthumanism in Japanese Visual Culture*.[44] For example, the black stain marking the absence of Yabe, which functions as a metaphor for the viral spread of Internet-facilitated suicide, assuming apocalyptic proportions by film's end as hundreds of thousands, perhaps millions, of residents disappear from cities all across Japan, evokes the trauma of the atomic bombs dropped on Hiroshima and Nagasaki and the intense thermal rays that literally burnt human shadows into stone, which could clearly be seen for ten years after the explosions.[45] Although commonly referred to as "Pulse" in English, this is actually a poor translation of *Kairo*. A better translation would be "circuit," as in "electronic circuit." *Kairo* takes up the mantle of viral techno-horror made famous by Nakata Hideo's *Ringu*, but goes beyond *Ringu* in terms of both the sense of uncanny unease that it evokes through sound design and the sort of philosophical questions it raises, exploring the increasingly complex circuitry of relations between modernity, technology, and human communication. *Kairo* won the International Federation of Film Critics' Prize at the Cannes Film Festival in 2001 for presenting "an original view on the 'virtual' danger of the world of computers."[46] Both *Ringu* and *Kairo* broke new ground by visualizing the viral aspects of technology in the space of horror, making technology an issue for horror in ways that go well beyond traditional Japanese horror cinema. In the wake of *Ringu* and *Kairo*, ghosts appearing in Japanese techno-horror films often function like telemarketers from the dead, haunting their victims by means of available imaging and telecommunication technologies, whether it be through videotape, telephone, cell phone, e-mail, or the Internet, and spreading like a virus from one person to the next.

By linking ghosts to the Internet, *Kairo* addresses the isolation of the modern individual and offers an allegory for our loss of connection with one another in an increasingly technological world as we become increasingly ghost-like in our virtual interactions with one another. In this regard, the retro-sounding noise of a dial-up modem connecting to the Internet plays a crucial role. At the outset of *Kairo*, before the very first shot, as the distribution and production credits start to appear, for a full 17 seconds we hear nothing but the chirping, squealing sounds of a computer modem handshaking with a server to establish a connection so that the transfer of information may occur. In other words, what we hear at the outset of the film and at key moments throughout are the voices of electronic "circuits" (the literal meaning of the word "*kairo*") communicating with each other. Such sounds are used by the film to suggest not only the automated process by which different systems and forms of technology establish a communication channel and negotiate telecommunication protocols based on information transfer rates and other parameters, but also a correlation between the transfer rate of ghosts into the world and the rate of disconnection experienced by Internet-addicted web users, who contract a virus spread via the Internet that increases their sense of isolation and fills them with the desire to commit suicide.

Modem dial-up sounds are not the only electromechanical noises that are used to good effect in the soundscapes of Kurosawa's horror cinema, as is evident in a terrifying scene that appears towards the end of *Kairo*.

In the film's final act, after the parallel storylines of two survivors, Michi and Kawashima, have intersected, Kawashima has an encounter with a ghost in an abandoned factory. As is often the case in Kurosawa's films, settings that evoke an aesthetics of architectural decay—especially rundown hospitals, abandoned factories, and dilapidated warehouses—may serve as spatial metaphors for the decaying state of Japanese modernity following the collapse of the bubble economy, evoking double-edged connotations in the form of both a nostalgia for the past and an ambivalence over what has taken its place. In the context of an abandoned factory mise-en-scène in which Kawashima encounters a ghost face-to-face, a variety of electro-mechanical noises are employed, from low- and mid-frequency machine hums and drones to glitching, high-pitched electronic chirps and feedback squeals, from electric locking noises to electronically filtered voices. In interviews, Kurosawa has indicated that he specifically wanted it to sound as if Kawashima had been trapped in a machine when he enters the factory room in *Kairo*. The ghost's electronic-sounding voice and breathing, recalling the acousmatic voice of Yabe, is made all the more strange by the application of reverse reverberation, which makes the attack of the ghost's voice swell at the beginning of each word.

As is often the case in scenes from the cinema of Kurosawa Kiyoshi that make use of ambient drones, the characters who are on-screen while such drones are audible appear transfixed, seemingly disconnected from their environments and temporarily suspended in time. What I am calling a "drone" is different from the low-frequency "rumble" so often used in contemporary Hollywood films to take advantage of the subwoofer channel in a surround sound mix. An ambient drone (not to be confused with drones of the flying variety) is a continuous or repeated pitch or cluster of frequencies that establishes a sustained tonality over a period of time, thereby creating a sonic atmosphere. Drones are also employed to good effect in the soundtracks of numerous John Carpenter films, such as *The Fog* (1980), *Escape from New York* (1981), and *The Thing* (1982), but Carpenter's mostly synthesized drones differ insofar as they are typically part of the nondiegetic musical score. In contrast, the ambient drones in Kurosawa's films are often non-musical and frequently blur the boundaries between diegetic and nondiegetic.[47] The sustained droning sounds that we hear during Kawashima's encounter with the ghost in the factory scene (and at other times during the film) are more complex than simply low-frequency subwoofer effects since they are modulated by a slow pulse or sweep; yet, they are not functioning as music either. Such ambient drones are *non-signifying*—they have neither meaning nor obvious source object; however, as the sound-image relations in such scenes suggest, that does not mean that the affective impact of such drones on the spectators watching the film is insignificant.[48] Far from it. Even if we are not consciously aware of such drones, they nonetheless impact us as audio spectators, producing resonance effects on the edge of meaning.[49]

Sonic Drones and Temporal Suspensions

With its improved dynamics, greater frequency range, and significant noise reduction, the introduction of Dolby Stereo in 1975 greatly enhanced our ability to hear such sonic drones and other ambient noises. According to Michel Chion, Dolby effectively "changed the balance of sounds, particularly by taking a great leap forward in the reproduction of noises" and heralding a "new sensory cinema."[50] In her analysis of European horror films that critics have grouped under the label "New Extremism," Lisa Coulthard underscores the importance of Chion's conceptualization of this cinema of noises:

> Chion anticipates this link between Dolby digital and a more haptic, tactile cinematic noise when he argues that Dolby stereo heralded a "new sensory cinema" focused on the sound effects associated with everyday actions of the body (breath, skin touches, cloth movements, footsteps), technology (machine hums, traffic noise, engine rumbles), and the environment (animal cries, bird songs, cricket chirps). This new sensory cinema communicates sensations of physical, bodily life through an intensification of its sounds. This last point is crucial: we hear not only with our ears, but our entire bodies. Whether it is the purr of rumbling engines or the unbearable intimacy of a closely miked breath played loud in the mix, sound can send shivers up one's back, increase the rapidity of a heartbeat, or create nausea, anxiety, or uneasiness.[51]

There is no question that continued advances in cinema sound technology, including Dolby Stereo in 1975, followed by Dolby Surround in 1982, Dolby Digital in 1991, and Dolby Atmos in 2012, have significantly expanded the ability of horror filmmakers to make evocative use of ambient noise to alter our perception of cinematic space, but it must also be acknowledged that such noise has been an integral part of sound cinema in the genre of horror practically from the very beginning.

One of the earliest horror films to make extensive use of ambient noise and sonic drones was James Whale's *Frankenstein* (1931). Although a film titled *The Terror* (1928) directed by Roy Del Ruth was the first horror film to be released with sound utilizing the Vitaphone sound-on-disc system and featured an array of scary noises—from howling wind to creaking doors—*Frankenstein* is probably the earliest horror film to incorporate electrical sounds in the creation of ambience and the sonic mediation of cinematic space. As is clear from the shooting script for *Frankenstein*, James Whale wanted the production design of Dr. Frankenstein's laboratory to rival that of Rotwang in Fritz Lang's *Metropolis* (1927)—an influence that Whale inherited from the uncredited shooting script written by Robert Florey upon which Whale's screenplay was based. In the stage directions for *Frankenstein*, Dr. Frankenstein's laboratory is described as follows:

> At one side of the room, covering a vast amount of wall-space, is an intricate electrical machine—a glittering, mysterious apparatus with generators, transformers, wave charger, diffusers, a large rotary spark gap, etc.—very impressive looking, as it looms large and forbidding in the gloom of the room.... In actuality, it is more impressionistic than scientific, and designed to create a feeling of modern scientific "magic"—something suggestive of the laboratory in "Metropolis."[52]

However, where Whale's *Frankenstein* surpassed Lang's *Metropolis* was through the inclusion of ambient noise designed to suggest a sonic sense of place. The buzzing, arcing, crackling, and humming sounds of electricity that fill Dr. Frankenstein's laboratory and give life to his monster were the creation of Kenneth Strickfaden, a visual and audio special effects technician, who developed a whole range of Tesla-inspired special effects equipment for Frankenstein's laboratory.[53]

The cinema of Kurosawa Kiyoshi may seem worlds apart from James Whale's *Frankenstein*, but one thing that Kurosawa has repeatedly underscored in his interviews and lectures on the history of horror is the importance of the early horror films made by Universal Studios to his conception of horror, including films such as *Frankenstein, Dracula* (dir. Tod Browning, 1931), *The Mummy* (dir. Karl Freund, 1932), and others.[54] Indeed, it is hard to imagine J-horror's distinctive sonic atmospheres, which are replete with ambient noise, drones, and low-frequency effects, without such non-Japanese precursors. Many of the filmmakers that I have mentioned, from James Whale to Stanley Kubrick to William Friedkin, have exerted a transnational influence on the development of ambient noise in contemporary J-horror where ambience frequently functions as a tool not simply of "worldizing," in the language of renowned film editor and sound designer Walter Murch, but more importantly as a tool of "other-worldizing": i.e., ambient soundscapes are used to *defamiliarize* the diegetic worlds inhabited by the characters in J-horror just as much as they are to create the impression that the characters exist in a real acoustic space or environment. Nowhere is this more apparent than in Kurosawa's acclaimed horror-thriller *Cure*.

Cure is the film that put Kurosawa Kiyoshi's name on the map of cutting-edge international filmmakers, having received numerous awards and accolades, including Best Film at the Japanese Professional Movie Awards in 1998 and three Best Actor Awards for Yakusho Kōji's portrayal of Detective Takabe. In addition to directing the film, Kurosawa wrote the screenplay and novel upon which it was based.[55] *Cure* offers an unusual twist on the serial killer film by introducing an amnesiac mesmerist named Mamiya who never kills anyone himself, but instead hypnotizes others into doing so, using techniques that he has derived from research on Franz Anton Mesmer's (1734–1815) theory of animal magnetism. By repeatedly posing the existential question—"Who are you?"— to the agents of modernity (in the guise of teachers, doctors, psychiatrists, police officers, and detectives), Mamiya throws into question metaphysical conceptions of the subject, demystifying notions of stable self-identity as fictions, thereby, making his listeners more vulnerable to hypnotic suggestion. "There is no real you here either [*hontō no anata wa koko ni mo inai*]," Mamiya suggests to Detective Takabe, rejecting Takabe's conflation of his identity with either his occupation as detective or the social role he plays as husband. Sounding more like an unabashed nihilist than a wayward Zen Buddhist, Mamiya celebrates the fact that there is no stable or metaphysical self, no fixed or timeless identity, but only unstable, fragmented subjects who are definitely not masters of their own houses. He tells his victims that if they make themselves empty as he has done, they will feel born again.

One such victim is psychiatrist Sakuma Makoto (played by Ujiki Tsuyoshi), who experiences a trance-like hallucination in his apartment after showing Takabe the oldest extant film of a hypnotism session in Japan that dates back to 1898, which presents an unidentified man hypnotizing a woman by drawing an "X" in the air.[56] After explaining to Takabe that government authorities during the Meiji period would have suppressed such a technique due to its association with occultism, Sakuma's trance commences with a low-frequency electromechanical drone that runs throughout the entire hallucination. In quick succession, we see and hear a junkyard incinerator whose abrupt amplitude fluctuation startles the viewer followed by various animals in small cages, some of which are emitting sounds of distress and discomfort. As recent studies by evolutionary biologists and bioacoustics specialists have demonstrated, nonlinear vocal phenomena in the form of animal cries and other sounds of distress that are produced by a variety of vertebrates are typically perceived by other vertebrates (especially mammals) as harsh, irregular, and disturbing precisely because of the nonlinear dynamics of such vocalizations.[57] The nonlinear dynamics of the animal cries heard in this introduction to Mamiya's lair are quite effective at evoking a sense of discomfort in the spectator.

As his hallucination develops, alternating between subjective and objective camera shots, Sakuma tours Mamiya's apartment while detectives collect evidence. Sakuma picks up a book titled *Heresies* (*Jakyō*) from Mamiya's desk. He flips to a chapter titled "Mesmerian" and examines its pages, which include the defaced photo of a man named Hakuraku Tōjirō who died in 1898, perhaps the same Meiji-era Japanese hypnotist seen performing in the short film analyzed in Sakuma's apartment. As the scene cuts to a long shot of Sakuma standing in a desolate field looking at a large, abandoned building (perhaps an old dormitory), a dissonant string cue drenched in reverb can be heard along with the howling wind and the ever-present droning sound. In the window peering out at Sakuma appears to be the man featured in the book on heresies. Then it cuts to Sakuma entering the cell of Mamiya at the psychiatric ward where he is being held. As the string cue is repeated in the background, the drone increases in volume and random violin plucks and scrapes raise the tension of the scene. Inside of Mamiya's cell, Sakuma encounters not Mamiya himself but Detective Takabe, who backs Sakuma into a corner, perhaps a foreshadowing of Takabe's eventual transformation into a Mamiya-like mesmerist at the end of the film. Sakuma is eventually aroused from his hallucination by the sound of Takabe's voice repeating his name. As he snaps out of his trance, the drone also becomes silent.

To better understand how drones modulate the soundscapes of *Cure*, it helps to view spectrographic snapshots of the soundtrack for this scene— Fig. 2.5 was taken just before Sakuma's hallucination, and Fig. 2.6 was taken during his hallucination. Earlier, we considered the spectral characteristics of the acousmatic voice in *Séance* through the lens of a spectrogram. Here,

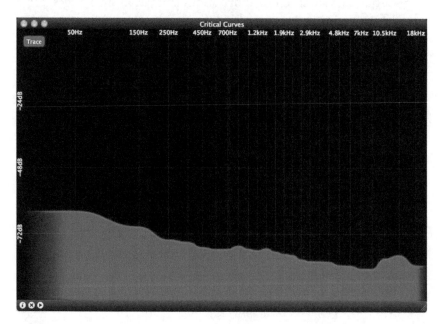

Fig. 2.5 Spectrographic snapshot before Sakuma's hallucination

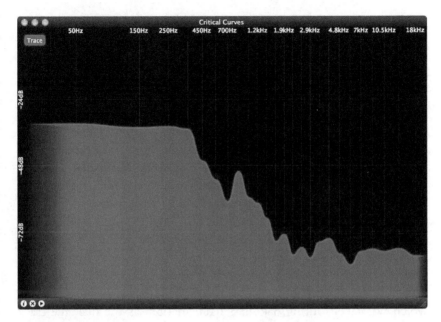

Fig. 2.6 Spectrographic snapshot during Sakuma's hallucination

I have applied a spectrograph to the audio track. The difference between a spectrogram and a spectrograph is that whereas a spectrogram displays the frequency content of the audio over time, with the x-axis showing time in seconds, the y-axis showing frequency, and color showing intensity of frequency, a spectrograph displays the frequency content of the audio mapped to volume at a given instant of time, with the x-axis showing frequency measured in hertz and the y-axis indicating volume level measured in decibels. By analyzing the sound flows of this scene by means of a spectrograph, it becomes obvious just how much the drone is contributing to the sound-image relations of the scene. Before Sakuma's hallucination, the frequency levels are relatively flat and the dynamics compressed. However, during Sakuma's hallucination, a low-to-mid frequency drone in the 20 Hz to 400 Hz range is introduced and the volume level dramatically increases a full 34 dB. Keep in mind that a mere 6-dB change would be perceived as twice the volume. In the spectrograph in Fig. 2.6, the drone appears as a plateau or shelf. We can also see the random violin plucks and scrapes in the 1.2 kHz range and higher.

It is also quite instructive to look at the same scene through a vector-scope, which displays coherence between two audio channels in the form of Lissajous curves or figures, which in the world of mathematics are typically used to graph a system of parametric equations that describe complex harmonic motion. In the realm of acoustics, the vectorscope is typically used to show the distribution of sound across the stereo space and detect any possible phase issues in a dual-channel signal. As is the case with many of Kurosawa's low-budget films, the soundtrack for *Cure* was originally in Dolby Digital two-channel stereo. Nevertheless, within the limitations of stereo, Kurosawa is still able to accomplish quite a lot simply by manipulating the stereo field. In the snapshot in Fig. 2.7, which was taken just before Sakuma's hallucination as Sakuma is telling Takabe about the government suppression of hypnotism in Meiji Japan, Sakuma's spoken words appear in the center of the stereo field, as indicated by the cone-shaped figure, which is where one would normally expect diegetic speech to be placed. However, in the snapshot in Fig. 2.8, which was taken during Sakuma's hallucination, as the dialogue track drops out and the ambient drone rises in the mix, notice how much of the stereo space is filled by the drone. The stereo space has suddenly become extraordinarily wide, and this widening of the stereo signal contributes to the feeling that the sound is all-enveloping.

Responding to an interviewer's question about the role of droning sounds in his films, Kurosawa remarked, "In my films I don't like to use sound to elaborate the story. The story is the story and sound operates on a slightly different plane. As I mentioned, film to me is somewhere in between reality and fiction and I think of sound as defining the world that I've created in that film. Sound is what defines the place that is neither story nor reality, but in between. Because I think when you're telling the story in visual images you reflect the characters and they can only be what they are. They are two-dimensional. But in a way sound can give you a three-dimensional signal of the world."[58] By examining Kurosawa's use of drones through the lens of both a spectrograph and a vectorscope, it becomes apparent how sound flows operate at the acoustic level to create the "three-dimensional signal of the world" that Kurosawa is trying to evoke.

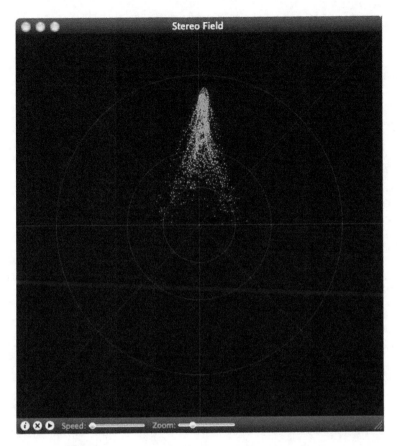

Fig. 2.7 Vectorscope image before Sakuma's hallucination

The soundscapes of *Cure* include diverse electromechanical sounds associated with modern industrialized life, such as the incessant spinning of an empty washing machine, the flickering of fluorescent lights, the dinging of a train crossing signal, and so forth, but it is the electromechanical drones in scenes such as Sakuma's hallucination that have prompted a number of reviewers to attach the label "trance films" to Kurosawa Kiyoshi's genre-bending experiments with horror. If Kurosawa's horror films warrant such an appellation, it has much to do with the way

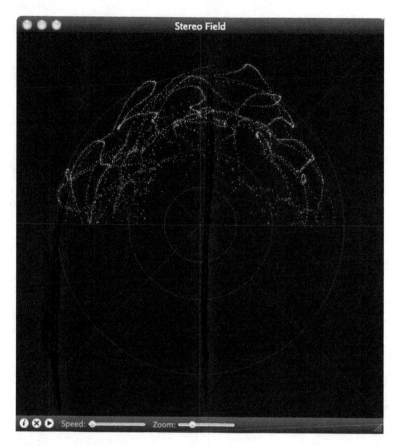

Fig. 2.8 Vectorscope image during Sakuma's hallucination

in which their drone-filled soundscapes put the audio spectator in an affective state of suspension similar to the films of Italian director Michelangelo Antonioni, such as *Red Desert* (*Il deserto rosso*, 1964).

Awarded the Golden Lion at the 25th Venice Film Festival in 1964, *Red Desert* was Antonioni's first color film and one of the most effective at showing how industrial noise and ambient drones can modulate affect in cinema. Monica Vitti plays a character named Giuliana, who, after a suicide attempt, has just been released from the hospital and is having trouble adjusting to life with her husband in a polluted industrial area of

Ravenna, where her husband is director of a national chemical plant. Giuliana is suffering from an anxiety disorder that makes her afraid of just about everything associated with the industrialized postwar world of Italy in the 1960s.

In addition to employing a variety of industrial sounds, including the din of chemical plant machinery and hum of a power station, as well as the sound of steam erupting from factory pipes, the soundtrack of *Red Desert* also includes an electronic music score composed by Vittorio Gelmetti that makes use of analog synthesizers to provide sound effects at key moments to suggest Giuliana's mental confusion. By overlaying industrial sounds with electronic drones, the soundtrack of *Red Desert* makes audible Giuliana's anxieties vis-à-vis the modern world, which are swirling around the protagonist's alienated mind (see Fig. 2.9). As Italian film scholar David Forgacs has noted, the entire "atmosphere grows oppressive" once the electronic noise "become[s] prominent."[59] Blurring the boundary between music and sound effects, Gelmetti's electronic score for *Red Desert* does an effective job of expressing Giuliana's affective states of anxiety, confusion, and isolation. Moreover, the electromechanical drones of *Red Desert* work together with the images "to create the sense

Fig. 2.9 Giuliana suspended in time in *Red Desert* (1964)

that time itself seems to be momentarily suspended, for both the film's characters and its viewers," as Andy Birtwistle has remarked, thereby underscoring Giuliana's "psychological disconnection from the immediate environment."[60]

Something similar is at work in the sound-image relations of Kurosawa's *Cure*. As in Antonioni's *Red Desert*, the ambient drones in Kurosawa's films frequently do not have an identifiable source object, making it unclear whether they are diegetic or nondiegetic. But it is precisely this indeterminacy that makes Kurosawa's drones all the more disturbing. Likewise, the characters that are on-screen while such drones are audible frequently appear transfixed, seemingly disconnected from their environments and temporarily suspended in time (see Fig. 2.10).[61] Although other directors of Japanese horror, such as Nakata Hideo, Shimizu Takashi, Miike Takashi, Sono Sion, and Tsuruta Norio, have also made use of ambient noise and low-frequency drones, few directors of horror employ such sound design techniques as effectively as Kurosawa Kiyoshi.

Fig. 2.10 Sakuma suspended in time in *Cure* (1997a)

Absolute Silence

As deft as Kurosawa is at manipulating noise and drones to modulate the soundscapes of his horror films, perhaps his boldest experiments with sound design involve his use of absolute silence. By absolute silence I do not mean merely diegetic silence (in which selected diegetic parts of the soundtrack are silenced and filled by music or nondiegetic sounds); nor do I mean dialogue silence (in which dialogue is suppressed while ambient sounds and nondiegetic music continue to be heard); nor am I referring to musical silence (in which music is suppressed where one would otherwise expect to hear it).[62] By absolute silence I mean the total suspension of sound, as occurs in an early scene from *Séance*, in which the spiritual medium Junko witnesses a footless ghost follow a customer out the door at the restaurant where she works (Fig. 2.11). This scene pays homage to

Fig. 2.11 A footless ghost follows a customer exiting a restaurant in *Séance* (1999)

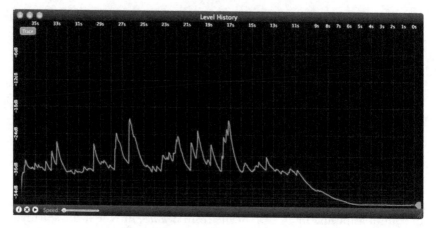

Fig. 2.12 The suspension of sound in *Séance* (1999)

the so-called "footless ghost" motif visualized in the Japanese hanging scroll and woodblock print traditions, in which ghosts are depicted without feet (or in some cases even lower legs) since they occupy a liminal zone between this world and the next. As Tim Screech has remarked, "Legs serve to join creatures to the soil, they root beings to the earth, and so to be [footless or] legless is in a sense to be disengaged."[63]

In my opinion the most impressive aspect of this scene from *Séance* is Kurosawa's use of silence. As the snapshot from a level history meter in Fig. 2.12 shows, which displays the level of the scene's audio over time, the ambient noise of the restaurant drops to absolute silence for almost a full ten seconds as the ghost in red follows the restaurant diner out the door. Ten seconds of absolute silence is an eternity in film. As scholar of film sound Paul Théberge has commented, "silence holds an ambivalent status in theories of film sound" primarily insofar as "it is conventionally held that absolute silence cannot be allowed to occur in film" lest it risk "being interpreted, by audiences, as a technical breakdown."[64] If there is no sound, many spectators think there is something wrong with a film. Given the relative rarity of absolute silence in the history of sound cinema, which is largely restricted, as Théberge has noted, to "instances where intensely dramatic or violent acts are depicted,"[65] it is, therefore, highly significant that absolute silence can be found in almost every horror film directed by Kurosawa Kiyoshi and, in some cases, it is used more than once in the same film. Kurosawa tends to employ the total suspension of sound at those moments where a Hollywood director of a mainstream horror film would insert a stinger chord or sudden blast of noise designed to elicit the startle response and make the audience jump out of their seats.[66] But Kurosawa is not interested in musical stingers. In fact, stinger chords and startle effects are largely absent from his films. Rather than underscoring a scene of horror with stingers, Kurosawa prefers to let the moment of horror speak for itself either suspended in time against the backdrop of an ambient drone (as noted in relation to *Cure*) or suspended in silence (as is the case in the scene from *Séance*).

Although Kurosawa generally eschews the clichéd use of stinger chords and startle effects that one encounters in contemporary Hollywood horror cinema, his employment of absolute silence owes a considerable debt to British and American horror from a different era, particularly British director Jack Clayton's deft use of silence in the Twentieth Century Fox film *The Innocents* (1961), a film that Kurosawa has praised for its chilling depiction of ghosts:

> Clayton's influence on me was very important. In fact, it wasn't important only for me, but for many filmmakers who belonged to what has been called the "Japanese Horror." When I saw *The Innocents* for the first time, I was deeply impressed by its way of representing phantoms, a way I had never seen before. The movie by Clayton was essential for me, not necessarily because of its beauty, not necessarily even because of its greatness, but simply because it is scary...I see *The Innocents* as the first film that managed to make visible a blurry, uncertain existence—to make that somehow real. It's the first film that shows ghosts as being *present*, existing truly, irrefutably.[67]

The interplay of sound and silence plays an enormously important role in how ghosts are presented in *The Innocents*. But here it is also noteworthy that, like *Ringu*-screenwriter Takahashi Hiroshi whose questioning of the "Japaneseness" of "J-horror" I quoted in the introduction, Kurosawa similarly underscores the transnational impact of British ghost films on the development of contemporary Japanese horror.

Regarding the interplay of sound and silence in horror, it should also be pointed out that for absolute silence to be effective it must be relational.

Interrupting sound flows with the suspension of sound only works if the contrast between sound and silence is contextual. As Michel Chion has suggested in his study *Audio-Vision: Sound on Screen*, "the impression of silence in a film scene does not simply come from an absence of noise. It can only be produced as a result of context and preparation...[S]ilence is never a neutral emptiness. It is the negative of sound we've heard beforehand or imagined; it is the product of a contrast."[68] In the case of the scene of the footless ghost from *Séance*, silence is especially effective because of the contrast it sets up with the mundane sounds that previously infused the scene of people talking during lunch at the restaurant where the ghost appears. The absolute silence that Kurosawa inserts suspends the everydayness of the mise-en-scène and underscores the temporal suspension that Junko must also feel each time she encounters a ghost.[69]

In this connection, the increased clarity, superior noise reduction, better dynamics, and excellent frequency separation offered by Dolby Digital ensure that the absolute silence of this scene from *Séance* (and others like it) is truly silent—without the hiss or ground noise associated with classical sound cinema in the pre-Dolby era. As Chion has pointed out, "Dolby cinema thus introduces a new expressive element: the silence of the loudspeakers, accompanied by its reflection, the attentive silence of the audience. Any silence makes us feel exposed, as if it were laying bare our own listening, but also as if we were in the presence of a giant ear, tuned to our own slightest noises. We are no longer merely listening to the film, we are as it were being listened to by it as well."[70] In the horror cinema of Kurosawa Kiyoshi, it is not simply the film that listens to us; it is also the abyssal clarity of absolute silence. With a nod to Chion (and to paraphrase Nietzsche), when the audience listens to the abyss of silence in a Kurosawa Kiyoshi film, sometimes the abyss uncannily listens back...

Reinventing the Scream

Along the continuum of sonic events presented to the horror spectator in the mediated space of cinema, at the opposite end of absolute silence is what Chion calls the "screaming point" (*le point de cri*). If the "silence of the loudspeakers" invites the audience's quiet attention, the "screaming point" commands it. The final sonic technique that I would like to consider is Kurosawa's reinvention of the "screaming point" in his 2006 film *Sakebi* and how it relates to what I call "haptic sonority."[71] *Sakebi* deals with a police detective named Yoshioka (performed by Yakusho Kōji, the same actor who played the sound technician Satō in *Séance*), who is haunted by a mysterious ghost in red after he starts investigating a series of murders and the evidence points to the detective himself as the prime suspect. Although the English title of *Sakebi* is "Retribution," the Japanese title of the film is closer to "Scream" or "Shriek." In addition to directing *Sakebi*, Kurosawa also wrote the screenplay upon which it was based. *Sakebi* was originally commissioned for a series of six films titled "J-Horror Theater," which was the brainchild of legendary J-horror producer Ichise Takashige.

The reason for the English mistranslation of *Sakebi* as "Retribution" was probably to distinguish Kurosawa's film from Wes Craven's 1996 horror parody titled *Scream*, which was marketed in Japan as *Sukurīmu* (スクリーム). Rather than being a tongue-in-cheek exercise in postmodern irony à la Craven, Kurosawa's title references an altogether different "scream": namely, Edvard Munch's earliest painted version of *The Scream* (*Skrik* in Norwegian) from 1893, whose original title was *Der Schrei der Natur* (The Scream of Nature). In Japan, "*Sakebi*" is how the title of Edvard Munch's most famous painting has been translated into Japanese ever since it was first introduced to a Japanese audience in the April 1912 issue of the Japanese literary magazine *Shirakaba* (White Birch).

There is no question that Munch's painting (along with its later versions and variations) is a significant intermedial text for Kurosawa's film *Sakebi*. Although *The Scream* is perhaps most often interpreted as an artistic expression of modern alienation and existential angst (and it certainly is that on some level), researchers at the Munch Museum in Oslo have speculated that for Munch himself, it may have been inspired by a literary passage from Dostoevsky's *Crime and Punishment* (1867), which had been translated into Norwego-Danish in 1884 and which Munch considered one of the most profound works of literature he had ever read.[72] The passage in question occurs after the novel's protagonist Raskolnikov, who had carried out the murders of an elderly moneylender and her sister only two chapters earlier, is awakened at dusk by a horrible, fearful scream, composed of "unnatural sounds," such as "he had never heard" before:

> It was dusk when he was waked up by a fearful scream. Good God, what a scream! Such unnatural sounds, such howling, wailing, grinding, tears, blows and curses he had never heard.
>
> He could never have imagined such brutality, such frenzy. In terror he sat up in bed, almost swooning with agony. But the fighting, wailing and cursing grew louder and louder. And then to his intense amazement he caught the voice of his landlady. She was howling, shrieking and wailing, rapidly, hurriedly, incoherently, so that he could not make out what she was talking about...Raskolnikov sank worn out on the sofa, but could not close his eyes. He lay for half an hour in such anguish, such an intolerable sensation of infinite terror as he had never experienced before.[73]

When Raskolnikov makes inquiries about the source of the scream, it becomes clear that he has experienced an auditory hallucination and that his guilty conscience has started to overwhelm him.

Although Munch never explicitly associated the mise-en-scène of *The Scream* with murder per se, in a text he composed in 1908 to accompany the 1893 painting (and other variants in the series), Munch synesthetically interweaves visual metaphors of violence involving "a flaming sword of blood [that] slashed open the firmament" with auditory recollections of hearing "a great scream" of nature:

> One evening I am walking down a mountain road near Christiania— together with two friends. It was a time when life had torn my soul asunder.
>
> The sun went down—had dipped quickly below the horizon—
>
> Then it was as though a flaming sword of blood slashed open the firmament—the air became like blood—with dazzling strands of fire—the hills grew deep blue—the fjord—sliced across in cold blue—yellow and red hues—the garish blood red—on the road—and the fence—my friends' faces became waxen—I felt as though I heard a great scream—and truly I did hear a great scream—

The colours in nature—broke the lines in nature—the lines and colours shimmered in movement—these vibrations of the light not only set my eyes vibrating—they also set my ears vibrating—so that I actually heard a great scream.[74]

Contemporary astronomers have speculated that the blood-red sky evoked by Munch in *The Scream* was caused by the eruption of the Krakatoa volcano on August 27, 1883, which discharged dust and gas into the atmosphere, creating a glowing red twilight that reportedly could be seen in Norway from the end of November 1883 until mid-February 1884.[75] However, the atmospheric effects created by the volcano are not enough to explain why Munch also felt that his ears were "vibrating" such that he "actually heard a great scream." It is this auditory dimension of *The Scream*—whose wave-like cloud bands have been interpreted by some art historians as "visualizations of sound waves"[76]—that has prompted some Munch scholars to point to the artist's fascination with *Crime and Punishment* as a likely source of inspiration.

However, it should also be pointed out that for the lithograph version of *The Scream* created in 1895, Munch added the German title "*Geschrei*" (screams, shrieks, screaming) along with the following caption: "*Ich fühlte das grosse Geschrei durch die Natur* [I felt the great screaming through nature]." Although Munch claims not to have read the works of German philosopher Arthur Schopenhauer (1788–1860) until much later in life, respected Munch scholar and former director of the Munch Museum Arne Eggum sees in Munch's choice of title and caption for the lithograph an allusion to the great philosopher of pessimism: "The fact that Munch chose the word 'Geschrei' (instead of 'Schrei') may very well stem from the German philosopher Schopenhauer's comment that the ultimate for pictorial art lay in the possibility of depicting precisely 'das Geschrei.'"[77] In his magnum opus *The World as Will and Representation* (*Die Welt als Wille und Vorstellung*, 1818/9; 2nd ed. 1844), Schopenhauer takes up the aesthetic debate between Johann Joachim Winckelmann (1717–1768) and Gotthold Ephraim Lessing (1729–1781) concerning the question of whether the famous marble sculpture depicting the death of Laocoön (*Laocoön and His Sons*, c. 27 BCE–68 CE) at the hands of giant serpents shows Laocoön crying out or not.

Winckelmann, the German Hellenist and historian of ancient art, had famously argued that the figure of Laocoön expressed "the tried spirit of a great man writhing in agony who tries to hold back the expression of feeling and shuts it up within himself: he does not break out into a loud scream [*lautes Geschrei*], as in Virgil; only worried sighs escape from him."[78] Here Winckelmann is responding to Virgil's depiction of Laocoön in the *Aeneid* (2.220–24), who, while trying to break free from the serpents' grasp, is described as having "simultaneously raised to the heavens horrendous screams [*clamores simul horrendos ad sidera tollit*]"[79] in response to the "black venom" of their bite. Since Winckelmann thinks it beneath Laocoön's dignity to cry out in this manner, he interprets the sculpture as showing the noble Trojan priest stoically suppressing the natural urge to cry out. In his polemic against Winckelmann, Lessing takes issue with Winckelmann's psychological interpretation of Laocoön's emotional restraint as an expression of Greek Stoicism. According to Lessing, if Laocoön does not cry out, it is due to both the limitations of the sculptural medium itself, which can only depict a single moment that has been frozen in time, and the unaesthetic qualities of an open mouth, which Lessing thinks would compromise the beauty of the sculpture. "Pain, in its disfiguring extreme," writes Lessing, "was not compatible with beauty, and must therefore be softened."

> Screams must be reduced to sighs, not because screams would betray weakness, but because they would deform the countenance to a repulsive degree. Imagine Laocoon's mouth open, and judge. Let him scream, and see. It was, before, a figure to inspire compassion in its beauty and suffering. Now it is ugly, abhorrent, and we gladly avert our eyes from a painful spectacle, destitute of the beauty which alone could turn our pain into the sweet feeling of pity for the suffering object. The simple opening of the mouth, apart from the violent and repulsive contortions it causes in the other parts of the face, is a blot on a painting and a cavity in a statue productive of the worst possible effect.[80]

Both poetry and drama, according to Lessing, have their respective limitations, but they offer more suitable temporal mediums than sculpture or painting for such intense and prolonged expressions of pain.

When Schopenhauer enters this debate in *The World as Will and Representation*, he immediately takes issue with Lessing's position that "screaming is not compatible with beauty [*das Schreien mit der Schönheit nicht zu vereinigen sei*]."[81] Moreover, although Schopenhauer agrees with Lessing's basic argument that what prevents Laocoön from screaming are the limitations of the artistic medium of sculpture itself, he cannot go so far as to accept Lessing's point that "a stationary work of art cannot portray a wholly ephemeral state that is incapable of duration."[82] In contrast, Schopenhauer contends that "there are hundreds of counter-examples of superb figures held fast in fleeting movements, dancing, wrestling, playing catch, etc."[83] One need only think of the Discobolus of Myron, a renowned bronze sculpture from fifth-century Greece that depicted a discus thrower about to release his throw, to realize the truth of what Schopenhauer suggests about sculpture's ability to evoke kinetic movement. In Schopenhauer's view, the limitations of the Laocoön sculpture have more to do with the inability of the plastic arts to reproduce sound, insofar as "the essence, and consequently the effect, of screaming on the spectator lies exclusively in the sound, not the gaping mouth."[84] In this vein, Schopenhauer adds that a "silent screamer [*stummer Schreier*] in painting or stone" would be "even more ridiculous."[85]

If Munch's choice of "*Geschrei*" for the German title of the 1895 lithograph is any indication, then *The Scream* series offers Munch's response to Schopenhauer et al. on the aesthetic limits of expressing a scream in the visual arts. Even if the gaping mouth of Munch's screamer would have repulsed Lessing and cannot lay claim to reproducing the sound waves constituting a sonic scream, surely *The Scream* evokes the act of screaming itself. If the sculpture of a wrestler or discus thrower can suggest implied movement, why cannot the painting of someone screaming suggest implied sound? From the sculptural figuration of Laocoön's travails in *Laocoön and His Sons* to poetic descriptions of his struggles in Virgil's *Aeneid*, from the fierce theoretical debates about the scream (or silence) of Laocoön waged among luminaries in the history of German aesthetics[86] to Munch's various painted and graphic versions of *The Scream*, the *Geschrei* of Laocoön (whether voiced, suppressed, or silent) demands our attention as it reverberates across multiple cultures, periods, languages, genres, and mediums.

Whether or not Kurosawa is aware of this long history of aesthetic debates surrounding the scream of Laocoön, *Sakebi* resonates with this history by way of Munch. That Kurosawa effectively invokes Edvard Munch's *Scream* in his film of the same name (translated into Japanese) by repeatedly showing the ghost of a murdered woman emit a spine-chilling shriek seems clear (Fig. 2.13). However, the question that I would like to consider in the remainder of this chapter is the function of the scream, both as an artistic citation and a sonic motif, in the context of Kurosawa's film. Does the scream in *Sakebi* simply recapitulate the "screaming point" in Michel Chion's sense of the term, or does it offer something different? Let us start with Chion's definition of the "screaming point":

> So let us define the *screaming point* [le *point de cri*] in a cinematic narrative as something that generally gushes forth from the mouth of a woman, which by the way does not have to be heard, but which above all must fall at an appointed spot, explode at a precise moment, at the crossroads of converging plot lines, at the end of an often convoluted trajectory, but calculated to give this point a maximum impact. The film functions like a Rube Goldberg cartoon mechanism full of gears, pistons, chains and belts—a machine built to give birth to a scream.[87]

Fig. 2.13 A ghost (*left*) emits a spine-chilling shriek that evokes Edvard Munch's *The Scream* in Kurosawa Kiyoshi's *Sakebi* (2006b).

Chion concludes that "it's not so much the sound quality of the scream that's important, but its placement," which he describes as "a point of the unthinkable inside the thought."[88]

In *Sakebi*, Kurosawa employs his usual array of sound design techniques, including the effective use of ambient noise, low-frequency drones, and sonic palimpsests, but then offers a fresh twist on the sound design of the scream. Although Kurosawa regularly uses Dolby Digital because of its increased clarity and excellent frequency separation, he rarely utilizes surround sound. Most of his horror films to date have been in Dolby Digital 2.0—i.e., two-channel stereo. However, the sound design of *Sakebi* is in surround. Perhaps the most interesting aspect of *Sakebi*'s surround sound is how the voice of the shrieking ghost is situated. The ghost's voice is close-miked and lacks reverb, which makes it sound more intimate. But even more interesting is Kurosawa's choice to mix the ghost's scream across all five channels of surround sound. Typically, speech and dialogue are reserved for the center channel, but Kurosawa distributes the ghost's scream across every channel of the surround sound field except the subwoofer: i.e., left, center, right, left surround, and right surround. The fact that the ghost's scream can be heard in all channels of the surround sound mix at the same time in *Sakebi* creates the sonic effect of enveloping the listener, making it seem both inescapable and perhaps internal to Detective Yoshioka's mind. It is as if we are inside of Yoshioka's head and can hear the ghost address his innermost thoughts. No other character's voice utilizes the surround channels in this way. Heavy reverb is applied to other aspects of the ghost's visitation, but her voice remains close-miked, lacking reverb, yet coming out of every channel. She is sonically very close yet all-encompassing.

Last but not least, in contrast to Chion, who suggests that "it's not so much the sound quality of the scream that's important, but its placement,"[89] I would argue, on the contrary, that if we are going to take seriously the materiality of film sound, then the sonic characteristics of the scream itself are just as important as its placement. In particular, the fundamental frequency and harmonics of the ghost's scream, which registers its strongest intensity at 2.5 kHz with secondary peaks at 4 kHz and 9 kHz, are essential aspects of how the screaming point is used in *Sakebi*. Human beings typically perceive high-frequency sonic phenomena in the

8 to 12.5 kHz range (equivalent to notes in the ninth octave of the chromatic scale of an equal-tempered instrument) to be especially piercing, but even high middle frequencies around 2.5 kHz (in the neighborhood of D#7 on the chromatic scale) can cause pain and discomfort if the amplitude is high enough. It is probably no accident that the peak frequency most strongly associated with the ghostly scream in Kurosawa's *Sakebi* is 2.5 kHz, which is the specific frequency targeted by the sonic weapon dubbed appropriately enough "The Scream" by the Israeli Defense Force.

As Steve Goodman notes in his study, *Sonic Warfare: Sound, Affect, and the Ecology of Fear* (2009), the Israeli Defense Force has utilized the "non-lethal" sonic weapon known as "The Scream" to control and disperse Palestinian protesters by "target[ing] a specific frequency toward the inner ear."[90] When such sonic weapons (or "Long Range Acoustic Devices," as they are also known) have been deployed, Associated Press journalist Amy Teibel reported that "Protestors covered their ears and grabbed their heads, overcome by dizziness and nausea, after the vehicle-mounted device began sending out bursts of audible, but not loud, sound at intervals of about 10 seconds. An Associated Press photographer at the scene said that even after he covered his ears, he continued to hear the sound ringing in his head."[91] And the Israeli Defense Force is hardly the only group to deploy such weapons. Long Range Acoustic Devices have been used by police and military forces against protesters all around the world, from Pittsburgh to Warsaw, from Ferguson to Delhi. In addition, such sonic weapons have also been used against pirates off the coast of Somalia and anti-whaling activists near Australia.

Although it is unclear if Kurosawa Kiyoshi had such Long Range Acoustic Devices specifically in mind when he wrote the screenplay for *Sakebi*, I would suggest that more than simply offering "a machine built to give birth to a scream," as Chion describes the screaming point, the shriek emitted by the vengeful ghost in *Sakebi* functions as a sort of sonic weapon, making both the character of the police detective who witnesses the scream and the audience subjected to watching the scene recoil in discomfort. However, rather than functioning as a sonic weapon in the hands of the powerful to control and suppress the disempowered, as is the case when Long Range Acoustic Devices are deployed against protesters and activists, the ghost of *Sakebi* turns the sonic weapon of her scream against the figure of the police detective Yoshioka, who is shown again and again during the course of the movie using excessive force in the arrest and interrogation of suspects. Although the shrieking ghost of *Sakebi* resembles the banshee from Irish lore, whose piercing shriek typically heralded the passing of a prominent family member, the screaming ghost in *Sakebi* more often than not protests the death of a disempowered individual who has been murdered or abandoned. It is here, on the sonic threshold of pain, just as the sonic frequency designed to keep protesters, pirates, and activists in check is effectively deterritorialized and turned against the powers that be, that haptic sonority comes to the fore.[92]

Conclusion

In closing, it is worth underscoring how much Kurosawa's experiments with haptic sonority have in common with film theorist Laura Marks's notion of "haptic visuality" developed in *The Skin of the Film* (2000), the term she gives to those modes of cinematic seeing whose characteristic traits evoke memories of the non-visual senses, such as touch, taste, or smell. According to Marks, it is possible for cinema to open up filmic visuality to haptic modes of seeing when it includes one or more of the following elements:

1. Sensuous or richly textured imagery that evokes memory of the senses.
2. Panning across the surface of objects in a way that underscores their materiality.
3. Under- or overexposure, shifts in focus or speed, or any technique that draws attention to the grain or flow of film.
4. Characters shown engaging in sensory activity (e.g., touching, smelling, tasting, licking, etc.).
5. Close-to-the-body camera positions and sound design that underscore the body's movement and corporeality on-screen.[93]

In short, by inviting the spectator to consider the textured materiality of the filmic image along with the corporeality of filmic characters rather than simply reducing on-screen images to their representational function within the narrative, cinema has the power to create a space for haptic visuality, which Marks interprets as a "non-instrumental," "anti-utilitarian" way of seeing.

Although Marks is the first to acknowledge that her theory of haptic visuality gives "short shrift to the power of nonverbal sound to have meaning in ways that cannot be reduced to simple signification,"[94] nevertheless she does offer helpful suggestions for sound theorists to pursue, especially in relation to the haptic nature of ambient and textural sound. For Marks, insofar as "all the senses work together in the embodied experience of cinema," a fuller consideration of haptic visuality must also include the role played by sound.[95] This broader notion of the haptic—one that is not restricted to visuality—is more in keeping with the philosophical texts and subtexts that have inspired Marks.

Twenty years before *The Skin of the Film* was published, Deleuze and Guattari offered groundbreaking engagements with the haptic in *A Thousand Plateaus* (1980). In their wide-ranging, unapologetically rhizomatic philosophical text, Deleuze and Guattari were ahead of the curve when it came to engaging the concept of the haptic. In their discussion of nomad art in the plateau on "The Smooth and the Striated," Deleuze and Guattari differentiate between "haptic space" (*l'espace haptique*), which they situate in relation to their concept of "the smooth" (*le lisse*), and "optical space" (*l'espace optique*), which they position in relation to what they call "the striated" (*le strié*).[96] For Deleuze and Guattari, such smooth, haptic space, which they conceive as a a space-time one occupies without counting, involving non-metric, anexact yet rigorous multiplicities, in which points are subordinated to lines and there is no top or bottom or center but only middle, is filled by events (or what they call "haecceities") "far more than by formed and perceived things."[97] According to Deleuze and Guattari, it is "a space of affects, more than one of properties" and is "occupied by intensities, wind and noise," forces with "sonorous and tactile qualities."[98] However, rather than reducing the smooth and the striated to an opposition between the ear and the eye, Deleuze and Guattari also insist that haptic space "may be as much visual or auditory as tactile."[99]

I would argue that the sonic weapon associated with the ghost's shriek in Kurosawa Kiyoshi's *Sakebi* occupies just such a haptic space, offering forces and intensities with "sonorous and tactile qualities." The shriek of *Sakebi* is where we encounter haptic sonority—a liminal space (or zone of indiscernibility) that blurs the boundaries between the sonic and the tactile and compels us to bear witness to the ineluctable molecularity of sound waves vibrating our bodies as if they were resonance chambers.[100] In J-horror cinema, such haptic sonority opens an intensive space where one does not so much hear sounds as one feels them in one's body in ways that are by turns bone-rattling, gut-wrenching, and hair-raising. It is here that film touches our bodies and invites us to enter into composition with the micropolitics of sound as resonant subjects in a "cinema of sensations."[101]

Notes

1. For example, see Michel Chion, *Audio-Vision: Sound on Screen*, translated by Claudia Gorbman (New York: Columbia UP, 1994); Michel Chion, *The Voice in Cinema*, translated by Claudia Gorbman (New York: Columbia UP, 1999); Michel Chion, *Film, A Sound Art*, translated by Claudia Gorbman (New York: Columbia UP, 2009); Elisabeth Weis and John Belton, eds., *Film Sound: Theory and Practice* (New York: Columbia UP, 1985); Elisabeth Weis, *The Silent Scream: Alfred Hitchcock's Sound Track* (Rutherford, N.J.: Fairleigh Dickinson University Press, 1982); Rick Altman, ed., *Sound Theory/Sound Practice* (New York: Routledge, 1992); Jay Beck and Tony Grajeda, eds., *Lowering the Boom: Critical Studies in Film Sound* (Urbana, IL: University of Illinois Press, 2008); Jay Beck, *Designing Sound: Audiovisual Aesthetics in 1970s American Cinema* (New Brunswick, New Jersey: Rutgers University Press, 2016); William Whittington, *Sound Design & Science Fiction* (Austin, TX: University of Texas Press, 2007); Anahid Kassabian, *Hearing Film: Tracking Identifications in Contemporary Hollywood Film Music* (New York: Routledge, 2001); Kevin Donnelly, *Film and Television Music: The Spectre of Sound* (London: British Film Institute, 2005); Andy Birtwistle, *Cinesonica: Sounding Film and Video* (Manchester: Manchester University Press, 2010).

2. Birtwistle, xii, 1.

3. Ibid., 6.

4. Gilles Deleuze, *Cinema 1: The Movement-Image*, translated by Hugh Tomlinson and Barbara Habberjam (Minneapolis: University of Minnesota Press, 1986); Gilles Deleuze, *Cinema 2: The Time-Image*, translated by Hugh Tomlinson and Robert Galeta (Minneapolis: University of Minnesota Press, 1989).

5. Gilles Deleuze and Félix Guattari, *A Thousand Plateaus: Capitalism and Schizophrenia*, translated by Brian Massumi (Minneapolis: University of Minnesota Press, 1987), 474–500.

6. "The Conversation (1974)," *Internet Movie Database*, n.d., http://www.imdb.com/title/tt0071360/?ref_=nv_sr_1 (accessed September 7, 2015).

7. See film critic and historian Carrie Rickey quoted in Sheila Weller Hoffmann, "What should Edward 'I'm a brave martyr but I wanna go home' Snowden do now?" *The Washington Post*, July 15, 2013, https://www.washingtonpost.com/blogs/she-the-people/wp/2013/07/15/what-should-edward-im-a-brave-martyr-but-i-wanna-go-home-snowden-do-now/ (accessed January 25, 2016).

8. After completing this chapter, I learned that Wes Folkerth also briefly uses the term "sonic palimpsest" in his study *The Sound of Shakespeare* to describe the different layers of acoustic technology that are audible in a recording of the opening speech of *Richard III*. In contrast, my usage focuses exclusively on sound design in horror cinema. See Wes Folkerth, *The Sound of Shakespeare* (London; New York: Routledge, 2002), 6. On the role of visual palimpsests in film, see David Bordwell, *Narration in the Fiction Film* (Madison, Wis.: University of Wisconsin Press, 1985), 322–332. On palimpsests in literature, see Gérard Genette, *Palimpsests: Literature in the Second Degree* (Lincoln: University of Nebraska Press, 1997).

9. For Kurosawa on Friedkin, see Kurosawa Kiyoshi, *Eizō no karisuma* (Tokyo: Ekusu Narejji, 2006a), 213, 217. For Kurosawa on Kubrick, see *Eizō no karisuma*, 16, 177–78, 183, 211, 216.

10. Tom Service, "Krzysztof Penderecki: Horror Film Directors' Favourite Composer," *The Guardian*, November 3, 2011, http://www.guardian.co.uk/film/2011/nov/03/krzysztof-pendercki-horror-soundtracks-david-lynch/print (accessed April 29, 2015).

11. Robynn J. Stilwell, "The Fantastical Gap between Diegetic and Nondiegetic," in *Beyond the Soundtrack: Representing Music in Cinema*, edited by Daniel Goldmark, Lawrence Kramer, and Richard Leppert (Berkeley: University of California Press, 2007), 184–202.

12. Claudia Gorbman, *Unheard Melodies: Narrative Film Music* (Bloomington: Indiana University Press, 1987), 22–23.

13. See Peggy Monastra, "Krzysztof Penderecki's *Polymorphia* and *Fluorescences*," in *The Rosaleen Moldenhauer Memorial: Music History from Primary Sources: A Guide to the Moldenhauer Archives*, edited by

Jon Newsom and Alfred Mann (Washington: Library of Congress, 2000), 350–57. On Penderecki's goal of "liberating sound beyond all tradition," see Mieczyslaw Tomaszewski, "Orchestral Works Vol. 1 Liner Notes," in Krzysztof Penderecki, *Penderecki: Orchestral Works, Vol. 1/Symphony No. 3/Threnody*, with Antoni Wit and Polish National Radio Symphony, Naxos, 2000, compact disc, liner notes.

14. Wolfram Schwinger, *Krzysztof Penderecki: His Life and Work*, translated by William Mann (London: Schott, 1989), 28–29, 124–28, 131–34, 140–41.

15. On "sound events" in Penderecki's early sonorist compositions, see Danuta Mirka, *The Sonoristic Structuralism of Krzysztof Penderecki* (Katowice: Music Academy in Katowice, 1997), 23, 51, 89, 131–33, 141, 168, 194; Danuta Mirka, "To Cut the Gordian Knot: The Timbre System of Krzystof Penderecki," *Journal of Music Theory* 45, no. 2 (Autumn, 2001): 435–456; Danuta Mirka, "Texture in Penderecki's Sonoristic Style," *Music Theory Online* vol. 6, no. 1, January 2000, http://www.mtosmt.org/issues/mto.00.6.1/mto.00.6.1.mirka.html (accessed May 7, 2015).

16. James Helme Sutcliffe, "Devil's Advocate," *Opera News* vol. 33, no. 27 (June 14, 1969): 15.

17. Deleuze and Guattari, *A Thousand Plateaus*, 142.

18. Ibid., 142.

19. Ibid., 136.

20. The foregrounding of a color lithograph by Alexander Calder titled *Calder Fleches* (1968) in the mise-en-scène of the doctor's office in *The Exorcist* may also be a visual allusion to the graphic notation of Penderecki's *Polymorphia*. Thanks to Jenifer Presto for calling my attention to this possible correlation.

21. Gordon Stainforth, "The Shining Music—Introductory Note," July 2015, http://www.gordonstainforth.co.uk/shining-music-intro (accessed August 2, 2017).

22. Gordon Stainforth, e-mail message to author, August 11, 2017.

23. Gordon Stainforth, e-mail message to author, August 29, 2017. Mr. Stainforth confirmed via e-mail the "density of layering" when editing musical excerpts for the soundtrack of *The Shining*, recalling that "In the last reel, #15 during the dubbing, three tracks were definitely played at the same time at several moments. I laid an extra track (there were already two overlaid at once) because Stanley said 'You've got to beef it up.'"

24. Stainforth, "The Shining Music—Introductory Note." See also Christine Lee Gengaro, *Listening to Stanley Kubrick: The Music in His Films* (Lanham, Md.: Scarecrow Press, 2013), 192, 202–205.

25. Wendy Carlos quoted in Vincent LoBrutto, *Stanley Kubrick: A Biography* (New York: Da Capo Press, 1999), 448.

26. Chion, *Film, A Sound Art,* 471–72.

27. Ibid., 489–90.

28. Ibid., 487; see also Chion, *Audio-Vision,* 25–34; Pierre Schaeffer, "Acousmatics," in *Audio Culture: Readings in Modern Music,* edited by Christoph Cox and Daniel Warner (New York: Continuum, 2004), 76–81.

29. Birtwistle, 15.

30. Ibid., 15. On sonorous objects, see also Schaeffer, "Acousmatics," 79–81.

31. Chion, *Film, A Sound Art,* 465; see also Chion, *The Voice in Cinema,* 18; *Audio-Vision,* 71–73. The term "acousmatic" (*acousmatique*) was coined by Pierre Schaeffer. See Pierre Schaeffer, *Traité des objets musicaux* (Paris: Seuil, 1966), 91–99.

32. Chion, *The Voice in Cinema,* 21. On the the *acousmêtre,* see Chion, *The Voice in Cinema,* 17–29; *Audio-Vision,* 129–31.

33. Chion, *Film, A Sound Art,* 365.

34. Ibid., 493. Although Chion himself numbers the seven telepheme types from 0 to 6—designating the first type as "type 0" because "it belongs to the silent era"(366)—I will refer to the seven types of telepheme from 1–7 to avoid confusion.

35. Ibid., 493.

36. Ibid., 493.

37. Ibid., 493.

38. Ibid., 493.

39. Ibid., 494.

40. Ibid., 494. For further discussion of all seven types of telepheme, see Chion, *Film, A Sound Art,* 365–71.

41. William Whittington interprets the voice of Yabe as sounding like an answering machine recording, but the syntheticness of Yabe's voice far exceeds that of an answering machine in my opinion. See William Whittington, "Acoustic Infidelities: Sounding the Exchanges between J-Horror and H-Horror Remakes," *Cinephile,* vol. 6, no. 1 (Spring 2010): 12.

42. Chion, *The Voice in Cinema*, 27.

43. Whittington, "Acoustic Infidelities," 11 n. 1.

44. Steven T. Brown, *Tokyo Cyberpunk: Posthumanism in Japanese Visual Culture* (Palgrave Macmillan, 2010), 113–32. This paragraph and the next one draw from my extended analysis of *Kairo* in *Tokyo Cyberpunk*.

45. In late July 2015, I had the opportunity to visit the Hiroshima Peace Memorial Museum, where the Sumitomo Bank steps showing a "Human Shadow Etched in Stone" (*hitokage no ishi*) have been preserved as a reminder of the unimaginable trauma experienced on that day. I was shocked to discover that seventy years later, a faint shadow is still visible where it is believed a customer who was waiting for the bank to open was sitting on the steps outside the bank when the bomb detonated.

46. "FIPRESCI Prize," http://www.fipresci.org/festival-reports/2001/cannes-film-festival (accessed January 15, 2016).

47. For an interesting discussion of ambient drones in a musical context, which I discovered after I had already completed this chapter, see Paul Roquet, *Ambient Media: Japanese Atmospheres of Self* (Minneapolis: University of Minnesota Press, 2016), 56, 72–73. Whereas Roquet focuses on ambient music and the aesthetics of comfort, I am more interested in this chapter in exploring the role played by ambient noise and other techniques of sound design utilized in Kurosawa Kiyoshi's horror cinema to create an aesthetics of *discomfort*.

48. In contrast, Lisa Coulthard has argued that, in the context of European New Extremist cinema, drones operate as a "thematically and aesthetically charged trope" that signifies "violent sexuality, psychological dissociation, death." See Lisa Coulthard, "Dirty Sound: Haptic Noise in New Extremism," in *The Oxford Handbook of Sound and Image in Digital Media*, edited by Carol Vernallis, Amy Herzog, and John Richardson (New York: Oxford University Press, 2013), 115–26.

49. On the sociological, psycho-physiological, musical, architectural, and acoustic aspects of drones, see Jean-François Augoyard and Henry Torgue, *Sonic Experience: A Guide to Everyday Sounds*, translated by Andra McCartney and David Paquette (Montreal: McGill-Queen's University Press, 2005), 40–46.

50. Chion, *Audio-Vision*, 149–50.

51. Coulthard, "Dirty Sound," 118.

52. Philip J. Riley, ed., *MagicImage Filmbooks Presents Frankenstein* (Absecon, N.J.: MagicImage Filmbooks, 1989), 20–21. See also Robert Spadoni, *Uncanny Bodies: The Coming of Sound Film and the Origins of the Horror Genre* (Berkeley: University of California Press, 2007), 98–99.

53. See Harry Golman, *Kenneth Strickfaden, Dr. Frankenstein's Electrician* (Jefferson, North Carolina: McFarland & Company, 2005).

54. Kurosawa Kiyoshi and Shinozaki Makoto, *Kurosawa Kiyoshi no kyōfu no eigashi* (Tokyo: Seidosha, 2003), 22–24, 64–65, 91–92, 112, 129, 133–34, 173. On Kurosawa's list of the "50 best horror films," *Frankenstein* appears at #18. See Kurosawa Kiyoshi, *Eiga wa osoroshii* (Tokyo: Seidosha, 2001a), 33–34.

55. For the novel, see Kurosawa Kiyoshi, *Cure (kyua)* (Tokyo: Kadokawa Shoten, 1997a).

56. For an insightful analysis of the "X" in *Cure* as "a mark or erasure… through which interiority escapes to the outside, and the exteriority enters inside," see Akira Lippit, *Atomic Light (Shadow Optics)* (Minneapolis: University of Minnesota Press, 2005), 143–57.

57. See Daniel T. Blumstein, Richard Davitian, and Peter D. Kaye, "Do Film Soundtracks Contain Nonlinear Analogues to Influence Emotion?" *Biology Letters* 6 (2010): 751–54; W. Tecumseh Fitch, Jürgen Neubauer, and Hanspeter Herzel, "Calls out of Chaos: The Adaptive Significance of Nonlinear Phenomena in Mammalian Vocal Production," *Animal Behaviour* 63.3 (2002): 407–418.

58. Tom Mes, "Interview with Kiyoshi Kurosawa," *Midnight Eye*, March 20, 2001, http://www.midnighteye.com/interviews/kiyoshi-kurosawa (accessed September 17, 2015).

59. David Forgacs, "Commentary," *Il deserto rosso*, directed by Michelangelo Antonioni (1964), translated as *Red Desert*, subtitled Blu-Ray (Irvington, NY: Criterion Collection, 2010).

60. Birtwistle, 108.

61. In their discussion of the sociology of drones, Augoyard and Torgue note that "when the intensity of a background sound exceeds a certain threshold, mental activity can become paralyzed"(41).

62. For an insightful discussion of the different types of silence in cinema, see Paul Théberge, "Almost Silent: The Interplay of Sound and Silence in Contemporary Cinema and Television," in *Lowering the Boom: Critical Studies in Film Sound*, edited by Jay Beck and Tony Grajeda (Urbana, IL: University of Illinois Press, 2008), 51–67.

63. Tim Screech, "Japanese Ghosts," *Mangajin*, no. 40 (1994), http://www.mangajin.com/mangajin/samplemj/ghosts/ghosts.htm (accessed September 27, 2014).

64. Théberge, 52.

65. Ibid., 53.

66. Stinger chords are "sudden musical blasts that coincide with moments of shock and revelation." See Joe Tompkins, "Mellifluous Terror: The Discourse of Music and Horror Films," in *A Companion to the Horror Film*, edited by Harry M. Benshoff (Malden, MA, USA: Wiley Blackwell, 2014), 190. On sound design that elicits the startle response, see Robert Baird, "The Startle Effect: Implications for Spectator Cognition and Media Theory," *Film Quarterly* vol. 53, no. 3 (Spring, 2000): 12–24; Peter Hutchings, *The Horror Film* (Harlow, England; New York: Pearson Longman, 2004), 134–41.

67. See Kurosawa Kiyoshi, "Interview with Kiyoshi Kurosawa about His Double Feature Choices," interview by Diane Arnaud and Lili Hinstin, Entrevues Belfort International Film Festival, October 9, 2014, http://www.festival-entrevues.com/sites/default/files/images/archives/inter-view_kurosawa_hd.pdf (accessed November 13, 2015). On Kurosawa's list of the 50 best horror films, *The Innocents* appears at #2. See Kurosawa, *Eiga wa osoroshii*, 28. It is probably no accident that *Kairo* (*Pulse*, 2001b), one of the scariest ghost movies ever made by Kurosawa, bears a title that evokes the Japanese translation of *The Innocents*, which is titled *Kaiten* in Japanese (meaning "turning"), probably in reference to Henry James's novel *The Turn of the Screw* (1898) upon which *The Innocents* is based.

68. Chion, *Audio-Vision*, 57.

69. Kurosawa employs a similar suspension of sound in his V-Cinema revenge tale *Serpent's Path* (*Hebi no michi*, 1998) in a scene in which one of the protagonists, an ex-yakuza named Miyashita (Kagawa Teruyuki), who is seeking justice for the death of his own daughter, happens to encounter a young girl who may or may not be the ghost of another yakuza victim whose death he himself may have inadvertently caused by participating in a child pornography ring. As Miyashita gazes long at the young girl, whom he sees in the street, his expression changes from a smile to something else, perhaps fear. Like most ghosts in Kurosawa Kiyoshi films, the girl does not say a word to him. At the very moment their gazes lock together, Kurosawa suspends sound completely to let the scene resonate before the silence is interrupted by the sound of a commuter train roaring past.

70. Michel Chion, "The Silence of the Loudspeakers, or Why with Dolby Sound it is the Film that Listens to Us," in *Soundscape: The School of Sound Lectures, 1998–2001*, edited by Larry Sider, Jerry Sider, and Diane Freeman (London ; New York: Wallflower Press, 2003), 55.

71. My usage of the term "haptic sonority" is informed by Lisa Coulthard's thought-provoking engagement with "haptic aurality." However, I prefer "sonority" over "aurality" both to avoid potential confusion with the homophone "orality" and to underscore the Deleuzoguattarian register in which I have situated my use of the term. See Lisa Coulthard, "Haptic Aurality: Resonance, Listening and Michael Haneke," *Film-Philosophy* 16.1 (2012): 16–29; "Dirty Sound: Haptic Noise in New Extremism," 115–126.

72. Arne Eggum, *Edvard Munch: The Frieze of Life from Painting to Graphic Art* (Oslo: Stenersen, 2000), 235; Sue Prideaux, *Edvard Munch: Behind the Scream* (New Haven Conn.: Yale University Press, 2005), 54.

73. Fyodor Dostoyevsky, *Crime and Punishment*, translated by Constance Garnett (New York: Vintage Books, 1950), Part II, Chapter 2, 105–06.

74. Munch quoted in Eggum, 225; see also *Edvard Munch's Writings*, Digital archive, published by the Munch Museum, MM T 2785-077-080, Dated 1909–1911, Sketchbook, http://emunch.no/TRANS_HYBRIDMM_T2785.xhtml (accessed November 13, 2015).

75. Donald W. Olson, Russell L. Doescher, and Marilynn S. Olson, "When The Sky Ran Red: The Story Behind *The Scream*," *Sky & Telescope* (February 2004): 20–35.

76. Thomas M. Messer, *Edvard Munch* (New York: H.N. Abrams, 1971), 84.

77. Eggum, 225. Here I am persuaded by Eggum that either Munch had read Schopenhauer earlier than he had remembered (a pocket edition of excerpts from Schopenhauer's theory of art was published in 1891 under the title *Philosophie der Kunst*) or he became aware of the debate by way of Scandinavian commentators, such as Lorentz Dietrichson (1834–1917), Norway's first professor of art history, in pioneering studies such as *Det skönas värld: Estetik och konsthistoria med specielt afseende på den bildande konsten. Populärt framställda* [The World of Beauty: Aesthetics and Art History, with Special Regard to the Fine Arts Popularly Produced] (Stockholm: Oscar L. Lamms förlag, 1870–79).

78. Winckelmann quoted in Arthur Schopenhauer, *The World as Will and Representation*, translated by Judith Norman, Alistair Welchman, and Christopher Janaway (Cambridge; New York: Cambridge University Press, 2010), 252. See also Johann Joachim Winckelmann, *History of the Art of Antiquity*, translated by Harry Francis Mallgrave (Los Angeles, Calif.: Getty Research Institute, 2006), 313–14.

79. Translation mine.

80. Gotthold Ephraim Lessing, *Laocoon: An Essay upon the Limits of Painting and Poetry*, translated by Ellen Frothingham (Boston: Little, Brown and Co., 1910), 13–14.

81. Arthur Schopenhauer, *Die Welt als Wille und Vorstellung* (Zürich: Haffmans Verlag, 1988), Bk. 3, Sec. 45, 302 (translation mine).

82. Schopenhauer, *The World as Will and Representation*, 252.

83. Ibid., 252–53.

84. "*Das Wesen, und folglich auch die Wirkung des Schreiens auf den Zuschauer, liegt ganz allein im Laut, nicht im Mundaufsperren.*" Schopenhauer, *Die Welt als Wille und Vorstellung*, Bk. 3, Sec. 46, 304 (translation mine).

85. Ibid., Bk. 3, Sec. 46, 305 (translation mine).

86. A number of other writers in the history of German aesthetics have also weighed in on this debate, including Johann Wolfgang von Goethe, Johann Gottfried von Herder, and Karl Philipp Moritz, but it would go beyond the scope of this chapter to address them all.

87. Chion, *The Voice in Cinema*, 76–77.

88. Ibid., 77.

89. Ibid., 77.

90. Steve Goodman, *Sonic Warfare: Sound, Affect, and the Ecology of Fear* (Cambridge, MA: MIT Press, 2009), 21.

91. Amy Teibel, "Israel May Use Sound Weapon on Settlers," *USA Today*, June 6, 2005, http://usatoday30.usatoday.com/news/world/2005-06-10-israel-soundweapon_x.htm# (accessed September 18, 2015).

92. As a student of horror cinema history, Kurosawa may also be paying homage to the 1964 sf-horror *Children of the Damned*, directed by Anton M. Leader, which was the sequel to the 1960 classic *Village of the Damned*, directed by Wolf Rilla. In *Children of the Damned*, a group of six children with telekinetic powers defend themselves against soldiers and government officials with a sonic weapon that makes use of an enormous pipe organ from the abandoned church they have chosen as their hideout.

93. Laura U. Marks, *The Skin of the Film: Intercultural Cinema, Embodiment, and the Senses* (Durham and London: Duke UP, 2000).

94. Ibid., xv.

95. Ibid., xv–xvi.

96. Deleuze and Guattari, *A Thousand Plateaus*, 474–500.

97. Ibid., 479.

98. Ibid., 479.

99. Ibid., 493.

100. On the human body as resonance chamber, see Jean-Luc Nancy, *Listening*, translated by Charlotte Mandell (New York: Fordham University Press, 2007), 8, 31, 38; Augoyard and Torgue, 106–08.

101. On the "resonant subject," see Nancy, 21 and Veit Erlmann, "Descartes's Resonant Subject," *differences: A Journal of Feminist Cultural Studies* vol. 22, nos. 2–3 (2011): 10–30. On the "cinema of sensations," see contributions to *The Cinema of Sensations*, edited by Ágnes Pethő (Newcastle upon Tyne: Cambridge Scholars Publishing, 2015).

3

Double Trouble: Doppelgängers in Japanese Horror

> Film is in its essence a world of doubles.
> —Nicholas Royle[1]

One of the most recognizable motifs of J-horror cinema involves vengeful ghosts who impersonate the shape, appearance, and/or voice of a potential victim's family member or friend to beguile that person into an encounter. Such scenes of doubling may be found in J-horror classics ranging from *Ju-on: The Grudge* (*Ju-on*; dir. Shimizu Takashi, 2002) to *Dark Water* (*Honogurai mizu no soko kara*; dir. Nakata Hideo, 2002) to *One Missed Call* (*Chakushin ari*; dir. Miike Takashi, 2003). In each case, the ghost takes the form of a double to gain access to a potential victim by exploiting that individual's personal ties and affections. On one level, such figurations draw upon Japan's long history of beliefs in restless spirits and vengeful ghosts. Tenth-century Heian aristocrats used the terms "*ikiryō*" and "*ikisudama*"—meaning "living spirit"—to describe the spirit likeness of a living person, which it was widely believed could exit a person's mouth and wander around without the person realizing it. The doubling aspect of the living spirit plays a significant role in the *Tale of Genji*

© The Author(s) 2018
S. T. Brown, *Japanese Horror and the Transnational Cinema of Sensations*,
East Asian Popular Culture, https://doi.org/10.1007/978-3-319-70629-0_3

(*Genji monogatari*, early 11th century), authored by Murasaki Shikibu, in which the living spirit of Lady Rokujō—one of the most famous restless spirits in the history of Japanese literature—assaults and kills in a fit of jealous rage Genji's lover Yūgao and wife Lady Aoi. Living spirits are also featured in the poetry and diaries of other Heian female literati such as Izumi Shikibu and Sei Shōnagon. It was believed that the only way to prevent a person's *ikiryō* from wandering forth and possibly possessing someone else's body was by tying a fold in the skirt underneath the person's kimono.[2]

During the Edo period (1603–1868), a variation on the *ikiryō* phenomenon known as "*rikonbyō*," or "soul separation illness" (the term used in modern Japanese for "somnambulism"), was used to describe the condition in which a person's spirit or soul becomes detached from the body and takes on the exact likeness of the person suffering from the illness.[3] Tales circulated during this period of individuals suffering from "soul separation illness" who either came face-to-face with their *rikonbyō* double themselves or whose family and friends encountered it, thinking that it was the actual person. Doubling also figures into the pantheon of Japanese *yōkai* (legendary creatures) involving the "*nopperabō*," or faceless ghost, a notorious shapeshifter that can temporarily adopt the appearance of someone resembling a family member or friend and then in the next instant make its face "completely featureless, lacking eyes, nose, mouth, and any kind of expression—a face as smooth as an egg."[4] All of these figurations of doubling have influenced the traits and behavior of vengeful ghosts in J-horror cinema. However, on another level, given J-horror's transnational hybridity, it is just as important to take into consideration non-Japanese engagements with the doppelgänger whose characteristics have also left their transcultural mark on the diegetic worlds of Japanese horror cinema.

A Brief Doppelgänger Lexicon

The term "doppelgänger" (originally spelled "*Doppeltgänger*" in German with a "t") was first coined in 1796 by German Romantic author Jean Paul (1763–1825) in his humorous novel *Siebenkäs*.[5] In the pages of *Siebenkäs*, Jean Paul defines the "*Doppeltgänger*" (literally, "double-goer") as a term for "people who see themselves in person [*Leute, die sich selber sehen*]."[6] He uses the term to describe the character Leibgeber (literally, "body-giver"), the alter ego of the eponymous hero Firmian Stanislaus Siebenkäs, who bears such an uncanny resemblance to Siebenkäs that he agrees to exchange names and trade places with his friend so that the latter may escape an unhappy marriage and pursue other romantic goals. In their *Deutschen Wörterbuch* (1838), which they hoped would one day become the definitive German dictionary, the Brothers Grimm cite Jean Paul's usage, but expand his definition as follows: "DOPPELGÄNGER, also known as *doppeltgänger*, someone of whom one imagines he can manifest himself at the same time in two different places."[7] Whereas Jean Paul's definition underscores the doubling of the self's vision and appearance, the Grimms shift attention toward the spatiality of the doppelgänger's bilocation. According to Thea Brejzek and Lawrence Wallen, "rather than focus on the physiognomic aspects of the doppelgänger, Jacob and Wilhelm Grimm's dictionary entry proposes a topological definition that speaks of a person who is present and is seen in two different ways simultaneously."[8] This differentiation in how the double is conceived and situated is repeated in a multitude of ways around the world depending on the author, culture, and sociohistorical period. Although the German origins of the term "doppelgänger" and its German Romantic literary history might lead one to believe that the double is a Western concept with little resonance for non-Western cultures, it is worth underscoring that the concept is one that is shared by numerous cultures and ages, both Western and non-Western, and dates back to the ancient Egyptians.

Cultural articulations of and engagements with the figure of the doppelgänger have appeared all around the world in mythology, folklore, literature, art, and film. Comparative linguistic research quickly yields numerous words for the concept of the double. For example, the ancient Egyptians conceived of "*ka*," the vital spark or life force, as a "spirit double" that possessed memories and feelings that were identical to the human being to whom the "*ka*" belonged. In his famous essay on "The Uncanny" (*Das Unheimliche*, 1919), Sigmund Freud (following Otto Rank) interprets the invention of the "immortal" soul in ancient Egypt as "the first double of the body [*der erste Doppelgänger des Leibes*]" and "a defence against annihilation."[9] However, Freud also points out that this "energetic denial of the power of death [*energische Dementierung der Macht des Todes*]" (Rank) later changes meaning: "having once been an assurance of immortality, it becomes the uncanny harbinger of death [*unheimlichen Vorboten des Todes*]."[10]

The hieroglyph for "*ka*" consists of two joined arms that are outstretched for an embrace. In ancient Egypt, "*ka*" statues were constructed as a place where a person's spirit double could rest after death rather than aimlessly roam the earth. According to Egyptian mythology, it was the "*ka*" (or spirit double) of the famously beautiful Helen of Troy—the "Face That Launched a Thousand Ships"—not Helen herself whom Paris unwittingly brought back to Troy after being separated from Helen's body by Hermes (the god of boundaries and transitions), thereby triggering the start of the Trojan War. In his fifth-century drama *Helen*, the Greek playwright Euripides drew upon this Egyptian variant of Helen's story by way of the Greek poet Stesichorus (c. 640–555 BCE) while adding a unique spin of his own. Here's how the character Helen describes what happened to her in Euripides' play of the same name, which was first performed at the Dionysia festival in Athens in 412 BCE:

> My name is Helen.
> Now let me tell you my sad history.
> The three goddesses, Hera, Aphrodite,
> and Zeus-born, virgin Athene, went one day
> to Paris's valley hide-out on Mount Ida
> quarreling about their beauty and determined
> to have the issue judged. And Aphrodite
> offered my beauty—if anything can be called
> beautiful that brings misery—as a bribe,
> and me as a wife, to Paris, and so won.
> Paris quitted his mountain herds and came
> to Sparta to collect his bride; but then
> Hera, disgruntled in defeat, deprived
> her rival's solid promise of all substance:
> she gave the Trojan prince not the real me
> but a living likeness [*eidōlon*] conjured out of air,
> so that believing he possesses me
> he possesses only his belief.[11]

In classical Greek, the word for the "living likeness" of Helen that was created by Hera to deceive Paris is "*eidōlon*." "*Eidōlon*" is a term that can be used to describe a phantom, ghost, reflection in the mirror or water, or any insubstantial form that bears a strong likeness to someone or something.

Centuries later, in Norse mythology and Scandinavian folklore, the word "*vardøger*" was used to describe a premonitory double that preceded a living person and could be seen performing that person's actions in advance with the same voice, scent, or appearance.[12] People who encountered a "*vardøger*" believed they had encountered the actual person before (s)he arrived on the scene. Similarly, in Finnish folklore, the term "*etiäinen*" has long been used to describe something very similar: a sort of proactive doppelgänger that "goes ahead of a person, doing things the person in question later does."[13] In Celtic mythology and Norman French folklore, the term "*Ankou*" designates the double as a harbinger or personification of death. In Scottish folklore, the doppelgänger is referred to as a "cowalker," which is a phantasmic (or "astral") body that is able to separate from the physical body and act independently from it. Finally, in Irish folklore, the term "fetch" is defined as the "supernatural double" or "apparition" of a living person, whose spectral appearance is viewed as an ominous warning of imminent death.

With so many terms used to conceptualize the double in mythology and folklore in societies ranging from ancient Egypt to classical Greece, from premodern Japan to the age of the Vikings and beyond, it is no wonder that cultural expressions of the double have appeared in literature, art, and film all around the world. In this chapter, I am especially interested in the role of cinema as a productive cultural medium for doubles. As media theorist Friedrich Kittler and others have noted, from its very inception, cinema has been haunted by doubles through the "celluloid ghosts of the actors' bodies."[14] Considered both in terms of its evocations of the uncanny and with respect to the ghostly effects of the cinematic apparatus itself, this chapter investigates the figure of the doppelgänger primarily in relation to the J-horror films *Bilocation* (*Bairokēshon*; dir. Asato Mari, 2013) and *Doppelgänger* (*Dopperugengā*; dir. Kurosawa Kiyoshi, 2003). In a coda to this chapter, I also consider an instructive variation on the double in the form of conjoined twins in the short film *Box* (dir. Miike Takashi, 2004), which was included in the omnibus *Three ... Extremes* (aka *San geng yi* or *Three, Monster*, 2004) that also included short films by Park Chan-wook (*Cut*) and Fruit Chan (*Dumplings*). Although conjoined twins are not simply equivalent to the doppelgänger, I argue that they exist along the same continuum as doubles, sharing similar codes, conventions, and problems, while also differing from doppelgänger narratives in some important respects.

A Cinema of Doubles

That "film is in its essence a world of doubles,"[15] as Nicholas Royle has remarked, is evidenced by how often the figure of the double (and its variations: clones, twins, and split personalities) has appeared in almost every period and genre of film history. From German Expressionist classics such as *The Student of Prague* (*Der Student von Prag*; dirs. Hanns Heinz Ewers and Stellan Rye, 1913) and *Metropolis* (dir. Fritz Lang, 1927) to early Hollywood monster movies such as *Dr. Jekyll and Mr. Hyde* (dir. Rouben Mamoulian, 1931); from film noir such as *The Dark Mirror* (dir. Robert Siodmak, 1946) to Hitchcockian psychological thrillers such as *Vertigo* (dir. Alfred Hitchcock, 1958) and *The Man Who Haunted Himself*[16] (dir. Basil Dearden, 1970); from McCarthy-era sci-fi-horrors such as *Invasion of the Body Snatchers* (dir. Don Siegel, 1956) to contemporary clone dramas such as *The Prestige* (dir. Christopher Nolan, 2006) and *Moon* (dir. Duncan Jones, 2009); from espionage thrillers such as *The Double Man* (dir. Franklin J. Schaffner, 1967) to samurai classics such as *Kagemusha* (dir. Kurosawa Akira, 1980); from existentialist meditations such as *Persona* (dir. Ingmar Berg, 1966), *Solaris* (dir. Andrei Tarkovsky, 1972), and *The Double Life of Véronique* (dir. Krzysztof Kieslowski, 1991) to twin horrors such as *Sisters* (dir. Brian De Palma, 1973) and *Dead Ringers* (dir. David Cronenberg, 1988); from split personality thrillers such as *The Dark Half* (dir. George A. Romero, 1993), *Fight Club* (dir. David Fincher, 1999), and *Black Swan* (dir. Darren Aronofsky, 2010) to Lynchian neo-noir such as *Lost Highway* (dir. David Lynch, 1997), *Mulholland Drive* (dir. David Lynch, 2001), and *Inland*

Empire (dir. David Lynch, 2006)—engagements with the doppelgänger have frequently crossed genre boundaries and been shaped by the specific sociopolitical anxieties and pressures associated with the periods in which they were produced. However, the year 2013 marks the first time in the history of global cinema when over half a dozen doppelgänger films were released in the same year.

In an article titled "Why are There So Many Doppelgangers in Films Right Now?" BBC Entertainment reporter Emma Jones noted the plethora of films released in 2013 that focus on the figure of the doppelgänger. The doppelgängers presented in films such as *Enemy* (dir. Denis Villeneuve, 2013), *The Double* (dir. Richard Ayoade, 2013), *Coherence* (dir. James Ward Byrkit, 2013), *The Congress* (dir. Ari Folman, 2013), *Oculus* (dir. Mike Flanagan, 2013), and *The Face of Love* (dir. Arie Posin, 2013), as well as television series such as *Orphan Black* (dir. John Fawcett et al., 2013–2017), resonate with contemporary audiences in part because of the peculiar anxieties amplified by social media such as Facebook, Instagram, and Twitter. As film critic Alissa Wilkinson notes, "We're afraid we're not enough and so we're creating our own doubles in our Facebook profiles. Those whom we wish would love us might prefer us if we were better, prettier, sexier, more likeable. I call it the idea of our better double...Ask yourself this: is my Facebook self really me?...In real life we're constructing them for ourselves now. You're facing the possibility you could lose your real self to your Facebook self."[17]

One movie noticeably absent from Jones's list of doppelgänger films that was also released in 2013 is the J-horror film *Bilocation*, directed by Asato Mari. *Bilocation* is an adaptation of the novel of the same name by Hōjō Haruka that was published in 2010 and that received first prize for the best Japanese Horror Novel of the year. What sharply distinguishes both the movie and the novel *Bilocation* from all the other doppelgänger films listed above is that both were the creative products of women. *Bilocation* was directed by a woman director (Asato Mari) based on a novel by a female author (Hōjō Haruko) in which the primary protagonist is a woman (Shinobu) trying to deal with her doppelgänger. In sharp contrast, most doppelgänger films in the history of cinema have been directed by men based on screenplays that were written by men about protagonists who are also typically male.

Although female novelists are not uncommon in a country whose most renowned writer was a woman—namely, Murasaki Shikibu, the author of the acclaimed eleventh-century *Tale of Genji*—female directors are still relatively rare in the conservative Japanese film industry. Even outside of Japan, female horror directors are not abundant; however, with the recent successes of *The Babadook* (2014), directed by Jennifer Kent, and *A Girl Walks Home Alone at Night* (2014), directed by Ana Lily Amirpour, along with the emergence of annual film festivals such as the "Scream Queen Filmfest Tokyo," which features horror films directed by women from all around the world, perhaps we are starting to see both an increase in directorial opportunities for women in the genre of horror as well as greater recognition of the work already being done by women horror directors. In this context, Asato Mari has started to carve out quite a niche for herself, having directed a dozen movies since 2004, including *The Boy from Hell* (*Jigoku kozō*, 2004), *Ju-on: Black Ghost* (*Ju-on: Kuroi shōjo*, 2009), *Ring of Curse* (*Gomennasai*, 2011), *The Chasing World* (*Real oni gokko*, 2012), and *Fatal Frame* (*Gekijō-ban: Zero*, 2014). That the female sensibilities of both the director and author of *Bilocation* significantly alter the way in which the problem of the doppelganger is situated becomes apparent during the course of the film.

The fact that gender will become an issue in the film is signaled at the very outset. While the screen is still black following the production and distribution credits, we hear a voiceover in a language that is not Japanese. Quite unusual for a J-horror film, *Bilocation* begins with a prologue spoken entirely in Russian and left almost entirely unsubtitled (apart from a parenthetical indication that a woman is speaking a foreign language). After four seconds of voiceover without visuals, it cuts to a close-up of a non-Japanese woman dressed in nineteenth-century period clothing who continues to recite a passage in Russian from a book that she is holding. The period and location are finally identified simply as "19th century. A church in Europe." Once the sequence cuts to a long shot, it becomes apparent that the woman is reading aloud a passage from the Bible to children during Sunday school in the setting of a Russian Christian church. Although the crosses that decorate the mise-en-scène look vaguely Russian Orthodox, this cannot be since the Russian Orthodox Church does not permit lay readers to recite the Bible or parishioners to sit. In any case, as the woman continues to recite, scattered pages from some unidentified text blow from the back of the church towards the altar where she is standing. The pages dissolve into particles that then reassemble into the form of the woman's doppelgänger, who begins reciting passages from the same text in sync with her other self as soon as this transformation of text-into-flesh is complete. Given that this is a Japanese film created by a Japanese cast and crew, based on a Japanese novel by a Japanese author, the choice of a Biblical prologue spoken entirely in Russian requires some unpacking, especially since what is said in the prologue resonates with other issues engaged by the film.

During the prologue, the unidentified Russian woman and her doppelgänger read aloud excerpts from the story of Cain and Abel included in the Book of Genesis (4:1–16). After repeating a few sentences together, the first woman stops reading to look over at the double beside her, whose eyes are completely white and lack irises. The doppelganger's voice is pitch-shifted an octave lower and the vocal formants sound masculine as she repeats again and again (in Russian): "And Cain said to Abel, and Cain said to Abel, and Cain said to Abel." As the doppelgänger returns the gaze, eerie silver pupils appear in her eyes and her irises blacken. The Russian woman is startled by her doppelganger and the doppelganger mirrors her startled reaction (Fig. 3.1).

Fig. 3.1 A Russian woman (*left*) is startled by her doppelgänger (*right*) while reading the story of Cain and Abel in the prologue to *Bilocation* (2013)

What does the story of Cain and Abel have to do with doppelgängers in Japan? Cain and Abel resonate with the doppelgänger narrative in *Bilocation* on a number of levels. First, it is noteworthy that some scholars have interpreted the somewhat odd phrasing used to describe the birth of Abel to imply that Abel was born immediately after Cain and was, therefore, not simply Cain's brother, but his twin brother—in effect, a biological doppelgänger.[18] Second, as is the case with the story of Cain and Abel, almost every doppelgänger narrative involves a crisis of differentiation in which the original tries to distinguish itself from the double before it is supplanted by the double. Invoking the Cain and Abel intertext at the outset of *Bilocation* raises issues of rivalry, jealousy, displacement, and murder that foreshadow how a number of characters in *Bilocation* respond to their doubles (and how some doubles respond to their originals). Although the Russian woman and her doppelgänger who recite the story of Cain and Abel at the outset of *Bilocation* are not twin sisters per se, the threat posed by the doppelgänger and the rivalry that develops between self and double hearkens back to Cain and Abel in ways that are repeated throughout the movie. However, *Bilocation* also recasts this paradigmatic narrative of male rivalry as a story about female rivalry and a woman's struggle with her own self-image come to life.

At the end of the prologue, the scene fades to white accompanied by chilling string glissandi and then cross-dissolves to the view of a town with a mountainous backdrop in contemporary Japan. The camera tilts down and pulls back to reveal the interior space of an apartment studio belonging to an artist named Shinobu (the film's narrator), who is hard at work creating a charcoal drawing of the very same scene (Fig. 3.2). Shinobu,[19] played by Mizukawa Asami (a veteran of J-horror films such as *Dark Water* [*Honogurai mizu no soko kara*; dir. Nakata Hideo, 2002] and *The Locker* [*Shibuya kaidan*; dir. Horie Kei, 2004]), draws a scene that mirrors the view outside her apartment and even includes in her work the sliding glass door that enframes her view. Shinobu's drawing strongly evokes paintings by surrealist René Magritte (1898–1967) that blur the boundaries between "depicted space and real space,"[20] between the virtual and the actual.

In paintings from *The Human Condition* (*La condition humaine*, 1933/1935) and *The Fair Captive* (*La belle captive*, 1931/1947/1948)

Fig. 3.2   Blurring the boundaries between inside and outside in *Bilocation* (2013)

series that show "pictures within a picture," Magritte depicts "a window, or some other opening to the outside, in front of which stands a canvas on an easel. On the canvas is depicted the same landscape as, theoretically, exists in reality as the view through the window."[21] One's initial assumption may be that the painting depicts that part of the landscape outside the window that is either visible or hidden from view. However, after further analysis, one comes to the realization that this is based on the false premise that "the imagery of Magritte's painting is real, while the painting on the easel is a representation of that reality."[22] Since this involves a painting within a painting, both the painting on the easel and the landscape behind it belong to the same painting and there is no difference between the two in an ontological sense—i.e., neither is more nor less real than the other. In this way, Magritte chips away at our knee-jerk dedication to realism, which positions images as more or less faithful representations or duplications of reality. Magritte's point seems to be that no matter how closely an object seems to be represented, we are never able to capture the material thing itself. In a letter to André Breton in 1934, Magritte wrote that his objective in such paintings "was to eliminate the difference between a view seen from outside and from inside a room."[23] Shinobu's picture-within-a-picture does not blur the boundaries to the same degree as Magritte's surrealist explorations; however, by invoking Magritte in this way, *Bilocation* does make clear at the outset that it will be engaging similar issues involving the ambiguity between interior and exterior, depicted space and real space, virtual and actual, in connection with the complicated relations between self and double. As we discover during the course of the movie, mirrors and other reflective surfaces offer a liminal zone that both confirms and challenges the boundaries between the two.

Shinobu first discovers that she has a double when she goes to pay for items at a local grocery store and the clerk refuses to accept her money because he claims it is counterfeit. He shows her a security video of someone who looks exactly like Shinobu making the earlier purchase with a counterfeit bill. A detective named Kano Takashi arrives, but rather than arrest her, he acknowledges that he knows it was not her in the security video. As he holds up the two 10,000 yen bills retrieved from Shinobu and her double, one of the bills disappears into thin air. Kano explains that it is the same with the person on the security video, whom he calls a "*nisemono*"—meaning "fake," "sham," "impostor," "pretender." Instead of taking Shinobu to the police station for processing, Kano drives her to a special location where she is introduced to a support group for people like her who are haunted by their doubles. Before entering, she must first pass a test to determine if she is the original or the counterfeit. The test involves entering a special room by herself that contains an enormous framed mirror. In addition to the large mirror, the room contains a number of strange artifacts, most notably a life-sized doll depicting conjoined twins who are joined at the shoulder (Fig. 3.3)—a striking image that was also featured on posters in the marketing campaign for *Bilocation*. As she pauses before the mirror, Shinobu is startled by her reflection, as is the audience. At the level of sound design, this moment is underscored by a sudden drop in ambient noise that dissolves into absolute silence, such as discussed in relation to the films of Kurosawa Kiyoshi in Chap. 2.

Since the mirror is a device that has haunted doppelgänger cinema from the very beginning, it is worth pausing to briefly consider its history. In what is arguably the earliest feature-length doppelgänger film ever made, the 1913 silent film classic *The Student of Prague* (*Der Student von Prag*), which was codirected by Hanns Heinz Ewers and Stellan Rye and loosely based on Edgar Allan Poe's short story "William Wilson"

Fig. 3.3 A life-sized doll depicting conjoined twins is featured in the special mirror room of *Bilocation* (2013), as well as on posters advertising the movie

(1839),[24] the significance of the mirror is underscored in the film's most pivotal scene. This early German expressionist horror film, along with others such as *The Golem* (*Der Golem*; dirs. Henrik Galeen and Paul Wegener, 1915) and *The Cabinet of Dr. Caligari* (*Das Cabinet des Dr. Caligari*; dir. Robert Wiene, 1920), reached Japan just a few years after its release and was quite popular with Japanese audiences (novelist Tanizaki Jun'ichirō was an ardent fan).[25]

The Student of Prague tells the story of an impoverished university student named Balduin (played by Paul Wegener), who makes a deal with the sorcerer Scapinelli (John Gottowt). In exchange for 100,000 gold coins, Balduin agrees to sign a contract giving Scapinelli the right to take whatever he wants from his room. Balduin thinks this is a great deal since he leads the Spartan existence of an impoverished student and his largely empty boarding room contains only the most basic of furnishings. Despite entering into this deal with the Devil, Balduin thinks it is a joke until the sorcerer proposes taking Balduin's image from the mirror as payment. Balduin is shocked as he watches his reflection literally step out of the mirror into the room (Fig. 3.4) and follow Scapinelli out the door—a cinematic trick accomplished by means of double exposure techniques that astounded audiences at the time.

Fig. 3.4 Balduin encounters his double emerging from a mirror in *The Student of Prague* (1913)

The most challenging aspect of such double exposure shots (decades before the advent of blue-screen chroma key compositing) was getting the timing, eyelines, and actor blocking just right. The camera had to be static and the performances nearly perfect; otherwise, the entire scene would have to be filmed and double exposed all over again. The advent of motion control cinematography in the early 1970s improved things considerably by enabling the cinematographer working on doppelgänger films such as *Bilocation* to employ computer-controlled cameras that permitted precise adjustment of multiple axes of camera motion along with automated manipulation of lens focus and shutter control and the duplication of those settings across multiple takes. The multiple takes are then composited into a single sequence either optically (via an optical printer) or in a digital editor. If cinema has been haunted by doubles from its very inception, it is in part due to the uncanny effects of the cinematic apparatus itself, which made such techniques possible. Indeed, as Paul Wegener, the actor playing Balduin, remarked in relation to *The Student of Prague*, the technique employed "to double the actor on the divided screen, superimposing other images," is precisely what "gives the content its real meaning."[26]

Following the departure of Scapinelli and Balduin's double, Balduin's worst fears are realized when he approaches the mirror to inspect it and discovers that he no longer has a reflection, that his mirror image has left the room along with his double. Not surprisingly, all manner of chaos is unleashed once Balduin's doppelgänger takes on a life of its own. One of the primary framing devices by means of which the problem of the doppelgänger is engaged and visualized in films such as *The Student of Prague* along with numerous other films that have followed in its wake is the liminal space created by mirrors and other reflective surfaces.[27]

As Otto Rank points out in his landmark survey *The Double: A Psychoanalytic Study* (1925), an earlier version of which Sigmund Freud cites approvingly in his famous essay on "The Uncanny" (1919), the significant role played by mirrors in films such as *The Student of Prague* draws upon the long history of superstitions surrounding reflective surfaces that are recorded in mythology and folklore.[28] As far back as the Greek myth of Narcissus, if not earlier, mirrors and other reflective surfaces have been a source of of both dread and fascination. In this connection, it is no accident that the same ancient Greek word that was used to refer to one's "reflection" (*eidōlon*) in a mirror or water was also used for the "living likeness" (*eidōlon*) of Helen's double when she was pursued by Paris in Euripides's play. In mythology and folklore from around the world, mirrors often function as gateways or portals for supernatural entities (whether ghosts, gods, demons, or spirits) to pass into the world of the living. In other traditions, mirrors have been utilized as tools of magic and divination that can either show one the future or permit one to revisit the past.

The association between mirrors and death is equally longstanding. Breaking a mirror is thought to cause seven years of bad luck or presage the death of a loved one. In some cultures, after the death of a family member, mirrors are covered up around the family's home—a common practice during the Victorian era while the coffin of the deceased was on display in the family parlor—because of a fear that the soul of the dead might become trapped in the mirror and rendered unable to proceed to the afterlife. It is probably related to such a superstition that some cultures prohibit infants from looking at mirrors until after they have been alive for at least one year. Even when it is not associated with death per se, mirrors often function in folklore as tools of either rejuvenation or aging. Oscar Wilde's scandalous novel *The Picture of Dorian Gray* (1891), which has been adapted for the cinema numerous times, draws upon such beliefs in its telling of the story of the eponymous libertine Dorian Gray, who sells his soul so that only his painted portrait will age while he maintains his youthful beauty.

There is no question that mirrors play an equally significant role in the doppelgänger assemblages offered by *Bilocation*. Once she has taken the mirror test, Shinobu is invited to enter a meeting for "bilocation victims." There she meets others like her who have their own doppelgängers, or "bilocations," as the film terms them, including the detective Kano Takashi who first introduced Shinobu to the doppelgänger support group, whose bilocation carried out a vicious attack against an abusive boss; a mother named Kadokura Mayumi, whose bilocation keeps abducting her sick son from the hospital by pretending to be his mother; and a student named Mitarai Takumi, whose bilocation has slept with his girlfriend. *Bilocation* stands apart from most other doppelgänger films in terms of the sheer number of doubles who appear.

Of course, in the history of doppelgänger narratives, it must be acknowledged that the possibility of multiple doppelgängers had already been conceived by renowned Russian writer Fyodor Dostoevsky (1821–1881) in his brilliant, psychologically penetrating novella *The Double* (*Dvoinik*, 1846/1866). In the following scene from Dostoevsky's dopplegänger novella, the protagonist Goliadkin—a paranoid government clerk who is losing his mind—has a horrifying nightmare about a proliferation of doubles:

> Forgetting himself, in shame and despair, the lost and perfectly righteous Mr. Goliadkin rushed off wherever his legs would carry him, as fate willed, whatever turn it might take; but with every step, with every blow of his feet on the granite pavement, there sprang up as if from under the ground—

each an exact and perfect likeness and of a revolting depravity of heart—
another Mr. Goliadkin. And all these perfect likenesses, as soon as they
appeared, began running after each other, and stretched out in a long line
like a string of geese, went hobbling after Mr. Goliadkin Sr., so that there
was no escaping these perfect likenesses, so that Mr. Goliadkin, worthy of
all compassion, was left breathless with horror—so that, finally, a frightful
multitude of perfect likenesses was born—so that the whole capital was
flooded, finally, with perfect likenesses, and a policeman, seeing such a
violation of decency, was forced to take all these perfect likenesses by the
scruff of the neck and put them in the sentry box that happened to be there
beside him…Stiff and frozen with horror, our hero would wake up and,
stiff and frozen with horror, feel that he was hardly going to have a merrier
time of it when awake. It was painful, tormenting.[29]

However, in the case of Dostoevsky's *The Double*, this "multitude of perfect likenesses" revolves around Goliadkin alone, who is apparently taken
to a mental asylum at novel's end. With the exception of clone narratives
such as *Invasion of the Body Snatchers* (1956/1978), *The Prestige* (2006),
Moon (2009), and the *Orphan Black* (2013–2017) television series, in
which the multiplication of doubles is a common motif, conventional
doppelgänger movies mostly center around a single doppelgänger belonging to a single person rather than a multiplicity of different doppelgängers belonging to different people.[30] If doppelgängers proliferate like
rabbits in *Bilocation*, what difference does it make? When the number of
doppelgängers is multiplied, it is no longer the problem of a single person, who may or may not be suffering from some form of mental illness.
The problem of the doppelgänger now applies to a whole group of people, who cannot all be suffering from the same mental illness unless it is
a form of mass hysteria. Nevertheless, although *Bilocation* deals with a
multiplicity of different doppelgängers belonging to different people,
there is no escaping the fact that the film's narrator, Shinobu, who provides interior monologue voiceovers at various points during the film, is
our primary focus.

At the bilocation support group meeting that Shinobu attends, the
group's organizer, Iizuka Makoto, defines "bilocation" (*bairokēshon* or
bairoke for short) as "another self that is generated near oneself [*jibun no
chikaku ni hassei suru mō hitori no jibun*]" out of conflicting emotions.

Shinobu is told that these "simultaneously existing incarnations" of oneself "are perfect mimics, even of voices": "They appear, assume physical form, and take action...But being fakes [*nisemono*], they eventually disappear. Bilocations have the memories of the original person. They also obtain their new memories. Other people can't tell the difference between them." However, bilocations tend to have more intense, sometimes violent personalities than the originals because they are like "concentrated versions," which, as we later learn, certainly applies to the bilocations of the detective, mother, and student. Moreover, Iizuka notes that, however the bilocation behaves, the original self "doesn't share the bilocation's experiences. They are unaware that their life is being altered."

Although Iizuka insists that the term "bilocation" be defined in contradistinction to "doppelgänger," since he asserts that "doppelgängers don't interact with humans, but bilocations do," this definition of doppelgänger is far too restrictive. In fact, in most doppelgänger films, doppelgängers *do* interact with their models. Moreover, as suggested by the Grimm Brothers' expanded definition of the doppelgänger discussed above ("someone of whom one imagines he can manifest himself at the same time in two different places"), the dual spatiality of the doppelgänger and self—the fact that they occupy two distinct places (or locations) simultaneously—is an attribute that defines both the doppelgänger and the bilocation. However, things get increasingly complex in the movie *Bilocation* when it becomes apparent that it is not always easy to ascertain whether a figure is or is not a bilocation.

Upon departing the support group for bilocation victims, Shinobu passes the large mirror once again, except this time her bilocation is also present (Fig. 3.5). Scenes of doubling, such as are visualized in this mirror scene and elsewhere throughout the film, would never have succeeded if not for the cinematic technologies that made them possible. In the case of *Bilocation*, two technologies were essential: green-screen chroma key compositing combined with motion-control camerawork. In a wide shot of Shinobu and her bilocation as they encounter each other for the first time, only Shinobu's reflection (on the left) appears in the mirror, whereas, her bilocation (on the right) has no reflection. This is how the mirror test works. Kano provides a pocket mirror to Shinobu and instructs her to check it whenever they meet to confirm that he is the "real thing."

Fig. 3.5 Shinobu encounters her doppelgänger in the mirror room of *Bilocation* (2013)

The housewife Kadokura Mayumi likewise tells her son Susumu to use the pocket mirror to check to see if she is really his mother. If there is no reflection, she advises him to ignore whatever her bilocation tells him. When Susumu tries this trick later and refuses to accompany the bilocation because she is a "*nisemono*" (counterfeit), the bilocation appears to be confused, as if she does not know what she is.

However, although a mirror is often a useful tool for detecting bilocations since they have no reflection, the differentiation between "counterfeits" (*nisemono*) and the "real thing" (*honmono*) is not foolproof. Iizuka later explains that using mirrors is not enough since "only originals and ordinary human beings ... can see if there's a reflection or not." As it turns out, bilocations *are* able to see their own reflections "because they mistake themselves for the real person," according to Iizuka. On the day that Shinobu first encountered her doppelgänger, she saw only herself in the mirror. According to the logic of mirroring in the film, if Shinobu only saw her own reflection, then that would indicate that she was the original. However, if she saw both reflections, then that would mean she was the bilocation. Late in the film, Shinobu is asked by Iizuka to try and remember what she saw on the day she first encountered her bilocation in front of the mirror. Since the Shinobu who is being addressed by Iizuka at that moment recollects seeing both reflections, it means that she is actually a bilocation. Shocked by this revelation, Shinobu collapses to the ground, and the audience is equally dumbfounded. The Shinobu we thought was the original turns out to have been a bilocation all along.

As it turns out, there are actually two support groups—one for originals and one for bilocations. Depending upon the outcome in the mirror room, originals are directed to the room on the right (the red room) and bilocations are told to enter the room on the left (the green room). When Shinobu later returned to what she thought was the bilocation victims support group, she entered the green room, indicating that the version of Shinobu appearing at that moment in time was a bilocation. For both groups two rules apply: (1) upon entering the building, one must be checked in the mirror at the entrance before one is told which room to enter; (2) when they meet, each member must recite the names of all members in the group. Besides the fact that the two groups are distinguished according to their ontological status (whether they are material beings or phantom doubles), there is one other significant difference: the support group for bilocations has one additional member named "Kagami," a cypher-like character who wears a black scarf over his mouth to cover a large scar. As the longest standing member of the group, Kagami only enters the green room. He is the one exception between the two groups because "those who use the red room don't know him." When an individual recites the members' names, if they exclude or include Kagami, it tells Iizuka whether he is speaking at that moment to an original (who does not know Kagami) or a bilocation (who does). In other words, Kagami (加賀美), whose name is a homophone for both "mirror" (鏡) and "model" or "pattern" (鑑), functions as a mirror of a different sort, helping to further differentiate copy from model.

In this context, it is tempting to conclude that the frequent staging of mirror scenes in doppelgänger films such as *Bilocation* functions as an illustration of Jacques Lacan's "mirror stage." This is precisely how scholars such as Caroline Ruddell have read similar mirror scenes in relation to *Black Swan* (2010), *Face/Off* (dir. John Woo, 1997), and *Buffy the Vampire Slayer* (dir. Joss Whedon et al., 1997–2003).

In many ways, the doubles explored in this chapter fit neatly into the model of Lacan's (narcissistic) ego because they are reminiscent of the "other" that is a reflection of the ego. The formation of the ego in the "mirror phase" is intrinsically linked to identification with a whole bodily image (gestalt) that is delusory and entails both misunderstanding and misrecognition; all the protagonists here are both fascinated, and to some extent, beguiled by their delusory images in the mirror and/or their double. The double in these texts also to some degree creates both erotic and aggressive tensions between the character and their counterpart; if read as one character, these characters all display the problems of the experience of identity that Lacan highlights in his psychoanalytic model."[31]

Lacan's theory of the "mirror stage" (*stade du miroir*) actually consists of two claims, one developmental and the other ontological: "The mirror stage is a phenomenon to which I assign a twofold value," writes Lacan. "In the first place, it has historical value as it marks a decisive turning-point in the mental development of the child. In the second place, it typifies an essential libidinal relationship with the body image."[32] The developmental claim is that between 6 and 18 months, infants uniformly come to recognize themselves in a mirror when a child "playfully experiences the relationship between the movements made in the image and the reflected environment, and between this virtual complex and the reality it duplicates—namely, the child's own body, and the persons and even things around him."[33] Such a claim pertaining to the mental development of the child has been largely debunked by Norman Holland and others, who have pointed out that "there is no evidence whatsoever for Lacan's notion of a mirror stage."[34]

Nevertheless, many Lacanians, such as Ruddell, continue to adhere to the ontological or structural value of his theory. According to Lacan's conception of the "ontological structure of the human world," which he outlines in his essay "The Mirror Stage as Formative of the *I* Function as Revealed in Psychoanalytic Experience" that was delivered at the Sixteenth International Congress of Psychoanalysis in 1949, what occurs during the mirror stage is an identification between the subject and the "specular image" (*image spéculaire*) in the mirror, such that "the *I* is precipitated in a primordial form, prior to being objectified in the dialectic of identification with the other, and before language restores to it, in the universal, its function as subject."[35] The formation of this "ideal-I," which Lacan insists occurs ontologically "prior to its social determination," allows the subject that is "caught up in the lure of spatial identification," to buy into the fantasy of wholeness that conceals through the function of "misrecognition" (*méconnaissance*) the "fragmented body" (*corps morcelé*) of the subject, which is "originally an inchoate collection of desires."[36] As such, the primary identification of the subject with its specular image that results in the formation of the ego is also the subject's introduction into the imaginary order.[37] Ruddell explains:

> *Méconnaissance* [misrecognition] refers specifically to the formation of the ego; at the time the ego is formed the subject profoundly misrecognises and misunderstands as she/he is beguiled by the other and believes in the delusional whole image which negates the more truthfully experienced fragmentary nature of existence. According to Lacan, *méconnaissances* "constitute the ego, the illusion of autonomy to which it entrusts itself" (Lacan 2001: 7). It is in the sense that the mirror can provide an image that is unrecognisable as well as being recognisable that many of the examples discussed here locate the double. In Lacanian thought, an image of wholeness seems or feels alien to the subject as the body feels fagmented and in "bits and pieces" which Lacan refers to in terms of the "fragmented body" (this is also often referred to as *le corps morcelé*). Misrecognition of the "whole" image leads to the seduction of the subject by the image as they desire to be this unified person and not a fragmented body.[38]

The problem with applying Lacan's ontology of the mirror stage to the numerous mirror scenes that appear in *Bilocation* and other doppelgänger films is that if such scenes fit a little too "neatly into the model," one wonders what is being ignored in the process. It is hard to disagree with the half-veiled criticism of Lacan's mirror stage offered by Deleuze and Guattari in *A Thousand Plateaus*: "Too much has been written on the double, haphazardly, metaphysically, finding it everywhere, in any old mirror, without noticing the specific regime it possesses both in a mixed semiotic where it introduces new phases, and in the pure semiotic of subjectification where it inscribes itself on a line of flight and introduces very particular figures."[39] If one attends to the specific regime that is at work in a film such as *Bilocation*, something is definitely at issue in relation to mirrors, but I would suggest that it is not the mirror stage per se.

In the context of *Bilocation*'s exploration of the dynamics between self and double in relation to the series of mirror scenes that are staged, it is not the gaze of the self in the mirror that creates the "specular I" of Lacanian identity formation, but rather the gaze of the other, who witnesses whether or not the self even has a reflection in the mirror. The mirror scenes in *Bilocation* cannot function as illustrations of the mirror stage because seeing oneself in the mirror is not a confirmation of the "ideal I." Both the bilocation and self see themselves in the mirror, but only a non-bilocation can detect that the bilocation has no actual reflection. When the bilocation sees its own reflection, this is not a confirmation because it cannot see that it has no reflection. In other words, in a Lacanian register, although the bilocation may very well be caught up in the misrecognition of regarding its insubstantial, fragmented body as an imaginary wholeness, the ontological structure of this mirror scene is shown to be a delusion and is demystified as such. At another level, although misrecognition in some sense may also occur in terms of the audience's uncertainty about whether what we are seeing is the self or its double, this is not the misrecognition of Lacan's mirror stage either.

In contrast, I would argue that what such mirror scenes stage in relation to the problem of the doppelgänger is not a confirmation of the "ideal I" in the process of identity formation, but rather its destabilization or deterritorialization—a line of flight away from subjectification rather than its misrecognized validation. Instead of a mirror stage, what is offered by such scenes is a circuit or exchange in which, as Deleuze argues in *Cinema 2: The Time-Image*, "the mirror-image is virtual in relation to the actual character that the mirror catches, but it is actual in the mirror which now leaves the character with only a virtuality and pushes him back out-of-field."[40] Rather than validating identity, the virtuality of the mirror image threatens to "absorb the entire actuality of the character, at the same time as the character is no more than one virtuality among others."[41] In this sense, the double is not simply a reduplication or exact copy of the self but rather a performative repetition with a difference. It is this repetition with a difference, which makes the double appear stronger, bolder, and more successful, that threatens the self most of all.

In the end, the Magrittean implications discussed earlier involving Shinobu's art are drawn out further in relation to the ambiguity of relations between Shinobu and her double.

Throughout much of the film, Shinobu and her double are differentiated by the fact that the original Shinobu is a single artist, who has retained her maiden name "Kirimura," whereas her double is a married housewife, who has adopted her husband Masaru's surname "Takamura." This occupational and matrimonial differentiation is preserved in long shots of Shinobu and her bilocation occupying two different apartments in the same building, showing the former as a solitary figure passionately devoted to creating art in her studio on the top floor while the latter enjoys dinner with her husband in the apartment below. However, this differentiation begins to unravel at the end of the film when the original Shinobu attends the art competition to which she has submitted her Magrittean charcoal drawing only to discover that another work—titled *Window* (*Mado*)—that closely resembles hers has been selected and is on display. Executed in much warmer colors than Shinobu's original charcoal drawing, *Window* is attributed to her bilocation (Takamura Shinobu). Ironically, Shinobu's original work was rejected because the judges presumed that she had copied her bilocation's motif. To make matters worse, the bilocation's art is awarded the Grand Prize. Needless to say, the original Shinobu is quite shocked and distraught that her doppelgänger won the Grand Prize instead of her. Kagami, who meets the original Shinobu at the competition, tells her not to cry since "that's her up there" on the award dais. According to Kagami, "Between you and her, there's no difference. No difference at all! [*Anata to are ni "sai" nanka nai. "Sai" nanka nai n da*]."

By invoking the Magrittean ambiguity between interior and exterior, image and reality, depicted space and real space, *Bilocation* emphatically affirms that the bilocation has become its own model on par with the original self, thereby freeing the doppelgänger's similitude from "its old complicity with representative affirmation," as Michel Foucault puts it in his insightful study of Magritte's paintings.[42] According to Foucault, Magritte's paintings "perfidiously mix ...the painting and what it represents" as a way of "affirming that the painting is indeed its own model."[43] However, rather than implying "an interior distance, a divergence, a disjuncture between the canvas and what it is supposed to mimic," for Magritte, "there exists from the painting to the model a perfect continuity of scene, a linearity, a continuous overflowing of one into the other."[44] This "continuous overflowing of one into the other" is re-staged in *Bilocation* not only in terms of the ambiguous relationship between depicted space and real space that is offered by the respective art works of Shinobu and her bilocation, but also between the two versions of Shinobu. The relationship between doppelgänger and self is as ambiguous as that between Shinobu's charcoal drawing and the scene it depicts. The film does not privilege one over the other.

In the wake of the art competition, a meeting is arranged between Shinobu and her bilocation in the red room that is typically reserved for originals (see Fig. 3.6). As it turns out, the primary objective of the two support groups—one for originals and the other for bilocations—was not simply to protect originals from their bilocations or vice-versa, but, more importantly, to help them coexist with each other—a radical departure from most doppelgänger narratives in which the double is typically a harbinger of death for the self. When the two Shinobus meet face-to-face, the bilocation offers to give up her life: "I want you to have my life. I'm … someone who doesn't exist. I'll give up my life. It's the right thing

Fig. 3.6 Shinobu's double (in black) offers to give up her life to the original (in white) in *Bilocation* (2013)

to do." On the surface, this may seem like an act of self-sacrifice that is quite uncharacteristic for the doppelgänger genre, but Shinobu herself is hardly enamored with the idea, since it comes with a catch: the bilocation begs Shinobu to live her [the bilocation's] life and become Masaru's wife. Moreover, the bilocation insists that Shinobu take on the role of Masaru's wife without disclosing the substitution to Masaru. Shinobu responds quite negatively, since it turns out that having both a successful art career and a husband are not at all what Shinobu wants. In fact, she is horrified: "You want me to marry some guy I've never met?" she exclaims. The bilocation offers Shinobu her wedding ring and tells her that she can have it all (including the art prize) if she will just accept the ring (and Masaru). The artist Shinobu rejects the ring offered to her, proclaiming, "I've never been with a man!" It is at this moment that the gender politics of *Bilocation* become particularly heightened as Shinobu forcefully questions why she should feel compelled to adopt the heteronormative model of marriage that is being forced upon her by her bilocation. Shinobu's only desire is to be an artist: "Art's been the only life I've known!" Between a rock and a hard place, Shinobu's response in the end is made tragically clear when she returns to her apartment and—looking around her studio at her desk, mixing jars, and easel—begins to cry.

During this poignant sequence, as the tears start to flow down Shinobu's face, the soundtrack is once again absolutely silent: no music, dialogue, sound effects, or ambient noise can be heard. Then it cuts back to Masaru and his bilocation wife in their apartment below. The bilocation Shinobu also starts to cry since she can feel whatever the original Shinobu is feeling. The bilocation apologizes to Masaru, telling him, "Only I can decide what I'll do." At that very moment, a body can be seen falling outside their window from the apartment above. When Masaru goes to investigate, it becomes clear that the original Shinobu has committed suicide. When Masaru looks back to where Shinobu was sitting inside, there is no one there. The bilocation has already dematerialized. It is uncertain if the bilocation's last spoken words were even heard by Masaru: "Only one thing's true: I love you." Although Iizuka confides in Shinobu's bilocation late in the film that one of his secret goals was to help Masaru, "a man who fell in love with an illusion [*maboroshi*], like I did," in the end that goal proves to be as elusive as the coexistence of bilocations and originals.[45]

Frame Games

In the previous section, I talked at some length about the important role played by mirror scenes in the framing of doppelgänger narratives such as *Bilocation*. Another J-horror film that pushes the limits of how framing can be used in creative ways that go beyond mirrors is the aptly titled 2003 film *Doppelgänger* (*Dopperugengā*), directed by Kurosawa Kiyoshi. In Chap. 2, I analyzed the role of sound design in the films of Kurosawa Kiyoshi with special attention given to sonic palimpsests and haptic sonority. Here I am more concerned with the complex framing techniques that Kurosawa employs to help visualize the unstable dynamics between self and double.

Kurosawa not only directed the film, but he also wrote the screenplay upon which it was based and oversaw the film's editing. *Doppelgänger* stars the accomplished Japanese character actor Yakusho Kōji.[46] In addition to appearing in numerous films directed by Kurosawa, including *Cure* (*Kyua*, 1997), *Charisma* (*Karisuma*, 1999), *Séance* (*Kōrei*, 2000), *Pulse* (*Kairo*, 2001), *Retribution* (*Sakebi*, 2006), and *Tokyo Sonata* (*Tōkyō sonata*, 2008), Yakusho has also starred in a number of notable films by other directors that display his wide range and talents, including director Itami Jūzō's *Tampopo* (1985), Suo Masayuki's *Shall We Dance?* (*Shall We dansu?*, 1996), Imamura Shōhei's *The Eel* (*Unagi*, 1997), Aoyama Shinji's *Eureka* (*Yurīka*, 2000), and Alejandro González Iñárritu's *Babel* (2006). Kurosawa has said in interviews that whenever he needs an actor who can convey the sensibility and anxieties of someone from his generation—i.e., someone with what he describes as "an ambiguous sense of values" born in the early years of Japan's postwar period as the country struggled to regain its footing politically, socially, and economically—he chooses Yakusho Kōji.[47]

Doppelgänger begins with two parallel narratives that eventually intersect. In the first, a young woman named Yuka (played by Nagasaku Hiromi) accidentally sees her brother Takashi in her rearview mirror and offers to give him a ride home, but he declines without offering an explanation and proceeds on his way. When Yuka returns home, she is surprised to discover that her brother is already home watching TV. Before she can figure out how Takashi beat her home, the phone rings and the police inform Yuka that her brother has just committed suicide and she needs to go to the hospital to identify his body. Yuka is both shaken and nonplussed since her brother was clearly at home, but when she calls Takashi to the phone, he has suddenly disappeared. After hanging up, Yuka hears someone typing on a computer and discovers that it is her brother's doppelgänger, who has reappeared again. We later learn that her brother's doppelgänger is writing the novel that Takashi always wanted to write.

The second narrative involves a medical device researcher named Hayasaki Michio (Yakusho Kōji), who is stressing out over the slow development of an "Artificial Human Body Chair," which would permit a patient suffering paralysis after a spinal cord injury to control a robotic chair via neck sensors. Hayasaki and his assistants run numerous experiments with the chair, but it still needs fine-tuning. Hayasaki fears the chair will be useless unless it can obey commands universally, reaching the point where it can replicate the complexity of human behavior and function as a sort of mechanical doppelgänger for the human body. Meanwhile, Hayasaki's boss is growing impatient with the slow progress and amount of research funds being spent.

It is while suffering from such work-related stress that Hayasaki first catches a glimpse of someone who resembles him from the back at a local restaurant. The next day at work, his female assistant, Takano (Satō Hitomi), asks Hayasaki if he believes in paranormal phenomena. She recounts a story she heard from a friend (Yuka) whose brother committed suicide. Takano recounts Yuka's story that her brother died because he had seen his doppelgänger, referencing the long-held belief that if one encounters one's doppelganger, death is close at hand. Takano asks Hayasaki what he thinks, but he feigns ignorance about such matters.

Later at home, Hayasaki is quite astonished when he encounters his own doppelgänger. The doppelgänger (also played by Yakusho Kōji) approaches him and inspects him up and down like a predator about to pounce on its prey, but says and does nothing (see Fig. 3.7). Hayasaki is quite shaken, but when he looks for the doppelgänger, he has disappeared. The set design of the mise-en-scène for this encounter, especially the yin-yang-patterned couch cover that is clearly visible, underscores the intertwinement of Hayasaki's self and doppelgänger

Fig. 3.7   Hayasaki encounters his double in *Doppelgänger* (2003)

and the interconnected nature of their contrary forces that will play itself out over the course of the movie.

After this encounter with his double, Hayasaki becomes increasingly angry that he is unable to make progress with his invention. The more agitated Hayasaki becomes, the more often his doppelgänger reappears. At a local restaurant, as Hayasaki starts to wonder if he is cracking up, his doppelganger shows up, sits behind him in the next booth and orders the same thing as Hayasaki. In response, Hayasaki rushes out of the restaurant and returns home. At home, Hayasaki's doppelganger is already there waiting for him, perusing his research notes. Hayasaki tries to kick him out of his house, but the doppelganger just makes himself at home. He confronts his doppelganger and demands to know who he is, but the doppelgänger simply responds, "I'm Hayasaki Michio, too." The doppelganger explains that he showed up because he felt sorry for him. It is at this point in the narrative that Kurosawa starts to employ advanced framing techniques to help visualize the complex dynamics between Hayasaki and his doppelgänger.

To get a handle on the director's frame games in *Doppelgänger*, it is useful to review some of the fundamental distinctions introduced by Gilles Deleuze in *Cinema 1: The Movement-Image.* One of the most basic concepts that Deleuze introduces in the opening pages of *Cinema*

1 is that of the frame and the forms of framing encountered in the image-machines of cinema. Deleuze notes that the cinematic concept of the frame has a number of distinctive traits. First, Deleuze defines the frame as "*a relatively closed system which includes everything which is present in the image,*" such as sets, characters, props, and so forth.[48] In cinema, the elements of this closed system often form subsets.

Second, the frame is characterized by two tendencies—either it is "towards saturation or towards rarefaction."[49] A saturated frame is one in which multiple elements come into focus due to increased depth of field and compete for the spectator's attention. A rarefied frame is one in which the focus is "placed on a single object," while the rest of the frame is mostly empty.[50] The classic example of rarefaction offered by Deleuze is the famous shot of a darkened window in Hitchcock's *Rear Window* (1954), from which one can detect a single glowing cigarette that stands out against the blackness of the rest of the frame.

Third, Deleuze notes that the cinematic frame provides a geometric or spatial composition of the elements that it contains in relation to horizontal and vertical lines, parallel lines, and diagonal lines. However, this does not mean that the geometry of the frame is fixed, since framing also offers a dynamic construction of elements that varies from shot to shot. In any case, it is the frame that composes the elements that fill it, either separating or bringing together the parts of a closed system.

Fourth, although the film screen as a whole may be said to be the "frame of frames,"[51] there are often different frames within frames, as well as frames beside frames, across the screen. "Doors, windows, box office windows, skylights, car windows, mirrors, are all frames in frames,"[52] according to Deleuze. Through the interaction of these secondary and tertiary frames, individual elements (or subsets of elements) are either brought together or separated. The interaction of these multiple frames in frames produces what Deleuze calls "zones or bands"[53] whose gradations may be precise or imprecise. "Here, it is by degrees of mixing," writes Deleuze, "that the parts become distinct or confused in a continual transformation of values."[54]

Fifth, the frame is always related to an angle of framing or point of view. Since the frame is a closed set in an optical system, there must always be an angle or point of view of some sort or another. However, Deleuze also acknowledges that there exist in cinema so-called "deframings" (*décadrages*) that express impractical angles or abnormal points of view that suggest other dimensions to the image.[55] Finally, just as important to what the frame frames is what the frame excludes: i.e., what is not inside the frame—what is offscreen or outside the frame. For Deleuze, the term "out-of-field" (*hors-champ*) refers "to what is neither seen nor understood, but is nevertheless perfectly present."[56] In other words, what is out of the picture (or offscreen) is just as significant to a film as what is inside the frame, especially when what is offscreen implies a larger set that extends what is in the frame. Insofar as the frame is constantly open to reframing from shot to shot, what is outside the frame is also constantly shifting. It is because this dynamic interplay between what is in the frame and what is out-of-frame continues throughout the duration of a film that the closed system inside the frame of a given shot is only relatively closed, never absolutely closed. According to Deleuze, "when a set is framed, therefore seen, there is always a larger set, or another set with which the first forms a larger one, and which can in turn be seen, on condition that it gives rise to a new out-of-field, etc."[57]

All of these distinctions are helpful when trying to come to terms with the complex framing techniques employed by Kurosawa in *Doppelgänger*.[58] Framing plays a very significant role in *Doppelgänger*, frequently amplifying unspoken elements of the narrative. Kurosawa typically manipulates the framing of *Doppelgänger* by dividing up the screen into multiple frames in the form of frames within frames and frames beside frames. Numerous permutations are played out during the course of the movie across the divided surface of the framed screen. The two most common ways in which the frame is divided and multiplied in *Doppelgänger* is when it is split into two panels (forming a diptych) or three panels (a triptych).

Since Kurosawa obviously did not invent the split-screen technique, some scholars have suggested that the director, who is an avid student of American cinema, may have borrowed the technique from earlier directors whose films he admires.[59] Indeed, a number of Kurosawa's cinematic heroes have employed split screen to good effect, such as Sam Peckinpah in the opening credits to *The Ballad of Cable Hogue* (1970) and *Junior Bonner* (1972). Likewise, Robert Aldrich, another director greatly admired by Kurosawa, uses a four-way split to dramatize the countdown to a terrorist-controlled missile launch in *Twilight's Last Gleaming* (1977). And Richard Fleischer uses the technique extensively in *The Boston Strangler* (1968)—one of Kurosawa's favorite films—to juxtapose interrogation scenes in the present and the past.[60] In addition, it is worth pointing out that split screen has occasionally been used in other films involving doppelgängers, evil twins, and split personalities, such as Robert Siodmak's *The Dark Mirror* (1947), as well as Brian De Palma's *Sisters* (1973) and *Carrie* (1976). As an avid student of film history, Kurosawa is undoubtedly familiar with all of these examples.

However, it is also important to consider the intermedial influence and significance of other art forms, such as the diptych and triptych in the history of Japanese woodblock printmaking. During the late Edo (1603–1868) and early Meiji (1868–1912) periods, kabuki actors were a popular subject of the two-panel diptych, such as in prints by Konishi Hirosada (fl. c. 1819–1863) devoted to the portraits of popular actors such as Utaemon IV and Tomosa II. In addition, *ukiyo-e* artists also embraced the triptych framework first introduced by hanging scroll painters as a way of dealing with larger scenes that exceeded the standard dimensions of Japanese paper and the cherry-wood boards that were used to print woodblock prints. For example, nineteenth-century woodblock print artists from Utagawa Kuniyoshi (1797–1861) to Toyohara Chikanobu (1838–1912) typically utilized the triptych to portray warriors and courtesans in works such as Kuniyoshi's *The Great Battle of Takadachi Castle in Mutsu* (1856) and Chikanobu's *Popular and Prosperous Pleasure Quarters: The Inamoto House* (1879). Actors performing famous scenes from kabuki plays were another popular subject for the triptych, such as in Toyohara Kunichika's *Tadamitsu, Kiheiji, and the Princess* (1879).

Although the separate prints making up a diptych or triptych typically constituted a unified design that formed a complete work with respect to both form and content, they were composed in such a way that individual panels could stand on their own artistic merit, since they were often broken up and sold individually. An interesting aspect of some triptychs is that certain figures are sometimes scaled out of proportion with other figures as a way of visualizing their unique strength, heroism, or social status, such as in Kuniyoshi's *Hako-o-maru and Kudō Suketsune at Hikone* (c. 1850), which depicts legendary warrior Kudō Suketsune as a figure who dwarfs his companions. If one considers Kurosawa's use of diptych and triptych framing techniques in *Doppelgänger*, a number of questions arise, such as: What sort of function is served by such split-screen techniques in the context of the film? How are relations between the figures inhabiting individual frames within frames or frames beside frames situated? How do such framing techniques influence our reception of the film as a whole?

First, it is noteworthy that the framework of the diptych and triptych split screen is frequently used in *Doppelgänger* to show the splitting of Hayasaki's subjectivity into different parts of himself engaged in different actions occurring simultaneously across multiple locations. For example, the triptych frame in Fig. 3.8 juxtaposes medium and close-up shots of Hayasaki at his laboratory in the left and right panels, while the doppelgänger occupies the middle panel at an exterior location as he wrestles with a man he is trying to rob. Although the left and right panels occur at different but closely related moments, the general timeframe seems to be roughly contemporaneous with the crime that is being committed in the middle panel. Rather than editing the shots together in a linear fashion, the triptych framework permits us to view parallel (or at least roughly contemporaneous) timelines and subjectivities in shots that are presented simultaneously. When viewing a sequence enframed in this way, so many

Fig. 3.8   The splitting of Hayasaki's subjectivity in a triptych frame in *Doppelgänger* (2003)

things unfold at once across different frames (from parallel time streams) that it can be difficult to process it all. In some cases, one does not quite know what to focus on. In other cases, the manipulation of scale or the number of panels occupied directs the viewer's attention to a particular focal point.

Kurosawa employs such framing techniques as a way to evoke the complexity of life occurring outside the frame, which is something that especially interests him as a filmmaker. In interviews, Kurosawa has been quite explicit about trying to suggest action outside the frame: "So when I capture space in a frame of film, I always try to convey a sense that space continues outside the frame. In other words, what's visible is definite, but the invisible part of space outside the frame should have some effect on the visible part captured in the frame.... The invisible part of space outside the frame must be affecting the visible part in some way. I always have that in mind when I clip space to fit into a frame."[61] In a number of his films, such as *Cure, Séance,* and *Tokyo Sonata,* Kurosawa strongly implies action taking place outside of the film frame, which nonetheless impacts those within the frame. This is not simply to draw attention to negative space within the frame, but space outside the frame altogether—the "out-of-field" discussed by Deleuze that refers "to what is neither seen nor understood, but is nevertheless perfectly present."[62]

However, in a film such as *Doppelgänger,* in addition to implying action "out-of-field," Kurosawa also utilizes the split-screen framework to achieve other effects. Besides the permutations already discussed, one may point to other examples, such as Fig. 3.9, in which medium close-up shots of Hayasaki are doubled across two horizontal panels stacked on the left from similar but not identical angles, while his doppelgänger appears in a medium long shot in the vertical panel on the right. In yet other variations, one figure may appear tripled across all three panels or one panel may be blacked out while the other two are divided between Hayasaki and his doppelgänger. Such techniques have the effect of foregrounding the framing, shot selection, and editing of a given scene.

In some scenes that make use of triptych framing, the eyelines strangely do not match. For example, in the scene shown in Fig. 3.10, after the doppelgänger has complained to Hayasaki about his inflexibility dragging him down, Hayasaki demands that his doppelgänger leave. When the

Fig. 3.9   Variations on the triptych frame in *Doppelgänger* (2003)

Fig. 3.10   Eyeline mismatches in *Doppelgänger* (2003)

doppelgänger (in the middle and right panels) looks up and to the right of the frame to respond, the eyeline of the doppelgänger does not match up with that of Hayasaki, who appears in medium close-up on the far left looking down. Kurosawa deliberately mismatches the eyelines in such scenes, breaking the 180-degree rule and subverting the conventions of Hollywood continuity editing. This is a good example of what Deleuze refers to as "deframing" (*décadrages*), which expresses impractical angles or abnormal points of view that suggest other dimensions to the image. In so doing, Kurosawa throws the audience off balance and draws our attention to the constructedness of the film's image-machine.

Kurosawa also plays with scale in some of the diptych/triptych shots in a manner that is strongly reminiscent of the woodblock print tradition, making either Hayasaki or his doppelgänger appear out of proportion with the other. For example, in Fig. 3.11, Hayasaki's panel on the right is a close-up that makes him look much larger than the doppelgänger who sits in medium shot on the left. In this same sequence, Kurosawa not only alternates between non-split screen, diptych, and triptych compositions, but also plays with scaling across panels with the doppelgänger sometimes appearing in close-up while Hayasaki appears in medium shot, thereby reversing the size difference. In this way, Kurosawa invokes the conventions of scaling that one encounters in woodblock print triptychs, but rather than visualizing the unique strength, heroism, or social status of the figure who is scaled out of proportion, here it seems to be used to emphasize who is in control (or has the upper hand) at a given moment in the sparring that unfolds between self and double. In other words, scale is manipulated to visualize the micropolitics of their exchange.

Fig. 3.11 Playing with scale in *Doppelgänger* (2003)

In one of the most poignant scenes later in the film, after the decision has been made to sell the Artificial Body Chair to a powerful medical instrument manufacturer, the doppelgänger pours champagne to celebrate. A non-split frame divides into two to form a diptych (Fig. 3.12) with Hayasaki appearing on the right and the doppelgänger on the left. As self and double discuss what they had hoped to get out of the robotic chair, it is interesting that both seem to occupy the same chair within the room. Moreover, when they speak, both address the camera, suggesting that the two frames of the diptych are the POVs of one another. Hayasaki insists that his doppelgänger never really existed in this world and the two start to fight. The doppelgänger tells Hayasaki that he accepts "the you inside of me" and that Hayasaki must accept "the me inside of you." "Sooner or later we'll merge as one self again. Give up. Accept your fate." The fight escalates and one of them ends up dead. Although we are initially led to believe that Hayasaki has disposed of his doppelgänger, like the return of the repressed, it is not so easy to get rid of one's doppelgänger.

Later in the film, the character whom we thought was Hayasaki resumes whistling a tune that only the doppelgänger had whistled previously. If this musical leitmotif is to be trusted, then either it was the

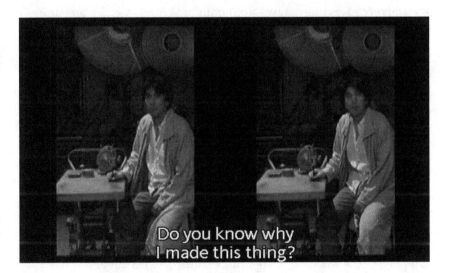

Fig. 3.12 Double vision in *Doppelgänger* (2003)

doppelgänger who killed the original—thereby affirming the double's traditional role as a harbinger of death—or the two have, in fact, merged, as the doppelgänger implored they must. In either case, when one considers the innovative ways in which diptychs and triptychs are used throughout the film, it becomes clear that such framing techniques foreground the double vision that is an essential trait of the doppelgänger narrative, in which the "subject beholds its other self as another, as visual object, or is beheld as object by its other self."[63]

Although *Doppelgänger* starts out as a straightforward J-horror film and was marketed internationally by Tartan Films as "The Most Frightening Film Yet From the Director of *Bright Future* and *Séance*," by the end of the movie, Kurosawa has effectively deterritorialized the genre conventions of horror and crossed over into other territories, including science fiction, comedy, thriller, family melodrama, romance, and road movie. By straddling multiple genres in this way (which is not uncommon for a Kurosawa Kiyoshi film), *Doppelgänger* turns out to be just as split as the diptych and triptych frames that are used to visualize the fractured subjectivity of Hayasaki. However, such genre mixing is not limited to *Doppelgänger*. Indeed, it would not be going too far to say that one of the most compelling aspects of J-horror's hybridity is how often it intermixes conventions drawn from multiple genres, thereby presenting a form of horror that is not only transnational but also transgeneric (a topic to which I will return in relation to surrealist horror in Chap. 4).

Coda: Hyphenated Subjectivities

In my discussion of *Bilocation* above, I noted in passing the appearance of a life-sized doll depicting conjoined twins who are joined at the shoulder that appears in the mirror room (see Fig. 3.3). Despite the fact that we never encounter conjoined twins as characters in *Bilocation*, the same image is also featured on posters for the movie's marketing campaign. Although conjoined twins are not simply equivalent to the figure of the doppelgänger, *Bilocation*'s juxtaposition of doppelgängers with the image of conjoined twins suggests that they exist along the same continuum of doubles, and, as such, may share similar codes, conventions, and problems. With this in mind, I would like to bring this chapter to a close by considering Miike Takashi's conjoined twin horror *Box* (2004) as a sort of borderline case that has much in common with doppelgänger narratives while offering unique twists of its own. Although it may not be a doppelgänger narrative in the conventional sense, there is no question that *Box* is infused with motifs of doubling and shares many traits with conventional doppelgänger narratives.

Coming from a director known for his stylistic excesses and graphic violence (see my discussion of *Gozu* in Chap. 4 and *Audition* in Chap. 5), *Box* not only stands apart from the two other films included in *Three …* *Extremes* from directors Park Chan-wook and Fruit Chan but also stands out as one of the most restrained and poetic horror films Miike has ever made. As Nikki Lee remarks, *Box*'s "poetically beautiful and surrealistic scenery, its images of dreamy and weird fantasies, and its atmosphere of fear and psychological pressure" are more reminiscent of the best J-horror fare from Nakata Hideo, such as *Ringu* and *Dark Water*, than Miike himself.[64] Miike has acknowledged that he deliberately set out to make a very quiet film with minimal dialogue and restrained sound design: "The story develops very slowly, but for the depth of each piece of information, I intentionally made the story progress very slow, so it can be felt deeply…. As much as possible, those things used in horror movies to make it scarier—sound effects, musical elements—were avoided as much as possible…. More than the story, it's about layering images that people can react to."[65]

Box is strikingly different in tempo and tone from *Bilocation* and *Doppelgänger*, yet, in its own way, also engages the peculiar uncanniness associated with doubles, whether conceived in supernatural, psychological, or biological terms. An identical twin, whether conjoined or not, is, after all, a sort of biological doppelgänger. It is for this reason that films about identical twins—e.g., *A Stolen Life* (dir. Curtis Bernhardt, 1946), *The Parent Trap* (dir. David Swift, 1961/dir. Nancy Meyers, 1998), *Dead Ringer* (dir. Paul Henreid, 1964), *Dead Ringers* (dir. David Cronenberg, 1988), *Adaptation* (dir. Spike Jonze, 2002), and *The Prestige* (dir. Christopher Nolan, 2006)—often engage similar issues. Drawn in the broadest of strokes, the figure of the doppelgänger often functions as a sort of id, doing all the things the self would like to do but dare not do because to do so would break laws and transgress social mores. Alternatively, it may also function as a sort of conscience or censoring agency, telling the self what it should not do and making it feel guilty about misdeeds.[66]

In his study of the figure of the doppelgänger in German literature titled *The Doppelgänger: Double Visions in German Literature*, Andrew J. Webber expands upon this basic understanding of the figure of the doppelgänger by singling out a number of traits that are commonly associated with it, including:

1. "double vision," in which the "subject beholds its other self as another, as visual object, or is beheld as object by its other self";
2. "double talk," or divisive language in which the doppelgänger "echoes, reiterates, distorts, parodies, dictates, impedes, and dumbfounds" what the self is trying to say by saying something contrary;
3. "performance," in which the double is "an inveterate performer of identity," such that identity is "always mediated by the other self";
4. "double-bind" involving the embodied stake "which epistemology and sexuality have in each other";
5. "power-plays" between ego and alter ego, which show the ego's inability to attain mastery of the self because it is constantly being displaced by its other self;
6. "material and sexual displacement," in which the doppelgänger functions as an economic and/or sexual rival;
7. "repetition and the return of the repressed," in which the double and the self switch places, as well as incorporating aspects of each other, creating new hybrid identities that blur the boundaries between self and other.[67]

Most of these traits are at work to varying degrees in how the double is situated in J-horror films such as *Bilocation* and *Doppelgänger*, but they also resonate with how the double is reconceived in the conjoined twin horror *Box*. However, *Box* adds a few new wrinkles of its own in its engagement with the peculiar doubling of concorporation.

Although it is not fully revealed until the end of the movie that twin sisters, Kyoko and Shoko, are fused side-by-side with a shared pelvis (Fig. 3.13), their conjoinment is intimated numerous times during the course of the film's brief 40-minute running time. In a series of surreal dreams in which they occupy separate bodies, ten-year-olds Kyoko and Shoko (played by identical twins Suzuki Mai and Suzuki Yuu, respectively) perform a dance routine that is part of a magic act presented by a man (who may or may not be their father) for an itinerant entertainment that takes place in a small circus tent. Both the performance and the venue are highly reminiscent of the "*misemono*" shows that travelled around Japan and were popular during the Edo and early Meiji periods. During Kyoko and Shoko's *misemono* spectacle, they adopt contortionist poses to suggest various forms of conjoinment, including fusion at the chest and neck (Fig. 3.14), even if their dreams ultimately present them in nonconjoined form. As the show proceeds, the sisters contort themselves into two small boxes, which are locked tight by the magician. The magician then casts a dart at each box, the lids of the locked boxes pop open, and it is revealed that the girls have disappeared and been replaced by red and white flowers.

Fig. 3.13 Final revelation of Kyoko and Shoko's conjoinment in *Box* (2004)

Fig. 3.14 Multiple forms of conjoinment are suggested during the performances by Kyoko and Shoko in *Box* (2004)

The choreography of the sisters' synchronized dance routine is elegantly beautiful, yet the strange forms of conjoinment that their contortions suggest also bring to mind the spectacle of freak shows that were part and parcel of the *misemono* tradition. As Andrew Markus observes in his study of *misemono* spectacles:

> Exhibits of freaks and deformities are among the oldest and most universal, if least laudable forms of entertainment. In Japan, however, the exhibitor of freaks not infrequently presented his subjects as object lessons in the Buddhist doctrine of karmic causation. A sinful act in a previous life or a more recent parental transgression was held responsible for a penal, deformed present existence—an attitude diametrically opposed to the popular Christian sentiment that the poor, the infirm, or the mentally insane are by virtue of their debility closer to God…To the Japanese entrepreneur, however, all freaks were *inga-mono* "karma acts."[68]

Freaks and natural curiosities of varying types played a significant role in *misemono* spectacles. In flashbacks of their contortionist performances, the young sisters in *Box* are not conjoined physically but only dramatically;

nevertheless, the "freakishness" of some of their contortions strongly suggests conjoinment. Moreover, a sense of karmic causation haunts the film in the form of a three-eyed, blue demon surrounded by flames that adorns the performance backdrop, which symbolizes a wrathful Buddhist deity associated with negative karma (Fig. 3.15).

Of course, conceiving conjoined twins as "freaks" and "monsters" has a long and complicated history that is intersected by medical, legal, ethical, and religious discourses and issues. As Susan Stewart has argued, "The physiological freak represents the problems of the boundary between self and other (Siamese twins), between male and female (the hermaphrodite), between the body and the world outside the body (the *monstré par exces*), and between the animal and the human (feral and wild men)… Ontology is not the point here so much as the necessity of exploring these relations, either through the fantastic or the 'real.'"[69] In his lectures at Collège de France on the discursive differentiation between "normality" and "abnormality" and how such a distinction correlates with power relations specific to the epoch that conceived it, Michel Foucault argues that the figure of the monster often presents "a legal labyrinth, a violation of and an obstacle to the law, both transgression and undecidability

Fig. 3.15 Kyoko and Shoko perform as directed by the magician/father figure against the backdrop of a wrathful three-eyed Buddhist deity in *Box* (2004)

at the level of the law."[70] Since each epoch privileges certain forms of monstrosity, according to Foucault, one must attend to the characteristics specific to the epoch and the monster. For example, in the Middle Ages, the privileged form of monstrosity was the "bestial man," or "the monster that is both man and beast."[71] During the Renaissance, a new form of monstrosity became privileged: viz., "Siamese twins," or "the one who is two and the two who are one."[72] In literary, medical, legal, and religious texts at the end of the sixteenth and beginning of the seventeenth centuries, Foucault notes the frequency of references to "the individual who has one head and two bodies, or one body and two heads."[73]

In a European context, Foucault shows how the problem of conjoined twins plays itself out in interesting ways with far-reaching legal, medical, and religious implications:

> When a monster with two bodies or two heads is born, should we give it one or two baptisms? Should we consider it a case of one child or two? I have found the trace of a story of two Siamese twin brothers, one of whom had committed a crime.... The problem was whether one or both of them should be executed. If one were executed, then the other would die; but if the innocent brother was allowed to live, then the other also had to be allowed to live. This is how the problem of monstrosity really appeared.[74]

For Foucault, conjoined twins present a "double breach, of law and nature."[75] If the concorporation of conjoined twins is perceived as defying the law, it is because of their morphological irregularity and the fact that modern law insists on conceiving the legal subject "as a single embodied mind" in possession of "a body with clear boundaries."[76] The conjoined twins' simultaneous lack of bodily integrity and lack of separateness go against modern legal conceptions of personhood, individual agency, and personal identity.[77] As Andrew Sharpe puts it in his study *Foucault's Monsters and the Challenge of Law*, "In the eyes of law, conjoined twins represent bodily confusion because, understood as two, it is difficult to delineate the precise bodily contours of each twin."[78] In other words, from the perspective of the law, conjoined twins present "two distinct persons with distinct identities [which] have, as it were, become trapped in a single morphology."[79] It is for this reason that surgical separation is often pursued as both a medical and legal solution no matter how deleterious the effects on one or both twins may be.

Although Foucault uses the dated term "Siamese twins" to refer to conjoined twins, it is worth pointing out that the term derives from conjoined twins Chang and Eng Bunker—the original Siamese twins—who are alluded to in *Box* by means of the association that is established between conjoinment and itinerant entertainment. Chang and Eng Bunker (1811–1874), who adopted the surname "Bunker" when they became naturalized American citizens in 1839, were twin brothers conjoined at the chest. Their condition made them famous around the world as they traveled with P. T. Barnum's circus and other exhibitors. The term "Siamese twins" derives from the fact that Chang and Eng were born near Bangkok in the Kingdom of Siam (today known as Thailand). The brothers were connected primarily at the sternum by a fleshy piece of cartilage, but their livers were also fused. They moved to the United States in 1839 and lived on a 110-acre plantation that they had purchased in North Carolina from the profits they earned touring the world as human curiosities. Chang and Eng lived a long and productive life, married two young American sisters in a double ceremony, and together fathered 21 children total.

A French journalist who met Chang and Eng when they visited Paris in 1835 described their unique bond as a "hyphen-mark between the two brothers":

The Siamese twins have never been sold, they belong to no one, they travel on their own expenses, in their own coach, with their own servants, and when they arrive in a big city, they depose their passport to the police, go to a good hotel, take a commodious and well-heated apartment; they move in and dine well, without waiting for someone to throw them a crust of bread after the exhibition. They hire an interpreter, and inform the public that they will receive them at certain hours…Dressed in European clothes, they wear little open vests, and the only visible part of their bodies is the band which unites them; a little opening in the shirt suffices to show this communal part which forms as a hyphen-mark between the two brothers…When one is hungry, the other is hungry, when one is tired, the other rests; they both like to eat well, and in this, as in everything, they have the same tastes…This double man is, in all respects, but one and the same man, and we are more burdened to find individual facts by action of community between two beings so ultimately united, and at the same time so complete, each in his own. When it comes to purely intellectual phenomena, it is clearly evident that they are equally double and independent, the one does not know the thoughts of the other; thus one can read a novel while the other studies history; but it is true that they don't like to do different things at the same time; in general, they read the same book together, as together they execute all the actions of their life.[80]

The hyphen-mark that showed "the communal part" between the two brothers also marked their differentiation—a "double man" that is a repetition with a difference. As transnational subjects who were born and raised in Siam, traveled and worked around the world as free men, and eventually became Siamese-American citizens of the United States, the hyphenated identities of Chang and Eng were truly modern, "equally double and independent." In their hybridity, the Siamese twins exemplified the doubleness that Foucault argued in *The Order of Things: An Archaeology of the Human Sciences* (*Les mots et les choses: Une archéologie des sciences humaines*, 1966) haunts modern subjectivity: "Identity separated from itself by a distance which, in one sense, is interior to it, but, in another, constitutes it, and repetition which posits identity as a datum, but in the form of distance, are without doubt at the heart of that modern thought to which the discovery of time has so hastily been attributed."[81]

And yet it was also the hyphenated nature of Chang and Eng's concorporation that elicited a great deal of controversy. Despite the fact that Chang and Eng were by all accounts respected members of their community, the appellation of "monster" and "freak" dogged them during their travels around the world. While being exhibited in Boston in 1829, the first posters that were printed to advertise the event billed Chang and Eng as "THE MONSTER." It was only after their sponsors objected that the poster was revised to "THE SIAMESE DOUBLE BOYS."[82] Although it is often assumed that P. T. Barnum coined the label "Siamese Twins" in 1853 to advertise the twins when they traveled with Barnum's circus, biographers have determined not only that it was the brothers themselves who came up with the designation but that it was also their preferred self-appellation, which they had been using since 1832.[83] However, the label was never meant to be applied to all conjoined twins irrespective of their ethnic origins.[84] Nonetheless, as the original Siamese twins traveled around the world, it was their monstrosity that was more frequently noted than their ethnicity. When famed French naturalist, professor of zoology, and founder of teratology (the study of monstrosities) Étienne Geoffroy Saint-Hilaire applied on behalf of the brothers for an entry visa and permit to exhibit Chang and Eng in Paris in 1831, the French government refused entry, claiming that their appearance might be harmful to pregnant women and the impressionable minds of children.[85] Four years later, with the continued advocacy of Geoffroy Saint-Hilaire, the French government finally relented and permitted the Bunkers to come to Paris. An early French reviewer for the newspaper *La Quotidienne* admitted to being impressed with Chang and Eng's grace and intelligence, yet continued to resort to metaphors of monstrosity in talking about them even as he placed into question the very use of such biased expressions: "These monsters, since we must call them by their name, are not monstrous at all."[86]

This unfortunate history of association between conjoined twins and freakish monstrosity is intimated as a subtext at several points in *Box,* especially in the dreamy flashbacks of the young sisters who are compelled to perform in *misemono*-type exhibitions before a paying audience. Nevertheless, what is most remarkable is that despite such associations, it is not their conjoinment per se that is problematized so much as it is the twins' double fear that their shared embodiment provokes, which intertwines displacement anxiety and separation anxiety.[87] In traditional doppelgänger literary narratives, such as E. T. A. Hoffmann's *The Devil's Elixirs* (*Die Elixiere des Teufels*, 1815), Fyodor Dostoevsky's *The Double* (*Dvoinik*, 1846/1866), and Edgar Allan Poe's "William Wilson" (1839), the self is typically most afraid of being displaced or supplanted by the double. However, *Box* reconceives the doppelgänger narrative through the lens of conjoined twins with respect not only to the unique bond that conjoined twins share but also the differing anxieties experienced by Kyoko and Shoko.

In *Box*, one encounters a poignant confrontation between displacement anxiety—the fear of being confused with one another, of not having an identity that can exist separately from the other—and separation anxiety—the fear that they will lose each other, that the special bond they share will be severed if they undergo separation and will no longer be able to experience the unique sense of wholeness that only conjoined twins can feel. During the film, Kyoko's desire to separate, which exemplifies displacement anxiety, is motivated by her increasing jealousy of Shoko for being the object of the magician/father figure's affections. In a dreamy flashback to Kyoko and Shoko's performance in the *misemono* exhibitions, the magician praises Shoko and presents her with a necklace as reward, but says nothing to Kyoko. Shoko encourages Kyoko to keep trying, but it is obvious that young Kyoko is both disappointed and jealous, since she concludes that the magician/father figure loves Shoko more than her. As is often the case in doppelgänger narratives, Kyoko's identical twin Shoko functions as a rival for the desired attentions of another character (in this case, the magician/father figure).

In what is perhaps her most traumatic dream, Kyoko's jealousy of her sister and desire for separation is violently expressed in a scene that is framed by the wrathful Buddhist demon adorning the performance backdrop, which evokes the power of negative karma haunting Kyoko. Young Kyoko stares at the Buddhist demon before gazing at her sister, who is practicing her routine. The moment that Shoko enters the box, Kyoko runs and locks her sister inside, telling her to "bear it for one night." At this point, the young and mature voices of Kyoko merge: "I want to be you, to sleep like you, to have nice dreams." When the magician walks in and discovers what Kyoko has done, he violently reprimands her, knocking her down. In response, Kyoko picks up one of the darts used in the routine and scrapes it across his face. As the magician stumbles around bleeding, Kyoko accidentally knocks over a nearby kerosene heater, igniting the box containing her sister. The magician tries to save Shoko, but it is too late. As the entire tent catches fire, young Kyoko escapes outside, fleeing into the snowy woods until she stumbles and arises as the mature Kyoko.

The nightmare of Shoko's death (which is also Kyoko's hidden desire) is preceded by a complementary dream that opens the film and is experienced repeatedly by the adult Kyoko (played by Hasegawa Kyoko) during the course of the film, evoking karmic connotations as the narrative unfolds. The mature Kyoko dreams of being buried alive by her magician/

father figure as punishment for the untimely death of her sister. In his influential essay on "The Uncanny," Freud goes so far as to assert that for many people being buried alive is the crowning example of the uncanny. Freud viewed the fear of being buried alive as a "terrifying fantasy" that was a darker variant on "the fantasy of living in the womb,"[88] but what makes the fear of being buried alive truly uncanny is that it involves the blurring of boundaries between the living and the dead, since the living is effectively treated as dead. In the case of *Box*, Kyoko's repeated dream of being buried alive (in the same type of box in which she also fantasized her sister perished) not only offers a fantasy of punishment for her desire to be separated from her conjoined sister but also the figurative means by which she may bury her guilt over harboring such transgressive desires.

In a related dream, the adult Kyoko returns to the *misemono* scene of her sister's death where she is joined by the magician, who compels her to look at the charred remains of the box that became her sister's coffin. At that precise moment, the box opens and the burned corpse of the young Shoko gazes accusingly at the mature Kyoko. Although Kyoko apologizes repeatedly, an apology is not enough. After sharing a passionate kiss, the magician slips a large, clear plastic bag over Kyoko's head and entire body, shouting: "Can't have one without the other! Shoko and Kyoko—together, a perfect pair. You're one and the same to me!" Dragging Kyoko over to Shoko's box, the magician forces her inside, even though she appears much too large to possibly fit. Nevertheless, this is the very box in which she repeatedly dreams of being buried alive by the magician. Just before dying from suffocation, Kyoko awakens from the dream and in voiceover indicates (as she has previously) that "The dream always ends just there." However, after this final awakening and just before the reality of their conjoinment is revealed (Fig. 3.13), Kyoko adds: "In reality, we've been together since birth…But then our dreams differ slightly."

Haunted Leitmotifs

At the level of the film's soundtrack, the fraught relations between the twins as they compete for the attentions of the father-figure magician is expressed by means of a musical leitmotif that is repeated at crucial moments during the course of the film. In my analysis of Kurosawa

Kiyoshi's *Doppelgänger* above, I touched briefly upon that film's use of a musical leitmotif to differentiate self from double. In *Box*, a musical leitmotif plays an even more significant role and requires some contextualization in relation to film music history to unpack its significance.

As is widely recognized, the role of the leitmotif in the film soundtrack owes much to Wagnerian usage. In his study of Wagner's *Ring* cycle (1876), William Cord defines the "leitmotif" as follows:

> A leitmotif is a short, uncomplicated musical phrase or theme, usually one to three measures, which is employed, and reused, by the composer when he deems it important to the composition. In the case of Wagner and his *Ring*, the leitmotif became a musical theme representative of a figure, an event, an emotion, a thought, an idea, or a concept in the drama, which theme he repeated, often in subtle but distinct, varying, and often tempered pitch, tone, and/or intensity according to the interpretive demands of his dramatic argument.[89]

In the realm of cinema, the clearest indicator that a musical leitmotif is doing its job in a film is if one cannot imagine a given scene without it: i.e., when the leitmotif becomes so catchy and the movie that features it so popular that the leitmotif is practically burned into cultural memory in relation to the global reception of the film that it serves, making such films practically indissociable from their sonic leitmotifs. In the history of cinema, there are certain leitmotifs, such as the famous stabbing strings leitmotif composed by Bernard Herrmann for the shower scene in *Psycho* (dir. Alfred Hitchcock, 1960) or the attacking shark leitmotif composed by John Williams for *Jaws* (dir. Steven Spielberg, 1975), which have become so famous and so profoundly absorbed by the pop cultural imaginary that one need only hear a few bars (or, in some cases, just a few notes) to recognize the source of the leitmotif and what it signifies. In the case of *Jaws*, Williams described the shark leitmotif, which revolves around repeating E and F bass notes performed on a tuba and accompanied by six double basses, eight cellos, and four trombones, as "so simple, insistent and driving, that it seems unstoppable, like the attack of the shark" itself.[90] According to Williams, the leitmotif could be performed either "loud and fast if he was attacking" or "soft and slow if he was lurking."[91] Either way, the shark leitmotif always sounds menacing and has practically become indissociable from the reception of the movie itself. However, as far as Frankfurt school theorist Theodor Adorno was concerned, that is precisely the problem with leitmotifs in film music.

When musical leitmotifs become overused in cinema or too mechanical in their application, argued Adorno, "The degeneration of the leitmotiv is implicit in this … it leads directly to cinema music where the sole function of the leitmotiv is to announce heroes or situations so as to allow the audience to orient itself more easily."[92] In a study titled *Composing for the Films* (1947) cowritten with Hanns Eisler a few years earlier, Adorno's objections to the leitmotif in film music were boiled down to a few essential points of criticism. Although Adorno and Eisler acknowledged the possibility of certain benefits associated with leitmotifs, such as "the ease with which they are recalled," providing "definite clues to the listener," functioning "as trademarks, so to speak, by which persons, emotions, and symbols can instantly be identified," they insisted that "cinema music is so easily understood that it has no need of leitmotifs to serve as signposts, and its limited dimension does not permit of adequate expansion of the leitmotif," which they argue is better suited to large-scale musical forms such as opera and Wagnerian music drama.[93] Moreover, according to Adorno and Eisler, the way in which leitmotifs are "drummed into the listener's ear by persistent repetition" suggests that the function of the leitmotif has been reduced "to the level of a musical lackey, who announces his master with an important air even though the eminent personage is dearly recognizable to everyone."[94] As far as Adorno and Eisler were concerned, "There is no place for [the leitmotif] in the motion picture," since narrative film, according to them, "seeks to depict reality," as opposed to the metaphysical significance endowing dramatic events in Wagnerian music drama.[95]

Although Adorno and Eisler's lambasting of the leitmotif in cinema has attracted a great deal of attention, other film theorists and historians of film music have not been so quick to dismiss the function of the leitmotif. As Mervyn Cooke points out in his landmark study, *A History of Film Music* (2010), Adorno and Eisler's comments "reveal strikingly basic misapprehensions about the function of music in narrative cinema, which can scarcely be said to depict 'reality.'"[96] Moreover, "these misapprehensions are tainted by an elitist dogma which views functional film music as a poor cousin to art music."[97] Given Adorno's criticism of the entire mass culture industry, which he blames for making consumers of mass-produced entertainment passive and docile, such a low opinion of the formulaic quality of the leitmotif in film music is hardly surprising. However, other theorists, such as Gilles Deleuze, have suggested that the leitmotif is considerably more complex than Adorno acknowledges, that there is more going on than simply announcing "heroes or situations," even if that is one of its primary traits.[98]

Rather than prematurely dismissing the function of the leitmotif, Deleuze offers a different approach, unpacking how the leitmotif mechanism works and introducing other aspects of the leitmotif that I will argue resonate strongly with its functioning in the context of a horror movie soundtrack, even one as minimalist as *Box*. In a seminar on music that Deleuze taught in 1977, he singled out a number of traits associated with the leitmotif in the context of a discussion of Wagner. First, Deleuze argued that the leitmotif is characterized by "pulsed time" (*temps pulsé*) that offers "a sonorous form with a strong intrinsic or interior property."[99] Typically, this takes the form of a simple musical phrase that is repeated, but for Deleuze pulsed time is distinguished not simply by its regularity or periodicity, since there are also irregular pulsations, but rather by its mode of temporality, which offers a "time of measure that situates things and persons."[100] Second, the leitmotif offers "the signpost of a character," which entails the formation of that character.[101] In this case, the pulsed time of the leitmotif marks the temporality of a subject in development—it is the time that "marks, measures, or scans, the formation of a subject."[102] Lastly, Deleuze suggested that insofar as the leitmotif is "fundamentally and functionally in the music, it serves as a function of sonorous territorialization, it comes and comes again."[103] By signaling movements of territorialization, the leitmotif "will be imposed on you, you will be forced to comply with it and from another side, it will order you."[104] For Deleuze, the pulsed time of the leitmotif is "always a territorialized time; regular or not, it's the number of the movement of the step that marks a territory…Each time there is a marking of territoriality, there will be a pulsation of time."[105] In sum, for Deleuze, both the character's formation and territoriality are signaled by the leitmotif. Deleuze does not deny that the leitmotif offers a signpost for a particular character, but he complexifies our understanding of its functioning by drawing our attention to the pulsed time of the leitmotif, which Deleuze associates not only with its sonorous form, but also with its role in marking a territory.

Applying Deleuze's conceptualization of the leitmotif to horror cinema, I would suggest that when it is used to express the character formation of a malevolent force, such as a vengeful ghost, serial killer, monster, or demon, the leitmotif not only guides our reception as spectators, but also signals to us both the moment when one character deterritorializes another character's territory within the film (and the ensuing chaos that is unleashed) and also the accompanying reterritorialization that marks out and takes control of a newly organized space (even if that newly organized space seems like the space of chaos for the victims of that force). In short, the issue of territory and the corresponding perception of chaos that are sonically signaled by the leitmotif's movements of deterritorialization and reterritorialization are just as essential to an understanding of how the leitmotif operates in the soundtrack of a horror film as is its functioning as "the signpost of a character." Although the musical form of the leitmotif is often anything but chaotic, since it typically makes use of a short, distinctive musical phrase that is repeated with only the slightest of variations, in the moment of deterritorialization, the leitmotif signals the threat of chaos that is already present or soon to be unleashed and whose perception is clearly dependent upon context and perspective.

Box may seem worlds apart from *Psycho* and *Jaws*, but what the leitmotifs of all three films share is the issue of territory and the processes of deterritorialization and reterritorialization that are implied. As the first and only piece of music heard repeatedly during what is otherwise quite a minimalist film, the leitmotif composed by Endō Kōji for *Box* is first introduced when the adult Kyoko, who also dreams of herself in nonconjoined form as a successful novelist, receives a small music box as a gift from her editor (played by Watabe Atsuro, who also doubles as the fatherly magician) in recognition of her achievements. More than anything else, boxes are the key to deciphering the audiovisual riddle that is *Box*. Indeed, Miike has acknowledged that "this is a movie where the story is connected by boxes."[106] The film titled *Box* is itself structured like a set of Chinese nested boxes, including the music box, the box that Kyoko repeatedly imagines herself buried alive inside, and the boxes that Kyoko and Shoko disappear into during their performance.

The first time Kyoko opens the music box, the diegetic sound of the leitmotif—a delicate, plaintive melody—alerts Kyoko to the spectral presence of her sister Shoko, who appears in nonconjoined form as a vengeful ghost who has returned to exact retribution for her untimely demise. As is often the case in J-horror films involving vengeful ghosts, the uncanniness of Shoko's appearance disturbs not only by producing an estrangement of the everyday—suggesting that something long repressed has returned to bring chaos to Kyoko's world—but also by evoking the anachronism that is an essential trait of spectrality itself. In other words, the figure of Shoko's vengeful ghost is herself a disjointed timeline insofar as she is an entity from another temporality (the past) that irrupts into Kyoko's present as the return of the repressed, haunting the present from a past that is no longer here. Neither simply past nor present, both past and present—exemplifying both absence and presence—Shoko's ghost is uncannily anachronistic and untimely.[107] However, even when the ghost of Shoko haunts Kyoko's waking hours, this, too, turns out to be a dream as the final epiphany of conjoinment reveals. In this sense, the uncanny also enters into *Box* by blurring "the line between between dreams and reality," as Miike acknowledges.[108] "What is dreaming and what is reality is usually depicted more clearly," observes Miike, "but maybe it's all dreams [*subete ga yume*]. That depends on how you feel when seeing the last shot, the last scene. That, too, I am leaving up to the audience's free sensibilities. As much as possible, I created many openings [*sukima*] in this work."[109]

The music box leitmotif is repeated twice more during the film: first, in a dreamy flashback when the young Kyoko gazes with envy upon Shoko as she sleeps quietly in the protective embrace of the father-magician and then again when their conjoined form is fully revealed at the end. On one level, this leitmotif functions as a signpost for the char-acter of Shoko, whose association with her is established in the first instance by Shoko's humming along to the music as it plays diegetically. However, on another level, the leitmotif signals that territory is very much at issue, as Deleuze suggests. In the case of *Box*, the territory in question is the hybrid space of the twins' conjoined corporeality itself.[110]

If the leitmotif belongs to Shoko, then its performance also expresses the extent to which Kyoko feels deterritorialized from their conjoined body. In short, their concorporation gives rise to mutually conflicting anxieties/fantasies of displacement and separation, which are experienced differently by each half of the conjoined whole.

In the end, although *Box* belongs to the continuum of doubling that includes doppelgängers, clones, and other variations such as concorporation, what it offers most of all is a haunting meditation on the myriad challenges facing conjoined twins whose hyphenated subjectivities and shared embodiment are inextricably bound together—doubled, yet independent. Perhaps the greatest challenge for conjoined twins is that, as Margrit Shildrick so eloquently puts it, "the other is also the self—a transgressive and indeterminate state in which corporeal, ontological and ultimately ethical boundaries are distorted and dissolved."[111] Until we learn to acknowledge (and accept) the paradox that "being conjoined is part of conjoined twins' individuality,"[112] the concorporation of "the one who is two and the two who are one"[113] will continue to haunt conceptions of the modern subject.

Notes

1. Nicholas Royle, *The Uncanny* (New York: Routledge, 2003), 76.
2. I discuss the role played by *ikiryō* in classical Japanese literature and medieval drama in my study *Theatricalities of Power: The Cultural Politics of Noh* (Stanford, Calif.: Stanford University Press, 2001), 37–87.
3. The illness was also known as "shadow sickness" (*kage no yamai*). See Konno Ensuke, *Nihon kaidanshū: Yūrei hen* (Tokyo: Chūō Kōron Shinsha, 2004), 64–66.
4. Michael Dylan Foster, *The Book of Yōkai: Mysterious Creatures of Japanese Folklore* (Oakland, California: University of California Press, 2015), 208.
5. The full title of Jean Paul's novel is *Blumen-, Frucht- und Dornenstücke oder Ehestand, Tod und Hochzeit des Armenadvokaten F. St. Siebenkäs im Reichsmarktflecken Kuhschnappel* (Flower, Fruit, and Thorn Pieces; or, the Married Life, Death, and Wedding of Siebenkäs, Poor Man's Lawyer).

6. Jean Paul, *Sämtliche Werke*, vol. 1, edited by Norbert Miller (Munich: Hanser Verlag, 1960), 67 (translation mine).

7. "*DOPPELGÄNGER, auch wol* doppeltgänger, *m. jemand von dem man wähnt er könne sich zu gleicher zeit an zwei verschiedenen orten zeigen.*" Jacob Grimm and Wilhelm Grimm, "DOPPELGÄNGER," *Deutsches Wörterbuch von Jacob Grimm und Wilhelm Grimm*, vol. 2 (Leipzig: S. Hirzel, 1860), 1263 (translation mine).

8. Thea Brejzek and Lawrence Wallen, "Derealisation, Perception and Site: Some Notes on the Doppelgänger Space," in *Perception in Architecture: Here and Now*, edited by Claudia Perren and Miriam Mlecek (Newcastle upon Tyne, UK: Cambridge Scholars Publishing, 2015), 2.

9. Sigmund Freud, *The Uncanny*, translated by David McLintock (New York: Penguin Books, 2003), 142.

10. Ibid., 142. On psychoanalytic theories of the double, see also Steven Jay Schneider, "Manifestations of the Literary Double in Modern Horror Cinema," in *Horror Film and Psychoanalysis: Freud's Worst Nightmare*, edited by Steven Jay Schneider (Cambridge: Cambridge University Press, 2004a), 107–110.

11. Euripides, *Helen*, translated by James Michie and Colin Leach (New York: Oxford University Press, 1981), 21–22 (lines 22–39).

12. Reimund Kvideland and Henning K Sehmsdorf, eds., *Scandinavian Folk Belief and Legend* (Minneapolis: University of Minnesota Press, 1988), 64–66; Lily Weiser-Aall, "En studie om vardøger," *Norveg* 12 (1965): 73–112.

13. "Etiäinen," *Wikipedia*, https://en.wikipedia.org/wiki/Etiäinen (accessed October 7, 2016).

14. Friedrich Kittler, "Romanticism—Psychoanalysis—Film: A History of the Double," in *Literature, Media, Information Systems*, edited by John Johnston (New York: Routledge, 1997), 96.

15. Nicholas Royle, *The Uncanny* (New York: Routledge, 2003), 76.

16. Although directed by Basil Dearden not Alfred Hitchcock, *The Man Who Haunted Himself* is based on the novel *The Strange Case of Mr. Pelham* (1957) by Anthony Armstrong, which was first adapted as an episode for the television series *Alfred Hitchcock Presents* in 1955. Hitchcock was not involved with the film adaptation, but the movie has an undeniably Hitchcockian flair.

17. Alissa Wilkinson quoted in Emma Jones, "Why are There So Many Doppelgangers in Films Right Now?" *BBC Culture*, April 10, 2014, http://www.bbc.com/culture/story/20140410-why-so-many-doppelgangers

(accessed January 19, 2015). See also Alissa Wilkinson, "What's With All the Movies About Doppelgängers?" *The Atlantic*, March 14, 2014, http://www.theatlantic.com/entertainment/archive/2014/03/whats-with-all-the-movies-about-doppelg-ngers/284413/ (accessed January 19, 2015).

18. H. D. M. Spence-Jones, ed., *The Pulpit Commentary* (New York, Toronto: Funk & Wagnalls Co., 189-?), 77.

19. Shinobu's name is spelled with the kanji 忍 (meaning "conceal oneself," "hide," or "endure"). In addition, it is also homophonic with the verb "*shinobu*" (偲ぶ), which may be translated as "recollect," "remember," "reminisce," "be nostalgic for." During the course of the film, all of these senses come into play in one way or another in Shinobu's character development.

20. David Sylvester, *Magritte* (Brussels: Mercatorfonds, 2009), 88.

21. Jacques Meuris, *René Magritte: 1898–1967* (Los Angeles: Taschen, 2007), 41. For further examples of Magritte's exploration of the ambiguity between interior and exterior, image and reality, see *The Key to the Fields* (*La clef des champs*, 1936), *The Call of the Peaks* (*L'appel des cîmes*, 1943), and *Where Euclid Walked* (*Les promenades d'Euclide*, 1955).

22. From an overview for *La condition humaine* (1933) provided by the National Gallery of Art, http://www.nga.gov/content/ngaweb/Collection/art-object-page.70170.html (accessed December 12, 2016).

23. Sylvester, 386.

24. Edgar Allan Poe's famous doppelgänger short story "William Wilson" (1839) ends with a terrifying mirror scene in which the protagonist thinks he sees the bloodied body of his doppelgänger in the mirror only to realize that he sees himself: "*You have conquered, and I yield. Yet henceforward art thou also dead—dead to the world and its hopes. In me didst thou exist—and, in my death, see by this image, which is thine own, how utterly thou hast murdered thyself.*" See Edgar Allan Poe, "William Wilson," in *The Complete Poems and Stories of Edgar Allan Poe, with Selections from His Critical Writings* (New York: A. A. Knopf, 1982), 292.

25. Donald Richie, *A Hundred Years of Japanese Film* (Tokyo: Kodansha International, 2005), 86.

26. Quoted by Lotte Eisner in *The Haunted Screen* (London: Secker & Warburg, 1973), 40.

27. On the role played by the divided space of mirrors in *The Student of Prague*, see Leon Hunt, "*The Student of Prague*," in *Early Cinema: Space, Frame, Narrative*, edited by Thomas Elsaesser and Adam Barker (London: BFI Publishing, 1990), 389–401.

28. Otto Rank, *The Double: A Psychoanalytic Study*, translated by Harry Tucker Jr., (Chapel Hill: University of North Carolina Press, 1971), 8–33, 49–68. See also Freud, *The Uncanny*, 142. The earlier version of Rank's research on the double that was cited by Freud in his essay "*Das Unheimliche*" had originally been published in the journal *Imago*, which was devoted to the application of psychoanalytic theory to the humanities and was edited by Freud. See Otto Rank, "*Der Doppelgänger*," in *Imago: Zeitschrift für Anwendung der Psychoanalyse auf die Geisteswissenschaften*, edited by Sigmund Freud (Leipzig, Vienna, and Zürich: Internationaler Psychoanalytischer Verlag, 1914), Vol. III, 97–164.

29. Fyodor Dostoevsky, *The Double and The Gambler*, translated by Richard Pevear and Larissa Volokhonsky (New York: Vintage, 2007), 111.

30. Another exception is the sci-fi thriller *Coherence* (2013), directed by James Ward Byrkit, about a group of friends who are confronted with their own doppelgängers when a passing comet tears a fissure in the space-time continuum that creates an opening for a parallel universe. In the realm of painting, I am also reminded of Dante Gabriel Rossetti's Pre-Raphaelite work *How They Met Themselves* (1864), which shows a couple wearing medieval dress who are startled by an encounter with their doppelgängers in a dark forest at twilight.

31. Caroline Ruddell, *The Besieged Ego: Doppelgangers and Split Identity Onscreen* (Edinburgh: Edinburgh University Press, 2013), 77.

32. Jacques Lacan, "Some Reflections on the Ego," *The International Journal of Psycho-Analysis*, vol. 34, no. 1 (1953): 14.

33. Jacques Lacan, "The Mirror Stage as Formative of the *I* Function as Revealed in Psychoanalytic Experience," in *Écrits: The First Complete Edition in English*, translated by Bruce Fink (New York: W.W. Norton & Co., 2006), 75.

34. Norman N. Holland, "The Trouble(s) with Lacan," http://users.clas.ufl.edu/nholland/lacan.htm (accessed October 21, 2015).

35. Lacan, "The Mirror Stage," 76.

36. Ibid., "The Mirror Stage," 76–78, 80; Jacques Lacan, *The Seminar of Jacques Lacan: Book III. The Psychoses, 1955–1956*, translated by Russell Grigg (London: Routledge, 1993), 39.

37. Dylan Evans, *An Introductory Dictionary of Lacanian Psychoanalysis* (London; New York: Routledge, 1996), 114–16.

38. Ruddell, 77.

39. Gilles Deleuze and Félix Guattari, *A Thousand Plateaus: Capitalism and Schizophrenia*, translated by Brian Massumi (Minneapolis: University of Minnesota Press, 1987), 587.

40. Gilles Deleuze, *Cinema 2: The Time-Image*, translated by Hugh Tomlinson and Robert Galeta (Minneapolis: University of Minnesota Press, 1989), 70.

41. Ibid., 70.

42. Michel Foucault, *This is Not a Pipe* (Berkeley: University of California Press, 1983), 50.

43. Ibid., 50.

44. Ibid., 50.

45. However, an alternate cut of the film, titled *Bairokēshon ura* (Bilocation Reverse Side), which was released in Japan just two weeks after the original cut's wide release on January 18, 2014, includes an alternate (much happier) ending in which Shinobu's bilocation (Takamura Shinobu) *does not* dematerialize—much to her surprise—after the original (Kirimura Shinobu) has committed suicide. The alternate version ends with a flash forward to Shinobu's pregnant bilocation, who apparently lives happily ever after with Masaru. In voiceover, Kagami reflects that he believes in a world in which humans and bilocations coexist (*kyōzon suru sekai*).

46. Kurosawa Kiyoshi briefly employs the figure of the doppelgänger in his earlier film *Séance* (1999), in which the character of Satō (also played by Yakusho Kōji) is silently confronted by his double after accidentally killing a young girl. In response, Satō sets the double on fire in particularly dramatic fashion in his backyard in a manner that probably references the apocryphal story of Catherine the Great (1729–1796), the eighteenth-century Empress of Russia (1762–1796), who is said to have once ordered her soldiers to set on fire her own doppelgänger when she saw it approach her.

47. "Interview," *Kyua*, directed by Kurosawa Kiyoshi (1997), translated as *Cure*, subtitled DVD (Chicago, IL: Home Vision Entertainment, 2003).

48. Gilles Deleuze, *Cinema 1: The Movement-Image*, translated by Hugh Tomlinson and Barbara Habberjam (Minneapolis: University of Minnesota Press, 1986), 12. In film criticism, the term mise-en-scène is practically synonymous with this aspect of the frame.

49. Ibid., 12.

50. Ibid., 12.
51. Ibid., 14.
52. Ibid., 14.
53. Ibid., 14.
54. Ibid., 14.
55. Ibid., 17. See also Pascal Bonitzer, *Peinture et cinéma: Décadrages* (Paris: Editions de l'Etoile, 1985).
56. Deleuze, *Cinema 1*, 16.
57. Ibid., 16.
58. Kurosawa Kiyoshi also makes use of split-screen techniques in *Bright Future* (*Akarui mirai*, 2003), which was released just nine months before *Doppelgänger*, but there it is used to visually underscore the generational gap between two characters rather than enframe the split between self and double.
59. Andrew Scahill, "Happy, Empty: On Authorship and Influence in the Horror Cinema of Kiyoshi Kurosawa," *Asian Journal of Literature, Culture and Society* vol. 4, no. 2 (October 2010): 76 n. 14.
60. It is noteworthy that when Kurosawa Kiyoshi was invited to choose films by other directors to complement some of his own for a series of double features organized by the Entrevues Belfort international film festival held on November 22–30, 2014, the director singled out Peckinpah, Aldrich, and Fleischer among others. See http://www.festival-entrevues.com/fr/retrospectives/2014/double-feature-kiyoshi-kurosawa (accessed October 29, 2015). For Kurosawa on Peckinpah, see Kurosawa Kiyoshi, *Eizō no karisuma* (Tokyo: Ekusu Narejji, 2006a), 5, 15, 26, 34, 36, 92, 101–02, 107, 166, 170, 238, 247, 261, 264, 268–70, 309, 326, 336. For Kurosawa on Aldrich, see *Eizō no karisuma*, 5, 166–69, 208, 239, 264, 284, 289–90, 296–99, 313, 326, 337. For Kurosawa on Fleischer, see *Eizō no karisuma*, 5, 92, 94–95, 104, 121, 140–67, 226, 264–65, 326, 337.
61. "Interview," *Kyua*.
62. Deleuze, *Cinema 1*, 16.
63. Andrew J. Webber, *The Doppelgänger: Double Visions in German Literature* (New York: Oxford University Press, 1996), 3.
64. Nikki J. Y. Lee, "'Asia' as Regional Signifier and Transnational Genre-Branding: The Asian Horror Omnibus Movies *Three* and *Three … Extremes*," in *East Asian Cinemas: Regional Flows and Global Transformations*, edited by Vivian P. Y. Lee (New York: Palgrave Macmillan, 2011), 111.

65. Miike Takashi, "Audio Commentary for *Box* by Director Takashi Miike," *Three … Extremes*, directed by Miike Takashi, Park Chan-wook, and Fruit Chan (2004), subtitled DVD (Santa Monica, CA: Lions Gate Home Entertainment, 2006).
66. See Freud, "The Uncanny," 142.
67. Webber, 2–5.
68. Andrew L. Markus, "The Carnival of Edo: *Misemono* Spectacles From Contemporary Accounts," *Harvard Journal of Asiatic Studies*, vol. 45, no. 2 (December 1985): 529.
69. Susan Stewart, *On Longing: Narratives of the Miniature, the Gigantic, the Souvenir, the Collection* (Durham; London: Duke University Press, 1993), 110.
70. From a lecture Foucault gave on January 22, 1975. See Michel Foucault, *Abnormal: Lectures at the Collège de France 1974–1975*, translated by Graham Burchell (London: Verso, 2003), 65.
71. Ibid., 66.
72. Ibid., 66.
73. Ibid., 66.
74. Ibid., 65.
75. Andrew N. Sharpe, *Foucault's Monsters and the Challenge of Law* (New York, N.Y.: Routledge, 2010), 111. See also Foucault, *Abnormal*, 324.
76. Sharpe, 127.
77. Margrit Shildrick, *Embodying the Monster: Encounters with the Vulnerable Self* (London: Sage, 2002), 56.
78. Sharpe, 115.
79. Shildrick, 58.
80. Quoted in Irving Wallace and Amy Wallace, *The Two* (New York: Simon & Schuster, 1978), 150–51.
81. Michel Foucault, "Man and His Doubles," *The Order of Things: An Archaeology of the Human Sciences* (London; New York: Routledge, 1989), 370.
82. Wallace and Wallace, *The Two*, 59.
83. Ibid., 75.
84. Alice Domurat Dreger, *One of Us: Conjoined Twins and the Future of Normal* (Cambridge, Mass.: Harvard University Press, 2004), 22.
85. Wallace and Wallace, *The Two*, 98–99.
86. Ibid., 150.
87. Another film that evokes the original Siamese twins, Chang and Eng, is David Cronenberg's twin horror *Dead Ringers* (1988). Cronenberg's

film includes a nightmarish dream sequence involving nonconjoined identical twins Elliot and Beverly Mantle (both played by Jeremy Irons) who appear suddenly conjoined in the dream. What haunts the dreamer most of all is not the conjoinment per se but rather the threat posed by a woman named Claire (Geneviève Bujold)—the romantic interest of the twin who is having the dream—who bites into the fleshy mass that conjoins the two brothers in the dream with her teeth, severing the bond that binds them. During the course of *Dead Ringers*, the twins experience both displacement anxiety and separation anxiety.

88. Sigmund Freud, *The Uncanny*, translated by David McLintock (New York: Penguin Books, 2003), 150.

89. William Cord, *An Introduction to Richard Wagner's* Der Ring des Nibelungen: *A Handbook* (Athens, Ohio: Ohio University Press, 1995), 133.

90. John Williams quoted in Jon Burlingame, "John Williams Recalls *Jaws*," *The Film Music Society*, August 14, 2012, http://www.filmmusicsociety.org/news_events/features/2012/081412.html?isArchive=081412 (accessed April 4, 2017).

91. Ibid.

92. Theodor Adorno, *In Search of Wagner*, translated by Rodney Livingstone (London: Verso, 2009), 36.

93. Theodor Adorno and Hanns Eisler, *Composing for the Films* (New York: Continuum, 2010), 2.

94. Ibid., 2–3.

95. Ibid., 3.

96. Mervyn Cooke, *A History of Film Music* (Cambridge: Cambridge University Press, 2010), 82.

97. Ibid., 82.

98. Adorno, *In Search of Wagner*, 36.

99. Gilles Deleuze and Timothy S. Murphy, "Vincennes Seminar Session, May 3, 1977: On Music," *Discourse* vol. 20, no. 3, *Gilles Deleuze: A Reason to Believe in This World* (Fall 1998): 213.

100. Gilles Deleuze and Félix Guattari, *A Thousand Plateaus: Capitalism and Schizophrenia*, translated by Brian Massumi (Minneapolis: University of Minnesota Press, 1987), 262.

101. Deleuze, "Vincennes Seminar Session," 213.

102. Ibid., 211.

103. Ibid., 213.

104. Ibid., 214.

105. Ibid., 210.

106. "Audio Commentary for *Box* by Director Takashi Miike," *op. cit.*

107. On the anachronism of ghosts and their "deformation of linear temporality," see Peter Buse and Andrew Scott, "Introduction: A Future for Haunting," in *Ghosts: Deconstruction, Psychoanalysis, History*, edited by Peter Buse and Andrew Scott (New York: St. Martin's Press, 1999), 1.

108. "Audio Commentary for *Box* by Director Takashi Miike," *op. cit.*

109. Ibid. (translation modified).

110. Miike makes similar use of a musical leitmotif in *One Missed Call* (*Chakushin ari*, 2003) involving a vengeful ghost who deterritorializes a cell phone's address book to select its next victim.

111. Shildrick, 63.

112. Alice Domurat Dreger, "The Limits of Individuality: Ritual and Sacrifice in the Lives and Medical Treatment of Conjoined Twins," *Studies in History, Philosophy, Biology and Biomedical Science*, vol. 29, no. 1 (1998): 26.

113. Foucault, *Abnormal*, 66.

4

Cinema Fou: Surrealist Horror from Face of Another to Gozu

> Surrealism is destructive, but it destroys only what it considers
> to be shackles limiting our vision.
> —Salvador Dalí[1]

> It is a film about mad love [*amour fou*] and people refuse to accept
> these two dimensions of love and madness.
> —Félix Guattari[2]

Other Surrealisms

When one hears the term "surrealist cinema," most students of film history will automatically think of Luis Buñuel and Salvador Dalí's quintessentially surrealist short film *Un chien andalou* (An Andalusian Dog, 1929). Despite its brief running time of 16 minutes, *Un chien andalou* almost instantaneously became the most influential film to come out of surrealism when it debuted in Paris in 1929, sending a shockwave through the French avant-garde film movement with its eye-slitting opening that practically invented the genre of body horror *avant la lettre*.[3] Although some

© The Author(s) 2018
S. T. Brown, *Japanese Horror and the Transnational Cinema of Sensations*,
East Asian Popular Culture, https://doi.org/10.1007/978-3-319-70629-0_4

scholars prefer to restrict surrealist cinema to the films made by members of the original Parisian Surrealist Group, including Buñuel, Dalí, Antonin Artaud, René Clair, Germaine Dulac, and Man Ray, others have argued that surrealist cinema is not reducible to a single style, genre, movement, or period.[4] As Maurice Blanchot writes in an essay titled "Le demain joueur" (Tomorrow at Stake), which was written shortly after the death of surrealism's founder André Breton in 1966 and included in *L'entretien infini* (The Infinite Conversation, 1969), "One cannot speak of what was neither a system or a school, nor a movement of art or literature, but rather a pure practice of existence [*pure pratique d'existence*]" whose potential has yet to be fully realized.[5] Blanchot's statement is provocative because surrealism has often been described as a school and movement in the past tense, if not a system per se. But what Blanchot tries to get us to see is that, although others may have spoken of surrealism in such terms, for Blanchot the history of surrealism does not tell the whole story, since surrealism is not merely a matter of the past, but is just as much a matter for the present and the future.

Indeed, if we follow Blanchot, not only is surrealism transnational, transgeneric, and intermedial, it is also as much a forward-looking experiment as it is a historically specific experience. In other words, although there is no denying that there is a surrealist tradition that dates back to the original Surrealist Group founded by André Breton, it is important to recognize that surrealism also offers a practical theory that seeks to transform the subject of surrealism as much as its object. As Luis Buñuel once remarked, "The real purpose of Surrealism was not to create a new literary, artistic or even philosophical movement, but to explode the social order, to transform life itself."[6] Whether or not surrealist cinema succeeds in this transformation is a matter of debate, but it is important to at least recognize at the outset of our investigations into surrealist horror in a Japanese context both the metamorphic changeability of surrealism and its implicit political impetus—its practical emphasis on transforming the present.

In this chapter, I analyze a pair of Japanese surrealist horror films situated in relation to the transnational and intermedial flows of international surrealist artistic production: viz., Teshigahara Hiroshi's *Face of Another* (*Tanin no kao*, 1966) and Miike Takashi's *Gozu* (*Gokudō kyōfu daigekijō: Gozu*, 2003). It is in the sense offered by Blanchot's expanded conception of surrealism that, although not a part of the original Surrealist Group, these two Japanese directors are also heirs to that practice, just as surely as are other contemporary directors such as Jan Švankmajer, Kenneth Anger, Alejandro Jodorowsky, Ōbayashi Nobuhiko, David Lynch, Peter Greenaway, Terry Gilliam, David Cronenberg, Michel Gondry, Jean-Pierre Jeunet, Yuasa Masaaki, Spike Jonze, Charlie Kaufman, Kon Satoshi, Darren Aronofsky, and Yamamura Kōji.

The Exquisite Corpse

Among the most oft-noted aspects of the early surrealists' artistic productions is the frequently collaborative nature of their experiments. The "exquisite corpse" (*cadavres exquis*) parlor game devised by André Breton and his cohorts in 1925 is an excellent illustration of the surrealists' collective art of unexpected combinations. Here is how the game of the exquisite corpse was defined in the *Dictionnaire abrégé du surréalisme* (Abridged Dictionary of Surrealism, 1938) that was edited by Breton and Paul Éluard:

> Game with folded paper that involves the composition of a sentence or a drawing by several people in which none of them can take account of the previous collaboration or collaborations. The example, that has become classic and gave its name to the game, was the first sentence obtained in this way: "The exquisite corpse will drink new wine."[7]

What Breton and his fellow surrealists valued most of all was how effective such collective experiments were at disrupting the instrumental rationality of everyday life through techniques of chance, collage, and automatism, thereby creating an opening for the most unexpected combinations and metamorphic hybridities. "With the *Exquisite Corpse*," proclaimed Breton, "we had at our disposal—at last—an infallible means of sending the mind's critical mechanism away on vacation and fully releasing its metaphorical potentialities."[8]

This emphasis on collaboration and collective experimentation was just as important to early surrealist filmmakers. One way in which surrealist filmmakers sought to undermine the class-marked pretensions and prejudices associated with bourgeois institutions was by throwing into question the patriarchal pretensions of directorial auteurship. The uncompromising vision of the Director-as-Auteur was gleefully undermined by the unabashedly collaborative process of surrealist filmmaking. Take, for example, the profoundly collaborative nature of Buñuel and Dalí's first experiment in surrealist cinema, *Un chien andalou*, in which they set out to create a film that would be a succession of surreal images and absurd, dream-like scenarios without a single person controlling the vision of the film. According to Buñuel, this hallmark of surrealist cinema was born "from an encounter between two dreams":

> When I arrived to spend a few days at Dalí's house in Figueras, I told him about a dream I'd had in which a long, tapering cloud sliced the moon in half, like a razor blade slicing through an eye. Dalí immediately told me that he'd seen a hand crawling with ants in a dream he'd had the previous night.
>
> "And what if we started right there and made a film?" he wondered aloud.
>
> Despite my hesitation, we soon found ourselves hard at work, and in less than a week we had a script. Our only rule was simple: No idea or image that might lend itself to a rational explanation of any kind would be accepted. We had to open all doors to the irrational and keep only those images that surprised us, without trying to explain why.[9]

Un chien andalou clearly exemplifies "the succession of images and the swift passage of ideas [*la succession des images, la fuite des idées*]," which fellow surrealist Max Morise described as the "fundamental condition of any Surrealist manifestation."[10] Even more collaborative was Buñuel and Dalí's follow-up to *Un chien andalou*, their surrealist comedy about sexual repression titled *L'âge d'or* (The Golden Age, 1930), which featured screenplay contributions from a number of other members of the original Surrealist Group, including Max Ernst, Gaston Modot, Jacques Prevert, and Jean Aurenche. As scholar of surrealist cinema Michael Richardson has noted, the fact that the script for *L'âge d'or* was passed around to various members of the Surrealist Group for comment and amendment "makes it not only the most surrealist film but also the most surrealist work *tout court*," since it went "beyond individual authorship to express a collective vision" of surrealism.[11]

This collaborative aspect of surrealist filmmaking is equally apparent in the first example of surrealist horror from Japan that I would like to consider in this chapter: *Face of Another* (*Tanin no kao*, 1966) directed by Teshigahara Hiroshi, which is based upon the 1964 novel of the same name by Abe Kōbō (who also wrote the screenplay) and features a haunting soundtrack by acclaimed composer Takemitsu Tōru.[12] The collaborations between Teshigahara, Abe, and Takemitsu, who also worked together on the films *Pitfall* (*Otoshiana*, 1962), *Woman in the Dunes* (*Suna no onna*, 1964), and *Man without a Map* (*Moetsukita chizu*, 1968), went much further than the credits might lead one to believe. As Peter Grilli notes,

Although Teshigahara, as director, was responsible for organizing and unifying these collaborations, it is otherwise difficult to distinguish absolutely the separate contributions of each of the three artists. To say that Abe wrote the screenplays, Takemitsu composed the musical scores, and Teshigahara provided the imagery is too simplistic. Each of the three challenged, provoked, and enhanced the work of the others.... Each artist involved himself deeply in the work of the others, and none of them hesitated to criticize or reshape the work of the others in order to strengthen it or give it deeper meaning.

"He gave me much more than just music," Teshigahara reminisced about Takemitsu, shortly after the death, in 1996, of the composer who provided the music for every one of his feature films. "He gave me ideas and energy and a kind of trust that never failed. He was always more than a composer. He involved himself so thoroughly in every aspect of a film—script, casting, location shooting, editing, and total sound design—that a willing director can rely totally on his instincts." Much the same was said by and about each member of this triangular collaboration. Both Abe and Takemitsu had strong visual instincts, as revealed in their private sketches and designs, and they were not hesitant to advise Teshigahara on the look of the films.[13]

Face of Another is unquestionably a Japanese heir to the tradition of the European Surrealist Group. Before making *Face of Another*, Teshigahara not only dabbled with surrealist painting in the style of works by Salvador Dalí and René Magritte, but was also a founding member of the self-avowed Japanese Surrealist Group called the Century Club (Seiki no kai), which also included Abe Kōbō, as well as a number of other aspiring Japanese surrealist artists, philosophers, and critics. Long after the Century Club had disbanded, surrealist issues and imagery continued to animate the works of both Teshigahara and Abe.[14]

Like Teshigahara's previous collaborations with Takemitsu and Abe, *Face of Another* mixes elements of surrealism and existentialism, offering a haunting meditation on the difference between face and mask in the performative presentation of the self.[15] Although such issues had been engaged by earlier horror films, most notably *The Phantom of the Opera* (1925) and *Eyes Without a Face* (*Les Yeux sans visage*, 1960)—both of which are echoed in Teshigahara's film—*Face of Another* has proven to be quite prescient in its anticipation of a wide range of issues confronting contemporary audiences. Viewed from the perspective of the early twenty-first century, in an era when both partial and full face transplantations are now surgically possible and cosmetic surgery has become so commonplace that it has spawned a slew of reality TV shows devoted to the topic,[16] the questions engaged by *Face of Another* have particular resonance for viewers fifty years after its release.

The Fragmented Body

The protagonist of *Face of Another* is a chemist named Okuyama, who, after suffering disfiguring burns and keloidal scars in an industrial accident while inspecting a new plant, receives a new face in the form of a mask that is modeled after the face of a complete stranger—the "*tanin*" (outsider or stranger who is not related by blood) of the film's title, *Tanin no kao*. Although his face is practically unrecognizable for the first 50 minutes of the film because he is wearing bandages, Okuyama is played brilliantly by one of the most acclaimed stars of Japanese cinema, Nakadai Tatsuya, who is still performing at the time of this writing, having starred in over 150 films since 1954. Nakadai is perhaps best known as the leading man in the films of two of Japan's most renowned directors, appearing in five films by Kurosawa Akira, including *Yojimbo* (*Yōjinbō*, 1961), *Kagemusha* (1980), and *Ran* (1985), and 11 films by Kobayashi Masaki, including *The Human Condition* trilogy (*Ningen no jōken*, 1959–61), *Harakiri* (1962), *Kwaidan* (1964), and *Samurai Rebellion* (*Jōi-uchi: Hairyō tsuma shimatsu*, 1967).

Although *Face of Another* was better received in Japan than it was abroad—receiving awards for best art direction and best film score at the 1967 Mainichi Film Concours—it is said to have exerted a profound influence on Andrei Tarkovsky's haunting meditation on the nature of reality and the status of the divided self in *Solaris* (*Solyaris*, 1972). Tarkovsky considered Teshigahara to be one of the greatest directors in film history and one of the few directors the Russian director esteemed as highly as Mizoguchi Kenji, the director of *The Life of Oharu* (*Saikaku ichidai onna*, 1952), *Ugetsu* (*Ugetsu monogatari*, 1953), and *Sansho the Bailiff* (*Sanshō dayū*, 1954).

Before the title credits appear, *Face of Another* begins with a creepy prologue in which a psychiatrist named Dr. Hori (played by Hira Mikijirō), who specializes in the treatment of accident victims via cosmetic prostheses, introduces one of the film's signature surrealist motifs in the form of fragmented body parts (Fig. 4.1). As Ghislaine Wood notes in her study *The Surreal Body: Fetish and Fashion*, "The body was a site for Surrealist experiment and a conduit for the transmission of ideas. It became the subject of intense scrutiny: dismembered, fragmented, desecrated, eroticized and eulogized in the pursuit of a range of psychological, sociological and sexual concerns."[17]

Surrealists have incorporated a wide range of body part imagery into their art, photography, and film—from parts of the face (eyes, mouth, lips, and ears) to body limbs (hands, legs, and feet) to erogenous zones (breasts, buttocks, and genitalia).[18] Of course, it goes without saying that such detached and fragmented body parts are not limited to surrealist art. As art historian Linda Nochlin argues persuasively in her study *The Body in Pieces: The Fragment as a Metaphor of Modernity*, the fragmented, mutilated, fetishized body is both a metaphor for modernity in art from the eighteenth century to the present and an expression of nostalgia for the

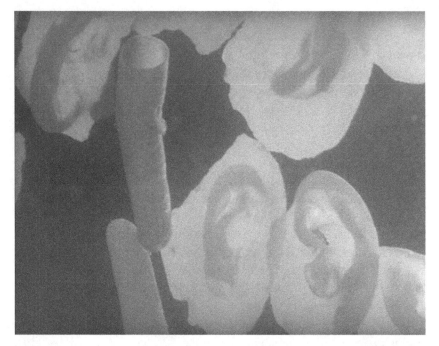

Fig. 4.1 The opening shot of fragmented body parts in *Face of Another* (1966)

perceived loss of some imagined utopian wholeness that has vanished.[19] However, it must be acknowledged that the fragmented body is something of a speciality for the surrealists.

The prevalence of the "body-in-pieces" in surrealist art has led some critics to attack the surrealists for phallocentrism, arguing that "the body (usually female) has been reduced to a projection of (usually male) desire … obliterating alterity and rejecting totality, in male gestures of narcissistic projection and totalitarian dismemberment."[20] However, taking into consideration the growing body of scholarship on female surrealists and the fluidity of gender in surrealist art, an increasing number of scholars, such as Elza Adamowicz, have begun to recognize that the status of the fragmented body is much more complex than that, insofar as it can also be read as deconstructing "the fetishistic construction of the female body" by rendering visible "the mechanisms of the psychological projection of the male self-image on to the female form."[21] And it is not just the processes of fetishization and masculinist desire that are thereby exposed (and frequently parodied), but also the mechanisms of consumption and "the alienation created by Capitalist consumer culture."[22]

In the prologue to *Face of Another*, as assorted artificial body parts (ears, fingers, hands, eyes, and so on) drift across the screen in extreme close-up, floating in an aquarium-like container and occasionally pulled out and inspected, the psychiatrist offers his perspective on the relationship between synthetic body parts and the psyche of the recipient: "Recognize these? You know what they are?... They're replicas of body parts [*jintai no mozōhin*]. You see? Sadly, this is not only a finger. It's an inferiority complex [*rettōkan*] in the shape of a finger. It's not that I specialize in treating fingers. I'm a psychiatrist, in fact. Inferiority complexes dig holes in the psyche, and I fill them in."

The fragmented body foregrounded at the outset of *Face of Another* is repeated throughout the film in scenes that incorporate body parts into the very texture of the mise-en-scène of the psychiatrist's office (Fig. 4.2). With its maze of glass partitions and other reflective surfaces designed by famed Japanese architect Isozaki Arata (b. 1931), which evokes Marcel Duchamp's enigmatic construction of glass, foil, wire, and dust known as *The Bride Stripped Bare By Her Bachelors, Even* (*La mariée mise à nu par ses célibataires, même*, 1915–23) that had been influential within Japanese art circles since the 1930s, the doctor's surrealist clinic creates an architectural collage of the fragmented body with detached and/or multiplied body parts (ears, hands, arms, legs, hearts, brains), separated from the organic wholeness of the body and resituated in frequently disturbing contexts that push the art of unexpected combinations into new realms of disfiguration and a critical awareness of the mechanisms of fetishization. In so doing, this collage of the fragmented body not only stands in stark contrast to the ideal human body associated with Leonardo Da Vinci's *Vitruvian Man* (*L'Uomo Vitruviano*, c. 1490) that adorns the transparent glass walls of the psychiatric clinic (Fig. 4.2), but also suggests that the clinic forms a kind of "glass cage or theater of cruelty," as James Quandt describes it.[23] In some scenes, characters who inhabit the clinic are incorporated into the design of the mise-en-scène as objects distributed across the clinic space, entering into composition with the clinic assemblage in a

Fig. 4.2 Fragmented body parts and Leonardo Da Vinci's *Vitruvian Man* are incorporated into the texture of the mise-en-scène in *Face of Another* (1966)

manner that makes them look like insects pinned inside an entomologist's glass-covered mounting box (Fig. 4.3).[24]

Here I am also reminded of Deleuze and Guattari's work in *A Thousand Plateaus* on the concept of "faciality" (*visagéité*).[25] For Deleuze and Guattari, perhaps the most important point about faciality is that one does not have a face, one slides into one: faces choose their subjects. Facial units are distributed across the grid of the face according to the facial traits organized by faciality. As such, the faciality machine involves the social production of a face through the decoding of a body and the overcoding of a head. Deleuze and Guattari underscore that the face not only overcodes (i.e., facializes) the head, but the rest of the body as well. In their view, concrete individualizations of faciality are combinations of facial units that choose one term or the other in binarisms such as man/woman, adult/child, white/non-white, rich/poor. In light of such

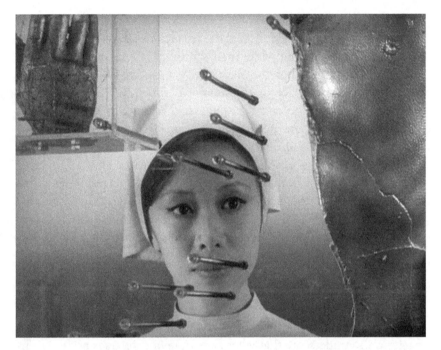

Fig. 4.3 The nurse (Kishida Kyōko) is incorporated into the mise-en-scène of the clinic assemblage like an insect mounted in an entomologist's collection box in *Face of Another* (1966)

overcoding, Deleuze and Guattari insist that "the face is a horror story," insofar as "there is even something absolutely inhuman about the face."[26] Although Deleuze and Guattari devote most of their attention to the abstract machine of faciality that they associate with the spread of Christianity and the global dominance of the "white-man" standard, which introduced a new relationship to the face—a new faciality machine—that overcoded the head in relation to a specific conception of signification and subjectification, it is important to point out that Deleuze and Guattari's critique of that particular faciality machine does not preclude the existence or emergence of other faciality machines that are non-Christian and non-white.

One of the most conspicuous examples of the faciality machine in *Face of Another* is the white-man standard embodied by the Vitruvian

Man that adorns the glass walls of the doctor's clinic. Although *Face of Another* does not explicitly address the pernicious effects of the faciality machine encoded by the white-man standard, it remains a significant subtext throughout. When the mask is first applied to Okuyama's face in the doctor's office, the doctor and nurse experiment with different combinations of moustache and beard across the grid of Okuyama's face, including some that are noticeably non-Japanese in style. Okuyama's numerous expressions of discomfort in relation to the mask—that he is experiencing a strange feeling "as if someone else has taken over" and that he feels "trapped in a hothouse"—may be construed as responses to the faciality machine of the mask that is overcoding his head. It is here that the inhumanness of faciality that prompted Deleuze and Guattari's assertion that "the face is a horror story" comes quite literally to a head.[27] From this perspective, the fragmentation of the body into the "body-in-pieces" that is on display alongside the *Vitruvian Man* in the clinic where Okuyama receives his new face helps visualize the decoding of the body that is an essential step on the way to overcoding.

The fragmentation of the body and the oppressiveness of the faciality machine also underscore that what *Face of Another* offers is not only surrealist cinema, but surrealist horror. It is with good reason that *Face of Another* is often compared to James Whale's *Frankenstein* (1931) and Georges Franju's *Eyes Without a Face* (1960). Whereas *Frankenstein* deals with a mad scientist (Dr. Henry Frankenstein) who assembles a living creature out of the body parts of corpses in an attempt to recreate human life and *Eyes Without a Face* tells the story of a homicidal surgeon (Dr. Génessier) who attempts to graft the faces of kidnapped women onto the head of his daughter, who was disfigured in an automobile accident,[28] *Face of Another* involves a psychiatrist (Dr. Hori) specializing in cosmetic prostheses who fits a disfigured man with a synthetic face modeled after another man so that he can feel human again. In the process, the assembled humans in *Frankenstein*, *Eyes Without a Face*, and *Face of Another* all eventually turn on the scientist/surgeon/psychiatrist who created them. All three films also share a mix of genre conventions, blending horror and science fiction, to create a hybrid genre of science-fiction horror (or the "*fantastique*," as the French like to call it).[29]

In so much surrealist visual art and film involving the fragmented body, it is eye imagery that dominates in the form of disembodied, all-seeing eyes (e.g., Max Ernst's *The Wheel of Light* [1925] and René Magritte's *The False Mirror* [1928]), multiplied voyeuristic eyes (Guillermo Meza' *Eyes-Paranoia* [1941] and Jindřich Štyrský's *Collage No. 5 from Emilie Comes to Me in a Dream* [1933]), sightless eyes (Marcel Jean's *The Spectre of the Gardenia* [1936]), eyes that are forced to gaze upon disturbing scenes (Max Ernst's *The Hundred Headless Woman* [1929]), and attacks on vision itself (*Un chien andalou*). As Dalí insisted, if surrealism is destructive, "it destroys only what it considers to be shackles limiting our vision."[30] The eye frequently functions in surrealist art and cinema as both a metaphor for the limits of vision and a parody of art construed as an imitation of nature. Perhaps Georges Bataille said it best when he argued (with a nod towards *Un chien andalou*) that the eye's "extreme seductiveness is probably at the boundary of horror."[31]

However, in *Face of Another*, although eye imagery is certainly included among the many visualizations of the fragmented body, of particular note is the confluence of severed or detached ears, both large and small, all of which were designed and sculpted by Japanese artist Miki Tomio (1938–1978). Inspired by Dadaist assemblages and surrealist objects, particularly the work of Marcel Duchamp, Miki Tomio sculpted his first ear in 1962 and then over the next 16 years (until his death at the age of 40) created literally hundreds of iterations, cast mostly in aluminum and occasionally in plaster and fired clay.[32] Although Miki was closely associated with Japanese Neo Dada, since he never formally joined the group, his work tends to be grouped together under the label of "Obsessional Art" instead, along with that of other Japanese avant-garde artists of a similar ilk, such as Kudō Tetsumi (1935–1990) and Kusama Yayoi (b. 1929), whose "source of obsessional imagery lies in a specific vision of infinite repetition and its force of self-negation that each experienced as a result of neurosis or existential reverie."[33] Miki was so obsessed with ears that he refused to create anything else throughout most of his career, producing endless iterations of human ears in all shapes and sizes, from life-sized ears to ears that are twice the size of a grown man. In some works, such as *Ear* (1968), he created grids displaying multiple ears in rows (Fig. 4.4); while in others, such as a piece that was commissioned for Expo '70, he produced ears that were large enough to fill up an entire plaza.

Miki's ears often appear as if they have been "amputated or torn from the head,"[34] as Alexandra Munroe aptly describes them, mere fragments

Fig. 4.4 Okuyama against a backdrop of ears arranged in a grid created by sculptor Miki Tomio for *Face of Another* (1966)

of the body that are no longer capable of hearing. In other cases, such as in a work titled *The Ear No. 1001* (1976), which was the last sculpture Miki created, the ears possess "intestine-like growths"[35] emerging from the base (possibly a visualization of the inner ear canal) and wings sprouting from the top as if preparing to take flight in search of another body to which they might reattach. For Miki himself, his fragmented ears functioned as images of the negation of hearing in particular and self-negation more generally.

In the context of *Face of Another*, the repetition of Miki's detached ear sculptures throughout underscores, on the one hand, the importance of sound design to the film, especially the artful contrast developed by composer Takemitsu between dissonant, eerie electronic noise and silence, which reinforces "the viewer's sense of alienation," as Keiko McDonald observes.[36] As film theorist Michel Chion has suggested in *Audio-Vision: Sound on Screen*, "[S]ilence is never a neutral emptiness. It is the negative of sound we've heard beforehand or imagined; it is the product of a contrast."[37] Interrupting the soundtrack with silence is especially effective in *Face of Another* because the contrast between noise and silence has been contextualized. In this connection, it is noteworthy that Okuyama complains that he has become extremely sensitive to noise since the accident and wonders if losing his face has deranged his senses. However, it might also be said that the ear motif works together with the accumulation of other body parts to suggest that the fragmentation of the body functions as a material analogue for the fracturing of subjectivity—the splitting of the subject into fragmented parts. When Okuyama complains that "everything around me seems fragmented," the doctor responds by saying that that is "the essence of the mask [*kamen no honshitsu*]." It is in this sense that the issues raised in relation to the distinction between face and mask that haunt the entire film intersect with the surrealist engagement with the fragmented body.

The Invisible Man

That the face/mask distinction will be interrogated throughout *Face of Another* is signaled during the title credits when we are presented with a series of illustrations and photos that emphasize the face, including a blank, featureless face surrounded by wavy lines (Fig. 4.5), a Chinese acupuncture face map, as well as composite pictures containing multiple face shots of unknown people whose number increases exponentially as the credits continue. These static shots dissolve into live-action footage of huge crowds shuffling slowly through the streets of Tokyo at night while the soundtrack features the first instance of an upbeat waltz (composed by Takemitsu) that will be repeated at key moments throughout the film and again at the very end, but which seems strangely out of sync with the affective mood of the title sequence.[38] Ironically, the first time we are introduced to *Face of Another*'s protagonist, it is done in such a way that Okuyama is effectively rendering both faceless and maskless. This is accomplished through a technique that has rarely been used in the history of cinema.

As Okuyama describes the circumstances surrounding the industrial accident in which he suffered disfiguring burns at a new factory he was

Fig. 4.5 During the title credits, a blank face underscores the issue of faciality in *Face of Another* (1966)

inspecting, a close-up of him speaking is presented entirely in the form of live-action X-ray footage (Fig. 4.6). Teshigahara employs a wide range of experimental techniques in *Face of Another*, including but not limited to the manipulation of aspect ratio; freeze frames and *La Jetée*-like photomontage sequences; stuttered editing and jump cuts; the creative use of rear projection[39] and repetition[40] (including the doubling of shots, settings, and dialogue); as well as more conventional techniques, such as fast zooms, whip pans, extreme close-ups, and tilted horizon shots. However, the inclusion of X-ray footage of a character speaking was quite novel for a film that debuted in 1966. In the history of cinema, one could probably count on one hand the number of times such a technique has been employed.

Given Teshigahara's surrealist inclinations and background, the live-action X-ray of Okuyama may have been inspired by Swiss surrealist Méret Oppenheim's (1913–1985) striking X-ray self-portrait, titled *X-ray of the Skull of Méret Oppenheim* (1964), which debuted just two years before *Face of Another*.[41] Perhaps best known for her fur-covered cup,

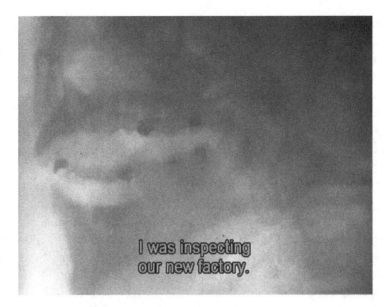

Fig. 4.6 X-ray footage of Okuyama describing the circumstances of his accident in *Face of Another* (1966)

saucer, and spoon, titled *Object: Breakfast in Fur* (*Object [Le Déjeuner en fourrure]*, 1936), Oppenheim was one of the most respected female surrealists associated with the original Surrealist Group founded by André Breton, known as much for her sculptural assemblages as for her paintings and photography.[42] Oppenheim's art explored issues of gendered identity and female sexuality with the characteristically "black humor" (*humour noir*) that was celebrated by her fellow surrealists. In her X-ray of herself, Oppenheim parodies the genre of portrait paintings in the history of European art and the presumption that such portraits reveal the internal character (or soul) of the subject portrayed.[43]

When read as an intermedial citation of Oppenheim's X-ray self-portrait, the X-ray footage of Okuyama at the outset of *Face of Another* functions in a similar way. Despite literally peering inside the head of Okuyama, reversing interiority and exteriority, the status of his identity is no more transparent. However, in addition to gesturing towards Oppenheim, *Face of Another*'s live-action X-ray also invokes the climactic scene from an earlier Universal Pictures horror classic. Although

Face of Another is often compared with Rupert Julian's *The Phantom of the Opera* (1925) and James Whale's *Frankenstein* (1931), another James Whale film that was released just two years after *Frankenstein*—the 1933 Universal Pictures adaptation of H. G. Wells' novel *The Invisible Man* (1897)—is even more relevant to *Face of Another*'s network of horror citations.

Like *Frankenstein*, *The Invisible Man* involves a mad doctor, Dr. Jack Griffin (played by Claude Rains), who performs unethical experiments, but rather than experimenting on others, the doctor in *The Invisible Man* experiments on himself, developing a drug called "monocaine" that triggers invisibility and turns him into a homicidal megalomaniac in the process. The bandages worn by Griffin, which, he tells an innkeeper, are intended to conceal his disfigurement from an accident, function as a mask to conceal his invisibility. However, once the bandages have been removed, the invisibility itself also functions like a mask in *The Invisible Man*, concealing Dr. Griffin's identity and giving him a sense of complete freedom, as well as the delusion that he will not be held accountable for anything he does, no matter how criminal, since "the whole world's my hiding place." "An invisible man can rule the world," proclaims Dr. Griffin. "Nobody will see him come, nobody will see him go. He can hear every secret. He can rob, and rape, and kill!" However, as Michel Chion points out,

> Although Griffin is invisible, the screenplay doesn't construct his body as immaterial; he can be nabbed. His invisibility is really the only trait that allows him to escape the servitude common to the human condition. He has other constraints that visible beings do not have: he must go naked when he does not want to be seen, hide in order to eat (since the food he takes in remains visible until completely digested), and so on. Everything in this character, from the disguise he must assume when he wishes to appear without giving himself away, which makes him look somewhat like a seriously wounded man, to the complaints he makes during his frequent tirades to say that he's cold or hungry or sleepy, everything shows us that what we have here is not a flying superhero but a suffering body, a "phantom" body whose organic character is accentuated rather than subtilized.[44]

The materiality of the invisible man's "phantom" body is fully revealed at the moment of his death. When Griffin's footprints in the snow give him away, the police detective who has been hunting him opens fire and Griffin suffers life-threatening injuries. He is taken to a hospital where on his deathbed the invisible man gradually regains visibility at the very moment of death (Fig. 4.7).

As Akira Lippit comments in his thought-provoking study *Atomic Light (Shadow Optics)*,

> The living, invisible body remains suspended in this realm of avisuality until death. In a trope that recurs throughout the invisible man phantasm, only death restores the body to a state of visibility. At the moment of death, the body returns to the visible world. Each death scene is almost always preceded by a final representation of invisible movement, tracked by footsteps on the ground, followed by a collapse, death, and the return of the

Fig. 4.7 The X-ray-like image of Dr. Griffin at the moment of his death in *The Invisible Man* (1933)

visible human figure. In Whale's film, Griffin returns to the visible spectrum inside out: first his skull returns, his skeletal interiority, followed by his exterior surface. An X-ray image mediates the return from invisibility to visibility— "a death in reverse," says Michel Chion.[45]

According to Lippit, such X-ray images, or "photographs in reverse," expose "the secrets of the body, its depths, collapsing the essential divide between surface and depth, and rendering the body a deep surface."[46] In her study *The Visible Human Project: Informatic Bodies and Post-Human Medicine*, Catherine Waldby explains how the X-ray reverses the relationship between depth and surface:

> The surface of the body, its demarcation from the world, is dissolved and lost in the image, leaving only the faintest trace, while the relation between depth and surface is reversed. Skeletal structures, conventionally thought of as located at the most recessive depth of the body, appear in coregistration with the body's surface in the x-ray image. Hence skeletal structures are externalized in a double sense: the distinction between inside and outside is suspended in the image, and the trace of the interior is manifest in the exteriority of the radiograph, the artefact itself.[47]

Although Okuyama is not invisible in the same way that Griffin is, differentiations between surface and depth, exteriority and interiority, visibility and invisibility are just as much at issue in *Face of Another* as they are in *The Invisible Man*. Not only does Okuyama's bandage-covered face strongly evoke that of Griffin (see Figs. 4.8 and 4.9)—both appearing to the world as "wounded" men—but the application of the prosthetic mask also renders Okuyama metaphorically and socially "invisible" in ways that bring to mind Griffin. In a private discussion with his nurse assistant about the "perilous" (*kikenna*) nature of the mask that they have constructed for Okuyama, the psychiatrist Dr. Hori asserts that "it's like a drug that turns one into an invisible man [*tōmei ningen ni naru kusuri mitai*]."[48]

Dr. Hori conveys as much to Okuyama himself, saying "once you're used to the mask you'll be a new man—one with no records, no past, a mind invisible to the world." As Hori explains the power of the facial mask to Okuyama, the camera does a 90-degree tilt to one side, as if to

Fig. 4.8   Dr. Griffin in bandages in *The Invisible Man* (1933)

visualize that a dramatic shift in perspective has just occurred. Although Okuyama insists that "I am who I am—that can't change," he also acknowledges a strange feeling, "as if someone else has taken over." Later, the doctor, who functions as an alter ego to Okuyama,[49] expounds further on the potential power and dangers associated with the mask: "What if the mask [*kamen*] lives on by taking over your body?" This concern that the mask might take over Okuyama's identity and body alludes to conceptions of the transformative power of masks in the Japanese performing arts tradition that first gained currency in the medieval period. As I have argued in my study of noh drama, *Theatricalities of Power: The Cultural Politics of Noh*, "The noh mask (*omote*) does not disguise the face of the actor; rather, the actor's face becomes the face of the other through the spirit of the mask. The mask is not worn like a hat, but is 'affixed' or 'joined' (*tsukeru*) to the actor's face, becoming 'a part of [his] body.'"[50] It is for this reason that the paradramatic space of the "mirror room" (*kagami no ma*) in which the noh actor performs a ceremonial donning of the

Fig. 4.9 Okuyama in bandages in *Face of Another* (1966)

mask before going onstage is described as a "space of transformation."[51] It is there that the noh actor undergoes becoming-other, as if possessed by the spirit of the mask.

In addition to alluding to Japanese performative practices, such concerns about the power of the mask also make reference to the history of world horror cinema, which is replete with mask-wearing monsters, including iconic figures ranging from Lon Chaney's phantom in *The Phantom of the Opera* (1925) to the bandaged mad scientist in *The Invisible Man* (1933), from Leatherface in *The Texas Chainsaw Massacre* (1974) to Michael Myers in *Halloween* (1978), from Jason Voorhees in *Friday the 13th Part III* (1982) to Hannibal Lecter in *The Silence of the Lambs* (1991), from Ghostface in *Scream* (1996) to Jigsaw in *Saw* (2004). In the context of horror cinema, it is noteworthy that the frozen expression of the mask-wearing monster seems to enhance rather than restrict the evocation of fear in the audience by making it difficult to read the monster's facial expression or feel a sense of identification.

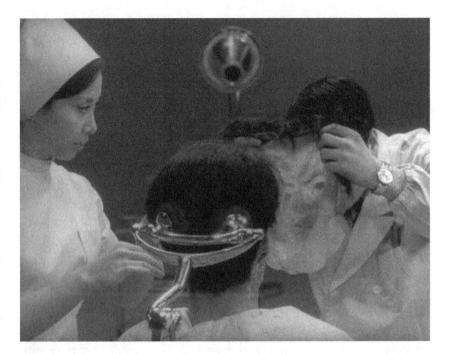

Fig. 4.10   Dr. Hori attaches the mask to Okuyama's face in *Face of Another* (1966)

Like the invisible man, Okuyama wears bandages for much of the film; however, when the bandages are removed, he dons a mask modeled after someone else's face to conceal his identity (Fig. 4.10). In the process of wearing a mask, Okuyama becomes drunk with delusions about the power he can wield through the concealment of his identity. Eventually, Okuyama discovers not only a newfound freedom from social constraints but also that the mask is slowly turning him into a "*bakemono*," or "monster." "*Bakemono*," literally "transforming thing," is a word with a long history that is used to describe all manner of ghosts, goblins, and monsters in Japanese folklore, literature, and horror. Connotations of disguise, transformation, and metamorphosis are quite apparent in *bakemono*'s derivation from the verb "*bakeru*," which means "(1) to take the form of (esp. in ref. to a spirit, fox, raccoon dog, etc.); to assume the shape of; to turn oneself into; to transform oneself into; (2) to disguise oneself as; (3) to change radically; to metamorphose."[52]

Early on in *Face of Another*, Okuyama confides to his wife his concern that "when the face is closed off, so too is the soul—it becomes the soul of a monster [*bakemono*], rotten to the core." Likewise, to his boss, Okuyama admits, "Sometimes I seem like a monster [*bakemono*] even to myself." However, Okuyama also defends the monster: "The monster [*bakemono*] is always to blame—what a convenient stereotype. Everything's the monster's fault." Reflecting further on the mindset of the sort of man who wears a mask, such as an executioner, Okuyama remarks, "There are monsters [*bakemono*] who act like people, and people who act like monsters. Even monsters [*bakemono*] have their pleasures." Towards the end of the film, Okuyama completes his transformation into a monster (thereby confirming the film's status as a horror film) when he sexually assaults a woman and is temporarily detained for that crime only to be released under his doctor's care, allowing him to commit another, more murderous one.

As Okuyama and his psychiatrist walk through the streets of Tokyo at night, the crowds of people pouring into the street as they exit the Shibuya train station echoes a similar shot from the title credits. However, whereas the people constituting the crowd during the title credits have faces with identifiable features, the crowds at the end of the film have blank faces, their facial features appearing to have been erased by a mask.[53] In addition to paying homage to earlier surrealist works of art such as René Magritte's *The Lovers* (*Les amants*, 1928) and Max Ernst's *Masks* (*Masques*, 1950), this scene of the faceless multitudes extends the idea of the mask to all social relations, so that the social space becomes "a masquerade, a dissembling of appearance,"[54] as James Quandt observes.

Earlier, Dr. Hori had fantasized about mass-producing masks and the social effects that would be elicited: "A face, easily removed. A world without family, friends, or enemies. There'd be no criminals, hence crime itself would disappear. Unbounded freedom, hence no yearning for it. No such thing as home, hence no dreams of escaping from it. Loneliness and friendship would bleed into one another. Trust among people, now so richly prized, would become obsolete. Suspicion and betrayal would no longer be possible." However, Dr. Hori becomes quite concerned that the mask will both strip one of individuality and at the same time allow one to evade personal responsibility by rendering one anonymous. Even if disguise is necessary in some sense for the sake of coexistence, Dr. Hori warns Okuyama that "some masks come off, some don't."

Although the doctor backs away from such speculations, concluding that a world like that could never really exist, as the affectless image of the faceless mob suggests, in a sense, it already does—it is the face of modern alienation (Fig. 4.11). In the end, Dr. Hori tells Okuyama that he is a free man and should do as he wishes. In their parting moment, which starts out as almost a tender embrace between the two, Okuyama responds "I will" and then proceeds to stab the doctor with a knife. As Okuyama walks away, blood starts to ooze out of his own mouth, suggesting both that the mask itself has started to die and that his transformation into a monster with a taste for blood is now complete. The final image is a freeze frame of Okuyama inspecting the contours of the mask on his face as a look of anxiety passes across his visage.

Fig. 4.11 Okuyama and Dr. Hori face off while surrounded by the faceless multitudes in *Face of Another* (1966)

Omote/Ura

As we have seen, some of the most fundamental questions raised by *Face of Another* involve the complex relations between face, mask, and self: What is the relationship between face and identity? How might one's identity change if the face one sees in the mirror (and the face shown to others) were to change significantly? Would one's moral sensibility change as well? Is one's face "only a layer of skin, a surface," as Okuyama repeatedly tells himself, or is it something more? Is it possible to have an identity without a face? Another way to approach such questions in *Face of Another* is through the lens of the conceptual distinction in Japanese between *omote* (surface, face, mask, public) and *ura* (underside, heart, mind, private). Broadly conceived, like two sides of a coin or "any other flat object with *omote* (the face) and *ura* (back)," as sociologist Sugimoto Yoshio explains, "*omote* represents the correct surface or front, which is openly permissible, whereas *ura* connotes the wrong, dark, concealed side, which is publicly unacceptable or even illegal."[55] Here *omote/ura* are construed not as an ahistorical national character trait, but rather as a discursive distinction that enframes the boundaries of social interaction without being exclusively or essentially "Japanese." Delving deeper into the social dynamics engaged by the dialectical relationship between the two, things become considerably more complex, as anthropologist Jane Bachnik points out:

> Two concepts which express these clusters of relationships are *ura* ("insideness," content, informality, everydayness) and *omote* ("outsideness," form, formality, difference from everydayness); both are major concepts in Japan…. None of these glosses is adequate as a definition, for my point here is that *omote* and *ura* are indexes, rather than referential terms—that they define a distance cline, between self and other, rather than naming or describing any characteristic of either. Index thus hinges on context, on the perceived relationships…. Most important of all, *omote/ura* … do not represent dichotomies. Rather than specifying some "thing," *omote* and *ura* index degrees of distance between self and other. Moreover, distance in turn also functions as an index—pointing out degrees of difference between self and other. Rather than formality versus informality, or "ordinariness" versus "non-ordinariness," *omote* and *ura* indicate the degree of formality (from formal to informal, along a continuum).[56]

Insofar as *omote* and *ura* are paired concepts with a dialectical relationship, they do not express a fixed dichotomy per se since the boundary between the two is relative and shifting, depending entirely upon context and point of view. As Doi Takeo has suggested, the *omote* of the face conceals the *ura* of the mind "even while expressing it," and at the same time, *omote* expresses the *ura* of the mind "even while concealing it—so as not to reveal it completely."[57] According to Doi,

> *Omote* can be seen, but *ura* is concealed behind *omote*. However, *omote* does not merely reveal only itself, and neither is it simply something that conceals *ura*. *Omote* is what expresses *ura*. Perhaps we could even say that *ura* performs *omote*. And, because this is true, when people look at *omote*, they are seeing not only *omote*, but also *ura* through *omote*. In fact, it may well be closer to the truth to say that they are looking at *omote* solely in order to see *ura*. In this way, although *omote* and *ura* are clearly distinguished conceptually, they are in fact closely related. Without *omote* there is no *ura*, without *ura* no *omote*—they are literally two sides (aspects) of a single entity. *Omote* and *ura* do not exist separately but, cojoined, form a single existence.[58]

And yet, as Doi recognizes, when the point of view shifts, the outsideness of *omote* that is visible and the insideness of *ura* that is hidden from view also shift. What is *omote* for one person may be *ura* for another.[59] The dialectical relationship between *omote* and *ura* is expressed in multiple scenes and levels throughout *Face of Another*, but two examples should suffice to illustrate its importance. The first involves Okuyama and his wife (played by Kyō Machiko). Fearing that Okuyama will use the mask to escape from both society and himself, Dr. Hori asks "what's the purpose of your double life with the mask?" Okuyama admits that he intends to use the mask to seduce his wife, who finds his disfiguration off-putting. Despite the doctor's warning that this would create a dangerous triangle between his wife, himself, and his masked self, Okuyama goes ahead with his plans. The masked Okuyama trails his wife (who is unnamed in the film and designated simply as "wife" [*tsuma*] in the screenplay) through the streets of Tokyo and strikes up a seemingly random conversation by pretending to return something that she had dropped. Eventually, he invites her to join him for tea, and they engage in flirtatious conversation.

With remarkable ease, Okuyama coaxes his wife back to an apartment he has rented for his masked self where the seduction continues (he rents a second apartment in the same building for his bandaged self).

The still masked Okuyama asks his wife if he seduced her or if she let herself be seduced. As the two of them appear in split screen, Okuyama remarks, "People aren't what they seem." However, she disagrees, saying that they must respect appearances. He complains that they are about to commit adultery and they don't even know each other's names. "I have so many selves, I can't even contain them all," she replies. The next morning, Okuyama pulls off the covers, exposing his wife's naked body, and starts arguing with her because the seduction was too easy. Okuyama is upset that his wife apparently slept with a stranger without protest. He starts to remove his mask to disclose his real identity, but she claims to have known it all along: "You think I didn't know?" she reveals. She thought they both knew they "were taking part in a masquerade." In fact, that is the reason she put on so much makeup, so that they would both "be wearing masks." "In love," she remarks, "people try to unmask one another. But I thought we must strive to keep the masks on." Furthermore, she asserts that women do not hide the fact that they are wearing makeup, "but pretending that the mask is your real face—that I'll never accept." In effect, Okuyama has cuckolded himself.

If the fake face that the mask permitted Okuyama to present to his wife functioned as the *omote* that he showed to his wife, then his goal of seduction was the *ura* behind the *omote*. However, Okuyama's wife was playing her own game of *omote/ura*. Although she pretended to go along with the seduction—feigning not to be aware that the masked Okuyama was actually her husband—in fact, she was aware and went along anyway because "we were taking part in a masquerade." In other words, the wife presented an *omote* of feigned ignorance to her husband, while concealing her *ura*, which was to rekindle relations with him. In each case, context is everything, since the dialectic between *omote* and *ura* is not referential but rather expresses degrees of distance between self and other in a complex network of shifting perspectives and situated relations. If, as Doi remarks, "a person who presents an artificial front in order to deceive others is a 'person with *ura-omote*,'"[60] then Okuyama and his wife each presented an "*ura-omote*" to the other.

Even monsters
have their pleasures.

Fig. 4.12 The main narrative is interrupted by a film-within-a-film in *Face of Another* (1966)

The second example of *omote/ura* involves *Face of Another*'s film-within-a-film. In Chap. 2, I discussed the concept of the sonic palimpsest in relation to the history of horror cinema and the films of Kurosawa Kiyoshi. *Face of Another* offers a visual palimpsest in the form of a film-within-a-film that interrupts the primary narrative just as Okuyama is having a discussion with his wife about the power of masks (Fig. 4.12). This interruption occurs in the form of a wash-away wipe that introduces a parallel narrative involving a young woman (played by Japanese-Russian fashion model Irie Miki) with disfiguring keloidal scars on her face (not unlike Okuyama's), who has an incestuous relationship with her elder brother (Saeki Kakuya). One of the most significant formal clues about how to position this parallel narrative in relation to the main narrative is provided by the differing aspect ratios that distinguish the two. In Fig. 4.12, which shows the moment the wash-away wipe begins, as the parallel narrative is unveiled, a different aspect ratio is also revealed. In his essay "*The Face of Another*: Double Vision," James Quandt incorrectly describes the aspect ratio of *Face of Another* as being "the squarish Academy ratio" (i.e., 1.375:1).[61] In fact, the aspect ratio of the film as a whole is 1.33:1. Both aspect ratios are full-frame, but the Academy ratio is more squarish. However, Quandt is quite right to point out that there is a formal tension between the old-fashioned full-frame aspect ratio used for most of the film and the letterboxed, widescreen 16:9 aspect ratio associated with the parallel narrative of the girl with the scars when she is first introduced.

So what does this formal tension between the two aspect ratios tell us about where the parallel narrative originated? It relates back to an earlier conversation between husband and wife about a movie Okuyama had just seen at a local theater, where he goes to escape the unkind stares of strangers. This is made even clearer in the novel by Abe Kōbō upon which the film was based where Okuyama describes the movie theater as "the only safe place for a monster."[62] Although Okuyama's description of the film, titled *One Side of Love* (*Ai no katagawa*), is restricted to a few pages late in the novel, Teshigahara's movie adaptation expands the role of this film-within-a-film (whose title is never revealed) with cross-cut editing that continuously juxtaposes scenes of Okuyama with scenes of the girl with scars, who is a *hibakusha* (atomic bomb) victim. The novel suggests that the young woman survived the bombing of Hiroshima, whereas the movie references Nagasaki. In one of the most poignant sequences of the film-within-a-film (which was closely adapted from the novel), when the girl walks down the street showing only the unblemished left side of her beautiful face to a group of young men, who wolf-whistle in appreciation, the movie utilizes a series of freeze-frame close-ups of the girl's face to stop time and crystallize the precise moment at which the keloidal scars disfiguring the right side of her face are revealed.[63] The unfeeling young men respond with horror and quickly disperse. During the day, the young woman works as a volunteer nurse at a "mental institution for old soldiers,"[64] as it is described in the novel, where inmates who were formerly soldiers in the Imperial Japanese Army continue to wear their World War II-era military uniforms and behave like soldiers—apparently unaware that Japan had lost the war some 20 years earlier.

In the film-within-a-film, as the girl walks around the grounds of the barracks-like asylum for old soldiers where she works, heavily distorted German-language audio clips of Hitler giving a speech at a Nazi rally can be heard. Later, when one of the inmates attempts to sexually assault the girl with the scars, we hear again what sound like Nazi political rants being replayed. The sound-image relations in such scenes and their political connotations are highly charged to say the least. As the film-within-a-film develops alongside the narrative of Okuyama's existential struggles with the mask, the girl repeatedly expresses anxieties to her brother that another war is imminent: "There won't be another war soon, will there?" Her brother (also unnamed) responds with uncertainty, since war is as unpredictable as the weather—"you don't even realize until it's already started." In the novel, the narrator suggests that it is not that the girl sought "revenge against those who were unblemished," but simply that she nurtured "the naïve hope that, if there were war, standards of value would be instantly reversed and people's interest would concentrate far more on the stomach than the face, on life itself rather than outer appearances."[65]

Seeking an escape from their humdrum lives, the girl and her brother travel to the coast and stay together in a room facing the sea. Cross-cut with shots from the sequence of Okuyama's seduction of his wife, the girl with the scars slowly seduces her brother at a seaside hotel, waking him up in the middle of the night and asking him to kiss her, since "I'm sure there'll be a war tomorrow." As the brother kisses his sister's scars with great passion, a freeze frame crystallizes their incestuous transgression. According to Keiko McDonald, the parallelism between Okuyama and his wife, on the one hand, and the girl with the scars and her brother, on the other, is further underscored visually toward the end of the scene when "the heads of brother and sister are aligned in the same way husband and wife were earlier and will be again when that scene returns."[66] Although McDonald interprets this visual parallelism as one of contrast between "real" and "unreal" love, it seems more likely to suggest the destructive lengths to which their desires have taken them and the complex masquerades at play in both relationships.

The next day, after sister and brother have transgressed the most ancient of taboos, the girl leaves a note for her brother and walks into the sea to drown herself. In one of the most surreal and disturbing scenes of this film-within-a-film, at the very moment that the brother looks out the window and witnesses his sister walking into the sea to drown herself, there is a bright, almost atomic-like flash as the brother is suddenly transformed into an animal carcass hanging from hooks that is crystallized in a freeze frame (Fig. 4.13). In addition to evoking the concept of *amour fou* (mad love)—the surrealists' concept of frenzied, obsessive love and uncontrollable sexual passion strongly associated with death and delirium[67]—students of British painter Francis Bacon (1909–1992) may also recognize in this scene an intermedial citation of the artist's grotesque work.

In a series of paintings that span his career from *Painting* (1946) to *Fragment of a Crucifixion* (1950), from *Figure with Meat* (1954) to *Three Figures and a Portrait* (1975), Bacon, who drew inspiration from early surrealism and whom some have considered a contemporary surrealist, uses the motif of meat hanging from hooks not only as a reminder of death but also as a point of identification with the animal in us:

Fig. 4.13 The brother of the atomic bomb survivor is transformed into an animal carcass after an atomic-like flash of light following his sister's suicide in *Face of Another* (1966)

Well, of course, we are meat, we are potential carcasses. If I go into a butcher's shop I always think it's surprising that I wasn't there instead of the animal. But using the meat in that particular way is possibly like the way one might use the spine, because we are constantly seeing images of the human body through X-ray photographs and that obviously does alter the ways by which one can use the body.... In my case, these things have certainly been influenced by X-ray photographs.[68]

In his study of Bacon titled *Francis Bacon: The Logic of Sensation*, Gilles Deleuze points out that "Bacon does not say, 'Pity the beasts,' but rather that every man who suffers is a piece of meat. Meat is the common zone of man and the beast, their zone of indiscernibility; it is a 'fact,' a state where the painter identifies with the objects of his horror and his compassion."[69]

In the context of *Face of Another*'s evocation of both X-ray and atomic bomb imagery, it is entirely fitting that Bacon's work should be cited. Just as the early surrealists responded to the horrors of the First World War in their art and film, so too, did surrealists of Bacon and Teshigahara's generation respond to the horrors of the Second World War in their art and film. Images within *Face of Another* that echo the atomic bombs dropped on Hiroshima and Nagasaki are painful reminders of how far humans will go in times of war to reduce the enemy to dehumanized pieces of meat and ash. As Keiko McDonald remarks, such powerful images "cannot fail to suggest a political metaphor connecting Teshigahara's grim tale of dehumanization with possibly the century's most potent image of anxiety: nuclear Armageddon."[70] It is from this perspective that *Face of Another*'s film-within-a-film about an incestuous survivor of Nagasaki, who works at a psychiatric hospital for war veterans where the delirium of Japanese wartime militarism continues to reverberate, functions as the dark underside (or "*ura*") of *Face of Another*'s surface (or "*omote*") narrative about a man going through an existential crisis after the disfiguration of his face in an industrial accident. In sum, *Face of Another* is deeply haunted by this unnamed film-within-a-film and the subtexts of World War II and its aftermath to which it returns again and again like the return of the repressed.

Yakuza Horror Theater

Nearly 40 years after the release of *Face of Another*, Miike Takashi unleashed *Gozu* (2003), considered by many critics to be one of Miike's most bizarre and controversial films, earning both praise and condemnation along with frequent comparisons with the filmmaking of Luis Buñuel, whose unforgettable short film cowritten with Salvador Dalí, *Un chien andalou* (1929), delivered quite a shock to the middle-class sensibilities of bourgeois viewers at the time it was released. Although originally intended as a straight-to-video V-Cinema release, *Gozu* made quite a splash when it debuted at the Directors' Fortnight (Quinzaine des Réalisateurs) section of the Cannes Film Festival in 2003 (Miike's first film to be invited) and quickly became a hit on the festival circuit, picking up awards for best film, best screenplay, and best visual effects. Film critic and punk rocker Chris D. has described *Gozu* as "a surreal parable à la Buñuel-on-LSD," "a shaggy dog version of *Alice in Wonderland* by route of David Lynch's *Lost Highway* with distant 'triangle' echoes from Truffaut's *Jules and Jim*."[71] But even Chris D.'s description does not do justice to just how truly bizarre *Gozu* is. Rather than making another genre film, Miike set out quite literally to shatter the formula of the yakuza movie: "Let's demolish accepted practice [*jōshiki o kowasō*]," the director proclaimed as the motivation behind making *Gozu*. "Let's destroy the yakuza movie from the past [*sono mukashi totta yakuza eiga o kowasō*]."[72] Miike himself has said that the creation of *Gozu* was so personally satisfying to him that he felt reborn after production wrapped, which is not hard to believe given that the imagery of rebirth plays such an important role in *Gozu* in relation to a scene that practically redefines the limits of body horror.

As Miike scholar Tom Mes has noted, the cast list for *Gozu* reads like a "Who's Who" of Miike movie alumni.[73] Aikawa Shō, who plays mentally unstable yakuza gang lieutenant Ozaki, has appeared in some of Miike's most acclaimed films, including *Rainy Dog* (*Gokudō kuroshakai*, 1997), *Ley Lines* (*Nihon kuroshakai*, 1999), *Dead or Alive* (*Dead or Alive: Hanzaisha*, 1999), *Zebraman* (*Zeburāman*, 2004), *Sun Scarred* (*Taiyō no kizu*, 2006), and *Like a Dragon* (*Ryū ga gotoku gekijōban*, 2007).

Meanwhile, Sone Hideki, who plays Ozaki's confused underling Minami (whose task it is to dispatch the off-the-rails Ozaki), has acted in such Miike standouts as *Agitator* (*Araburu tamashiitachi*, 2001), *Graveyard of Honor* (*Shin jingi no hakaba*, 2002), *Deadly Outlaw: Rekka* (*Jitsuroku Andō Noboru kyōdōden: Rekka*, 2002), and *Zebraman*. Other Miike regulars appearing in *Gozu* include Tanba Tetsurō (*Happiness of the Katakuris* [*Katakurike no kōfuku*, 2001], *Deadly Outlaw: Rekka*, *Demon Pond* [*Yasha ga ike*, 2005]), Ishibashi Renji (*Bird People of China* [*Chūgoku no chōjin*, 1998], *Audition* [*Ōdishon*, 1999], *Dead or Alive*, *Sukiyaki Western Django* [*Sukiyaki wesutān jango*, 2007]), Endō Ken'ichi (*Visitor Q* [*Bijitā Q*, 2001], *Happiness of the Katakuris*, *Great Yokai War* [*Yōkai daisensō*, 2005], *Sun Scarred*), Tomita Keiko (*One Missed Call* [*Chakushin ari*, 2003]), and Satō Sakichi (the screenplay writer of both *Ichi the Killer* [*Koroshiya 1*, 2001] and *Gozu*, who has a cameo in *Gozu* as a transgendered coffee shop manager). Even respected Japanese film critic Shiota Tokitoshi was given a role to play in *Gozu*, appearing as the titular ox-headed Gozu demon. The crew is also staffed with Miike regulars, most notably cinematographer Tanaka Kazunari and longtime editor Shimamura Yasushi. Like most Miike films, the collaborative production of *Gozu* was practically a family affair, even if the subject matter is hardly suitable for most families!

During a regular meeting of the Azamawari yakuza gang at a local restaurant, Ozaki becomes agitated when he catches sight of a Chihuahua in the arms of its owner outside.[74] In a state of paranoia, Ozaki warns the gang's boss (played by Miike regular Ishibashi Renji) that the diminutive dog is actually "a trained yakuza attack dog" in disguise that kills only yakuza "made" men and therefore poses a threat to the boss' life. The fact that Ozaki precedes this warning with a meta-level comment unheeded by the boss—"Everything I'm about to tell you is a joke—don't take it seriously"—announces to the audience at the outset that the surreal story that is about to unfold is not to be taken seriously.[75] As the boss looks on in disbelief, Ozaki rushes outside the restaurant to confront the helpless animal, violently dashing it onto the sidewalk and then hurling it against the restaurant window. As the poor animal's blood drips down the restaurant window, the expression of disapproval on boss Azamawari's face suggests that Ozaki's deranged behavior has just sealed his fate.

This bizarre outburst of violence is not only shocking (especially for dog lovers), it is also quite hilarious in a surrealist, absurdist sort of way. Tom Mes views *Gozu*'s dark sense of humor as "reminiscent of the kind employed by the kings of absurdist wit, Monty Python," whom Miike has acknowledged as an influence.[76] However, both Monty Python and Miike may be situated in a long line of dark satirists dating back to Jonathan Swift. What makes *Gozu* a profoundly surrealist horror is its peculiar sense of humor—what the early surrealists dubbed "black humor" (from "*humour noir*" in French)—which is evident to varying degrees in many of Miike's films. The term "black humor," which involves "laughter that arises from cynicism and scepticism,"[77] was first coined by surrealism founder André Breton in 1935 for his *Anthology of Black Humor* (*Anthologie de l'humour noir*). For Breton and other surrealists, black humor—a peculiar brand of comedy and satire that Breton attributes to Jonathan Swift—is "the mortal enemy of sentimentality."[78] By exploring topics related to death that are often considered taboo, black humor typically evokes in its audience a mixture of both cynical laughter and ethical discomfort. At its root, black humor is "a response to hopeless situations," as writer Kurt Vonnegut put it: "It's small people being pushed this way and that way, enormous armies and plagues and so forth, and still hanging on in the face of hopelessness...And the black humorists are gallows humorists, as they try to be funny in the face of situations which they see as just horrible."[79] Indeed, although it may be the apparent hopelessness of the victims of black humor that makes their plight so darkly funny, it is also by learning to laugh in the face of hopelessness that black humor makes the oppressiveness of life seem a little more bearable.

In response to Ozaki's over-the-top assassination of the yakuza attack dog, junior gang member Minami (Sone Hideki) is instructed to take Ozaki to the "yakuza dump" in Nagoya to dispose of his body without leaving a trace. What makes this an especially difficult job for Minami is that Ozaki—a man who once saved Minami's life—is Minami's senior (*senpai*), whom he addresses throughout the film as "*aniki*" (elder brother). In yakuza discourse, when Minami addresses Ozaki as "elder brother" (*aniki*), it is not because they are literally blood relatives, but rather because they are cohorts within the same yakuza social group.

"*Aniki*" is an honorific term in Japanese that can be used to address an older brother or any male superior. It is a term that is commonly used in yakuza circles (and movies) to address one's "big brother" in crime, as it were. Later in the film, after Ozaki undergoes a sudden metamorphosis into the body of a woman, it is noteworthy that Minami continues to address Ozaki as "*aniki*" even after the latter's body has undergone a spontaneous sex change.

On their way to the yakuza dump in Nagoya, Minami steps on the brakes suddenly, which causes Ozaki to hit his head against the dashboard of the car, apparently killing him in the process. Upon reaching Nagoya, things take an even stranger turn when Ozaki's body disappears from the car during a brief stop at a local restaurant. Minami begins to panic and questions the locals inside the restaurant, but his encounter with a trio of transgendered waitresses makes it clear that he is a stranger in a strange land, as he is repeatedly reminded ("Ya ain't from Nagoya, are ya!"). One of the most interesting aspects of *Gozu's mise-en-scène* is the fact that it is set in the port city of Nagoya, which functions as a counter-space where Minami encounters all manner of unexpected obstacles and unusual beings. In traditional yakuza films, the setting is usually Tokyo or Osaka. In contemporary Japan, there is nothing particularly strange or unusual about Nagoya. However, as a surreal place in the defamiliarized world of *Gozu*, it takes on meaning as a space of estrangement for a Tokyo-based yakuza such as Minami. By setting up Nagoya in this way, *Gozu* underscores the extent to which Minami is a fish out of water. Underscoring such estrangement is the way in which language is used. For example, in his exchanges with the Nagoyan locals, the dialogue becomes so thoroughly defamiliarized that it recalls David Lynch's handling of language as a sort of "sound effect" in *Eraserhead* (1977). Like *Eraserhead*, the strangely repetitive and vacuous dialogue emitted by native Nagoyans in their local dialect has less to do with the conveyance of narratival information in *Gozu* and more to do with the insertion of off-putting rhythms that continuously throw Minami off-balance.

The Azamawari boss advises Minami to seek help from an affiliated gang in Nagoya, the Shiroyama crew. Once he locates them, Minami's answer to a riddle ("What 'takes' but also 'passes'?" Answer: "Time") posed to him by the Shiroyama boss (a riddle that recalls Oedipus's encounter with the Sphinx) secures the assistance of a Shiroyama gang member named "Nosechi" (played by Hino Shōhei), also known as "Nose." Nose checks Minami into a local Japanese-style inn run by an elderly woman named Masa (Tomita Keiko) and her autistic brother Kazu (played by Sone Harumi—the real life father of the actor playing Minami and a veteran of a number of acclaimed yakuza films in the 1960s and 1970s, including Fukasaku Kinji's *Battles Without Honor and Humanity* series). Minami discovers to his surprise and horror that, despite her advanced age, the elderly innkeeper has a lactation problem (gift?) that requires her to regularly express her milk into bottles with her brother's assistance, which are then sold around town. Hyper-lactation is a motif that Miike has explored previously in *Visitor Q (Bijitā Q, 2001)*— his scathing deconstruction of the nuclear family—but *Gozu* pushes such mammary metaphors to a whole new level. Masa and Kazu's motto is: "Those who deliver milk are healthier than those who drink it [*Gyūnyū o haitatsu suru ningen wa kore o nomu ningen yori mo kenkō de aru*]." So that not a drop goes to waste, the hyper-lactating inkeeper offers her breast milk to Minami, but he nervously declines. However, when eating meals at the inn, not only is her milk served as a beverage but a milky substance dripping from the ceiling onto his food makes one wonder if Minami has been consuming the innkeeper's milk involuntarily the entire time. The fact that Minami is propositioned not only by the elderly innkeeper—who provocatively expresses her milk in front of him—but also by Nose—who is insulted that Minami will not allow him to spend the night with him at the inn—suggests that nearly everyone the virginal Minami (who had recently been circumcised) encounters in Nagoya seems to want to have sex him.

What is perhaps most peculiar about *Gozu*'s lactation imagery is that it takes something that is conventionally perceived as nourishing and life-giving and turns it into something "abject" (at least for Minami, judging by his reaction). In her study *Powers of Horror: An Essay on Abjection* (1980),[80] Julia Kristeva argues that abjection and its attendant emotions (revulsion, disgust, nausea, and horror) are felt when one is confronted with "an object that threatens to disrupt the distinction between self and other,"[81] crossing the boundary between subject and object in some disturbing way. The threat of such boundary crossing may come from outside or inside. Kristeva argues that when such boundaries are crossed, a collapse of meaning occurs that produces the feeling of revulsion, which is the tell-tale sign that one is in the presence of abjection. In *Gozu*, such boundary crossing is both transgressive and resonant.

Encounters with Monstrous Hybridity

Not long after an amusing but failed attempt by Masa to compel a spirit to enter her brother Kazu's body in order to divine the location of the missing Ozaki, Minami learns that someone resembling Ozaki stayed at the inn the previous night. After recognizing Ozaki's scent in the room, Minami insists upon staying in the same room in case he returns. In the middle of the night, blurring the boundaries between dream and reality, Minami has a vision that he is visited by the monstrous, ox-headed Gozu, who lasciviously licks Minami's face with its oversized tongue while drooling a semen-like saliva (Fig. 4.14). Although the eponymous creature of the film appears only once, it is unforgettable. Shots of the monster licking Minami are cross-cut with images of Kazu incestuously suckling the breast of his sister Masa.[82]

Fig. 4.14   Minami encounters the eponymous ox-headed creature in *Gozu* (2003)

A more literal translation of the film's full title, *Gokudō kyōfu daigekijō: Gozu*, which means "Grand Theater of Yakuza Horror: Ox Head," underscores the importance of this strange creature, which demands further unpacking. The word "Gozu" is a dual allusion to both Buddhist and Shintoist religious mythologies. On the one hand, Gozu alludes to "Gozu Rasetsu," a Buddhist demon with a human body and the head of an ox charged with keeping order in one of the many levels of Buddhist hell—a sort of prison guard of hell—in the service of Bishamonten, protector of Buddhism and defender of the nation. In scroll paintings, Gozu frequently appears alongside his companion, the horse-headed guardian of hell known as "Mezu Rasetsu." Together the Gozu-Mezu team of Buddhist guardians feed on the flesh of the damned, extracting their intestines and removing their tongues as punishment. On the other hand, Gozu also refers to the Shinto deity "Gozu Tennō," an ox-headed god of epidemic disease and plague that is the syncretic product of Shinto-Buddhist intermixing, who has been honored and appeased in annual purification rituals performed at the Yasaka (Gion) Shrine in Kyoto since the year 869 to prevent the spread of plague and pestilence. Such religious tropes reinforce the impression that the strange inn where Minami encounters Gozu is the "gateway to the netherworld," as Mes puts it.[83]

However, equally significant are the film's various allusions to the bull-headed figure of the Minotaur and other hybrid monsters in surrealist iconography. It may have been merely a coincidence that *Gozu* was released close to the seventieth anniversary of the publication of the first issue of the acclaimed surrealist magazine titled *Minotaure*, but it is no accident that Miike's cinematic visualization of the ox-headed Gozu, along with the crouching pose of the creature that graces some of the movie's marketing posters, are strikingly similar to the symbol of the bull-headed Minotaur that became synonymous with the surrealist journal of the same name and whose image frequently graced its cover. No less an artist than Pablo Picasso was responsible for the design of the Minotaur that graced the cover of issue no. 1 that was published in 1933.[84]

Surrealists of every generation have expressed a fascination with hybrid creatures and constructed monstrosities, especially those zoological-botanical fantasies that blatantly subvert scientific taxonomies. Moreover, as

Elza Adamowicz suggests in her study *Surrealist Collage in Text and Image: Dissecting the Exquisite Corpse*, the surrealist "collage-monster as a literal agglomeration of parts" not only overturns hierarchies and transgresses taboos, but in its "joyous collision of limbs" and celebration of hybridity also unleashes the eroticism of jouissance.[85] Such artistic citations and their psychosexual connotations clearly identify Miike's *Gozu* as an unabashedly surrealist film and in so doing effectively resonates with the entire tradition of surrealist filmmaking and art. As Tony Rayns remarks, "it's all about seeing through the veil of the everyday to the perversity beneath."[86] The ox-headed Gozu hands to Minami a letter signed by Ozaki that says he will wait for him at the yakuza dump. The next day, Minami heads to the yakuza disposal site—a "recycling plant for dead yakuza, which produces buckets of entrails and neatly starched 'suits' of tattooed skin"[87]—whose boss repeatedly poses the same question to Minami: "Who da ya want disposed of?" When Minami demands to know what they have done with the body of Ozaki, he is shown racks of steam-pressed yakuza bodies, including one that is identified as Ozaki's and bears his signature tattoo of a jealous female demon on the back (Fig. 4.15).

Fig. 4.15 Racks of steam-pressed yakuza bodies, including Ozaki's (on the far right), are shown to Minami at the yakuza dump in *Gozu* (2003)

Gender Ambiguity

However, things become even more surreal when Minami prepares to depart the yakuza dump only to discover a woman he has never met before sitting in the back seat of his convertible, who claims to be the female version of Ozaki. Initially, Minami finds this beyond belief, but the female Ozaki (Yoshino Kimika) knows personal secrets about Minami that only Ozaki would know, such as the details of his circumcision (after which Ozaki had told Minami that his penis "looks just like Frankenstein's") or the fact that he is still a virgin. He drives her back to Tokyo where she allows herself to be seduced by boss Azamawari himself, who has a sexual predilection for long-handled ladles stuck up his rear end. In a fit of jealousy, Minami interrupts them *in flagrante delicto* and violently confronts his boss, who ends up perishing by ladle in the skirmish.

Minami and the female Ozaki—whom Minami continues to address as "*aniki*" (elder brother)—run off together to spend the night in a hotel where they have sex for the first time (and Minami loses his virginity). As they make love, Minami's penis gets stuck inside of the female Ozaki. To his shock and horror, Minami discovers that his penis is firmly grasped by a hand inside of the woman's uterus, which belongs to the male Ozaki. After much struggle, Minami attains release and the head of the male Ozaki pokes his head out of the female Ozaki's vagina. At that point, Ozaki's adult male self emerges from her body, his rebirth complete with his signature tattoo of a jealous female demon on his back (Fig. 4.16). Throughout the birth scene, Minami repeatedly addresses the reborn Ozaki as "*aniki*" (elder brother). At the very moment that Ozaki's body is released from the birth canal of the female Ozaki, a loud, cartoon-like popping sound can be heard, and Ozaki slides across the room towards Minami, who is cowering in the corner. *Gozu* features a number of distinctive sound design choices throughout, including bowed and scraped string sounds and low-frequency drones that reinforce an overarching sense of dread, but perhaps the most memorable is the "popping" sound heard at the precise moment when the male Ozaki is released from the birth canal of the female Ozaki, which provides a comical sonic exclamation point that helps release all the tension (sexual and otherwise) that has built up over the course of the entire film.

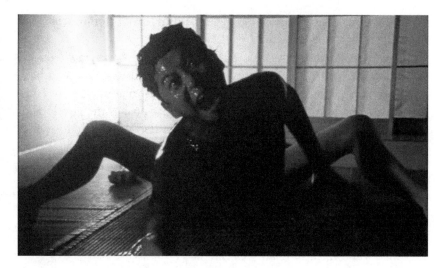

Fig. 4.16   Ozaki's rebirth in *Gozu* (2003)

By far the most puzzling and complex questions raised by the film have to do with its sexual politics, especially the film's surreal engagement with gender confusion, transgressive sexuality, and grotesque rebirth. In particular, the monstrous birthing scene in which the female Ozaki gives birth to the adult male Ozaki has been the focus of a great deal of critical attention. Miike was certainly not the first director to visualize a monstrous birth involving a baby with an adult's head. Danish *enfant terrible* Lars von Trier caused quite a bit of controversy in episode four (titled "De levende døde" or "The Living Dead") of his supernatural hospital drama *The Kingdom* (*Riget*, 1994), which aired on Danish television in 1994, by showing the grotesque birth of a character named "Little Brother" (played by German actor Udo Kier), the alleged son of a murderer (also played by Udo Kier) and a nurse at the hospital. Although the birth of Little Brother in *The Kingdom* probably inspired Miike's visualization of Ozaki's birth in *Gozu*, there are enough distinctions to suggest that Ozaki's birth is not simply derivative. First, although Lars von Trier's grotesque Little Brother is born with a mature adult head, the rest of his body is not mature at birth. Second, the birth of Little Brother does not blur gender boundaries or flirt with intersexual imagery in the manner of *Gozu*. Third, Lars von

Trier's hospital drama does not engage the problem of homosociality to the same extent that *Gozu* does.

To get a handle on what Miike (and his screenplay writer Satō Sakichi) are visualizing with Ozaki's surreal rebirth, we need to take a step back and contextualize the gender confusion and intersexual imagery of *Gozu* in terms of the long history of surrealist art that pushes the envelope of gender and sexual identity. Surrealism's founder André Breton once famously remarked, "I wish I could change my sex the way I change my shirt,"[88] and his fellow surrealists could not have agreed more. Surrealists of every stripe have long been interested in border crossings and boundary transgressions of one sort or another, and this applies no less to the blurring of gender boundaries than it does to the exploration of alternative sexualities. As Penelope Rosemont notes in her introduction to *Surrealist Women: An International Anthology*,

> In matters of gender and sex, as in everything else, the first surrealist generation—men and women—were rebels and revolutionaries.... [T]he early surrealists' questioning and challenging of gender stereotypes went much deeper than even the most radical of their contemporaries were willing to go (Breton 1937). At a time when Marxist and anarchist organizations either downplayed sexuality or ignored it entirely, surrealists carried out a long series of open group discussions on sexual activity—excerpts of which appeared in their journal. As these discussions confirm, tolerance of so-called sexual deviance was much higher in the surrealist milieu than elsewhere. In the lives and work of several early surrealists—including Marcel Duchamp, Man Ray, and Claude Cahun—gender ambiguity was a large factor. Several surrealists engaged in homosexual relations (Rene Crevel, Georges Malkine, and Claude Cahun openly, Louis Aragon more discreetly, and others, in France and elsewhere, in later years). Because of its pronounced sexual openness, the Surrealist Group as a whole was for many years—well into the 1940s—widely accused of being homosexual.[89]

Among the most famous examples of such surrealist border crossing is Man Ray's series of photographs of the transgendered Marcel Duchamp adopting the feminine persona "Rrose Selavy" (a pun on the French phrase *"Eros, c'est la vie,"* or "Eros, that's life"). Duchamp's transgendered portrait has become so iconic that it has often been imitated by later photographers, ranging from Morimura Yasumasa to Robert Wilson. In the wake of Duchamp's Rrose Selavy, *Gozu* certainly does not shy away from using gender ambiguity as a technique to get the audience to think about the performativity of gender, as the scene in the restaurant featuring *Gozu* screenplay writer Satō Sakichi demonstrates (he is the bald one in the middle in Fig. 4.17). However, *Gozu* also explores border crossings that push the envelope even more, embracing figurations and desires that verge on the intersexual. In such cases, the early surrealists again paved the way. From René Magritte's painting *The Titanic Days* (*Les Jours gigantesques*, 1928), which shows the struggle of male and female within the same body, to Salvador Dalí's *The Great Masturbator* (*Visage du Grand Masturbateur*, 1929), whose enormous distorted face cast downward is a self-portrait of the artist out of which emerges a nude female figure resembling Dalí's muse and lover Gala, the early surrealists were utterly fascinated by the intersexual mixing of male and female within the same body. Indeed, as art critic Brian Sewell confirms in the documentary *Dirty Dalí: A Private View* (dir. Guy Evans, 2007a), although Dalí was attracted to both men and women

Fig. 4.17   Gender ambiguity in *Gozu* (2003)

(and was known to have had affairs with both), his "physical ideal was the hermaphrodite."[90]

Hans Bellmer (1902–1975) was another early surrealist interested in gender instability and intersexual mixing, as suggested by photos from Bellmer's *The Doll* (*La Poupée*, 1935–1938) series that intermix male and female limbs at the waist. Bellmer was quite explicit in his view that masculine and feminine images are "interchangeable," arguing in his essay "A Brief Anatomy of the Physical Unconscious, or The Anatomy of the Image" that the sexes tend "towards their amalgam, the hermaphrodite."[91] As is frequently the case with Bellmer, such images are both grotesque and erotic. Bellmer's engagement with intersexual mixing is even more pronounced in his drawings, such as *The Crimes of Love* (*Les Crimes de l'amour*, 1961), which "fuse male and female forms to create ambiguous, fluid organisms."[92] Peeling away the flesh of his female self in an untitled work from 1947–48, Bellmer reveals his own face. Bellmer's greatest desire seems to have been for his male self to make love to his female self, thereby giving new meaning to the term "auto-eroticism." Although such examples explore intersexual imagery as a space for auto-eroticism, Bellmer was also interested in situating intersexual desire in the context of quasi-birth imagery, such as in Bellmer's *Study for "Transfer of the Senses"* (*Etude pour "Transfert des Sens,"* 1949), which flirts with self-birthing imagery in a way that uncannily anticipates Miike's visualization of Ozaki's self-birth in *Gozu*.

Homosociality and *Amour Fou*

Taking into consideration the history of surrealism's engagement with such border crossing, how does *Gozu* make use of such imagery to explore questions of gender and sexuality in the context of the homosocial sphere of the yakuza underworld? As the film's full Japanese title suggests, *Gozu* is a self-described "yakuza horror film." What makes it a horror film, in part, is *Gozu*'s engagement with the horror of homophobia in the homosocial context of the yakuza social space. Here I am using the term "homosocial" as defined by scholars in the field of gender studies, especially the work of Eve Kosofsky Sedgwick and David William Foster. According to Sedgwick and Foster, "homosociality is not homosexuality":

> Indeed, the two are mutually exclusive. Homosociality is understood to refer to the way in which patriarchal society forges bonds between men for the orderly transference and maintenance of masculinist power: these bonds not only allow for men to transmit power from one to another (along any number of social axes of class, caste, race, religion, profession, and the like), but also they allow for the process of inclusion of some men in power and exclusion of others from it, and they allow for the vigilant scrutiny of men to determine if they are abiding by the conditions of the patriarchy—that is, if they are worthy exponents of it. It is here, of course, that homophobia comes in, since homophobia works against those men who do not abide by the heteronormative rules of the patriarchy, and it works both to punish and to exclude them, often by violent death. In homosociality, women are tokens of the exchange of power between men: appropriate and adequate heterosexual relations with women are taken as a guarantee of one's conformance with the patriarchy, and it is frequently through women that patriarchal power is transmitted—for example, from a powerful man to his son-in-law. The bonds between men range over the sociocultural spectrum between what, popularly, we call the buddy system to, in a more formal and professional context, the old-boy network.[93]

Gozu raises challenging questions concerning the horror of homophobia in the exceedingly homosocial space of the yakuza underworld. But rather than simply recapitulating homophobia in a mindless heterosexist sort of way, *Gozu* actively explores the problem of homophobia in a manner that is quite distinctive when viewed in relation to the pronounced homosocial history of the yakuza genre. Perhaps the most difficult question for any viewer of *Gozu* to answer is whether Miike's surrealist yakuza horror succeeds in overcoming the homosocial baggage weighing down decades of traditional yakuza cinema.

More than simply dramatizing the horror of homophobia, *Gozu* offers a nontraditional yakuza love story—or, more to the point, given its surrealist leanings—a celebration of *amour fou* in the surrealists' sense of the term. This is confirmed by the strange incantation—"*gean keruke mister amore*"—

that innkeeper Masa invites Minami to recite along with her in order to locate Ozaki with the help of her brother as spiritual medium. Later, Minami hears again the strange incantation, but this time emitted from the womb of the female Ozaki while she is sleeping. The first half ("*gean keruke*") of the incantation consists of nonsense syllables, but the second half ("*mister amore*") is anything but nonsense, since it addresses Minami himself as "Mr. Amore" (Mr. Love). As Tom Mes astutely observes, "sexual desire [is] the driving force behind the story of *Gozu*."

> Having made so many of them, Takashi Miike has had plenty of opportunities to toy around with the codes of the yakuza film and the genre's homoerotic subtext in particular has been a recurring feature in his films. It rears its head quite overtly in films like *Shinjuku Triad Society, Blues Harp, Ichi the Killer,* and *Agitator.* On the surface all the pushing around, yelling, punching, and shooting seem like typical displays of pumped-up machismo, but more often than not Miike dwells just that little bit longer on the fact that these men spend a lot more time with each other than with women. In a Miike film, members of the opposite sex are mere passers-by in a gangster's life. He goes so far as to show groups of these supposedly virile men living together in the same house, cooking communal meals, and doing the dishes and each other's laundry.
>
> *Gozu* continues this motif in what is perhaps its most direct expression yet. Stripped of its abundant absurdism, the film tells the simple tale of a man who wants his male companion to admit that he loves him and wants to sleep with him. It requires the illusion of heterosexuality, in the shapely form of actress Kimika Yoshino, to get him there, but once he has owned up to his true feelings this illusion quite literally splits apart to reveal its true face.[94]

What *Gozu* offers is nothing less than a nontraditional yakuza love story and coming-out film in the context of a surrealist horror. As film critic Tony Williams reminds us, although it is not hard to detect subtexts involving closeted homosexuality in "classical Hollywood gangster films such as *Little Caesar* (1931) and later examples such as *The Pawnbroker* (1965) as well as the traditional yakuza movie," *Gozu* brings such issues out of the closet in ways that are quite innovative for the genre.[95] After the rebirth of the male Ozaki, the female Ozaki certainly looks worse for wear, but Minami conveys in voiceover that they simply "put the girl in the tub and she was back to normal." *Gozu* ends with a touching shot of three toothbrushes side-by-side followed by the two Ozakis and Minami walking arm-in-arm down the street in a love triangle that calls to mind François Truffaut's *Jules and Jim* (*Jules et Jim*, 1962) but with less tragic consequences. The female side of Ozaki effectively serves as the bridge (or intermediary) between Minami and the male Ozaki that allows Minami to bring his love for Ozaki out of the closet, so to speak. Miike may not have succeeded in destroying the traditional yakuza movie as he set out to do, but at the very least it might be said that the homosociality that is one of the yakuza film's most defining and tenacious characteristics has been both recapitulated and transgressed by the end of *Gozu*'s yakuza horror theater.

Conclusion

This chapter shows a side of Japanese horror that is rarely discussed. Although *Face of Another* is not, strictly speaking, an example of contemporary Japanese horror, it is included here because it serves as a bridge that connects earlier Japanese surrealist filmmakers to contemporary J-horror directors, who have incorporated experimental surrealist filmmaking techniques and tropes into their films in often underappreciated ways. Despite being strikingly different in tone and style, what *Face of Another* and *Gozu* share with one another is an insistence on defying logic with unexpected combinations and disorienting juxtapositions; employing oneiric structures and scenarios that disrupt narrative continuity; and raising existential and sociopolitical questions about the shifting status of identity, body, and life. By confronting us with the strange, absurd, bizarre, and uncanny side of life, such surrealist horror films not only push the envelope of what a horror film can be but also defamiliarize the everyday to the point that the organizational powers of modernity that repress, control, and fragment the bodies of the films' protagonists are thereby exposed. Here most of all, on the "edge of meaning," to paraphrase Jean-Luc Nancy, the sound-image machines of these two films confront us with "resonant subjects" grappling with the "edgy meaning of extremity."[96]

Notes

1. Salvador Dalí quoted in Hans Richter, *Dada, Art and Anti-Art*, translated by David Britt (New York, N.Y.: Thames and Hudson, 1997), 194.
2. Félix Guattari, *Chaosophy: Texts and Interviews 1972–1977*, edited by Sylvère Lotringer (Los Angeles, CA: Semiotexte, 2009), 247. The concept of "*cinema fou*" (mad cinema), which serves as the main title of this chapter, is borrowed from an interview with Guattari on the role of *amour fou* in Terence Malick's *Badlands* (1973), which was first published in *Libération* (July 17, 1975) and later reprinted in Félix Guattari, *La Révolution moléculaire* (Fontenay-sous-Bois: Recherches, 1977).
3. For further discussion of *Un chien andalou*, including its influence on Japanese horror films such as *Tetsuo: The Iron Man* (*Tetsuo*; dir. Tsukamoto Shin'ya, 1989), see my *Tokyo Cyberpunk: Posthumanism in Japanese Visual Culture* (Palgrave Macmillan, 2010), 60–64.
4. On conceptions of surrealist cinema and its exemplars both narrowly and broadly defined, see Alison Frank's discussion in *Reframing Reality: The Aesthetics of the Surrealist Object in French and Czech Cinema* (Bristol: Intellect, 2013), 1–10.
5. Maurice Blanchot, "Tomorrow at Stake," in *The Infinite Conversation*, translated by Susan Hanson (Minneapolis: University of Minnesota Press, 1993), 407; Maurice Blanchot, *L'entretien infini* (Paris Gallimard, 1969), 597.
6. Luis Buñuel, *My Last Breath* (London: Flamingo, 1985), 107.
7. Quoted in Keith Aspley, *Historical Dictionary of Surrealism* (Lanham, Md.: Scarecrow Press, 2010), 267. See also André Breton, "The Exquisite Corpse, Its Exaltation (1948)," in André Breton, *Surrealism and Painting*, translated by Simon Watson Taylor (Boston: MFA Publications, 2002), 288–90. See also Elza Adamowicz, *Surrealist Collage in Text and Image: Dissecting the Exquisite Corpse* (Cambridge; New York: Cambridge University Press, 1998), 78–83, 160–62, 175–78.
8. Breton, "The Exquisite Corpse," 290.
9. Luis Buñuel, *My Last Sigh*, translated by Abigail Israel (Minneapolis: University of Minnesota Press, 2003), 103–04.
10. Morise quoted in Aspley, 8. From Morise's essay "Les yeux enchantés" (The Enchanted Eyes), which was included in the opening issue of the surrealist journal *La Révolution surréaliste* published in December 1924.
11. Michael Richardson, *Surrealism and Cinema* (Oxford; New York: Berg, 2006), 29.
12. Takemitsu's score for *Face of Another* received an award for Best Film Score at the 1967 Mainichi Film Concours.

13. Peter Grilli, "The Spectral Landscape of Teshigahara, Abe, and Takemitsu," *The Criterion Collection*, July 9, 2007, https://www.criterion.com/current/posts/607-the-spectral-landscape-of-teshigahara-abe-and-takemitsu (accessed November 19, 2016).

14. See Felicity Glee's comparative analysis of surrealist practice in Teshigahara's *Otoshiana* (*Pitfall*, 1962) and Buñuel's *Los Olvidados* (*The Forgotten Ones*, 1950): Felicity Glee, "Surrealist Legacies: The Influence of Luis Buñuel's 'Irrationality' on Hiroshi Teshigahara's 'Documentary-Fantasy,'" in *A Companion to Luis Buñuel*, edited by Rob Stone and Julián Daniel Gutiérrez-Albilla (Malden, MA: Wiley-Blackwell, 2013), 572–89.

15. John Woo would explore similar ideas in his 1997 action thriller *Face/Off*, but *Face of Another* offers a much more philosophically charged, surrealist engagement with such issues.

16. Examples include *Extreme Makeover* (2002–2007), *Dr. 90210* (2004–2008), *Miami Slice* (2004), and *I Want a Famous Face* (2004–2005).

17. Ghislaine Wood, *The Surreal Body: Fetish and Fashion* (London: V & A Publications, 2007), 6.

18. On the fragmented body in surrealist art and photography, see Wood, 6–17, 32–55; Sidra Stich, *Anxious Visions: Surrealist Art* (Berkeley: University Art Museum, 1990), 26–37, 42–47, 51–54, 74–79; Madeleine Cottenet-Hage, "The Body Subversive: Corporeal Imagery in Carrington, Prassinos and Mansour," in *Surrealism and Women*, edited by Mary Ann Caws, Rudolf E. Kuenzli, and Gloria Gwen Raaberg (Cambridge, Mass.: MIT Press, 1991), 76–95; Hal Foster, "Violation and Veiling in Surrealist Photography: Woman as Fetish, as Shattered Object, as Phallus," in *Surrealism: Desire Unbound*, edited by Jennifer Mundy (Princeton, N.J.: Princeton University Press, 2001), 203–26. On the fragmented body in surrealist cinema, see Richard Abel, *French Cinema: The First Wave, 1915–1929* (Princeton, NJ: Princeton University Press, 1984), 483–85; Robert Short, "Un Chien Andalou," in *The Age of Gold: Surrealist Cinema*, edited by Robert Short (London: Creation Books, 2003), 72; Phillip Drummond, "Textual Space in *Un Chien Andalou*," *Screen* vol. 18, no. 3 (1977): 55–119; Paul Sandro, "The Space of Desire in *An Andalusian Dog*," *1978 Film Studies Annual* (1979): 57–63.

19. Linda Nochlin, *The Body in Pieces: The Fragment as a Metaphor of Modernity* (New York: Thames and Hudson, 1995).

20. Adamowicz (178) summarizing the argument put forward by Xavière Gauthier in her study *Surréalisme et sexualité* (Paris: Gallimard, 1971).

21. Adamowicz, 181.

22. Wood, 56.

23. James Quandt, "Video Essay," *Tanin no kao*, directed by Teshigahara Hiroshi (1966), translated as *Face of Another*, subtitled DVD (Irvington, N.Y.: The Criterion Collection, 2007).

24. Such imagery resonates with the surrealist fascination with insect imagery. Here I am thinking not only of Buñuel and Dalí's visualization of ants crawling out of a hole in a man's hand in *Un chien andalou* (Dalí practically established swarming ants as a leitmotif for mortality, decomposition, and irrepressible sexual desire) but also the early surrealists' usage of the praying mantis as a figuration for the voracious sexuality of the femme fatale. In *Woman in the Dunes* (*Suna no onna*, 1964), which was released two years before *Face of Another*, Teshigahara and his collaborators Abe and Takemitsu pursued the surrealist implications of such entomological tropes as far as they would take them. The protagonist of *Woman in the Dunes* is an amateur entomologist named Niki Junpei who in the course of collecting rare bugs comes face-to-face with what it feels like to be treated like a bug himself by the unnamed "sand-woman" (*suna no onna*) played by Kishida Kyōko, who also plays the nurse at the clinic treating Okuyama in *Face of Another*.

25. Gilles Deleuze and Félix Guattari, *A Thousand Plateaus: Capitalism and Schizophrenia*, translated by Brian Massumi (Minneapolis: University of Minnesota Press, 1987), 167–91.

26. Ibid., 168, 170.

27. Ibid., 168.

28. On *Eyes Without a Face*, see Raymond Durgnat, *Franju* (Berkeley: University of California Press, 1968), 78–86; Kate Ince, *Georges Franju* (Manchester: Manchester University Press, 2005), 50–53, 67–75, 139–42. In *Ring 0: Birthday* (*Ringu 0: Bāsudei*, 2000)—a prequel to the *Ringu* series—Tsuruta Norio pays homage to *Eyes Without a Face* by having the young Sadako (before she turns into the vengeful ghost of *Ringu*) play the lead role in a play titled *Kamen* (Mask) that is supposed to be a stage adaptation of George Franju's unsettling classic.

29. On the genre of "*cinema fantastique*," see Ince, 47–61. As Richard Scheib points out in his review, "*The Face of Another* joins a number of other films from the late 1950s onwards that deal with surgeons engaged in facial experiments. This mini-genre began with the French arthouse hit *Eyes Without a Face* (1960) and quickly made its way to the province of B horror movies with the likes of *Atom Age Vampire* (1960), *Circus of Horrors* (1960), *The Awful Dr. Orloff* (1962) and *Corruption* (1968)." See Richard Scheib, "Review of The Face of Another," *Moria: Science Fiction,*

Horror and Fantasy Film Review, http://moria.co.nz/sciencefiction/face-of-another-1966-tanin-no-kao.htm (accessed December 3, 2016).

30. Salvador Dalí quoted in Hans Richter, *Dada, Art and Anti-Art*, 194.

31. Georges Bataille, "Eye," in *Visions of Excess: Selected Writings, 1927–1939*, edited by Allan Stoekl (Minneapolis: University of Minnesota Press, 1985), 17.

32. Miki's ear art may also have been inspired by Méret Oppenheim's bronze sculpture *Giacometti's Ear* (1933).

33. Alexandra Munroe, *Japanese Art After 1945: Scream Against the Sky* (New York : H. N. Abrams, 1994), 195.

34. Munroe, 198. See also Doryun Chong, "Tokyo 1955–1970: A New Avant-Garde," in *Tokyo 1955–1970: A New Avant-Garde*, edited by Doryun Chong (New York: Museum of Modern Art, 2012), 58.

35. Munroe, 198.

36. Keiko I. McDonald, "Stylistic Experiment: Teshigahara's *The Face of Another*," in *From Book to Screen: Modern Japanese Literature in Films* (Armonk, N.Y.: M.E. Sharpe, 2000), 278.

37. Michel Chion, *Audio-Vision: Sound on Screen*, translated by Claudia Gorbman (New York: Columbia UP, 1994), 57.

38. Later, when Okuyama meets Dr. Hori at a nightclub to discuss his experiences with the mask, the same waltz is played again but this time it is performed diegetically by a live band with a Japanese singer who sings German lyrics that resonate strongly with the discussion at hand: "I see your face before me,/Yet I no longer recognize you./Where are you? Where are you? The you I knew yesterday./I saw you in the fog/As if through frosted glass./You were so near and yet so far away./You glistened in the moonlight/As if your skin were made of glass./You were good to me and yet you were a stranger."

39. Rear projection is used to create a number of extraordinarily surreal scenes. In one scene, a door in the middle of the doctor's office (that seems to lead to nowhere) opens by itself to reveal an extreme close-up of a woman's long hair floating on the shoreline like seaweed—perhaps an intimation of the suicide that takes place later in the film involving a parallel narrative about an atomic bomb survivor from Nagasaki with disfiguring facial scars. In another example, a woman (probably the doctor's wife) flies around the city on a bed, dodging buildings. In each case, the surreal interrupts the everyday without forewarning, making us question what it is that we are seeing.

40. The doubling of shots, settings, and snippets of dialogue, in which Okuyama is reinserted into nearly identical scenes, creates a strong sense

of cinematic déjà vu that is strongly reminiscent of Buñuel's use of repetition in *The Exterminating Angel* (*El ángel exterminador*, 1962).

41. Also known as *X-ray of My Skull*. See https://www.sfmoma.org/artwork/96.188 (accessed July 31, 2017).

42. On Oppenheim, see Wood, 42–47; Renée Riese Hubert, "From *Déjeuner en fourrure* to *Caroline*: Meret Oppenheim's Chronicle of Surrealism," in *Surrealism and Women*, 37–49; and Robert J. Belton, "Androgyny: Interview with Meret Oppenheim," in *Surrealism and Women*, 63–75.

43. For a discussion of how the genre of the portrait is parodied in the art of other surrealists, see Adamowicz, 141–55. The fact that Oppenheim's X-ray self-portrait displays rings on her hand and earrings dangling from her ears probably also references the intersection of X-rays and fashion that accompanied the early introduction of X-ray technology. According to Stanley Reiser, "New York women of fashion had X-rays taken of their hands covered with jewelry, to illustrate that 'beauty is of the bone and not altogether of the flesh.' 'Women Not Afraid,' read one headline, as single women clasped hands with their beaux for sentimental X-ray photographs, and married women gave bony portraits of their hands to relatives as family souvenirs." See Stanley Joel Reiser, *Medicine and the Reign of Technology* (Cambridge; New York: Cambridge University Press, 1978), 61. See also Lisa Cartwright, *Screening the Body: Tracing Medicine's Visual Culture* (Minneapolis: University of Minnesota Press, 1995), 115.

44. Chion, 128.

45. Akira Mizuta Lippit, *Atomic Light (Shadow Optics)* (Minneapolis: University of Minnesota Press, 2005), 87.

46. Ibid., 29–30.

47. Catherine Waldby, *The Visible Human Project: Informatic Bodies and Post-Human Medicine* (London: Routledge, 2000), 91.

48. Translation mine.

49. Teshigahara remarked in interviews that the doctor was another part of Okuyama.

50. Steven T. Brown, *Theatricalities of Power: The Cultural Politics of Noh* (Stanford, Calif.: Stanford University Press, 2001), 27–28. See also Komparu Kunio, *The Noh Theater: Principles and Perspectives*, translated by Jane Corddry (New York: Walker/Weatherhill, 1983), 227–28; Nakamura Yasuo, *Noh: The Classical Theatre*, translated by Don Kenny (New York: Walker/Weatherhill, 1971), 214.

51. Komparu, 126.

52. WWWJDIC Japanese Dictionary Server, s.v. "*bakeru*," http://nihongo. monash.edu/cgi-bin/wwwjdic?1F (accessed on December 3, 2016).

53. Director Alan Parker would later pay homage to this scene in the movie *Pink Floyd: The Wall* (1982).

54. Quandt, "Video Essay."

55. Yoshio Sugimoto, *An Introduction to Japanese Society*, 3rd ed. (Cambridge: Cambridge University Press, 2010), 33.

56. Jane M. Bachnik, "Time, Space and Person in Japanese relationships," in *Interpreting Japanese Society: Anthropological Approaches*, edited by Joy Hendry (London; New York: Routledge, 1998), 107–08.

57. Takeo Doi, *The Anatomy of Self: The Individual Versus Society* (Tokyo; New York: Kodansha International, 1986), 25.

58. Doi, 26.

59. As Doi points out, the concepts of *omote* and *ura* are strongly correlated with the concepts of *soto* (outside) and *uchi* (inside). See Doi, 29; Bachnik, 108.

60. Doi, 33.

61. James Quandt, "*The Face of Another*: Double Vision," *The Criterion Collection.* https://www.criterion.com/current/posts/592-the-face-of-another-double-vision (accessed November 15, 2016).

62. Kōbō Abe, *The Face of Another*, translated by E. Dale Saunders (New York: Vintage, 2003), 62. For a more detailed comparison of the *Face of Another* novel and film adaptation, see McDonald, 269–86; Tomoda Yoshiyuki, *Sengo zen'ei eiga to bungaku: Abe Kōbō x Teshigahara Hiroshi* (Kyoto: Jinbun Shoin, 2012), 215–243.

63. On the significance of the young woman's keloidal scars and the function of this film-within-a-film, see Tomoda, 215–228.

64. Abe, 231.

65. Abe, 230.

66. McDonald, 283.

67. See André Breton, "Second Manifesto of Surrealism" (1930), in *Manifestoes of Surrealism*, translated by Richard Seaver and Helen R. Lane (Ann Arbor: University of Michigan Press, 1969), 180–81. In *The Phantom of Liberty* (*Le Fantôme de la liberté*, 1974), Buñuel uses incestuous relations between both aunt and nephew and brother and sister to illustrate the transgressive nature of *amour fou*. On *amour fou* in the films of Buñuel, see Peter William Evans, "An *Amour* still *fou*: Late Buñuel," in *The Unsilvered Screen: Surrealism on Film*, edited by Graeme Harper and Rob Stone (London: Wallflower, 2007b), 38–47.

68. David Sylvester, *The Brutality of Fact: Interviews with Francis Bacon* (London: Thames & Hudson, 1987), 46–47.

69. Gilles Deleuze, *Francis Bacon: The Logic of Sensation* (Minneapolis: University of Minnesota Press, 2004), 21.

70. McDonald, 284. However, I do not agree with McDonald's interpretation that "the young man's body is seen (in my view) as a vulture chained to the window"(284). The animal carcass hanging from hooks appears more bovine than avian in my opinion. See also discussion in Tomoda (236–241), who compares the scene to Luis Buñuel's surrealist comedy *L'âge d'or* (1930), in which a young woman discovers a cow in her bed.

71. Chris D., *Outlaw Masters of Japanese Film* (London; New York: I.B. Tauris, 2005), 198–99.

72. Miike Takashi, "Interview by Film Critic Wade Major," *Gozu*, directed by Miike Takashi (2003), subtitled DVD (United States: Cinema Epoch, 2009).

73. Tom Mes, "Review of *Gozu*," *Midnight Eye*, May 21, 2003b, http://www.midnighteye.com/reviews/gozu/ (accessed December 14, 2015).

74. In his crazed endeavor to take out the yakuza attack dog, Ozaki appears to have been inspired by a strange video (probably a parody of the *Ringu* video) that appears at the very outset of the film displayed on a television monitor in the restaurant. Ozaki is as mesmerized by the horribly distorted sound-image relations of the short video as he is by the dictum expressed in it, one of the most famous mottos attributed to influential Meiji-period educator William Smith Clark (1826–1886): "Boys, be ambitious [*Shōnen yo taishi o idake*]!" In the context of *Gozu*'s nontraditional, transgendered yakuza love story, "Boys, be ambitious!" effectively becomes "Boys, be ambiguous!"

75. This meta-level playfulness is reaffirmed again in a later scene when it is revealed to both Minami and the audience that the character of an American woman, who speaks Japanese very poorly, is actually reading aloud cue cards that are hanging just outside the frame, thereby demystifying the illusion of the cinematic construct even further.

76. Tom Mes, *Re-Agitator: A Decade of Writing on Takashi Miike* (Surrey, England: FAB Press, 2013), 46.

77. Jorge Bastos da Silva, "A Lusitanian Dish: Swift to Portuguese Taste," in *The Reception of Jonathan Swift in Europe*, edited by Hermann Josef Real (London, England: Thoemmes, 2005), 90.

78. André Breton, *Anthology of Black Humor*, translated by Mark Polizzotti (San Francisco: City Lights Books, 1997), xix.

79. Kurt Vonnegut, *Conversations with Kurt Vonnegut*, edited by William Rodney Allen (Jackson: University Press of Mississippi, 1988), 56.

80. Julia Kristeva, *Powers of Horror: An Essay on Abjection*, translated by Leon S. Roudiez (New York: Columbia University Press, 1982).

81. Brigid Cherry, *Horror* (London; New York: Routledge, 2009), 112.

82. Tom Mes has suggested that the incestuous sister and brother, Masa and Kazu, invoke Japanese creation mythology, offering "a degenerate version of Izanagi and Izanami, the brother and sister deities who descended from the heavens to Earth's primordial ooze and gave birth to the Japanese archipelago and its first emperor (after initially spawning a boneless miscreant named Hiruko, that is)." Mes, *Re-Agitator*, 50.

83. Mes, *Re-Agitator*, 50.

84. See Jillian Suarez, "Minotaure: Surrealist Magazine from the 1930s," Guggenheim.org, September 25, 2014, http://blogs.guggenheim.org/findings/minotaure-surrealist-magazine-1930s/ (accessed December 23, 2016).

85. Adamowicz, 97.

86. Tony Rayns, "Review of *Gozu*," *Sight & Sound*, vol. 14, no. 9 (September 2004): 64.

87. Rayns, 64.

88. André Breton quoted in Penelope Rosemont, "Introduction: All My Names Know Your Leap: Surrealist Women and Their Challenge," in *Surrealist Women: An International Anthology*, edited by Penelope Rosemont (Austin: University of Texas Press, 1998), xliv.

89. Rosemont, xliv–xlv.

90. Brian Sewell interviewed in *Dirty Dalí: A Private View*, directed by Guy Evans (2007), DVD (London: Channel 4, 2007a).

91. Hans Bellmer, *The Doll*, translated by Malcolm Green (London: Atlas Press, 2005), 125.

92. Michael Semff and Anthony Spira, "Introduction," *Hans Bellmer*, edited by Michael Semff and Anthony Spira (Ostfildern, Germany: Hatje Cantz Publishers, 2006), 10.

93. David William Foster, *Queer Issues in Contemporary Latin American Cinema* (Austin, TX: University of Texas Press, 2004), xiv–xv.

94. Mes, *Re-Agitator*, 50.

95. Tony Williams, "Takashi Miike's Cinema of Outrage," *Cineaction*, no. 64 (2004): 62.

96. Jean-Luc Nancy, *Listening*, translated by Charlotte Mandell (New York: Fordham University Press, 2007), 7.

5

In the Wake of Artaud: Cinema of Cruelty in *Audition* and *Oldboy*

> All words are lies, only pain can be trusted.
> —Asami[1]

> Without an element of cruelty at the root of every spectacle, the theater is not possible. In our present state of degeneration it is through the skin [*par la peau*] that metaphysics must be made to re-enter our minds.
> —Antonin Artaud[2]

From "Torture Porn" to "Spectacle Horror" to "Cinema of Cruelty"

In recent years, the term "torture porn," which was first coined by film critic David Edelstein for an article published in *New York Magazine* in 2006,[3] has been used to designate a subgenre of horror that emphasizes scenes of graphic, visceral violence and gore-filled imagery. Torture porn (along with the portmanteau word "gorno," combining "gore" and "porno") has been applied to ultra-violent films from around the world,

© The Author(s) 2018
S. T. Brown, *Japanese Horror and the Transnational Cinema of Sensations*,
East Asian Popular Culture, https://doi.org/10.1007/978-3-319-70629-0_5

including such standouts as *Saw* (dir. James Wan, 2004, USA/Australia), *Hostel* (dir. Eli Roth, 2005, USA), *The Devil's Rejects* (dir. Rob Zombie, 2005, USA/Germany), *Wolf Creek* (dir. Greg McLean, 2005, Australia), *Funny Games* (dir. Michael Haneke 1997/2007, Austria/USA/France/UK/Germany/Italy), *Inside* (*À l'intérieur*; dirs. Alexandre Bustillo and Julien Maury, 2007, France), *Frontier(s)* (*Frontière(s)*; dir. Xavier Gens, 2007, France/Switzerland), *Martyrs* (dir. Pascal Laugier, 2008, France/Canada), *The Human Centipede (The First Sequence)* (dir. Tom Six, 2009, Netherlands), *The Collector* (dir. Marcus Dunstan, 2009, USA), *Grotesque* (*Gurotesuku*; dir. Shiraishi Kōji, 2009, Japan), *Antichrist* (dir. Lars von Trier, 2009, Denmark/Germany/France/Sweden/Italy/Poland), *A Serbian Film* (*Srpski film*; dir. Srdjan Spasojevic, 2010, Serbia), *I Saw the Devil* (*Angmareul boatda*; dir. Kim Jee-woon, 2010, South Korea), *Cold Fish* (*Tsumetai nettaigyo*; dir. Sono Sion, 2010, Japan), *Tusk* (dir. Kevin Smith, 2014, USA), and many others.[4] According to Edelstein, "torture porn" includes the following traits: First, it contains "explicit scenes of torture and mutilation," which are gratuitous and excessive (with an emphasis on tight framing and close-ups of wounds, incisions, and various aspects of the fragmented body).[5] Second, it is part of mainstream movie culture—i.e., it is featured at the local multiplex rather than in adult movie theaters—and features solid production values and professional special effects. Third, it deals with victims who, rather than being expendable or interchangeable, are typically "decent people with recognizable human emotions."[6] Finally, torture porn places the spectator in a position to identify "with either the victim or the victimizer,"[7] or alternately shifts positions between the victim's and the victimizer's points of view, thereby "making the viewer complicit in brutal violence."[8]

Although some film scholars and critics (including Edelstein) have sought to restrict the designation "torture porn" to "a specific cycle of ultra-violent films that dominated the box office between 2004 and 2008," which express "a resounding surge in fear of terrorism and ...of our own ambivalence about torture and invasive government surveillance" in post-9/11 America,[9] the fact is that there are scores of films sharing similar traits with the subgenre of "torture porn" that both predate the most recent American cycle and have been produced in countries all over the world. Even if post-9/11 anxieties can be said to animate contemporary American horror films featuring torture and it is accepted that "the release of the Abu Ghraib prison photos did spur the escalation of uninhibited images of torture, degradation, and mutilation in film,"[10] as Isabel Pinedo has argued, that does not explain why similar films involving explicit body horror produced outside of the US both before and after 9/11 have also found audiences. In other words, while American torture porn may engage post-9/11 concerns, torture porn may also be construed as a global subgenre of horror that predates 9/11, not just an American response to the War on Terror or a cinematic allegory for American historical trauma.[11]

Moreover, it is worth noting that the term "torture porn" is not without its detractors. An increasing number of film critics and theorists have begun to openly debate the value of the term, pointing out its many shortcomings. For example, some have pointed out that the term is so imprecise as to be almost meaningless. Where is the "porn" in "torture porn"? "Torture porn" suggests an analogy between the simulated violence depicted in horror and the actual sex on display in pornography. However, there is an enormous difference between simulated violence and actual sex on film. Like the genre of melodrama, both horror and pornography may be construed as "genres of bodily excess," as Linda Williams has argued.[12] However, as Williams also suggests, insofar as horror and pornography differ both in terms of what is represented on the screen and the sort of responses that they are seeking to evoke from their respective audiences, it would be both misleading and reductive to simply conflate the two, as the term "torture porn" seems to do. More often than not, the formulation "torture porn" functions simply as an expression of moral disapproval of the role of violence in horror rather than signaling anything significant about the genre itself. By attaching the term "porn" to horror films in which sex often plays much less of a role than violence, the term "torture porn" ends up creating more confusion than clarification.

Another term, "Asia Extreme," was first introduced by UK-based distribution company Tartan Films during a marketing campaign to sell violent Asian horror around the globe between 1999 and 2008. Although Tartan Films declared bankruptcy in 2008, Kino Lorber bought the distribution rights from Palisades Tartan in 2014 and currently distributes films from the

"Asia Extreme" library. Tartan Films presented "Asia Extreme" as "A New Breed of Extreme. Extreme Action. Extreme Passion. Extreme Horror." The problem with such marketing hype is that it reduces films by diverse directors operating in different filmmaking contexts to a monolithic conception of Asian cinema that effaces their differences and cultural specificities in favor of an essentializing Orientalist stereotype that construes "extreme" Asian film as representing the inscrutable, violently irrational Orient. This is not to say that films categorized as belonging to the genre of Asian horror featuring stylized violence are unrelated, since such films frequently have transnational links with one another, freely borrowing styles, techniques, conventions, and imagery from one another, as well as from earlier horror films, both those produced across north and southeast Asia and outside of Asia altogether. However, acknowledging the transnational links between such films, which reach out to one another across their national cinema boundaries, is quite different from reducing them all to the Orientalist marketing hype associated with Tartan Films' "Asia Extreme" series.

In response to criticisms of both "torture porn" and "Asia Extreme," other terms, such as "spectacle horror" and "cinema of cruelty," have been proposed as alternatives to engage the issues raised by horror films that focus on graphic violence. For example, Adam Lowenstein defines the concept of "spectacle horror" as follows: "the staging of spectacularly explicit horror for purposes of audience admiration, provocation, and sensory adventure as much as shock or terror, but without necessarily breaking ties with narrative development or historical allegory."[13] Lowenstein argues that in spectacle horror, "identification with a victim or victimiser is not the exclusive form of viewer engagement with the film."[14] Instead of (or in addition to) identification, spectacle horror, according to Lowenstein, offers a "cinema of attractions" in film historian Tom Gunning's sense of the term, directly soliciting "spectator attention, inciting visual curiosity, and supplying pleasure through an exciting spectacle," in which "theatrical display dominates over narrative absorption, emphasizing the direct stimulation of shock or surprise at the expense of unfolding a story or creating a diegetic universe."[15]

Likewise, the term "cinema of cruelty" has also been proposed as a way of understanding such films. Cinema of cruelty is a term that is derived from the theories of surrealist poet and playwright Antonin Artaud

(1896–1948) and his conception of the Theater of Cruelty (Théâtre de la Cruauté). Artaud famously wrote in 1938 that *"without an element of cruelty [cruauté] at the root of every spectacle, the theater is not possible. In our present state of degeneration it is through the skin [par la peau] that metaphysics must be made to re-enter our minds."*[16] Artaud argued that it was only through spectacles of "cruelty" that one could "break through language in order to touch life [*briser le langage pour toucher la vie*]."[17] Much of the debate surrounding Artaud's conception of the Theater of Cruelty revolves around the status of the term "cruelty" itself. For example, in his essay "The Theater of Cruelty and the Closure of Representation," Jacques Derrida argues that, rather than calling for destruction, the cruelty evoked by Artaud is an affirmation of an "implacable necessity."[18] This position is supported by Artaud in a letter he wrote to a friend in 1932 defending his "Theater of Cruelty": "I employ the word 'cruelty' in the sense of an appetite for life, a cosmic rigor and implacable necessity [*nécessité implacable*], in the gnostic sense of a living whirlwind that devours the darkness, in the sense of that pain apart from whose ineluctable necessity [*nécessité inéluctable*] life could not continue; good is desired, it is the consequence of an act; evil is permanent."[19]

Derrida interprets this inescapable, implacable necessity as a necessary affirmation that does not yet exist, but that will be born "by separating death from birth and by erasing the name of man."[20] For Derrida, Artaud's Theater of Cruelty is not about representation, but rather that which "announces the limit of representation," "the extent to which life is unrepresentable."[21] Artaud, according to Derrida, is not interested in representing the life of an individual character, but of showing the nonrepresentable force that is life, which "carries man along with it, but is not primarily the life of man."[22] It is in this sense that Derrida reads the Theater of Cruelty as producing a "nontheological space" that is not subordinated to an author-creator or to an authorized text authored by an author-creator.[23] The playwright may be treated like God on Broadway, but not in Artaud's Theater of Cruelty. Instead of the stage serving as the mouthpiece for the playwright, Artaud envisions a theater that overthrows "the dictatorship of the writer" and "the tyranny of the text" with "the triumph of pure mise-en-scène"—privileging spectacle over speech, force over representation, and immersive spectatorship over passive consumption.[24]

Artaud defended his notion of the Theater of Cruelty against charges of sadism—"This Cruelty is a matter of neither sadism nor bloodshed, at least not in any exclusive way"—and went out of his way to redefine the term in a nonconventional sense to signify "rigor, implacable intention and decision, irreversible and absolute determination."[25] However, that is not all there is to it. As Derrida acknowledges, "Nevertheless, there is always a murder at the origin of cruelty, of the necessity named cruelty. And, first of all, a parricide. The origin of theater, such as it must be restored, is the hand lifted against the abusive wielder of the logos, against the father, against the God of a stage subjugated to the power of speech and text."[26] Even as Artaud sought to distance the Theater of Cruelty from "bloodshed," arguing that "it is not the cruelty we can exercise upon each other by hacking at each other's bodies, carving up our personal anatomies, or, like Assyrian emperors, sending parcels of human ears, noses, or neatly detached nostrils through the mail,"[27] the program of suitable topics that he outlined in his "First Manifesto" makes it clear that the Theater of Cruelty is not above violent spectacle, even if it does not require "bodily laceration."[28]

Among other suggestions, Artaud proposed adapting both "*the story of Bluebeard reconstructed according to the historical records and with a new idea of eroticism and cruelty*" and "*a Tale by the Marquis de Sade, in which the eroticism will be transposed, allegorically mounted and figured, to create a violent exteriorization of cruelty, and a dissimulation of the remainder.*"[29] How precisely Artaud would have staged adaptations of Bluebeard and Sade for the Theater of Cruelty is unknown since they were never produced, but at the very least his choice of subject matter is instructive since it suggests that the "cruelty" in Theater of Cruelty is not entirely devoid of "bloodshed" nor exclusively a matter of "rigor" and "implacable necessity." Artaud acknowledged as much in his "Second Manifesto" when he admitted that the cruelty he had in mind "will be bloody when necessary but not systematically so" and "is not afraid to pay life the price it must be paid."[30] In the last analysis, according to Artaud, if "it is consciousness that gives to the exercise of every act of life its blood-red color, its cruel nuance," it is also understood that, even if "cruelty is not synonymous with bloodshed," the cruelty of life is, nevertheless, "always someone's death."[31] For it is the "fundamental cruelty [*cruauté foncière*]" of "life itself," which "leads things to their ineluctable end at whatever cost."[32]

It is the rigorous cruelty of life itself that "exceeds all bounds and is exercised in the torture and trampling down of everything."[33] In this sense, Artaud's concept of cruelty = necessity = life, which "feeds upon contingencies," "cements matter together," and "molds the features of the created world," approaches something like an ontological principle: "evil is the permanent law [*le mal est la loi permanente*], and what is good is an effort and already one more cruelty added to the other."[34]

If cruelty is the ontological principle behind Artaud's Theater of Cruelty, there is also a praxis associated with the theory. Acting not simply as a reflection or representation of reality but as a force that assaults the audience's senses—"attack[ing] the spectator's sensibility on all sides"—the spectacles produced by the Theater of Cruelty perform what Artaud described as "a frightful transfer of forces from body to body [*un épouvantable transfert de forces du corps au corps*]."[35] By creating "violent physical images [to] crush and hypnotize the sensibility of the spectator" like "a whirlwind of higher forces," as he put it, Artaud sought to revolutionize theater and reconnect the audience to a more primal state of being.[36] Artaud proposed to accomplish this by deconstructing the division between stage and auditorium and placing spectators in the center of a "revolving spectacle" that would immerse them in "visual and sonorous fragments [*éclats visuels et sonores*]" of gesture, sound, light, and action.[37] By interweaving each of these elements into spectacles that physically envelop and surround the spectator—immersing the spectator "in a constant bath of light, images, movements, and noises"[38]—Artaud's Theater of Cruelty aspired to become a theater of sensations that "addresses itself to the organism by precise instruments"[39] and "wakes us up: nerves and heart."[40] It is a theater that, by "engulfing" and "physically" affecting the spectator, "gives the heart and the senses that kind of concrete bite [*morsure concrète*] which all true sensation requires."[41] Let us briefly consider each element and what it contributes to Artaud's Theater of Cruelty.

With respect to gesturality, Artaud sought to liberate "a new lyricism of gesture which, by its precipitation or its amplitude in the air, ends by surpassing the lyricism of words."[42] For Artaud, the force of gesture had the power to incite and reverberate in the very body of the spectator.[43] Similarly, Artaud proposed employing sound and music like a snakecharmer, treating "spectators like the snakecharmer's subjects and conduct[ing] them *by means of their organisms* to an apprehension of the subtlest notions" so that their bodies respond to sonic vibrations like the bodies of snakes touching the earth.[44] "In this spectacle," Artaud writes, "the sonorisation is constant: sounds, noises, cries are chosen first for their vibratory quality."[45] However, for such "sonorisation" to be most effective, Artaud advised that one must know "how to intersperse from time to time a sufficient extent of space stocked with silence and immobility."[46] Artaud saw a similar, albeit luminous, power in lighting: "*The particular action of light upon the mind, the effects of all kinds of luminous vibration must be investigated, along with new ways of spreading the light in waves, in sheets, in fusillades of fiery arrows. The color gamut of the equipment now in use is to be revised from beginning to end. In order to produce the qualities of particular musical tones, light must recover an element of thinness, density, and opaqueness, with a view to producing the sensations of heat, cold, anger, fear, etc.*"[47] Finally, Artaud believed in the "dynamism of action": "here the theater, far from copying life, puts itself whenever possible in communication with pure forces. And whether you accept or deny them, there is nevertheless a way of speaking which gives the name of 'forces' to whatever brings to birth images of energy in the unconscious, and gratuitous crime on the surface."[48]

Rather than invoking a Wagnerian conception of "*Gesamtkunstwerk*" ("total work of art") to express the ideal unification of all works of art through the theater (dance, music, and poetry along with architecture, sculpture, and painting), it is noteworthy that Artaud stresses instead the importance of "dissonance" to his conception of Theater of Cruelty:

> These means, which consist of intensities of colors, lights, or sounds, which utilize vibration, tremors, repetition, whether of a musical rhythm or a spoken phrase, special tones or a general diffusion of light, can obtain their full effect only by the use of *dissonances*. But instead of limiting these dissonances to the orbit of a single sense, we shall cause them to overlap from one sense to the other, from a color to a noise, a word to a light, a fluttering gesture to a flat tonality of sound, etc.[49]

Such dissonances are not confined to "a single sense," but pass synesthetically "from one sense to the other," sacrificing unity at the alter of discord and embracing inharmonious difference no matter how harsh it may be perceived.

Even in the most violent of actions staged in the Theater of Cruelty, Artaud saw the potential for "a kind of lyricism," which had the power to summon up "supernatural images, a bloodstream of images, a bleeding spurt of images in the poet's head and in the spectator's as well."[50] Artaud was convinced that the theater would "never find itself again" unless it learned to furnish the spectator "with the truthful precipitates of dreams, in which his taste for crime, his erotic obsessions, his savagery, his chimeras, his utopian sense of life and matter, even his cannibalism, pour out, on a level not counterfeit and illusory, but interior."[51] Artaud sought to rouse theater from its slumber and transform it into something "that will shake the organism to its foundations and leave an ineffaceable scar."[52] Rather than "lulling the viewer to sleep within the safe-zone of voyeuristic pleasure," Brent Strang has argued that the Theater of Cruelty is "designed to disrupt the spectator from indolent passivity."[53]

If Artaud sometimes likened the Theater of Cruelty to "plague," it was not because it was "contagious," but rather "because like the plague it is the revelation, the bringing forth, the exteriorization of a depth of latent cruelty by means of which all the perverse possibilities of the mind, whether of an individual or a people, are localized."[54] However, just as importantly, Artaud argued that it was only by witnessing spectacles of cruelty in the safe space of the theater that one could disarm the impulse towards violence that humans sometimes experience in life: "I defy any spectator to whom such violent scenes will have transferred their blood," wrote Artaud, "the violence and blood having been placed at the service of the violence of the thought—I defy that spectator to give himself up, once outside the theater, to ideas of war, riot, and blatant murder."[55]

Although Artaud distinguished such spectacles of cruelty from outright sadism and went out of his way to distance the Theater of Cruelty from cinema, which he criticized for "murdering us with second-hand reproductions,"[56] some have suggested that the best example of Artaud's Theater of Cruelty today may, indeed, be found in cinema, where filmmakers from Pier Paolo Pasolini to Sam Peckinpah, from Luis Buñuel to Quentin Tarantino, have extended Artaud's conception of the Theater of Cruelty to film. Take, for example, Pasolini, the director of the notorious *Salò, or the 120 Days of Sodom* (1975), which tracks the extreme violence and cruelty of a group of wealthy, sadistic fascists after the fall of Mussolini, who wrote that he conceived of *Salò* as "a film in the genre of Artaud's theater of cruelty, since it was designed to express that power that transforms individuals into objects, fascist power, the anarchy of power, the power of consumption."[57] It is in this sense Pasolini contended that "a film modeled on the theater of cruelty" could be "directly political."[58]

Likewise, in his essay "Toward a Cinema of Cruelty," William Blum, who was one of the earliest scholars to recognize the potential of Artaud's theories for film, has argued that by offering a "vehicle for cruelty" that approaches "the function of a social tool" in films such as *The Wild Bunch* (1969), Sam Peckinpah "pays life the price it must be paid by extolling the beauty in the horrible," such that "the more horrible it becomes, the more beautiful, and the more cathartic."[59] In this way, Blum argues, by "submitting to the experience of a work of Cruelty," Peckinpah compels the spectator to acknowledge "that forces exist inside you beyond your control, forces that can make you tear out a man's throat or burn his children."[60]

Although he does not acknowledge the influence of Artaud, the renowned French film critic and theorist André Bazin, who first coined the term "cinema of cruelty" (*cinéma de la cruauté*) in an essay about Erich von Stroheim published in 1949, was clearly thinking of Artaud when he suggested that directors such as Stroheim and Buñuel aim at a higher truth in their films that "transcends morality and sociology, at a metaphysical reality—the cruelty of the human condition."[61] For Bazin, the "presence of beauty in the midst of atrocity (and which is by no means only the beauty of atrocity)" in the cinema of cruelty is there to inspire "neither sadistic satisfaction nor pharisaical indignation in its audiences," but rather to transform "the taste for the horrible, the sense of cruelty, the seeking out of the extreme aspects of life" itself into a recognition of "human nobility" even in degradation.[62]

However, not everyone is convinced that the cinema is the best place for the Theater of Cruelty to work its magic. Indeed, some Artaud scholars have severely criticized attempts to extend Artaud's Theater of Cruelty to contemporary directors such as Quentin Tarantino. For example, in his essay "Cinemas of Cruelty?" Francis Vanoye argues:

If we want to stay close to Artaud while betraying him, as we must, since we are trying to promote a cinema of cruelty, we must exclude all pure and simple representations of cruelty (Sergio Leone?), all reductions of cruelty to violence, crude sadism and blood, we must therefore exclude a good part of the cinematographic production of the past and especially the present. Quentin Tarantino, for example, and his emulators, French or American, who make of cruelty an object of representation and of spectatorial pleasure.[63]

But was there ever a "pure and simple" representation of cruelty? Do not such attempts to exclude filmmakers from Leone to Tarantino, who explore the forces of cruelty so disturbingly in their films, end up sanitizing Artaud's Theater of Cruelty and its "bleeding spurt of images"? Is not violent cinema just as capable of "inspir[ing] us with the fiery magnetism of its images,"[64] as Artaud claimed for the Theater of Cruelty? Vanoye is free to select which proponents of the "cinema of cruelty" are most faithful to Artaud (he includes Buñuel, Pasolini, Ingmar Bergman, David Lynch, and Naruse Mikio) and whom he thinks should be excluded for their lack of faith to Artaud (in addition to Leone and Tarantino, he mentions Alfred Hitchcock, Oliver Stone, and Michael Haneke). However, as Derrida reminds us, we must always remember that the Theater of Cruelty remains an impossible theater: "[O]ne comes to understand very quickly that fidelity is impossible. There is no theater in the world today which fulfills Artaud's desire. And there would be no exception to be made for the attempts made by Artaud himself."[65]

The same could very well be said of the cinema of cruelty; and yet, as I argue in this chapter, the cinema of cruelty remains a productive concept that also resonates with the dynamics of violent spectacle on display in some forms of Asian horror cinema. With the twists and turns of Artaud's conception of the Theater of Cruelty and its application to cinema firmly in mind, the rest of this chapter will focus on the juxtaposition of two case studies—the boundary-pushing Japanese horror *Audition* (*Ōdishon*; dir. Miike Takashi, 1999) and the Korean horror *Oldboy* (*Oldeuboi*; dir. Park Chan-wook, 2003)—each of which offers engagements with extreme violence and cruelty but was released just before the American cycle of "torture porn" films. Here it should be acknowledged that Miike and Park are hardly strange bedfellows, since they both served as poster boys for Tartan Films' "Asia Extreme" series, an association that was cemented by their inclusion (along with Fruit Chan) in the omnibus *Three …Extremes* (aka *San geng yi* or *Three, Monster*, 2004) (see Chap. 3 for a discussion of Miike's contribution titled *Box* in the context of doppelgänger cinema). However, rather than conflating *Audition* and *Oldboy* with "torture porn" or "Asia Extreme," I develop the concept of "cinema of cruelty" as an alternative way to talk about how these unabashedly visceral horror films resonate with the aesthetics of sensation that Artaud developed in relation to the Theater of Cruelty, arguing that they offer just the sort of "concrete bite" addressed "to the entire organism" that Artaud sought in the Theater of Cruelty.[66] I am less interested in how faithful such filmmakers are to Artaud than I am in how their engagement with the cinema of cruelty resonates with what Artaud attempted to accomplish in the Theater of Cruelty. Perhaps the strongest evidence that the violent physical images offered by such films succeed in "crush[ing] and hypnotiz[ing] the sensibility of the spectator" in the manner to which Artaud aspired in his Theater of Cruelty—like "a whirlwind of higher forces"—is that they frequently send spectators scurrying for cover or escape, either covering their eyes and ears in fear or exiting the cinema altogether in a state of shock.

Miike's Cinema of Outrage

In an essay about Miike Takashi's diverse body of work, Tony Williams asserts that Miike's films "represent a particular cinema of outrage that symbolizes a rapidly changing world facing the Japanese population today in which the worst aspects of globalization and postmodernism have called former values into question."[67] "Rather than retreat into the values of past Japanese cinema," Williams argues, "Miike's films confront the nihilistic aspect of cultural change by recognizing their dangerous implications…Miike's films represent a cinema of outrage. But they often contain more than meets the eye on a visceral level."[68] Such a description is especially applicable to Miike's notorious *Audition* (*Ōdishon*, 1999), which was the controversial filmmaker's earliest film to garner worldwide attention. It is no exaggeration to say that *Audition*, which was adapted from the novel of the same name by Murakami Ryū that was published in 1997 (with a screenplay by Tengan Daisuke), remains one of Miike's most highly acclaimed and controversial films, winning not only a number of prizes at film festivals around the world but also, occasionally, the outrage of audience members, some of whom feel a strong desire to flee the theater as quickly as possible, especially in the film's last 20 minutes. Indeed, one of the most oft-recounted anecdotes about the film's reception relates that when *Audition* was screened at the International Film Festival Rotterdam in January 2000 with the director in attendance, a female audience member angrily confronted Miike after the screening, telling him "You're sick!"[69] That Miike proudly shares such anecdotes only reinforces the film's notoriety, but it also points to the "cinema of outrage" that Williams and others regard as a defining characteristic of Miike's body of work and that *Audition* clearly warrants.

Indeed, Miike's films exemplify numerous connotations of the word "outrage" that enframe the term's history of usage in English (and its derivation from the Old French word "*ultrage*"). The noun "outrage" is defined in the Oxford English Dictionary as follows:

1. a. Mad, passionate, violent, or disorderly behaviour; confusion caused by over-excitement, disorder; violence of language, insolence. Also occas.: an instance of this.
   b. Violent clamour; an outcry, a loud cry.

2. a. An act of violence, esp. one committed against a person or against society; a violent injury or wrong; a gross indignity or affront.
   b. Violence affecting others; violent injury or harm (sometimes spec. sexual assault or rape).
   c. In extended use: gross or malicious wrong or injury done to feelings, principles, etc.: an instance of this. Also in weakened use: an action or situation which provokes indignation, shock, anger, etc.
   d. A person of extravagant appearance or behaviour; a wild or eccentric person. Now rare.

3. a. The exceeding of established or reasonable bounds; lack of moderation, extravagance, excess, esp. of food or drink; exaggeration. Also: an instance of this.

b. Excess of boldness or pride; foolhardiness, rashness; presumption.

4. A violent effort or exertion of force.
5. Fierce and overwhelming indignation, anger, etc., experienced in response to some injustice or affront.[70]

Not only does a film such as *Audition* show the audience spectacles of outrage involving "mad, passionate, violent, or disorderly behaviour," including acts of violence and other injuries committed against more than one character, along with the confusion and "fierce and overwhelming indignation" experienced by characters "in response to some injustice or affront" that is generated by such acts, but it also evokes an "outcry" in the audience, who may feel anger over the shock of what is shown, perhaps even going so far as to regard the film as having done "injury" to their feelings or having offended their moral sensibility. Indeed, if a film such as *Audition* approaches something like a "cinema of cruelty," as I contend, then the outrage felt by spectators is an essential aspect of its reception, since Artaud argued that it is only by "attack[ing] the spectator's sensibility on all sides" with "violent physical images [to] crush and hypnotize the sensibility of the spectator" like "a whirlwind of higher forces" that the audience will awaken from their consumer culture-induced slumber and reconnect to a more primal state of being.[71] Films such as *Audition* best exemplify Linda Williams's argument that horror is a "genre of bodily excess," in terms of both what is represented on the screen and the sort of responses that it seeks to evoke from the audience.[72] However, *Audition* is no less brilliant for being viscerally disturbing.

Given that *Audition* was a Japanese-Korean co-production between Japan-based Omega Project and AFDF Korea, who had just enjoyed immense success with their collaboration on the J-horror classic *Ringu*, directed by Nakata Hideo, that was released the year before *Audition*, it is not surprising that *Audition* was marketed as a horror film.[73] However, its peculiar brand of horror is quite different from the viral ghost tale offered by *Ringu*. Although there is no question that there are dread-filled scenes in *Audition* that position the film as belonging to J-horror, other genre codes also enter into the warp and weft of the film's narrative. Like so many Miike films before and after, *Audition* embraces genre bending and hybridity.

On the question of genre, Miike has been quite explicit in his refusal to adhere to genre conventions: "I don't have the common sense to acknowledge genres. Genres are for people who have to promote or critique films. As long as you are human, the bottom line of everything creative is simply to ask: why do we exist? Every theme seems to go back to that point, although I don't necessarily use that as the central theme in my films. To me, genre doesn't impose any meaning, I just want to experiment and create."[74] However, Miike's consummate manipulation of genre conventions belies his insistence that he doesn't "have the common sense to acknowledge genres." What separates Miike from conventional genre directors is his fearless experimentalism—his insistence on pushing the boundaries of genre to the breaking point, as I noted in my analysis of *Gozu* in Chap. 4. This desire to shatter genre formulae is confirmed by those who have worked with him, such as veteran Miike actor Ishibashi Renji, who attests: "When it comes to Miike, he destroys everything first and thinks about how to put it back together…. That's the difference between him and other directors. Other directors try to build something, but Miike tries to destroy [*kowashiteiku*] something."[75] In the case of *Audition*, Miike's refusal to respect the boundaries of genre expresses itself in his extraordinarily deft splicing together of multiple genres (family melodrama, romantic comedy, and body horror), whose conventions he breaks apart to reassemble into something unique.

Audition begins with an unabashedly melodramatic flashback straight out of a soap opera, introducing us to protagonist Aoyama Shigeharu (played by Ishibashi Ryō) as he anxiously watches over his wife Ryōko, who barely clings to the last moments of her life. In the novel, it is explained that Ryōko was diagnosed with an aggressive form of cancer that had spread quite rapidly. Ryōko passes away in the hospital just moments before their ten-year-old son Shigehiko arrives to deliver a handmade "get well" gift to his mother. By drawing upon melodrama's characteristic temporality of "too late!" and attendant melancholy of loss,[76] Miike underscores Aoyama's acute loneliness and the gaping hole in his life that has been left by Ryōko's passing, which he will seek to fill seven years later with a suitable mate selected from the eponymous "audition."

The melodramatic opening of the film also helps set the stage for the development of Aoyama's "victim consciousness," which will make the cruelty he suffers in the film's climax all the more horrific. As Yoshimoto Mitsuhiro has remarked with respect to the history of Japanese cinema, "melodrama clears the space for the subject who does not act but only is acted upon; that is, the Japanese have negatively constructed a subject position from which they can fall into a delusion of being innocent victims of evil doings by others."[77] Yoshimoto views the victim consciousness constructed by Japanese melodrama as not only arising out of "a disparity between modernity and modernization" but also expressing "a specific type of the so-called *ressentiment* articulating the colonial mentality of the Japanese, which has never been overcome for almost a century and a half."[78] That Aoyama is not the only character in the film who suffers from "victim consciousness" is made abundantly clear when he becomes romantically entangled with a young woman named Yamazaki Asami (Shiina Eihi) as a result of the sham audition.

Seven years after his wife's passing, middle-aged widower Aoyama is encouraged by his high-school son Shigehiko (Sawaki Tetsu) to commence dating again and look for a new wife. During a dinner discussion, in which father and son compare catching women to catching fish, Shigehiko chides his father for starting to show his age and advises him to remarry. Aoyama confesses to his son that he prefers to wait for "the big one" (which, he acknowledges, is his form of "romanticism"), but Shigehiko encourages his father to be more pragmatic. In response to his son's suggestion, Aoyama, who runs a small video production company, hatches a plan with his longtime friend and former colleague Yoshikawa Yasuhisa (Kunimura Jun), a film producer. Echoing an earlier conversation that Aoyama had at work with a colleague who shared his concerns that "the whole of Japan is lonely," Aoyama's male chauvinist friend Yoshikawa offers an equally bleak diagnosis of Japan's future as a nation-state that he attributes to the current state of gender relations, pronouncing that "Japan is finished" because of the dearth of "decent women."

It is only after being urged by his son and friend to take action that Aoyama goes from a "subject who does not act but only is acted upon" to a subject who is not only acted upon but can act. Together, Aoyama and Yoshikawa conceive a plan to locate an ideal mate for Aoyama—a hidden gem not unlike Aoyama's first wife Ryōko with an impressive range of abilities who is not too young and has received extensive training in a respectable performance art such as concert piano, singing, or ballet. Yoshikawa impresses upon Aoyama that it is essential to find someone with such training, since training breeds confidence and confidence breeds happiness. Toward that end, Yoshikawa arranges a fake audition for a film production titled *The Day after Tomorrow's Heroine* (*Asatte no hiroin*), which will provide the opportunity for Aoyama to interview and observe as many suitably qualified women as he likes and select the ideal one to ask out on a date, and, if everything works out, to be his wife.

In another era and in the hands of a different director such as Garry Marshall (*Pretty Woman, Runaway Bride, The Princess Diaries*), such material might have been fodder for a slightly off-color romantic comedy. However, with Miike at the helm, this deal between two men is decidedly creepy. By underscoring the gendered dynamics of Aoyama's contract with Yoshikawa, the fictional audition that takes place foregrounds the characteristic traits of homosociality. As I discussed in Chap. 4 in relation to Miike's surrealist yakuza horror *Gozu*, homosociality refers "to the way in which patriarchal society forges bonds between men for the orderly transference and maintenance of masculinist power."[79] In the transmission of patriarchal power between men, the heteronormative exchange of women plays a crucial role, since "heterosexual relations with women are taken as a guarantee of one's conformance with the patriarchy."[80] Although homosociality is not challenged as frontally as it is in *Gozu*, *Audition* exposes its creepy mechanisms (at one point, Aoyama tells Yoshikawa that selecting applicants is like "choosing a car") in the very staging of the audition itself. The two men underscore the value of finding a woman who is "*sunao*." Although "*sunao*" is an adjective with connotations ranging from "honest" to "docile," given the patriarchal context in which the audition takes place, it is more likely that Aoyama is looking for a woman who is more "obedient" than "frank." Whether compared to cars or fish, women are reduced to objects and commodities. The audition thereby functions as a homosocial contract between men for the acquisition of a wife.

During the audition, much to the chagrin of his friend Yoshikawa, it becomes clear that Aoyama has already selected his ideal woman even before the interviews have begun based on a sensitively written application submitted by a young woman named Asami, who eloquently describes the challenges she faced after injuring her hip and being forced to give up her dreams of one day becoming a prima ballerina. Asami describes the process of coming to terms with her disappointment as being akin to learning how to accept death, which strikes a very deep chord in Aoyama, who is impressed with her maturity. Despite Yoshikawa's explicit reservations about Asami, whose references he has had no success confirming, Aoyama begins dating Asami and becomes completely smitten with her. After a number of successful dates, Aoyama invites Asami to a seaside hotel where he intends to propose to her. There, before making love, Asami reveals the scars, both physical and emotional, that she suffered as a child at the hands of an abusive aunt and stepfather. She emphatically requests that Aoyama promise to love only her, to which he consents.

In the middle of the night, Aoyama groggily awakens only to discover that Asami has suddenly left the hotel. He asks his friend Yoshikawa to help locate her, since she has disappeared and does not answer her phone, but Yoshikawa advises Aoyama to forget about her. Aoyama refuses and thus begins his phantasmagoric descent down the rabbit hole. In his search for Asami, Aoyama visits a creepy ballet studio where she once studied and where she may have been the victim of sexual abuse. There he encounters Asami's former ballet instructor, Shimada (Ishibashi Renji), a pedophilic elderly man with prosthetic feet who asks Aoyama if he saw Asami, heard her voice, touched her body, and smelled her. Tom Mes speculates that the ballet teacher might actually be Asami's stepfather, but this is never made explicit. However, at the very least, the two abusive male figures are conflated in the imagination of Aoyama.[81] A flashback shows Shimada torturing Asami as a young girl by burning her thigh with red-hot metal chopsticks—the "*hibashi*" or "fire chopsticks" used to handle charcoal in a Japanese brazier (*hibachi*).

Next, Aoyama visits Asami's place of work, the Stone Fish (Ishi no Sakana) bar, whose name evokes and continues the fish motif shared by father and son. There he encounters another strange guide who recounts the details of a gruesome murder that took place at the Stone Fish bar more than a year ago when the owner's body was chopped up into little pieces. Insofar as the floor of the old building was tilted, blood poured out into the hallway from the bar. When police investigated and attempted to assemble the pieces, they were puzzled by what they found: three extra fingers, an extra ear, and a tongue. Aoyama hears a strange sound and turns around to experience an uncanny vision of the dismembered body parts strewn across the floor, including a detached tongue that is still wiggling. According to Freud, dismemberment becomes uncanny when a severed body part moves on its own, blurring the boundaries between animate and inanimate: "Dismembered limbs, a severed head, a hand cut off at the wrist, as in a fairy tale of Hauff's, feet which dance by themselves...all these have something peculiarly uncanny about them, especially when, as in the last instance, they prove capable of independent activity in addition."[82] Before Aoyama withdraws from this gruesome fantasy, the unnamed guide remarks, "It's a scary world, isn't it?"

Aoyama returns home from the Stone Fish bar and drinks whiskey that has apparently been drugged by Asami. As he starts to collapse unconscious from the effects of the drugged whiskey, Aoyama begins to experience a series of hallucinations in which he replays in his mind earlier dates with Asami that feature significantly revised dialogue. In these revised recollections, Asami spares none of the heart-wrenching details about the physical and sexual abuse she suffered while growing up. One of the hallucinations takes place inside of Asami's apartment, where Aoyama trips over a large burlap sack from which emerges a deformed man (Ōsugi Ren) who is missing the extra body parts that were discovered by police at the scene of the murder at the Stone Fish bar. It is strongly implied that the man in the burlap sack (or "bag man," as some critics have dubbed him) is a missing record producer named Shibata, whom Asami had listed as one of her references in her application.

The scene cuts back to Aoyama's house, where Asami proceeds to torture Aoyama in his living room. After injecting a needle into Aoyama's tongue to paralyze his body without dulling his pain receptors and inserting acupuncture needles into his chest and eyelids, Asami gleefully amputates his left foot with a wire saw (thereby rendering him physically incapable of abandoning her) and throws it against the patio door, leaving a large red bloodstain on the window. Just as Asami is preparing to cut off Aoyama's other foot, this scene of unimaginable cruelty is interrupted by Aoyama's son Shigehiko, who has just returned home only to discover to his horror the disfigured body of his father. At this moment, the scene cuts back to the seaside hotel room, where Aoyama suddenly awakens and sits upright in bed. After splashing his face with water, Aoyama returns to bed with Asami. As they lie in bed together with the birds chirping in the background, Asami tells Aoyama that she has decided to accept his proposal for marriage, which he is slightly startled to hear since he does not remember offering one. Asami considers herself the luckiest woman from the audition, since even if she "didn't become the heroine of a film," she became one in real life. Just as Aoyama falls asleep again, the scene cuts back to the house of horrors where Aoyama experiences the torture of commitment all too literally. The sudden arrival of Aoyama's son interrupts this Theater of Cruelty, bringing the film to its climax. Asami chases Aoyama's son upstairs, attempting to spray him in the face with pepper spray, but as they reach the top of the stairs, Shigehiko kicks her away and Asami falls backwards down the stairs, snapping her neck in the fall. In the end, the torturer and the tortured, the dying Asami and the disfigured Aoyama, stare deeply into one another's eyes while Asami strangely repeats brief snippets of conversation from one of their earlier dates together. The film ends with a flashback to the young Asami sitting in her bedroom as she dons her ballet slippers.

As detailed as this synopsis of *Audition* has been, what it fails to adequately convey is how the film achieves such a viscerally unsettling effect on the audience. As Tony Rayns has perceptively noted, *Audition* is "like a machine—a mechanism, if you like—that allows the viewer to project into it what he or she wants and to find in it what he or she wants but to come out of it essentially aware of ambiguities.... It's a mechanism to provoke questions and uncertainties and doubts and fears and paranoias as well."[83] To understand what makes this sound-image machine work, we need to consider how non-narrative elements weave their spell on the audience, particularly lighting and sound design.

The Color of Cruelty in *Audition*

Numerous film critics, even those who express shock at the graphic nature of the climactic scene of torture, praise *Audition*'s cinematography by Yamamoto Hideo. For example, in his review for *Variety*, despite expressing uncertainty about whether *Audition* is "a harsh critique of possessive love or a gory celebration of outright misogyny," Ken Eisner acknowledges that *Audition* is "made even more disturbing by its haunting beauty," which he attributes to the cinematography of Yamamoto whose "exquisite work lulls the viewer" into a false sense of complacency.[84] In addition to serving as director of photography for some of Miike Takashi's most accomplished and controversial films, including *Happiness of the Katakuris* (*Katakurike no kōfuku*, 2001), *Ichi the Killer* (*Koroshiya 1*, 2001), *Visitor Q* (*Bijitā Q*, 2001), *Dead or Alive* (*Dead or Alive: Hanzaisha*, 1999), and *Fudoh: The New Generation* (*Fudō*, 1996), Yamamoto also handled lensing duties on Kitano Takeshi's *Fireworks* (*Hanabi*, 1997), Shimizu Takashi's Hollywood remake of *The Grudge* (2004), and Sono Sion's *Why Don't You Play in Hell?* (*Jigoku de naze warui*, 2013).

In a perceptive essay on *Audition* included in his study *Agitator: The Cinema of Takashi Miike*, Tom Mes underscores how a subtly "off-balance" impression is created by Yamamoto's unorthodox shot selection: "Aoyama and Asami sit facing each other at a restaurant table on their first date. The conversation is obviously shot from two camera standpoints, as is the custom for dialogue scenes. However, instead of assuming two neutral points of view, Miike chooses to do only one: an over-the-shoulder shot to represent Aoyama. For Asami he uses a subjective point-of-view shot. This puts the scene somewhat off-balance and hints at something not being quite as it should be."[85] Other cinematographic choices, such as breaking the 180-degree rule in a tense dialogue scene between Aoyama and Yoshikawa, the use of "tilted horizon" (or "Dutch angle") shots to convey Aoyama's sense of disequilibrium during hallucination sequences, and the employment of extreme close-ups during the torture scenes, all work to throw the audience off-balance.

Just before the torture of Aoyama commences, Yamamoto also appears to have applied tilt-shift photography to a couple of close-up shots of

Aoyama. Distinguished from conventional shallow focus because of how selective it is, this technique makes use of a special "tilt-shift" lens that enables the cinematographer to rotate the lens plane relative to the image plane (the "tilt") while simultaneously moving the lens parallel to the image plane (the "shift"), thereby manipulating both the orientation and positioning of the plane of focus. In this way, the cinematographer can control which elements of the frame appear sharp and which ones appear out of focus even if they occupy the same relative depth of field in actual space.[86] As Asami prepares her tools of torture, two quick shots show Aoyama lying on the ground immobilized from the drugged whiskey, his face appearing in focus while his clothes are out of focus, thereby underscoring the expression of sheer terror on Aoyama's face.

In addition to the various cinematographic techniques applied, the stylized use of colored lighting and color correction to express the complex emotional and psychological dynamics at work are equally important to the look of the film and the affective responses elicited. It is nearly impossible to overstate the importance of lighting in creating the atmospherics of horror, especially the play of light and shadow and what scholars such as Isabel Pinedo have described as "the prominence of blind space in the horror film, what lurks outside the frame or unclearly within it."[87] And it probably goes without saying that the cinematic significance of light is not limited to the genre of horror. Legendary Italian director Federico Fellini once remarked that "Film is light," and generations of cinematographers could not agree more.[88] For example, renowned cinematographer Vittorio Storaro, an ardent admirer of Fellini, followed the maestro's lead by incorporating Fellini's conception of film-as-light into his influential redefinition of the role of the cinematographer. According to Storaro, who served as the director of photography on such films as *Last Tango in Paris* (dir. Bernardo Bertolucci, 1972), *Apocalypse Now* (dir. Francis Ford Coppola, 1979), *Reds* (dir. Warren Beatty, 1981), *The Last Emperor* (dir. Bernardo Bertolucci, 1987), *Dick Tracy* (dir. Warren Beatty, 1990), and *The Sheltering Sky* (dir. Bernardo Bertolucci, 1991), insofar as cinema is a "spectacle of moving images" that is "revealed by the conflict and harmony of LIGHT and SHADOW," it is only fitting "that the person who executes this intellectual work should be known as a CINEMATOGRAPHER," whom

Storaro defines as "the author who writes with light in motion [*la scrittura della luce in movimento*]."[89]

Studies of film lighting tend to focus on basic elements such as types of light sources (and their varying degrees of intensity and warmth), placement and angle of light sources, the difference between key light, fill light, and back light, hard versus soft light, low key versus high key lighting, the techniques for diffused light, bounced light, and ambient light, and the impact of different types of film stock on the capture of light, but just as important, according to Storaro, is the role played by color in lighting a scene.[90] For Storaro, the problem of light is inseparable from the problem of color. For example, when developing the color scheme for Francis Ford Coppola's romantic musical *One from the Heart* (1981), Storaro gave serious consideration not only to the potential psychological and affective significance of different colors within the film but also to their impact on the human nervous system and rate of metabolism. In this context, although he does not explicitly invoke Artaud, Storaro's comments on the affective power of lighting recall Artaud's theories about the "*particular action of light upon the mind, the effects of all kinds of luminous vibration*" that are able to produce "*the sensations of heat, cold, anger, fear, etc.,*"[91] which Artaud argued were essential to the Theater of Cruelty.

In the context of Coppola's *One from the Heart*, Storaro suggests that a hot color such as red, which is used in *One from the Heart* to symbolize sexual desire and conquest, has a tendency to increase blood pressure and metabolism.[92] In contrast, Storaro uses the color blue and its association with night to suggest rest and "a regenerative effect" that leads the autonomic nervous system "towards a decrease of its functions" and "reduced hormonal secretions."[93] Although Storaro's general assertion that the psychological and affective connotations of different colors correlate in some sense to responses from the human nervous system is supported by research on the biological and developmental aspects of color reception, current research also suggests that color reception and preference are neither hard-wired nor universal and are just as influenced by culture, sex, and age as they are by neurology.[94] Proponents of the ecological valence theory of color preference have argued that the ecological associations of colors with objects and situations, which include symbolic associations with colors that are culturally constructed, are just as important, if not more, for understanding their impact on us and why we like some colors and dislike others than are strictly biological approaches to color reception and preference.[95]

Such a view is fundamentally in sync with the theoretical positions offered by Soviet filmmaker Sergei Eisenstein (1898–1948) on the role of color in cinema. In his lectures on color in the late 1940s, Eisenstein refuted the notion that there is a strict correspondence between a particular color and a specific sound, meaning, or emotional value in the realm of art. According to Eisenstein,

> What is unique in an image and what can blend essentially with it are absolute only in the conditions of a *given* context, of a *given* iconography, of a *given* construct. How can anyone look for absolute correspondence with a colour, when you are not dealing with a total abstraction but with the actual, objective reality, to say nothing of the emotional and intellectual reality, of an image! One only has to descend for a moment from the abstract to objective phenomena and one will see that there, too, colour assumes an endless multitude of forms and is bound up with a most complex set of phenomena.[96]

For Eisenstein, the same applies to the role of color in cinema: there can be no absolute equivalence or correspondence, but only differential correlations established by the conventions and conditions associated with a particular work of filmmaking. Nevertheless, Eisenstein insisted on the significance of color in cinema, arguing that it is "important to establish *the place of colour on an equal footing with the other elements of montage* within film-making. We have identified it as the necessary and uniquely all-embracing precondition for achieving *total and genuine synchronicity between the sonic and the visual image.*"[97]

Moreover, Eisenstein suggested that, with respect to color, cinema has much to learn "from its 'elder brother': literature."[98] Most notably, Eisenstein spoke approvingly of Gogol's dynamic use of color in works such as *Dead Souls* (*Mertvye dushi*, 1842) to suggest character conflict: "In other words, the drama itself, the struggle between the characters is not confined to the structure of the plot! It also 'shows through' in colour. The very clash of colours becomes an arena of the struggle and, echoing the drama, first one colour and then another 'captures' the characters."[99] Eisenstein espoused similar techniques for cinema, asserting that "the moving image in colour is no mere piece of frivolous amusement but a force capable of profound psychological revelation."[100] To create the conditions for the "expressive movement of colour" in cinema, Eisenstein argued that the filmmaker must "separat[e] colour from what necessarily lies beneath it, to draw it out into a general feeling and make this general feeling become a subject again."[101] That is, color must be differentiated from its object for it "to acquire different meanings" and emotional values.[102] Here Eisenstein almost seems to anticipate Deleuze and Guattari's aesthetics of sensation, which I discussed in the Introduction, for whom color functions as a principal modulator of sensation. More precisely, according to Deleuze and Guattari, insofar as sensation is not construed as a perception referring to an object, "the sensation is not colored but ...coloring."[103] Here color "operates as a force," according to Barbara Kennedy, with "each tone or modulation of colour excercis[ing] a force upon a corresponding body, both in and outside of any text."[104]

Eisenstein seems to have aspired to something similar in his limited cinematic experiments with color, such as in the second part of *Ivan the Terrible* (*Ivan Groznyi*, 1958) where he and Andrei Moskvin, the cinematographer who shot all the interior scenes, applied a subtractive bipack color processing technique restricted to red and blue hues to a 16-minute sequence late in the film and again in the epilogue to provide emotional coloring to the bleakest moments of what is otherwise a black-and-white film.[105] Eisenstein also experimented with non-photographic color techniques in earlier films, such as a hand-painted red flag that was originally inserted in early prints of *Battleship Potemkin* (*Bronenosets Potemkin*, 1925) and tinted sequences in *The General Line* (*Staroe i novoe* [*General'naia liniia*], 1929).[106]

In the genre of horror, Luciano Tovoli, the cinematographer behind the lens of Dario Argento's masterpiece *Suspiria* (1977), agrees with Eisenstein on the dynamic importance of color in film and its potential for affective impact. In this connection, Argento has readily acknowledged that the vibrant color palette of *Suspiria* was heavily influenced by Walt Disney's *Snow White and the Seven Dwarfs* (1937) with which it shares not only the saturated colors of Technicolor processing but also a narrative

Fig. 5.1 The tension between red and blue in the climactic scene of *Suspiria* (dir. Dario Argento; d.p. Luciano Tovoli, 1977)

about an innocent young woman who is persecuted by an evil witch (or coven of witches as is the case in *Suspiria*). With respect to the specific color symbolism at work in *Suspiria*, Tovoli asserts that among the "alphabet of colors" he helped orchestrate to give the film a fairytale-like appearance, "red" signifies "aggression and danger, the blood that the unknown pursuer will soon force out of [a character's] body with his knife."[107] In contrast, the color "blue" signifies "the terrifying death sentence already pronounced and a color that accompanies [a character] into the sinister world of death."[108] In some scenes, the tension between saturated red and blue is played out in the same frame, such as in the climactic scene from *Suspiria* shown in Fig. 5.1, in which the protagonist Suzy Bannion (played by Jessica Harper) confronts the queen of a witches' coven who is responsible for the strange events and gruesome deaths that have occurred at a dance academy where Bannion is studying.

The poetics of color plays an equally important role in a film such as *Audition*, where the vivid power of colored lighting helps illuminate the cinema of cruelty itself. Other elements in the construction of mise-en-scène, including composition, set design, props, and costumes, also play a role in the dynamic distribution of color, but color-coded lighting—orchestrated by Miike and his cinematographer Yamamoto to influence our perception of specific scenes—plays by far the most important role in

Audition's disturbing aesthetics of cruelty. In the broadest strokes, the film develops a contrast between scenes emphasizing cool colors and those that foreground warm colors. As relations between Aoyama and Asami become more intense, the film's colors become increasingly saturated. The dynamic distribution of color throughout *Audition* takes the form not only of colored lighting, but also other color-coded elements in the construction of the mise-en-scène, including composition, set design, props, and costumes. How do color shifts alter our perception of individual scenes? What, if anything, do particular colors come to signify? To answer such questions, a sampling of how colored lighting, set design, and costuming are used throughout the film is in order.

The fact that Aoyama's surname is itself color-coded and literally translates as "blue mountain" or "green mountain" (青山) is already an etymological clue as to how strongly cool colors, including a range of blue and green hues, are associated with the character of Aoyama. We first encounter such cool colors in the blue-lit hospital hallway leading to the room where Aoyama's wife Ryōko is clinging to life. Immediately after the movie's title, we are reintroduced to Aoyama and his son Shigehiko seven years later as they fish together on the coast: shots of the ocean foreground blue and green hues, while both father and son appear in blue with Aoyama wearing a blue-and-black jacket and blue cap and Shigehiko a blue-and-black jacket with blue gloves. Shots of Aoyama wearing his blue clothing and cap against a blue sky underscore this association. The blue sky is also echoed on the cover of the screenplay for the romantic drama (*The Day after Tomorrow's Heroine*) concocted by Aoyama and his friend for the sham audition. As Aoyama sits in his car listening to the radio ad for the audition, the car's interior is lit in midnight blue tones. Studies of the ecological aspects of color preference show that in most cultures, "people generally like saturated blue because it is mainly associated with things that most people perceive as positive (e.g., clear sky and clean water)."[109] In the context of a film such as *Audition*, the association of Aoyama with blue probably reinforces the initially positive impression of his character. Even if he is about to engage in deception to select a potential mate, he comes across, basically, as a decent guy.

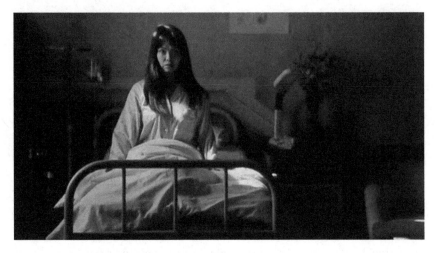

Fig. 5.2   Flashback to Aoyama's wife Ryōko in her blue-lit hospital room (*Audition*, 1999)

Back at home, when Aoyama and Shigehiko discuss women while eating the fish they caught earlier, they sit at a green dining room table. After dinner, Aoyama cleans dishes in a kitchen adorned with green cabinets. Further inside their home, Aoyama's study is decorated with blue drapes and includes a bed covered with a green bedspread. In a later scene that shows Aoyama taking the initiative to contact Asami, the blue drapes in his study occupy nearly half the screen, thereby underscoring that Aoyama is in his color-coded element. While reading Asami's application and thinking about her personal motto that "To live means to approach death gradually," a very brief flashback takes us back to Aoyama's wife sitting upright in her hospital bed with a disapproving look on her face in a scene that is bathed entirely in blue light (Fig. 5.2).

The first few audition files reviewed by Aoyama include face shots of applicants who have been photographed against blue and green backgrounds. However, by the time Aoyama gets to Asami's application, her photo stands out because she is wearing a white dress and is photographed against a mostly white background with only the slightest hint of yellow around the edges. During the audition itself, which is held in a nondescript room that is mostly white and black and lit with a slight bluish

Fig. 5.3 Asami's audition (*Audition*, 1999)

tint (including a blue door behind Aoyama and Yoshikawa), most of the applicants enter the space of the audition wearing colored clothing from across the spectrum. Asami alone is the exception, since she shows up wearing nothing but white (shirt, jacket, skirt, and shoes). She is dressed very simply—not even wearing makeup—and appears enframed by black and white geometric figures (Fig. 5.3). Through the use of shallow space and lack of a strong backlight, it almost looks as if Asami has been projected onto a screen. Indeed, Asami functions as a blank screen onto which Aoyama projects both his fantasies and fears.

Suggesting that both the novel and film versions of *Audition* were heavily influenced by early J-horror anthologies, such as the straight-to-video *Scary True Stories* (*Hontō ni atta kowai hanashi*, 1991–1992) directed by Tsuruta Norio, Tom Mes sees in the demeanor and hair styling of Asami a link with other figures from J-horror history, especially those creepy female ghosts "with long black hair hiding their face."[110] I do not doubt that this is the case, nor do I doubt Takahashi Hiroshi's claim (discussed in the introduction) that such figures also owe something to ghosts from American and British ghost movies from the 1960s and

1970s, but one should not overlook the Japanese cultural references that both precede contemporary J-horror and are interwoven with its transnational hybridity.

In addition to serving as a screen for Aoyama, Asami's white costume also functions as a citation of the figure of the vengeful female ghost with

Fig. 5.4 Sadako dressed in white in *Ringu* (1998)

Fig. 5.5 Asami dressed in white in *Audition* (1999)

long black hair wearing a white kimono that goes back to the tale of Oiwa from *Ghost Story of Yotsuya* (*Yotsuya kaidan*), arguably the best known Japanese ghost story of all time (adapted for stage and screen over 30 times), which was first performed on the kabuki stage in 1825 (written by Tsuruya Nanboku IV, 1755–1829). In Japan, white kimonos have traditionally been used to dress female corpses for burial, a centuries-old practice that continues even today. Nakata Hideo's 1998 J-horror classic *Ringu* effectively revived this motif in the costuming of Sadako (Fig. 5.4), the vengeful ghost who malevolently pursues the unlucky viewers of her cursed video. Although Asami in *Audition* never dons a white burial kimono per se, the fact that she often appears dressed in white and has long black hair resonates with this entire tradition (Fig. 5.5).

In fact, Asami dresses mostly in white throughout the entire film, but from the very beginning a poetics of color is also subtly introduced, such as in the photo that accompanies her application, which (as I noted above) includes a faint yellow halo outlining her face. In this connection, just as the etymology of Aoyama's surname is color-coded ("blue mountain"), so, too, is Asami's given name, whose etymology could be translated as "flaxen or pale yellow beauty" (麻美). Therefore, it should come as no surprise that a range of warm colors—from yellow to orange to red hues—are associated with Asami, whether produced by colored lighting, set design, or costuming. For example, although Asami dresses in white on their first date, she also wears a full-length blue-and-yellow plaid coat over the white as if to underscore her developing association with Aoyama and the fact that Aoyama is in the dominant position at this early stage of their relationship. However, when Aoyama invites Asami on a subsequent date (despite the protestations of his friend Yoshikawa, who finds it suspicious that he has not been able to reach any of her contacts to verify that she is who she claims to be), Asami wears a bright red jacket over her white dress as if to signal a change in the power dynamics between the two. It is a subtle hint that Asami is starting to gain the upper hand. As if to further underscore this shift in the dynamics of their relationship, the red that appeared only in her jacket on their previous date dominates the entire decor of the restaurant where they have dinner on their next date, appearing as a stripe across each tablecloth and completely covering the walls of the restaurant. Visually, Aoyama is enveloped on all sides by this crimson mise-en-scène. From this point forward, a tension between cool and warm colors is played out across the screen as if to suggest the struggle that is developing in the power relations between Aoyama and Asami.

As the film progresses, shots of Asami's apartment also begin to take on warmer colors. For example, when Aoyama takes Yoshikawa's advice and postpones calling her for awhile, there is a brief shot of Asami sitting in her apartment filmed diagonally from behind with the man in the burlap sack occupying the background. As Mes has noted, whether appearing as an adult or in flashbacks as a child, Asami is often filmed in a reverse diagonal shot emphasizing her back and neck, which foreshadows the broken neck she will suffer at the end of the film when she is kicked down the stairs by Shigehiko.[111] Although Asami's apartment is dominated by warm colors, especially yellow and brown hues, this color scheme is interrupted by a bedroom window illuminated by blue light with traces of bluish smoke rising up outside, suggesting that Aoyama is in Asami's thoughts even if he is presently staying away. That the blue-lit smoke outside Asami's window is strongly associated with Aoyama is further reinforced by the next two shots, which show Aoyama at home in bed, the entire scene bathed in blue. Then it cuts back to a head-and-shoulder shot of Asami in her warm-colored apartment followed by a close-up of Aoyama, who rolls over in bed looking slightly disturbed (and still bathed in blue light)—suggesting that the scenes of Asami in her apartment may be occurring in Aoyama's dreams. Then it cuts to a blue-tinted shot of Aoyama's dead wife appearing briefly from behind a tree and then receding back out of view.[112]

The next day, as Aoyama sits in his living room looking troubled, his housekeeper Rie asks him if he is ill, since he rarely takes a day off from work. Perhaps contemplating the previous night's dreams of Asami and his deceased wife, blue smoke rises from Aoyama's cigarette resting in an ashtray beside him, as if to suggest that his sense of control is also starting to dissipate. In this way, a very subtle, subconscious association is formed between the blue-hued smoke rising outside of Asami's bedroom window and the blue-hued smoke rising from Aoyama's cigarette. Mes interprets the smoke outside Asami's window as suggesting that Asami lives in an industrial area,[113] which is confirmed in the final shot of the film that flashes back to Asami's childhood where we see a large factory smokestack

Fig. 5.6 Aoyama gazes at Asami's scars in a blue-lit scene from *Audition* (1999)

outside her bedroom window; however, in terms of the poetics of color that is offered by the film, other associations are also at work.

Aoyama and Asami go to the coast for the weekend where he contemplates proposing to her. The hotel room where they are staying is initially lit in shades of blue and green with a large blue window enframing Aoyama's head as he reviews their options for the evening. However, when Asami suddenly turns off the lights to the room and offers herself to Aoyama, the dominant shade of the entire room shifts to blue. In the blue-lit hotel room, Asami asks Aoyama to gaze at her entire body, especially the scars inflicted upon her by previous abuse, and insists repeatedly that he promise to love only her (Fig. 5.6). At this crucial turning point in the film, if Asami is the one who initiates sexual relations with Aoyama, then why is blue lighting used? Perhaps it is simply that, insofar as this marks the very moment that Asami gives herself over completely to Aoyama, it appears to Aoyama that he is the one in control.

It is only when Aoyama is awakened by a telephone call from the front desk in the middle of the night to ask if he will be staying the rest of the night following the sudden departure of Asami that the cool blue-lit room suddenly takes on warm yellow, orange, and red hues. In other words, the dramatic shift in the color scheme from cool to warm colors coincides with Aoyama's discovery that Asami has suddenly departed the hotel without warning. It also signals Aoyama's gradually quickening descent down the rabbit hole as he begins to lose control of the direction his life is taking. In conjunction with the color shift, one of the things that makes *Audition* so very effective is its pacing—*Audition* lulls one into a false sense of security. Just when one starts to think that perhaps *Audition* is more romantic drama than horror, Miike pulls the rug out from underneath one. *Audition*'s film editor, Shimamura Yasushi, who has edited dozens of films for Miike, deserves substantial credit for modulating the intensity and pacing so deftly that it hits the audience like a ton of bricks when things start to go bad.

In an attempt to determine Asami's whereabouts, Aoyama visits places listed on her resume. The first stop is the Shimada Ballet Studio where Asami studied dance and where she may have been the victim of sexual abuse, which is introduced with a tilted horizon shot that is strongly color corrected in yellow-orange hues. Not only the exterior of the ballet studio but also the sky itself is bathed in unusually warm colors. The interior of the ballet studio raises the intensity a few more notches with pronounced orange-red lighting. Both the wheel-chair bound ballet instructor, Shimada, and Aoyama himself are bathed in intense blood-red lighting. Indeed, the entire ballet studio is almost completely dominated by an orange-red color scheme, the only exception being a few small windows appearing off to one side of the studio through which tiny specks of blue light dimly shine. As embers burning red-orange fly upward, we hear the crackling sound of a charcoal brazier followed by a close-up of the fire chopsticks (*hibashi*) Aoyama imagines Shimada wielded to torture the young Asami.

In his search for Asami, it is as if Aoyama himself has entered hell and Shimada is one of its demons. Given the abuses to which Asami was subjected by Shimada, this is no exaggeration. Shimada asks Aoyama if he has really looked at Asami—heard her voice, smelled her scent, and made love to her. Throughout most of their strange exchange, the ballet studio is practically burning up in red-orange lighting. However, during Aoyama's vision of Shimada torturing the young Asami with fire chopsticks, the warm color scheme suddenly shifts back to cool colors as

Shimada approaches Asami dressed in a blue kimono, as if to suggest that this nightmarish vision of Shimada the abuser is itself a projection of Aoyama's own feverish imagination. When the flashback of Shimada's abuse cuts back to the present, the orange-red lighting returns, and it is intimated that Shimada is not only the victimizer of Asami but also her victim: as he rises from his wheel chair, Shimada reveals grotesque leather prosthetic legs and feet, which imply that he, too, may have lost an appendage or two to the adult Asami.

The warm color scheme continues on the next stop of Aoyama's phantas-magoric journey to locate Asami: the Stone Fish bar where Asami claimed to work. The blinking exterior sign for the Stone Fish bar may be illuminated blue, but inside, the dominant colors are red, orange, and yellow. As Aoyama descends down the blood-red stairway in tilted horizon shots leading to the entrance of the Stone Fish bar, he encounters a strange guide who recounts the details of the gruesome murder that took place there. In blood-red lighting, Aoyama hallucinates the dismembered body parts strewn across the floor (all of which we later discover to our horror belong to the bag man who resides in Asami's apartment), including three extra fingers, an extra ear, and a tongue that is still wiggling.

Fig. 5.7 Aoyama's wife Ryōko (*left*) expresses her disapproval of Asami in a hallucination from *Audition* (1999)

After Aoyama returns home and starts hallucinating from the effects of the drugged whiskey, he begins to experience a series of flashbacks in which he replays in his mind snippets from earlier dates with Asami, featuring significantly altered dialogue. During one of those hallucinations, Aoyama recollects a previous dinner date, which is lit in an even more intensely hot fashion with the faces of both Asami and Aoyama colored dark blood-red. When Aoyama hears someone addressing him in a familiar fashion, he looks over at the next table and sees his dead wife Ryōko, his son Shigehiko, who is the same age he was when his mother died, and Shigehiko's high school girlfriend all seated with their faces lit in a similar fashion and offering looks of disapproval (Fig. 5.7). The ghost of Aoyama's wife openly expresses strong disapproval of Asami, insisting that she is not right for him and pleading with him not to marry her. A subtle low frequency rumble emerges from the subwoofer channel to reinforce the overall atmosphere of acute dread that permeates this scene, but it is the blood-red lighting that is most noticeable. Cross-cultural studies of the ecological aspects of color preference show that Americans tend to like dark red very much, whereas Japanese participants in such experiments tend to show a strong aversion to dark shades of red. The Japanese dislike of dark red stands in stark contrast to the positive symbolic associations that most Japanese have with saturated, bright red, which adorns the national flag of Japan commonly known as "Circle of the Sun" (*Hinomaru*) and is a color often used to celebrate happy occasions.[114] Although non-Japanese viewers may not respond in the same way as Japanese viewers to the dark red lighting in this scene,[115] the use of colored lighting to evoke a feeling of unpleasantness in the Japanese audience for the film is probably meant to suggest the guilt that increasingly plagues Aoyama as the movie progresses.

When Ryōko stands up from the table, the scene suddenly cuts to Asami's apartment, where Asami propositions Aoyama. This time, Asami's apartment is lit with even warmer colors (yellow, orange, and red) than previously, while the window is still illuminated blue. As Asami aggressively attempts to perform fellatio on Aoyama, her face changes first to that of Aoyama's female co-worker, Michiyo, with whom he had had a prior fling, then back to Asami, and then finally to Shigehiko's girlfriend, Misuzu, dressed in her high school uniform. The way in which the three women morph into one another in the context of Aoyama's nightmarish fantasies about Asami suggests that they function, in effect, as the dramatis personae populating Aoyama's unconscious imaginary. Moreover, their interchangeability demonstrates not only how the mechanisms of displacement and condensation operate in Aoyama's dream world, but also how deeply ingrained the sexual objectification of women is in Aoyama's unconscious.[116]

As Aoyama pushes away the sexually aggressive Asami-Michiyo-Misuzu, he trips over the man in the burlap sack. That this is the missing record producer, Shibata (played by Ōsugi Ren), who is lacking the very body parts that were found in excess at the Stone Fish bar, is confirmed by a cutaway shot that takes us back to the Stone Fish bar where Aoyama first learned of the extra body parts discovered at the crime scene. The affective tone of the scene shifts from sexual arousal to gruesome body horror to abjection as Asami vomits into a dog bowl to feed the footless bag man. The adult Asami then reverts to the young Asami in her ballet costume, who pets Shibata like a dog as he feeds on her flaxen-colored vomit. It is noteworthy that Shibata's surname is phonetically similar to "Shimada," the ballet studio owner. The phonetic association between the names of the two men suggests that those who have abused Asami (and have been abused by her) are being conflated together in Aoyama's mind in an act of displacement where multiple chains of association intersect not unlike the interchangeability of Asami, Michiyo, and Misuzu in the previous sequence. These various acts of displacement confirm that we are deep inside Aoyama's fevered unconscious, that these horrific hallucinations belong to none other than Aoyama himself, and that we should most definitely not trust the protagonist's point of view for the remainder of the film.

As the young Asami pets the disfigured Shibata, the ballet instructor Shimada emerges out of blue-hued shadows in Asami's apartment and arises from his wheelchair wearing a blue kimono. Shimada grabs a pair of fire chopsticks from the brazier (whose burning red-orange center is now enframed by a blue fringed container) and approaches Asami. As he approaches the adult Asami, the room transforms into the ballet studio, which is now bathed entirely in blue light. Shimada falls to his knees and first begs then demands that Asami dance for him. Rather than dance,

Asami sits down and spreads her legs so that Shimada may burn her inner thighs with the fire chopsticks. When Asami screams in pain, Aoyama calls out her name.

It is at this the point that the opposition that was previously established between the cool color scheme associated with Aoyama and the warm color scheme associated with Asami begins to deconstruct. That Shimada emerges from blue shadows wearing a blue kimono in a blue-lit ballet studio suggests that he is not only a construction of Aoyama's unconscious but also in some sense a substitute figure for Aoyama himself. In other words, the poetics of color that enframes this entire cinema of cruelty intimates that the abusive acts performed by Shimada against Asami, as well as the abuse to which Asami subjects him, are correlated fantasies desired by Aoyama himself. That Aoyama secretly desires both to abuse Asami and to be abused by Asami is what this cinema of cruelty illuminates most disturbingly through the play of colored light itself, bypassing the censorship of Aoyama's conscious mind and exceeding the continuity requirements of narrative cinema. Dialogue and meaning recede in importance as the Artaudian dynamics of lighting are foregrounded.

In the ballet studio—still bathed in blue light—Asami lovingly tells Shimada that "this wire cuts through bones so easily." As she decapitates Shimada with a wire saw and a cruel smile on her face, Shimada continues to play the piano. With a look of *jouissance* that crosses his face just before the moment of death, Shimada utters his last words: "You're wonderful." The color scheme quickly changes back to warm yellow and red hues in a rapid sequence of shots in which a naked Aoyama utters Asami's name while looking up at her; Aoyama's wife Ryōko says "stop" while lying on the blood-red floor of a restaurant; Aoyama's housekeeper Rie appears in a sexual embrace with Shibata (outside of his burlap sack) on the stairway inside of Aoyama's house; and Ryōko shouts "stop" again. "Men need women to support them, or they'll exhaust themselves," utters Rie as she embraces Shibata. In effect, Shibata becomes a substitute figure for Aoyama just as Rie becomes a substitute figure for Asami. The color scheme changes back to blue as Ryōko in close-up turns towards the camera while sitting on her hospital bed. This is followed by a shot of Aoyama sitting on the audition chair where Asami sat, but this time the set design has changed so that instead of being composed of a series of black squares against a white backdrop, we now see a series of blue squares against a white backdrop. The color of Aoyama's jacket also seems to have changed from black to blue. After a few more cutaway shots that demonstrate the complex pathways of association enacted by the dream-work inside of Aoyama's hallucinations, the sequence finishes with a return to the blue-lit ballet studio where Asami completes the decapitation of Shimada. As Shimada's head falls to the ground, we return to Aoyama's house, which is now infused with yellow, orange, and red hues, where Aoyama falls down backwards, the drugged whiskey finally taking full effect.

As Asami applies the wire saw to Aoyama's ankle and enthusiastically saws through the bone with the same sadistic pleasure that she decapitated Shimada, the warm-lit scene cuts to shots of Shimada (his head reattached) bathed in blue light as he pleasures himself. If Shimada is a substitute figure for Aoyama, which the lighting clearly suggests, then the masturbating Shimada intimates that this scene of torture is part and parcel of Aoyama's twisted fantasy of cruelty. Given Aoyama's feelings of guilt over betraying the memory of his dead wife, which is suggested repeatedly during the film, he must be punished for his desire to remarry.[117] Who better to punish Aoyama than Asami herself? In this sense, the figure of Asami the vengeful female torturer is a twisted masculinist fantasy haunting the dark recesses of Aoyama's unconscious.

When Aoyama's son Shigehiko returns home and discovers to his horror the disfigured body of his father, the scene cuts back to the blue-lit hotel room, where Aoyama suddenly awakens and sits upright in bed, relieved to discover that he still has two feet. This cutaway sequence back to the hotel suggests that Aoyama continues to hallucinate, but renders ambiguous what is dream and what is reality. After briefly awakening from his nightmare of torture, Aoyama goes to the hotel bathroom, which mixes warm and cool color schemes: the bathroom itself is lit pinkish-red and Aoyama's face is red; however, when Asami approaches Aoyama at the bathroom doorway to inquire about his well-being, she is enframed in blue. After splashing his face with water, Aoyama returns to bed with Asami, which is bathed in blue light. As they lie in bed together with the birds chirping in the background, Asami tells Aoyama that she has decided to accept his proposal for marriage, which he is startled to hear since he does not remember offering one. She considers herself the luckiest young woman in the world. Even if she "didn't become the heroine of a film," she became one in real life. To end it here would be a Hollywood ending of the most clichéd sort. Instead, it cuts from a close-up of Aoyama's sleeping face at the hotel to an extreme close-up shot of one of his eyes viewed upside down back home, which opens in response to Asami's sing-song mantra of "*kiri kiri kiri.*" As soon as the scene of torture resumes, the color scheme shifts back from cool blue to warm yellow, orange, and red.

Tom Mes interprets this sudden scene shift as suggesting that Aoyama has awakened from his dreamy slumber back at the hotel and is confronted by the horrific reality of his torture at the hands of Asami. Arguing against the "age-old and rather hackneyed 'it was all a dream' device," Mes views it simply as a moment of relief from the tension before returning to the unremitting reality of torture.[118] For Mes, "there simply is no escape from the reality."[119] However, one of the most challenging aspects of interpreting *Audition* is figuring out where reality ends and dreams (or hallucinations) begin, since the boundary between dream and reality is profoundly porous and ambiguous. For example, given that Asami's history of abuse is shown almost entirely in the context of Aoyama's hallucinations, doubt is cast on whether such abuse actually occurred or if Aoyama's paranoid, drug-induced mind simply imagined it. Does Aoyama really have his foot amputated? Is he still dreaming/hallucinating at the end of the film? As Robert Hyland has suggested, there are at least "two dream sequences—the drug induced metadream which occurs within the violent anxiety dream."[120] According to Hyland, one of the things that makes it so difficult to confidently ascertain the boundary between dream and reality is that "the film's expressive formal qualities are highly at odds with [its] realist sequences"[121]:

> After Aoyama has hit the ground, the film at this point reverts to a realist formal style. This treatment contrasts starkly with the overwhelming use of expressive lighting, color, music and grotesque violent imagery of the dream sequence. The film once again returns to naturalistic incandescent lighting, clear focus, long shots and long takes, and only uses close-up intercuts to reinforce certain images, that forcibly imply Asami's subsequent

"real" actions as opposed to the expressionistic depiction of violence in the dream sequence.[122]

On this view, the formal qualities of the amputation scene lead us to perceive it as real, whereas the editing of the sequence (enframed by waking up and going back to sleep) suggests otherwise. I agree with Hyland on the importance of *Audition*'s expressive formal qualities, but would argue that the poetics of color, which is established from the very outset, both reinforces and supersedes the distinction Hyland draws between "expressive lighting" and "naturalistic incandescent lighting." Construed in terms of Deleuze and Guattari's aesthetics of sensation, one might say that, if characters such as Aoyama and Asami exist as cinematic beings of sensation, it is not simply that they are symbolized by the colors associated with their characters, but rather that by entering into a resonant, color-infused mise-en-scène, they themselves become "part of the compound of sensations" that is presented by the film— they themselves become "colorized," as it were, by the film's bloc of sensations and the infernal cinema of cruelty that it presents.

Fig. 5.8   Asami prepares the syringe in a yellow-orange-hued scene from *Audition* (1999)

As Asami carries out the extended torture of Aoyama in his living room, which involves the insertion of a syringe needle into his tongue, the application of acupuncture needles to his chest and eyelids, and, finally, the amputation of his foot, the color scheme shifts back to the warm colors (yellow, orange, and red hues) that are so strongly associated with Asami (Fig. 5.8). This confirms not that the torture to which Aoyama is subjected is "real," but rather that the diegetic world is still being colored by Aoyama's imagination. In sum, if the character names are color-coded, the power relations between characters are also color-coded. In many (but not all) cases, it seems that whatever color dominates a particular scene indicates who has the upper hand in the sexual politics at that particular moment. However, as noted, it becomes increasingly difficult to decipher the power relations in scenes in which cool and hot colors are dynamically intertwined in the same shot or when the color scheme is reversed. On another level, blue may visualize Aoyama's sense of guilt over choosing a new mate; whereas, yellow-red may visualize Aoyama's masculinist anxieties about the monstrous-feminine. In other words, although warm colors are associated with Asami, they are also projections from Aoyama's unconscious, expressing his fears of a powerful woman who threatens Aoyama's control over his patriarchal world. As Hyland perceptively notes: "The film then can be read as presenting patriarchy as monstrous, but a patriarchy which is unable to face its own monstrosity, and consequently projects that monstrosity upon the innocent woman...Miike's film proposes that the monstrous feminine is in fact entirely a construct of patriarchal society's fears of the female other, compounded and confounded by male anxiety."[123]

A film such as *Audition* operates on multiple levels. On the diegetic level, what we see may be construed as both misogynist and sexist. However, at the meta-diegetic level, the film offers a critique of patriarchy and its misogynist fictions. Rather than advocating for misogyny, *Audition* exposes the very mechanisms by which women are objectified and commodified by men. Rather than being a masculinist fantasy, what *Audition* offers is a misogynist's worst nightmare about a woman scorned exacting revenge. In this dark cinema of cruelty, Aoyama comes face-to-face with the fractures of his own thinking and inability to control his life in a manner that evokes what Artaud considered the power of cinema. As

Gilles Deleuze points out in *Cinema 2: The Time-Image*, for Artaud, "what cinema advances is not the power of thought but its 'impower.'"[124] In Artaud's view, "more important than the dream" is the "powerlessness at the heart of thought."[125] According to Deleuze, Artaud "believes in cinema as long as he considers that cinema is essentially suited to reveal this powerlessness to think at the heart of thought."[126] What makes *Audition* Artaudian is that, going beyond the opposition between the abstract and the figurative, Miike's cinema of cruelty introduces us to the "dissociative force" that unlinks thought from the power of images and the "rhythm of metaphors," and confronts us instead with "multiple voices, internal dialogues, always a voice in another voice," which make it impossible "to think the whole and to think oneself."[127]

Nowhere is this "dissociative force" more apparent than in the time slippages experienced by Aoyama in the form of flashbacks and hallucinations about previous dates with Asami, Asami's childhood, and Asami's encounters with her ballet teacher in which Aoyama imagines the cruelty to which Asami has been subjected and to which she has subjected others. As Tony Rayns notes:

> I found the time slips between this reality and that reality, especially if the other reality was something that was a flashback or a reference back to something we'd seen earlier, actually more scary probably than the element of torture in the action ...but the time slips are so rapid and so momentous in their impact that actually they themselves add to the terror of the entire episode at the end of the film. You're never quite sure which is the reality... He's been tortured, is he now thinking back to that time and remembering it differently—is that why it's like that—or this torture that he's going through now, is this his fantasy—his paranoid fantasy—about what she might inflict on him, which goes through his mind at this earlier point. Are we now going back to the earlier point? Which way does the projection work? And the film doesn't make it clear. It leaves it deliberately ambiguous.[128]

It is the deft interweaving of such time slips with color-inflected scenes that gives us the keenest insight into the full extent of Aoyama's mental dislocation and his "powerlessness to think the whole."[129]

Auditioning Cruelty: Phonic Disarticulations

In an interview conducted in 2001 while *Audition* was still shocking audiences on the festival circuit, Miike was asked why he had made so few horror films. In response, Miike starts out by remarking that for him "*Audition* is not horror" because "there is no monster, it's not supernatural."[130] "It's a story about a girl who has just slightly strange emotions, so it's not impossible to understand her. She just wants the person she loves to stay by her side. She doesn't commit a big crime, she just cuts the guy's foot off."[131] However, Miike does admit that Murakami's novel (upon which the film was based) "really scared" him. As the interview develops, Miike changes his mind about whether *Audition* is or is not horror, acknowledging that he "accentuated the aspect of horror a bit more":

> In horror films, we think the horrific element is a special thing that doesn't exist in real life and that's why we can enjoy it. But there are terrifying things in life too and they are all made by human beings. Everybody has those things inside themselves. So by filming human beings, it naturally becomes a horror movie.... For example in *Audition* if the lead actress wasn't Eihi Shiina the film would be very different. She smiles when she cuts off the foot, and as a result that moment becomes real horror.[132]

Why does Asami's smile at the very moment she cuts off Aoyama's foot make it "real horror"? Quite simply because it underscores her monstrosity, much in the same way that Hannibal Lecter's wicked smile or Freddy Krueger's wry smirk in the very moment of committing horrific acts of violence confirms their status as monsters. It tells us that we are in the presence of malevolence that is self-consciously aware that it is malevolent and unabashedly affirms its malevolence. However, in the case of Asami, it is more than simply her smile while administering torture to the helpless Aoyama that underscores her figuration as the monstrous-feminine—there is also a sonic dimension that needs to be considered.

At the level of sound design, the horror of such scenes of cruelty are rendered all the more chilling by the cheerful, sing-song manner in which the actress playing Asami (Shiina Eihi) repeatedly utters the words "*kiri kiri*" as she performs her torture by acupuncture juxtaposed with

Aoyama's screams of pain and enhanced puncture sound effects. "*Kiri kiri*" is a Japanese onomatopoeia that is used to phonetically imitate the sound of something that rotates quickly or hurts sharply, probably derived from the noun "*kiri*," meaning "drill" or "auger." In Japanese, the expression "*kiri kiri itai*" is used to describe the feeling of piercing pain. In the soundtrack for *Audition*, the repetition of this word functions more as a sound effect than dialogue per se. Shiina's performance offers the perfect example of an "anempathetic effect" (*anempathique effet*) in the sense that film sound theorist Michel Chion has given to that term. According to Chion, whereas an "empathetic effect" (*empathique effet*) may be produced by music or sound that is "in harmony with the emotional climate of a scene: dramatic, tragic, melancholic, etc.," an "anempathetic effect" may be created by music or sound that is out of harmony with or indifferent to the emotional climate of a scene.[133] In the case of *Audition*, as Asami spins each acupuncture needle between her fingers during insertion into Aoyama, although the "*kiri kiri*" onomatopoeia that she repeats phonetically reinforces the impression of quick rotation and piercing pain, her cheerful intonation is emotionally out of sync with the scene of torture that Aoyama undergoes. By subjecting Aoyama to her auditory celebration of cruelty, Asami compels him to become a "resonant subject" in Jean-Luc Nancy's sense of the term, forcing Aoyama to confront the "edgy meaning of extremity [*un sens de bord et d'extrémité*]… as if the sound were precisely nothing else than this edge, this fringe, this margin."[134]

From another perspective, it may be said that Asami's "*kiri kiri*" leitmotif invokes the Artaudian potential of language to exceed its utilitarian use for the communication of meaning. As Asami herself remarks in between performing her signature onomatopoeia, "All words are lies, only pain can be trusted [*kotoba nanka uso da kedo, itami dake ga shinjirareru*]."[135] Artaud was acutely interested in the power of disarticulated speech in the Theater of Cruelty:

> To make metaphysics out of a spoken language is to make the language express what it does not ordinarily express: to make use of it in a new, exceptional, and unaccustomed fashion; to reveal its possibilities for producing physical shock; to divide and distribute it actively in space; to deal

with intonations in an absolutely concrete manner, restoring their power to shatter as well as really to manifest something; to turn against language and its basely utilitarian, one could say alimentary, sources, against its trapped-beast origins; and finally, to consider language as the form of *Incantation*.[136]

Earlier we considered Artaud's distancing of his conception of the Theater of Cruelty from the "the dictatorship of the writer" and "the tyranny of the text."[137] What Denis Hollier terms Artaud's penchant for "phonic disarticulation" is an essential technique in the Theater of Cruelty for privileging spectacle over speech and "short-circuiting representation."[138] Artaud sought to recover a notion of language that is "half-way between gesture and thought":

This language cannot be defined except by its possibilities for dynamic expression in space as opposed to the expressive possibilities of spoken dialogue. And what the theater can still take over from speech are its possibilities for extension beyond words, for development in space, for dissociative and vibratory action upon the sensibility. This is the hour of intonations, of a word's particular pronunciation. Here too intervenes (besides the auditory language of sounds) the visual language of objects, movements, attitudes, and gestures, but on condition that their meanings, their physiognomies, their combinations be carried to the point of becoming signs, making a kind of alphabet out of these signs. Once aware of this language in space, language of sounds, cries, lights, onomatopoeia, the theater must organize it into veritable hieroglyphs, with the help of characters and objects, and make use of their symbolism and interconnections in relation to all organs and on all levels.[139]

Juxtaposed with Aoyama's acute "language of cries," the anempathetic onomatopoeias expressed by Asami's "*kiri kiri*" exclamations are intoned in such a way that they take on an almost incantatory quality in the sense that Artaud sought for the Theater of Cruelty. By turning "words into incantations," Artaud argued that the voice could be expanded in such a way that words could go beyond meaning and approximate the importance they have in dreams.[140]

Nowhere is the power of phonic disarticulation—the power of deformed speech—as fully on display as it is when, just prior to losing his left foot, Aoyama hallucinates an encounter in Asami's apartment with the bag man—the record producer Shibata who is missing a tongue, two feet, and three fingers. As soon as Shibata emerges from his burlap sack and slurps down the vomit that Asami has served to him in a dog bowl, he utters, almost incomprehensibly, "Delicious [*Oishii*]!" The bag man's words are so distorted because of the loss of his tongue that his utterances sound more like babble than words conveying meaning. His thorough dehumanization is characterized by the loss of both voice and mobility. The bag man's language approaches the "glossolalia" celebrated by Artaud in the Theater of Cruelty. As Allen Weiss explains, "Glossolalia is a type of speech or babble characteristic of certain discourses of infants, poets, schizophrenics, mediums, charismatics."

> It is the manifestation of language at the level of its pure materiality, the realm of pure sound, where there obtains a total disjunction of signifier and signified. As such, the relation between sound and meaning breaks down through the glossolalic utterances; it is the image of language inscribed in its excess, at the threshold of nonsense. Thus, as a pure manifestation of expression, the meaning of glossolalia depends upon the performative, dramatic, contextual aspects of such utterances within discourse and action; meaning becomes a function of the enthusiastic expression of the body, of kinetic, gestural behaviour. In *Le Theatre et son double* Artaud already provides the rationale for the utilisation of such enunciations in his theatre of cruelty."[141]

Artaud sought to "to benumb, to charm, to arrest the sensibility" of the audience in the Theater of Cruelty by foregrounding "the vibrations and qualities of the voice" and transforming speech into something that could "pile-drive sounds."[142] The bag man's mode of utterance in *Audition* is all the more disturbing precisely because it foregrounds the materiality of language over signification, offering a "desublimation of speech into body, in opposition to the sublimation of body into meaningful speech."[143] In other words, it is the way in which the tongueless man struggles to speak—the distorted, guttural "grain of his voice"[144]—that elicits the strongest reaction rather than the meaning of what he says.

On the threshold of nonsense in *Audition*, in the midst of this scene of body horror that mixes sexual arousal with abjection, the adult Asami suddenly changes into the young Asami, who appears in her ballet costume. As the young Asami pets the bag man like a dog while he slurps up her vomit, she repeats to Aoyama the request she made in the seaside hotel room, but with the mature Asami's voice: "You'll love only me, right? Only me. [*Watashi dake o aishite kureru deshō. Watashi dake o*]." This dislocation of voice and body (an example of schizophonia)—of having the mature Asami's voice emitted from the immature Asami's body—creates an extremely uncanny effect. In response to this collapse of meaning, Aoyama collapses to the ground in horror and experiences additional visions of torture—both the torture of Asami at the hands of her ballet instructor, Shimada, and the torture and decapitation of Shimada at the hands of Asami. Soon, thereafter, the scene of cruelty returns to Aoyama's living room, where Asami resumes her torture of Aoyama before being interrupted by Aoyama's son, Shigehiko.

Audition's final example of phonic disarticulation occurs near the film's end. After Asami has been kicked down the stairs by Shigehiko in self-defense, snapping her neck in the fall, the dying Asami reiterates in a serene voice snippets of dialogue from previous dates as they gaze deeply into one another's eyes against a plaintive piano melody playing in the background: "I thought you were busy. I don't understand your business. You may think I'm a clingy sort of woman, but I've been waiting and waiting for your call. I thought I'd never see you again. I'm so happy, I can't stop smiling. I've been on my own all my life. I've never had anyone to talk to. I've never met anyone like you, so warm and comforting. You understand and accept me. No one ever did." With a similarly calm delivery, we hear Aoyama's response in voiceover (also a repetition from an earlier conversation): "It'll be hard [*tsurai*] to get over, but you'll find life is wonderful, one day. That's why we all carry on with our lives."[145] The final exchange between Asami and Aoyama is so strange that it must be either a dream or a hallucination. Their parting words offer a phonic disarticulation by dissociating the meaning of what is being said from the context of production—the horrific aftermath following a scene of cruel torture. Here intonation plays an especially important role by underscoring the enormous gap that separates the preternaturally relaxed tone of their delivery and the intense scene of cruelty that preceded and enframes it. And yet, at the same time, perhaps Aoyama's affirmation of life—even in its moments of greatest cruelty—also evokes the Nietzschean spirit that animates both Artaud's Theater of Cruelty and Miike's cinema of cruelty.

"My name is Oh Dae-su": The Mythical Force of Cruelty in *Oldboy*

Our second case study of the cinema of cruelty focuses on Park Chan-wook's notorious *Oldboy*, which was released in South Korea in 2003. *Oldboy* opens *in medias res* with an unnamed man holding onto the tie of another man, who dangles precariously backwards over the edge of a tall building in a suicide attempt. Rather than listen to the plight of the would-be suicide, the unnamed savior insists on telling his own story. Just as he is about to reveal his name, the scene flashes back to 1988, where we are introduced to a Korean businessman (the unnamed man in the prologue) who is being held at a local police station for drunkenness and disorderly conduct. The man slowly speaks his name while looking directly at the camera: "Oh Dae-su." After being released by the police, Oh Dae-su is suddenly kidnapped by someone whose identity is concealed and forced to spend the next 15 years in a prison cell that looks like a cheap hotel room. For 15 years, Oh Dae-su racks his brain in an attempt to figure out what crime he could have committed that would warrant such cruel treatment and who might seek such revenge. The passage of time is marked by a lengthy montage sequence that plays on the television in his cell, which shows a series of news events (most of them political or economic in nature) that have occurred both inside and outside of South Korea during Oh Dae-su's lengthy incarceration, including the arrest of former South Korean dictator Chun Doo-Hwan (1995), the British handover of Hong Kong to China (1997), the death of Princess Diana (1997), the International Monetary Fund's approval of South Korea's $21 billion credit line (1997), the inauguration of South Korean President Kim Dae-jung (1998), Kim Dae-Jung's visit to North Korea

(2000), the attack on the World Trade Center (2001), the World Cup co-hosted by South Korea and Japan (2002), and the election of South Korean President Roh Moo-hyun (2003). When he is finally released as inexplicably as he was kidnapped, Oh Dae-su spends the rest of the film searching for the identity of his kidnapper and the motives behind his imprisonment. In the process, Oh Dae-su suffers unimaginable cruelties—the worst of all being a revelation about his own identity and that of his lover that he will give anything to forget.

Oldboy is the second in a trilogy of films dedicated to the topic of vengeance that includes *Sympathy for Mr. Vengeance* (*Boksuneun naui geot*, 2002) and *Lady Vengeance* (*Chinjeolhan geumjassi*, 2005). *Oldboy* is loosely based on a Japanese manga of the same name written by Tsuchiya Garon and illustrated by Minegishi Nobuaki, which was first published in the Weekly Manga Action magazine between 1996 and 1998. The manga received a prestigious Eisner Award in 2007 for artistic achievement. Spike Lee directed a Hollywood remake of *Oldboy* that was released in 2013, starring Josh Brolin in the role of the ill-fated protagonist (renamed "Joe Doucett"). Park Chan-wook's *Oldboy* has been hailed by critics as "a Tarantino movie that Tarantino would be afraid to make,"[146] but this does not do justice to just how much *Oldboy* pushes the envelope and "subverts the rules of genre," as Richard Corliss put it,[147] mixing elements from different subgenres ranging from revenge horror to family melodrama, from suspense thriller to mystery, from prison film to martial arts. Like *Sympathy for Mr. Vengeance* and *Lady Vengeance*, *Oldboy* is characterized more by its genre hybridity than it is by its allegiance to any single genre; and yet it is quite instructive that it also shows up on most top ten lists for the best Asian horror films of all time. Scholars of Asian horror have been quick to recognize *Oldboy*'s singular contribution to the subgenres of revenge horror and horror of the abject. A case in point is the collection of essays edited by Jinhee Choi and Mitsuyo Wada-Marciano, titled *Horror to the Extreme: Changing Boundaries in Asian Cinema* (2009),[148] which devotes nearly 20 percent of the entire volume to essays that analyze *Oldboy* as a genre-bending illustration of revenge horror.

In addition to receiving the Grand Jury Prize at the 2004 Cannes Film Festival (the second highest award presented by the jury that was headed by Quentin Tarantino), *Oldboy* also swept the 2004 Grand Bell Awards

(South Korea's equivalent to the Academy Awards), winning five awards, including best director, best actor (for Choi Min-sik's riveting performance as Oh Dae-su), best editing, best lighting, and best music. Despite such critical acclaim, *Oldboy* the movie has also been dogged by controversy since it was learned that the perpetrator of the Virginia Tech massacre of 2007 posed for a photo holding a raised hammer in a manner similar to marketing posters for *Oldboy*. The news media immediately attempted to lay blame on *Oldboy*, even though investigators never found a shred of evidence that the mass murderer had ever even seen the movie. Needless to say, this is not the first time that cinematic violence has been blamed for real-world violence. One need only recall how quickly media critics blamed *The Matrix* (dir. Lana and Lilly Wachowski, 1999) for the Columbine massacre of 1999 or *The Basketball Diaries* (dir. Scott Kalvert, 1995) for the Paducah killings of 1997 to realize that the idea of "dangerous art"—even if it has no sociological or psychological evidence to support it—will continue to be exploited as long as it can attract an audience eager for sensationalism and easy answers to complex problems.

Is *Oldboy* a dangerous movie that will cause one to do terrible things to one's fellow human beings? I seriously doubt it. Is it a movie that will make one cringe in one's seat and provoke contemplation on the darker mysteries of the human heart in a manner similar to what Sophocles' *Oedipus Rex* did nearly 2,500 years ago when ancient Athenians presented on stage the tale of a king who killed his father, slept with his mother, and blinded himself out of shame? Perhaps we should view *Oldboy* as the modern equivalent of a Greek tragedy. If the Greeks never shied away from depicting artistic violence on stage, it is because they understood that dramatizing dysfunctional families and showing the human animal reduced to an abject state could be profoundly moving to the human spirit, provoking not a lack of compassion but a further deepening of it. Indeed, Park Chan-wook has asserted in interviews that in *Oldboy* he aspired to touch upon "the archetypes that people store in their unconscious,"[149] archetypes that the director himself views as having more in common with Greek mythology than cinematic realism. Furthermore, Park has acknowledged parallels with the myths of both Oedipus and Pandora's box: "I named Oh Daesu in *Old Boy* to remind the viewer of Oedipus. I was thinking of Greek myth or the classics."[150] For a Korean spectator, the name "Oh Dae-su" evokes the name of "Oedipus" through the phonetic proximity of the two names when "Oedipus" is transliterated into Korean, where it is pronounced "Oidipuseu."

Greek mythological analogues are also evoked by Oh Dae-su's antagonist Lee Woo-jin, the man who cruelly imprisons Oh Dae-su for 15 years without revealing his identity or purpose and orchestrates (with the help of a hypnotist) an act of incest between Oh Dae-su and his daughter, Mi-do. According to Park, Lee Woo-jin (played by Yoo Ji-tae) is "a surreal, godlike figure" whose esoteric yoga pose is supposed to evoke "the image of Apollo, based on a polytheistic religion like that of India or ancient Greece."[151] In Greek mythology, it is the oracle of Apollo at Delphi that prophesied to Laius that any son fathered by him would murder him. In an effort to elude the prophesy, when Oedipus was born to Laius's wife Jocasta, Laius had Oedipus's ankles pierced and bound together to limit his mobility, thereby providing the origin story for the name "Oidípous," which means "swollen foot." Although Laius and Jocasta intended to have the young Oedipus abandoned on a nearby mountain, he was saved by a shepherd from Corinth and eventually ends up at the house of Polybus, the king of Corinth, who adopts him as his own. Haunted by rumors that he is not truly the son of Polybus, the mature Oedipus travels to Delphi to consult the oracle of Apollo about his parentage, but the oracle ominously prophesies that he will kill his father and marry his mother.

Oldboy's mixture of Korean horror-melodrama with Greek mythology also calls to mind Artaud's embrace of *Oedipus Rex*. As Artaud argues in his essay "No More Masterpieces," "In *Oedipus Rex* there is the theme of incest and the idea that nature mocks at morality and that there are certain unspecified powers at large which we would do well to beware of, call them destiny or anything you choose. There is in addition the presence of a plague epidemic which is a physical incarnation of these powers."[152] For Artaud, the Theater of Cruelty must recover what he described as "the dark hour of certain ancient tragedies," which he saw as bringing forth "a depth of latent cruelty by means of which all the perverse possibilities of the mind, whether of an individual or a people, are localized."[153] Artaud was most interested in "extract[ing] the forces which struggle within" such ancient myths.[154] First and foremost for Artaud was "the idea of a perpetual conflict, a spasm in which life is continually lacerated, in which everything in creation rises up and exerts itself against our appointed rank."[155] By invoking "the terrible lyricism"[156] of Greek mythology, Artaud contended that the Theater of Cruelty "releases conflicts, disengages powers, liberates possibilities, and if these possibilities and these powers are dark, it is the fault not of the plague nor of the theater, but of life."[157]

By suggesting a strong analogy with Oedipus, the plight of Oh Dae-su in *Oldboy* similarly invokes such "terrible lyricism" by showing not only how Oh Dae-su becomes the plaything of dark forces beyond his comprehension, but also that as "a hero fighting against destiny," as Park Chan-wook describes him, Oh Dae-su "doesn't break but intends to go boldly to the end."[158] Like Oedipus, Oh Dae-su only learns the truth of his incest when it is too late to avoid. Also, like Oedipus, Oh Dae-su punishes himself for his transgression, but rather than gouging out his eyes, Oh Dae-su cuts out his own tongue in an effort to dissuade Lee Woo-jin from revealing his act of incest to his daughter/lover Mi-do (Kang Hye-jeong). In Artaudian terms, when Oh Dae-su is confronted by the "implacable necessity" of life's cruelty (as orchestrated by Lee Woo-jin), he does not wilt under the pressure but continues to affirm life in all its cruelty.

Spectacle of Faces

What ultimately humanizes Oh Dae-su's tragedy and its mythological proportions is the "spectacle of faces" that is paraded throughout the film, which in true Artaudian fashion privileges spectacle over speech. Even more than Teshigahara's *Face of Another*, which I discussed in relation to Deleuze and Guattari's concept of "faciality" in Chap. 4, *Oldboy* makes extensive use of close-ups of the face. As Kim Young-jin notes in passing regarding the frequent close-ups of actor Choi Min-sik, who plays the role of Oh Dae-su: "Rather than focusing on a rhythm of relaxation and tension, PARK immerses himself more and more in the use of extreme close-ups that seem to come pouring down on the screen. In the climax of *Old Boy*, close-ups of the face of CHOI as OH are edited in at regular intervals. In this film, which could be called a spectacle of faces, the close-ups of CHOI are the source of a decisive fascination."[159] Without unpacking their significance further, Kim draws our attention to such close-ups

Fig. 5.9 Close-up of Oh Dae-su's face obscured by shadows in the prologue to *Oldboy* (2003)

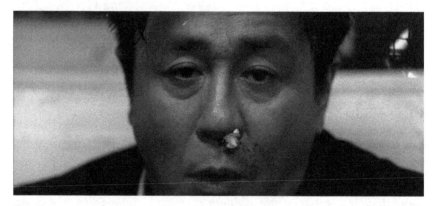

Fig. 5.10 Close-up of Oh Dae-su's face revealed at the very moment he speaks his name in a flashback at the outset of *Oldboy* (2003)

in the film's climax; however, as I will argue, the "spectacle of faces" is present throughout the film—from the very beginning.

In the film's prologue, when Oh Dae-su compels a suicidal man (played by Oh Kwang-rok) dangling off the edge of a building to listen to his story, the would-be suicide's face is shown in close-up while that of Oh Dae-su is obscured in backlit shadows (Fig. 5.9). Rather than undercutting the spectacle of faces, this concealment of Oh Dae-su's face at the outset underscores the importance of faciality all the more. Just as Oh

Dae-su is about to disclose his name ("My name is …"), the scene flashes back 15 years earlier to the police station where a drunken Oh Dae-su is being held. It is here that the past Oh Dae-su completes the sentence of the present Oh Dae-su: "My name is …Oh Dae-su." At that very moment, as both the face and name of Oh Dae-su are revealed simultaneously (Fig. 5.10), Oh Dae-su demonstrates the most important aspect of faciality, which is that one does not have a face, one slides into one: the production of a face is profoundly social, as Deleuze and Guattari observe.[160]

During the parade of close-ups that populate the screen in *Oldboy*, one of the most subtly compelling formal techniques that is selectively applied by the film's director of photography, Chung Chung-hoon, to some of the close-up shots is "tilt–shift" cinematography. As discussed earlier in relation to *Audition*, the use of tilt-shift photography enables the cinematographer to control which elements of the frame appear sharp and which ones appear out of focus even if they occupy the same relative depth of field in actual space. Tilt–shift cinematography is a technique employed in a number of Park Chan-wook's films to draw the spectator's attention to selected parts of the frame that the director chooses to emphasize for some dramatic purpose in a way that is not otherwise achievable with conventional focus techniques. For example, in his quirky twist on the vampire genre titled *Thirst*—literally, "*Bat*" (Bakjwi) in Korean—which was awarded the jury prize at the 2009 Cannes Film Festival (making Park the first South Korean director to be honored twice at Cannes, the previous time being for *Oldboy* in 2004), Park and Chung Chung-hoon, his frequent director of photography, use tilt–shift cinematography to convey the heightened senses of a Korean Roman Catholic priest-turned-vampire named Sang-hyun (Song Kang-ho), who struggles to come to terms with his newly expanding senses and desires. In one particularly memorable scene, when Sang-hyun encounters the wife (Tae-ju) of a childhood friend running barefoot at night on the empty streets outside her home to escape her boring husband and oppressive mother-in-law, the priest is aroused by the woman's pulsating veins, which come into focus while other parts of her body go out of focus, making it clear that, despite his ongoing internal ethical struggle, Sang-hyun is sizing her up as a potential lover/prey (Fig. 5.11).

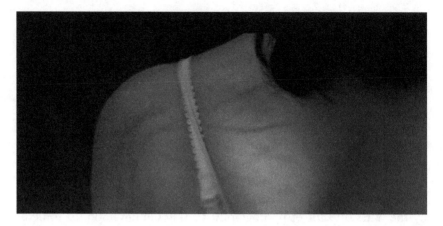

Fig. 5.11 Tilt-shift cinematography is used to selectively highlight the pulsating veins of a potential lover/prey for the priest-turned-vampire Sang-hyun in *Thirst* (2009)

In the context of *Oldboy*, tilt-shift cinematography is used quite effectively when Oh Dae-su encounters the first human face he has seen in person in 15 years: the suicidal man dangling off the edge of a building (Fig. 5.12). When Oh Dae-su first emerges from captivity and encounters another human being who is about to end his life, Oh Dae-su sniffs the man up close and presses his hands all over the man's face as if to confirm that he is human. Oh Dae-su then grabs the suicidal man's hand and rubs it across his own face to feel again the human touch that he has been sorely lacking for the past 15 years. In response, the suicidal man asks, "Even though I am no better than a beast, don't I have the right to live?" In the context of *Oldboy*'s cinema of cruelty, this practically becomes the mantra of the abject. Since Oh Dae-su himself is also profoundly abject, he repeats the world-weary man's words of wisdom back to him, but the selective focus of the tilt-shift shots at the outset of their encounter suggests that Oh Dae-su is not seeing the whole man in front of him. Oh Dae-su prevents the man from committing suicide long enough to compel him to hear his tale of imprisoned woe. However, just as the suicidal man starts to tell his own story, Oh Dae-su abruptly departs the scene, leaving the man to complete his desperate act of self-destruction alone moments later. The suicidal man's plea for compassion is echoed near the

Fig. 5.12 Tilt-shift cinematography is used to express Oh Dae-su's POV during his first encounter with another human being in 15 years in *Oldboy* (2003)

end of the film when Lee Woo-jin forces Oh Dae-su to confront his own act of incest that he has unwittingly committed with his daughter, Mi-do. Oh Dae-su repeats the suicidal man's words to Lee Woo-jin, begging him to treat him as his slave and dog in exchange for not revealing the fact of incest to Mi-do: "Even though I am no better than a beast, don't I have the right to live?" Lee Woo-jin finally relents and then takes his own life as he relives the moment of his sister's suicide in his head.

One of the most powerful close-ups of Oh Dae-su's face occurs just before Lee Woo-jin commits suicide. Lee Woo-jin had previously challenged Oh Dae-su to a cruel game: if Oh Dae-su correctly determined within five days the motives for his kidnapping and imprisonment by Lee Woo-jin, the latter would commit suicide. However, if Oh Dae-su was unable to ascertain the reason for such cruel treatment, then Lee Woo-jin would end Mi-do's life instead. In the process of his investigation, Oh Dae-su recalls that he had briefly attended the same high school as Lee Woo-jin and had once voyeuristically spied upon Lee Woo-jin and his sister Lee Soo-ah (Jin-seo Yun) engaging in incestuous relations after school in an unused classroom. Oh Dae-su spreads gossip about Lee Woo-jin and Lee Soo-ah without realizing that they are brother and sister. After Oh Dae-su transfers to another high school, the rumor becomes embellished further that Lee Soo-ah is pregnant with Lee Woo-jin's child. Despite the fact that she was probably not pregnant, Lee Soo-ah becomes

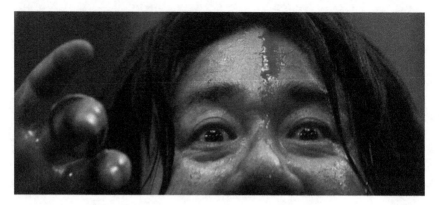

Fig. 5.13 Close-up of Oh Dae-su's face as he cuts off his own tongue in *Oldboy* (2003)

so tormented by the gossip that she started to believe in a phantom pregnancy. To end the torment, Lee Soo-ah commits suicide by falling off a bridge, which Lee Woo-jin helplessly tries to prevent in a series of close-ups that foregrounds their two faces at the tragic moment. As a result, Lee Woo-jin blames Oh Dae-su for his sister's pregnancy, telling Oh Dae-su, "Your tongue got my sister pregnant! It wasn't Lee Woo-jin's dick; it was Oh Dae-su's tongue!"

In an attempt to dissuade Lee Woo-jin from revealing Oh Dae-su's incest with Mi-do to Mi-do herself, who remains blissfully unaware, Oh Dae-su cuts off his own tongue in atonement, thereby rendering himself mute and even more abject than he already was (Fig. 5.13). Although this act of self-mutilation might be interpreted as Oh Dae-su's commitment to remain silent, the fact that he continues to emit utterly tormented and incomprehensible sounds after his tongue has been removed recalls the earlier discussion of Artaud on phonic disarticulation in relation to the bag man in *Audition*. There is no question that Oh Dae-su's disarticulated speech after removing his tongue "arrest[s] the sensibility" with the auditory language of sounds and cries, exercising the "possibilities for dynamic expression" beyond spoken dialogue (and meaning) that Artaud imagined for the Theater of Cruelty.[161] It is at such moments that, as Denis Hollier suggests, the soundtrack itself becomes "the battlefield between speech and noise, between articulated and nonarticulated sounds," where the "taming of the sound by the dialogue" and the reterritorialization of "the voice within the face on screen" become thoroughly deterritorialized, desublimating speech back into the materiality of the body.[162]

One of the most interesting aspects of the spectacle of faces in *Oldboy* is the way sound design is used to enhance the visuality of facial close-ups, giving the issue of faciality an auditory dimension. One particularly notable example will illustrate what I mean. As has already been noted, abjection plays an important role in *Oldboy* with Oh Dae-su practically functioning as the poster boy for the abject. As Julia Kristeva argues in her landmark study *Powers of Horror* (1982),[163] the abject is that which is in-between subject and object, self and other, human and animal. Abjection is linked to the emotions of revulsion, disgust, nausea, and/or horror that are felt when one is confronted with "an object that threatens to disrupt the distinction between self and other,"[164] crossing the boundaries between subject and object, the living and the dead, in disturbing ways. The abject involves that which "disturbs identity, system, order," and "does not respect borders, positions, or rules."[165] The threat of such boundary crossing may come from outside or inside. Kristeva argues that when such boundaries are crossed, a collapse of meaning occurs that produces the feeling of revulsion, which is the telltale sign that one is in the presence of abjection.

Abjection applies to all sorts of revolting figures and imagery in horror cinema, anything that confronts the self with its own mortality and potential disintegration. Classic illustrations of abjection include corpses, open wounds, decay, sewage, and all manner of bodily fluids, such as blood, vomit, urine, feces, semen, and pus. Anything a given culture describes as "dirty" or "taboo" is potentially abject. In this sense, incest, necrophilia, and bestiality are all profoundly abject. Abjection also applies to various food-related taboos, including the consumption of an animal while it is still alive,[166] as well as rotten food and spoiled milk, cannibalism, and coprophagia. Anything that makes one respond with disgust is potentially abject. In other words, the gross-out dimension to horror is not simply a cheap way of eliciting a response from the audience, it is also an engagement with the problem of abjection. According to Kristeva, the most profound modern literature and art explore "the place of the abject, a place where boundaries begin to break down, where we are confronted with an archaic space before such linguistic binaries as self/other or subject/object."[167]

In her study *The Monstrous-Feminine: Film, Feminism, Psychoanalysis* (1993), film critic Barbara Creed argues that the concept of the abject applies to horror cinema in three ways (one or more of which may be present in a given film): (1) by showing images of abjection; (2) by showing boundary crossing in the construction of the monster; and (3) by showing the maternal figure as abject, as a monstrous-feminine threat to men.[168] In analyzing the function of abjection in the horror film, Creed argues that "The horror film attempts to bring about a confrontation with the abject (the corpse, bodily wastes, the monstrous-feminine) in order finally to eject the abject and redraw the boundaries between the human and the non-human. As a form of modern defilement rite, the horror film attempts to separate out the symbolic order from all that threatens its stability."[169] According to Creed, just as important as the confrontation with the abject is the cleansing of it, the restoration of the status quo by casting out the abject or repressing it. In short, to live as human, the abject must be rejected. Which is not to say that the abject does not also serve as a source of fascination. The abject simultaneously repels and fascinates, which is why the horror genre continues to be one of the most successful in film history. Part of the appeal of the horror film, according to scholars such as Barbara Creed, is the way in which it engages the problem of the abject, creating a space in which to safely encounter the abject without falling victim to the threat posed by it, to trespass into the space of the abject without feeling the attendant shame that an association with the abject in everyday life would invariably bring.

Oh Dae-su exemplifies abjection in numerous ways—from incest to self-mutilation—but one of the film's most interesting illustrations of the abject is a strangely surreal scene that takes place while Oh Dae-su is still in captivity and has started to lose his mind. Just as Oh Dae-su learns from a television news broadcast about the brutal murder of his wife, which the police wrongly suspect was committed by the missing Oh Dae-su, an ant pokes a hole through his forearm and crawls from the inside out. This is followed by other ants that swarm all over his face. In this scene, *Oldboy* incorporates an explicit citation of the ant motif that appears in Luis Buñuel and Salvador Dalí's classic surrealist short *Un chien andalou* (An Andalusian Dog, 1929) as well as other works of surrealist art by Dalí involving ants. The surrealists were utterly fascinated—some might say obsessed—with insect imagery. Dalí practically established swarming ants as a motif, such as in the gouache-and-ink collage that was contemporaneous with *Un chien andalou*, aptly titled *The Ants* (*Las Hormigas*, 1929). In Dalí's work, ants symbolize death, decay, and irrepressible sexual desire. In the context of *Oldboy*, not only do the ants indicate that Oh Dae-su has started to hallucinate, they are also a sign of Oh Dae-su's abjection—ants crawl through Oh Dae-su's body as if he were a corpse or detritus.[170]

On the formal level, as we witness the spectacle of Oh Dae-su's abject face, a number of cinematic techniques are used to make this scene particularly disturbing, including violently shaking handheld and spin-around cinematography, extreme close-ups, adjustments to camera speed, as well as flickering lights and shadows. At the level of the soundtrack, we hear a man or animal howling, reversed voices, a jet airplane, electrical discharge noises, smashing glass, a ticking clock, as well as a plaintive string musical cue. However, what is most effective is the way in which the surround sound field is used to enhance the spectacle of Oh Dae-su's mental anguish over the murder of his wife and unjust attribution of guilt to him. By viewing the multichannel audio content of this scene through specialized surround sound meters, we can gain insight into how sound is being manipulated at the level of frequency, dynamics, and placement within the surround sound field.

In the snapshot in Fig. 5.14, the audio analysis software[171] that I have applied to this scene includes a number of different meters that visualize various aspects of the sound design. Of particular interest is (1) the vertical meter on the far left, called a "spatial spectrogram," which shows frequency mapped both along the vertical y-axis from 20 Hz–20 kHz and in terms of color (with red signifying the lowest frequencies and purple the highest), as well as the panning of sound across left, center, and right channels, and (2) the middle square meter on the bottom, called a "surround scope," which displays how a surround signal's various elements are distributed in a multichannel environment (with left, center, and right channels positioned at the top and surround channels arrayed in the middle and down towards the bottom) with frequency displayed using the same chromatic spectrum as the spatial spectrogram. As Oh Dae-su starts to suffer some sort of seizure or mental breakdown, the placement

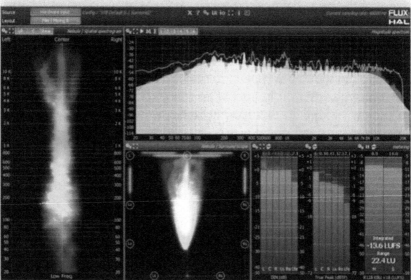

Fig. 5.14 Audio analysis software shows how sound is being manipulated at the level of frequency, dynamics, and placement within the surround sound field in *Oldboy* (2003)

of sound in the surround field starts to mimic the movement of Oh Dae-su's head in this scene—violently jerking back and forth from right to left, front to back. Sounds in the upper mid and high frequencies (3 kHz to 20 kHz) are whipped dramatically across multiple channels in the surround sound space. There is also quite a bit of activity in the bass frequencies in the 100–250 Hz range. As this happens, the spatial spectrogram in Fig. 5.14 starts to resemble a tornado, both figuratively and sonically. The impact such sound design has on audiovisual spectators is that it reinforces the feeling of disorientation as Oh Dae-su starts to lose his grip on reality.[172]

The spectacle of faces circulating throughout *Oldboy* also evokes a wide range of affective tonalities, in some cases even combining happiness and sadness in the same expression. As Deleuze notes in a discussion of the status of close-ups in *Cinema 1: The Movement-Image*, "*The affection-image is the close-up, and the close-up is the face.*"[173] For Deleuze, the face is "a large unit whose movements …express compound and mixed affections," with the "ambiguity of its expressions" capable of evoking a wide range of different affects and inviting us "to enter a 'system of emotions' which is much more subtle and differentiated, less easy to identify, capable of inducing non-human affects."[174] Nowhere is this system of compound and mixed affections more apparent than in Oh Dae-su's response to a work of art that hangs in his prison cell and with which it may be said he forms an assemblage of sorts. It is a reproduction of a famous tempera-on-canvas painting by nineteenth-century Belgian artist James Ensor, titled *The Man of Sorrows* (*L'Homme de douleurs*, 1891) (see Fig. 5.15).

Ensor (1860–1949) was a painter and printmaker known as "the painter of the masks" (*le peintre des masques*), who exerted a significant influence on twentieth-century artists belonging to the expressionist and surrealist movements. *The Man of Sorrows* combines Ensor's fascination with Japanese theatrical masks (especially grinning demon masks), Christian iconography showing the suffering Christ (dripping blood from the crown of thorns placed on his head), and figurations of the grotesque. As some viewers have noted, the expression on the face of *The Man of Sorrows* is profoundly ambiguous: is this grinning demon/suffering Christ figure laughing, weeping, or snarling? According to Herwig Todts, "Ensor, for his part, almost always used masks as a tool of revelation: the ridiculous, raw, evil, ugly or sad expression of the phantasmal masked being actually reveals their true nature."[175] But rather than conclude that "the purpose of these grotesque images [was] really to denounce bourgeois society as a whole," Todts argues instead that "research into the iconography of Ensor's work is not sufficiently advanced

Fig. 5.15 A reproduction of James Ensor's *The Man of Sorrows* (1891) hangs on the wall of Oh Dae-su's prison cell in *Oldboy* (2003)

to draw firm conclusions in this respect, for it is precisely the fundamentally grotesque nature of these representations that undermines their meaning."[176] Although I largely agree with Todts, I would suggest that it is not their "grotesque nature" that undermines meaning, but rather the mixed affections dancing upon the surface of the system of emotions presented by the face of *The Man of Sorrows* that makes meaning profoundly unstable. As Oh Dae-su stares at *The Man of Sorrows* and mimics his expression (Fig. 5.16), thereby producing resonance effects between the two, the mixed emotions conveyed by Oh Dae-su's own faciality machine are no less ambiguous. In a later scene, a dissolve between a close-up of *The Man of Sorrows* and Oh Dae-su's own face leaves no doubt as to the strong identification that has been established between the two.

Underscoring the ambiguity of *The Man of Sorrow*'s expression is an inscription in Korean that adorns the reproduction hanging on the wall in Oh Dae-su's prison cell but was never part of Ensor's painting: "Laugh, and the world laughs with you;/Weep, and you weep alone."[177] The inscription is a quotation (translated into Korean) from the poem "Solitude" by American poet Ella Wheeler Wilcox (1850–1919) from her collection *Poems of Passion* (1883). Although not quoted in *Oldboy*, the final lines of Wilcox's poem are just as applicable to the tragic plight of Oh Dae-su: "There is room in the halls of pleasure/For a large and lordly train,/But one by one we must all file on/Through the narrow aisles of pain."[178]

Fig. 5.16 Oh Dae-su mimics the facial expression of *The Man of Sorrows* in *Oldboy* (2003)

After the suicide of Lee Woo-jin, Oh Dae-su appeals to Yoo Hyung-ja (Lee Seung-shin)—the hypnotist who had hypnotized him while he was imprisoned so that he would be susceptible to post-hypnotic suggestion and commit incest with his daughter once released—to hypnotize him again so that he will forget his act of incest. In a handwritten letter to the hypnotist, Oh Dae-su reiterates the plea first made to him by the suicidal man who was about to jump off the building at the outset of the film: "Even though I am no better than a beast, don't I have the right to live?" Yoo Hyung-ja agrees and hypnotizes Oh Dae-su so that he splits into two people: the one who forgets and does not know the secret of his incestuous relationship with Mi-do will continue to live as Oh Dae-su; however, the other one who remembers this terrible secret—whom she describes in voiceover as "the monster"—will eventually disappear. In this way, the ending reiterates the film's repeated engagement with the plasticity of memory (the ability to erase and/or revise memories in acts of recollection) that has haunted the tale of Oh Dae-su since the very beginning. Indeed, the issue of memory's pliability is signaled loudly during the opening credits, where the visualization of watches and clocks that bend and twist like rubber offers a playful intermedial citation of another surrealist work by Salvador Dalí—viz., *The Persistence of Memory* (*La persistencia de la memoria*, 1931). Originally known as *Soft Watches*, Dalí's melting watches are often interpreted as offering a rejection of the conception of time as "rigid" and "deterministic," perhaps with a nod to Einstein's theory of relativity, which no longer conceived of time as uniform and absolute.[179] For Oh Dae-su, memory's pliability is a matter of life and death.

In the end, despite undergoing hypnosis to forget that Mi-do is actually his daughter so that they can go on living together without feeling guilty about the incestuous nature of their relationship, as Oh Da-esu embraces Mi-do in a snowy landscape and she tells him that she loves him (Fig. 5.17), his ambiguous expression—halfway between smiling and weeping—evokes both *The Man of Sorrows* that adorned his prison cell and the poetic caption that accompanied it, making it uncertain if the hypnosis has actually enabled Oh Dae-su to forget his cursed state or whether the mixed emotions expressed by his simultaneous laughing and weeping confirm that Oh Dae-su remains as imprisoned as ever by what Artaud described as the "fundamental cruelty [*cruauté forcière*]" of life itself, which "leads things to their ineluctable end at whatever cost."[180] In Park Chan-wook's cinema of cruelty, the liminal affective state expressed by Oh Dae-su, who is in-between smiling and weeping, suggests that even the plasticity of memory cannot exorcise Oh Dae-su's demons or enable him to avoid being haunted by the trauma of his past, since he appears destined to continue playing the role of the Man of Sorrows even if it is without the Christ figure's crown of thorns.

Fig. 5.17 Oh Dae-su mimics the ambiguous facial expression of *The Man of Sorrows* again at the end of *Oldboy* (2003)

Conclusion

Although there is no denying that the vast majority of vengeful ghosts appearing in J-horror are women, J-horror is not simply reducible to a genre devoted to "dead wet girls," as some have claimed. As is amply demonstrated by Miike Takashi's *Audition*, which is probably the most prominent J-horror film after *Ringu*, Japanese horror also creates a space for the tormented bodies and subjectivities of male characters, whose suffering is placed on display in a way that compels us to recognize that "resonant" subjects are not only gender-marked feminine. The comparative juxtaposition of *Audition* and *Oldboy* undertaken in this chapter is also instructive because it foregrounds the extent of J-horror's transnational regional influence on neighboring cinemas such as South Korea. That *Oldboy*'s director Park Chan-wook is, as he himself has readily acknowledged, a longstanding fan of Miike's body of work is confirmed by the range of techniques and tropes that Park shares with Miike's cinema of cruelty.

However, not all critics have viewed such points of contact as laudable. For example, *New York Times* film critic Manohla Dargis has famously lambasted extreme Asian cinema along the lines of *Audition* and *Oldboy* as "arty exploitation flick[s]": "Unlike the great cultural provocations, like the French theater director Antonin Artaud's Theater of Cruelty," writes Dargis, "most of what falls under the aegis of extreme cinema is devised just to distract and reaffirm the audience's existing worldview: an eye for an eye, it's a dog-eat-dog world, ad nauseam."[181] In contrast, I have argued in this chapter that the graphic violence and cruelty on display in films such as *Audition* and *Oldboy* do more than simply reaffirm the status quo or flatter "paying customers for whom the movie screen will never be anything more than a reassuring mirror."[182] Nor is the cinema of cruelty on display in such films evidence of the Orientalist stereotypes that Anglophone reviewers keep projecting onto them involving ethnic associations with sadism or "the Far East cinema's fixation on physical pain,"[183] which, as Daniel Martin points out in his study *Extreme Asia: The Rise of Cult Cinema from the Far East*, is "a stereotype that has existed in the West at least since the Second World War."[184] In sharp contrast, in this chapter,

I have tried to show how both *Audition* and *Oldboy* in their own way exemplify the very Artaudian spirit that Dargis complains is missing.

Rather than conflating *Audition* and *Oldboy* with "torture porn" or "Asia Extreme," the term "cinema of cruelty," as I have defined it, offers an alternative way to situate these unabashedly visceral horror films in relation to the aesthetics of sensation, which offer just the sort of "concrete bite" addressed "to the entire organism" that Artaud sought in the Theater of Cruelty.[185] Although *Audition* and *Oldboy* are often mentioned together as supreme examples of "Asia Extreme" cinema (and, indeed, Tartan Films' marketing campaign worked hard to foster such associations by means of the Orientalist fictions that I critiqued at the outset), such an approach barely scratches the surface of their significant areas of overlap in relation to the cinema of cruelty. Far more productive is to consider how the two films engage the cinema of cruelty in an Artaudian sense by privileging spectacle over speech, force over representation, and immersive spectatorship over passive consumption.

Both films foreground the extreme suffering of their male protagonists—Aoyama in *Audition* and Oh Dae-su in *Oldboy*—in an effort not simply to titillate or sensationalize but rather, by creating "violent physical images" that "crush and hypnotize the sensibility of the spectator" like "a whirlwind of higher forces" in the language of Artaud, to awaken audiences from their consumer culture-induced slumber and reconnect them to a more primal state of being.[186] By "giv[ing] the heart and the senses that kind of concrete bite [*morsure concrète*] which all true sensation requires,"[187] as Artaud hoped to attain in his Theater of Cruelty, such films create a cinema of sensations that "addresses itself to the organism by precise instruments"[188] that "wake us up: nerves and heart."[189] In the case of *Audition* and *Oldboy*, this is accomplished through a wide range of techniques—including effective use of extreme close-ups and the spectacle of faces, disarticulated speech and the "short-circuiting [of] representation,"[190] expressive lighting and the production of affect through luminous vibrations, as well as impactful sound design—that compels us to witness the fractures of thinking and inability to control their lives that haunts the protagonists to the point of recognizing the "powerlessness at the heart of thought."[191]

If the cinema of cruelty "releases conflicts, disengages powers, liberates possibilities, and if these possibilities and these powers are dark," as Artaud acknowledges, "it is the fault not of the plague nor of the theater, but of life."[192] According to the dark lyricism offered by both films, despite suffering so much when confronted by the "implacable necessity" of life's cruelty, the protagonists of *Audition* and *Oldboy* do not hesitate to reaffirm life in a manner that evokes the Nietzschean spirit of *amor fati* that animates Artaud's Theater of Cruelty. As Aoyama remarks in voiceover at the end of *Audition*: "It'll be hard to get over, but you'll find life is wonderful, one day. That's why we all carry on with our lives."

Notes

1. *Ōdishon*, directed by Miike Takashi (1999), translated as *Audition*, subtitled Blu-Ray (Shenley, England: Arrow Video, 2016) (translation modified).
2. Antonin Artaud, "The Theater of Cruelty (First Manifesto)," in *The Theater and Its Double*, translated by Mary Caroline Richards (New York: Grove Press, 1958), 99.
3. David Edelstein, "Now Playing at Your Local Multiplex: Torture Porn," *New York Magazine*, February 6, 2006, http://nymag.com/movies/features/15622/# (accessed February 9, 2016).
4. For a more extensive filmography of "torture porn," see Steve Jones, *Torture Porn: Popular Horror after* Saw (New York: Palgrave Macmillan, 2013), 217–222. For a discussion of earlier Japanese torture films prior to the "torture porn" cycle, see Jay McRoy, *Nightmare Japan: Contemporary Japanese Horror Cinema* (Amsterdam; New York, NY: Rodopi, 2008), 15–47.
5. Edelstein. Cf. Isabel C. Pinedo, "Torture Porn: 21st Century Horror," in *A Companion to the Horror Film*, edited by Harry M. Benshoff (Chichester, West Sussex, UK; Malden, MA, USA: Wiley Blackwell, 2014), 353.
6. Edelstein.
7. Ibid.
8. Pinedo, 345.
9. Pinedo, 345. See also Kevin J. Wetmore, "'Torture Porn' and What It Means to Be American," in *Post-9/11 Horror in American Cinema* (New York: Continuum Publishing, 2012), 95–115; Catherine Zimmer,

"Caught on Tape? The Politics of Video in the New Torture Film," in *Horror after 9/11: World of Fear, Cinema of Terror*, edited by Aviva Briefel and Sam J. Miller (Austin: University of Texas Press, 2011), 83–106; Matt Hill, "Cutting into Concepts of 'Reflectionist' Cinema? The *Saw* Franchise and Puzzles of Post-9/11 Horror," in *Horror after 9/11*, 107–123; Aaron Kerner, *Torture Porn in the Wake of 9/11: Horror, Exploitation, and the Cinema of Sensation* (New Brunswick, New Jersey: Rutgers University Press, 2015).

10. Pinedo, 357.
11. On national cinema and historical trauma, see Adam Lowenstein, *Shocking Representation: Historical trauma, National Cinema, and the Modern Horror Film* (New York: Columbia University Press, 2005), 10–12.
12. Linda Williams, "Film Bodies: Gender, Genre, and Excess," *Film Quarterly* vol. 44, no. 4 (Summer 1991): 2–13.
13. Adam Lowenstein, "Spectacle Horror and *Hostel*: Why 'Torture Porn' Does Not Exist," *Critical Quarterly* vol. 53, no. 1 (April 2011): 42.
14. Ibid., 43.
15. Tom Gunning, "The Cinema of Attractions: Early Film, Its Spectator and the Avant-Garde," in *Early Cinema: Space—Frame—Narrative*, edited by Thomas Elsaesser with Adam Barker (London: British Film Institute, 1990), 58–9.
16. Artaud, "The Theater of Cruelty (First Manifesto)," 99 (Artaud's italics).
17. Antonin Artaud, "Preface: The Theater and Culture," in *The Theater and Its Double*, translated by Mary Caroline Richards (New York: Grove Press, 1958), 13.
18. Jacques Derrida, "The Theater of Cruelty and the Closure of Representation," in *Writing and Difference*, translated by Alan Bass (London: Routledge, 2001), 292.
19. Antonin Artaud, "Letters on Cruelty," in *The Theater and Its Double*, translated by Mary Caroline Richards (New York: Grove Press, 1958), 102.
20. Derrida, 293.
21. Ibid., 294.
22. Ibid., 294.
23. Ibid., 296.
24. "The dictatorship of the writer [*la dictature de l'écrivain*]" is from Antonin Artaud, "The Theater of Cruelty (Second Manifesto)," in *The Theater and Its Double*, translated by Mary Caroline Richards

(New York: Grove Press, 1958), 124. "The tyranny of the text [*la tyrannie du texte*]" is Derrida's gloss from "The Theater of Cruelty and the Closure of Representation," 298. On "the triumph of pure mise-en-scène [*le triomphe de la mise-en-scène pure*]," see Antonin Artaud, *Œuvres complètes* (Paris: Gallimard, 1970), vol. 4, 305.

25. Artaud, "Letters on Cruelty," 101.

26. Derrida, 301.

27. Antonin Artaud, "No More Masterpieces," in *The Theater and Its Double*, translated by Mary Caroline Richards (New York: Grove Press, 1958), 79.

28. Artaud, "Letters on Cruelty," 101.

29. Artaud, "The Theater of Cruelty (First Manifesto)," 99 (Artaud's italics).

30. Artaud, "The Theater of Cruelty (Second Manifesto)," 122.

31. Artaud, "Letters on Cruelty," 101–02.

32. Ibid., 103.

33. Antonin Artaud, "Letters on Language," in *The Theater and Its Double*, translated by Mary Caroline Richards (New York: Grove Press, 1958), 114.

34. Artaud, "Letters on Cruelty," 103–04.

35. Artaud, "The Theater and Cruelty," 86; Artaud quoted in Derrida, 315.

36. Artaud, "No More Masterpieces," 82–83.

37. Antonin Artaud, "The Theater and Cruelty," in *The Theater and Its Double*, translated by Mary Caroline Richards (New York: Grove Press, 1958), 86 (translation modified).

38. Artaud, "The Theater of Cruelty (Second Manifesto)," 125.

39. Artaud, "No More Masterpieces," 83.

40. Artaud, "The Theater and Cruelty," 84.

41. Artaud, "The Theater of Cruelty (First Manifesto)," 96; "The Theater and Cruelty," 85.

42. Artaud, "The Theater of Cruelty (First Manifesto)," 91.

43. Artaud, "No More Masterpieces," 81.

44. Ibid., 81 (Artaud's italics).

45. Ibid., 81.

46. Artaud, "The Theater and Cruelty," 87.

47. Artaud, "The Theater of Cruelty (First Manifesto)," 95 (Artaud's italics).

48. Artaud, "No More Masterpieces," 82.

49. Artaud, "The Theater of Cruelty (Second Manifesto)," 125 (Artaud's italics). On "*Gesamtkunstwerk*," see Wagner's *Das Kunstwerk der Zukunft* ('The Art-Work of the Future," 1849).

50. Artaud, "No More Masterpieces," 82.

51. Artaud, "The Theater of Cruelty (First Manifesto)," 92.

52. Artaud, "No More Masterpieces," 77.

53. Brent Strang, "Beyond Genre and Logos: A Cinema of Cruelty in Dodes'ka-den and Titus," *Cinephile: The University of British Columbia's Film Journal* vol. 4 (Summer 2008): 29.

54. Antonin Artaud, "The Theater and the Plague," in *The Theater and Its Double*, translated by Mary Caroline Richards (New York: Grove Press, 1958), 30.

55. Artaud, "No More Masterpieces," 82.

56. Artaud, "The Theater and Cruelty," 84.

57. Pier Paolo Pasolini quoted in Kriss Ravetto, *The Unmaking of Fascist Aesthetics* (Minneapolis: University of Minnesota Press, 2001), 126.

58. Ibid., 126.

59. William Blum, "Toward a Cinema of Cruelty," *Cinema Journal* 10.2 (Spring 1971): 30, 32.

60. Ibid., 33.

61. André Bazin, *The Cinema of Cruelty: From Buñuel to Hitchcock*, edited by François Truffaut and translated by Sabine d'Estrée (New York: Arcade Publishing, 2013), 54.

62. Ibid., 58.

63. Francis Vanoye, "Cinemas of Cruelty?" in *Antonin Artaud: A Critical Reader*, edited by Edward Scheer (London and New York: Routledge, 2004), 181.

64. Artaud, "The Theater and Cruelty," 84.

65. Derrida, 313.

66. Artaud, "The Theater and Cruelty," 85, 87.

67. Tony Williams, "Takashi Miike's Cinema of Outrage," *Cineaction*, no. 64 (2004): 55.

68. Ibid., 55.

69. Recounted by Tony Rayns, "Damaged Romance: An Appreciation by Tony Rayns," *Ōdishon*, directed by Miike Takashi (1999), translated as *Audition*, subtitled Blu-Ray (Shenley, England: Arrow Video, 2016).

70. "Outrage," *Oxford English Dictionary Online*, Oxford University Press, http://www.oed.com.libproxy.uoregon.edu/view/Entry/133856?result =1&rskey=xKx1ma& (accessed May 10, 2017). I have outlined the

English usage of the word "outrage" since that is the term used by Tony Williams; however, it should be pointed out that there is considerable overlap between the connotations associated with the English "outrage" and the various Japanese terms for "outrage," such as *muhō, bōkō, bōgyaku, bōjō, daiaku, rōzeki,* etc.

71. Artaud, "The Theater and Cruelty," 86; Artaud, "No More Masterpieces," 82–83.

72. See Linda Williams, 2–13.

73. *Audition* appears on numerous lists for the best horror films in the history of cinema. For example, *The Guardian,* a respected British newspaper, ranks *Audition* as "the 21st Best Horror Film of All Time," positioning it just below *Dracula* (1931) and above *Blair Witch Project* (1999). See "The 25 Best Horror Films of All Time," *The Guardian* (October 22, 2010), http://www.guardian.co.uk/film/2010/oct/22/audition-miike-odishon-horror (accessed July 22, 2016).

74. Patrick Macias, *Tokyoscope: The Japanese Cult Film Companion* (San Francisco: Cadence Books, 2001), 221.

75. Interview with Ishibashi Renji, *Ōdishon,* directed by Miike Takashi (1999), translated as *Audition,* subtitled Blu-Ray (Shenley, England: Arrow Video, 2016).

76. Linda Williams, 11.

77. Mitsuhiro Yoshimoto, "Melodrama, Postmodernism, and Japanese Cinema," in *Melodrama and Asian Cinema,* edited by Wimal Dissanayake (Cambridge: Cambridge University Press, 1993), 108.

78. Yoshimoto, 106, 108.

79. David William Foster, *Queer Issues in Contemporary Latin American Cinema* (Austin, TX: University of Texas Press, 2004), xiv–xv.

80. Ibid., xiv–xv.

81. Audio commentary by Tom Mes, *Ōdishon,* directed by Miike Takashi (1999), translated as *Audition,* subtitled Blu-Ray (Shenley, England: Arrow Video, 2016).

82. Sigmund Freud, "The 'Uncanny,' " in *The Standard Edition of the Complete Psychological Works of Sigmund Freud,* edited and translated by James Strachey, vol. XVII (London: Hogarth Press, 1955), 244.

83. Rayns, "Damaged Romance."

84. Ken Eisner, Review of *Audition, Variety* (October 31, 1999), http://variety.com/1999/film/reviews/audition-1200459973/ (accessed July 27, 2016).

85. Tom Mes, *Agitator: The Cinema of Takashi Miike* (Surrey, England: FAB Press, 2003a), 184.

86. Outside of the genre of horror, tilt-shift cinematography is also used to good effect in films such as *Minority Report* (2002) and *The Assassination of Jesse James by the Coward Robert Ford* (2007).

87. Isabel Pinedo, *Recreational Terror: Women and the Pleasures of Horror Film Viewing* (Albany, NY: State University of New York Press, 1997), 53.

88. Fellini quoted in Kris Malkiewicz, *Film Lighting: Talks with Hollywood's Cinematographers and Gaffers*, 2nd ed. (New York: Simon & Schuster, 2012), 1. Fellini did, in fact, direct one horror film, titled *Toby Dammit* (1968), an adaptation of the Edgar Allan Poe story, "Never Bet the Devil Your Head" (1841), which was included in the film omnibus *Spirits of the Dead* (*Histoires extraordinaires*, 1968). Roger Vadim and Louis Malle contributed short film adaptations of other Poe stories to the same compilation.

89. Vittorio Storaro, "The Author of Cinematography; or Rather: The Right to Consider Ourselves Co-Authors of the Cinematographic Image," in Vittorio Storaro, Bob Fisher, and Lorenzo Codelli, *L'arte della cinematografia* (Milano: Skira, 2013), 8.

90. Storaro, "The Author of Cinematography," 8.

91. Artaud, "The Theater of Cruelty (First Manifesto)," 95 (Artaud's italics).

92. Vittorio Storaro quoted in "Mating Film with Video for 'One from the Heart,'" *American Cinematographer* vol. 63, no. 1 (January 1982): 24.

93. Storaro quoted in "Mating Film with Video," 24.

94. Anya Hurlbert and Angela Owen, "Biological, Cultural, and Developmental Influences on Color Preferences," in *Handbook of Color Psychology*, edited by Andrew J Elliot, Mark D Fairchild, and Anna Franklin (Cambridge: Cambridge University Press, 2015), 454–477.

95. On the ecological valence theory of color preference, see Karen B. Schloss and Stephen E. Palmer, "Ecological Aspects of Color Preference," in *Handbook of Color Psychology*, edited by Andrew J Elliot, Mark D Fairchild, and Anna Franklin (Cambridge: Cambridge University Press, 2015), 435–53. On biological approaches to color reception and preference, see Anya C. Hurlbert and Yazhu Ling, "Biological Components of Sex Differences in Color Preference," *Current Biology*, vol. 17, no. 16 (August 2007): 623–25.

96. Sergei Eisenstein, "On Colour," in *Color: The Film Reader*, edited by Angela Dalle Vacche and Brian Price (New York; London: Routledge, 2006), 107.

97. Ibid., 111 (Eisenstein's italics).

98. Ibid., 113.
99. Ibid., 113.
100. Ibid., 113.
101. Sergei Eisenstein, "From Lectures on Music and Colour in *Ivan the Terrible*," in *Sergei Eisenstein: Selected Works: Volume III: Writings, 1934–1947*, edited by Richard Taylor (London; New York: I.B. Tauris: 2010), 335.
102. Ibid., 335.
103. Gilles Deleuze and Félix Guattari, *What is Philosophy?*, translated by Hugh Tomlinson and Graham Burchell (New York: Columbia University Press, 1994), 167. See also Barbara M. Kennedy, *Deleuze and Cinema: The Aesthetics of Sensation* (Edinburgh: Edinburgh University Press, 2000), 115–117.
104. Kennedy, 117
105. On Eisenstein's use of bipack color processing, see Wheeler W. Dixon, *Black & White Cinema: A Short History* (New Brunswick, New Jersey: Rutgers University Press, 2015), 47–48; Jay Leyda, *Kino: A History of the Russian and Soviet Film* (London: Allen & Unwin, 1960), 382–384.
106. For an interesting discussion of Eisenstein's use and theories of color, see Eirik Frisvold Hanssen, "Eisenstein in Colour," *Konsthistorisk tid-skrift/Journal of Art History* vol. 73, no. 4 (2004): 212–227.
107. Tovoli quoted in Stanley Manders, "Terror in Technicolor," *American Cinematographer* vol. 91, no.2 (February 2010): 75.
108. Tovoli quoted in Manders, 75.
109. Schloss and Palmer, 436.
110. Mes commentary, *Audition*.
111. Ibid.
112. Aoyama's deceased wife Ryōko just stands there like a ghost from one of the so-called "true ghost stories" referenced by screenwriter Takahashi Hiroshi in his reflections on the early beginnings of J-horror discussed in the Introduction.
113. Mes commentary, *Audition*.
114. See Schloss and Palmer, 443; and Kazuhiko Yokosawa, Karen B. Schloss, Michiko Asano, and Stephen E. Palmer, "Ecological Effects in Cross-Cultural Differences Between U.S. and Japanese Color Preferences," *Cognitive Science* (2015): 1–27.
115. In Christian art history, the fires of hell are typically depicted as red-orange rather than dark red.

116. On fungibility as a trait of sexual objectification—i.e., treating a person as an object that is interchangeable with other objects of the same or other type—see Martha C. Nussbaum, "Objectification," *Philosophy & Public Affairs* vol. 24, no. 4 (October 1995): 257.

117. On the status of Aoyama's guilt and the film's suggestion "that Asami's 'lies' and violence are in fact created by the protagonist Aoyama's imagination in order to assuage his own guilt feelings for deceiving Asami and for letting go of his past love for his long deceased wife," see Robert Hyland, "A Politics of Excess: Violence and Violation in Miike Takashi's *Audition*," in *Horror to the Extreme: Changing Boundaries in Asian Cinema*, edited by Jinhee Choi and Mitsuyo Wada-Marciano (Hong Kong: Hong Kong University Press, 2009), 205.

118. Mes commentary, *Audition*.

119. Ibid.

120. Hyland, 213–14.

121. Ibid., 210.

122. Ibid., 212.

123. Ibid., 205. On the reception of *Audition* as a "feminist fable," see Daniel Martin, *Extreme Asia: The Rise of Cult Cinema from the Far East* (Edinburgh: Edinburgh University Press, 2015), 54–55, 57.

124. Gilles Deleuze, *Cinema 2: The Time-Image*, translated by Hugh Tomlinson and Robert Galeta (Minneapolis: University of Minnesota Press, 1989), 166.

125. Ibid., 166.

126. Ibid., 166.

127. Ibid., 167.

128. Rayns, "Damaged Romance." In his audio commentary on *Audition*, Tom Mes also notes the importance of playing with time and chronological order.

129. Deleuze, 167.

130. Miike Takashi interviewed by Kuriko Sato and Tom Mes, *Midnight Eye*, May 1, 2001b, http://www.midnighteye.com/interviews/takashi-miike/ (accessed August 14, 2016).

131. Ibid.

132. Ibid.

133. Michel Chion, *Film, A Sound Art*, translated by Claudia Gorbman (New York: Columbia UP, 2009), 477, 467.

134. Jean-Luc Nancy, *Listening*, translated by Charlotte Mandell (New York: Fordham University Press, 2007), 7; Jean-Luc Nancy, *À l'écoute* (Paris: Galilée, 2002), 21.

135. Translation modified.

136. Antonin Artaud, "Metaphysics and the *Mise-en-Scene*," in *The Theater and Its Double*, translated by Mary Caroline Richards (New York: Grove Press, 1958), 46.

137. "The dictatorship of the writer [*la dictature de l'écrivain*]" is from Artaud, "The Theater of Cruelty (Second Manifesto)," 124. "The tyranny of the text [*la tyrannie du texte*]" is Derrida's gloss from "The Theater of Cruelty and the Closure of Representation," 298.

138. Denis Hollier, "The Death of Paper, Part Two: Artaud's Sound System," in *Antonin Artaud: A Critical Reader*, edited by Edward Scheer (London and New York: Routledge, 2004), 164, 159. On "the triumph of pure mise-en-scène [*le triomphe de la mise-en-scène pure*]," see Antonin Artaud, *Œuvres complètes* (Paris: Gallimard, 1970), vol. 4, 305.

139. Artaud, "The Theater of Cruelty (First Manifesto)," 89–90.

140. Ibid., 91, 94, 85–86; Artaud, "The Theater of Cruelty (Second Manifesto)," 125.

141. Allen S. Weiss, "K," in *Antonin Artaud: A Critical Reader*, edited by Edward Scheer (London and New York: Routledge, 2004), 152–53.

142. Artaud, "The Theater of Cruelty (First Manifesto)," 91.

143. Weiss, 157. See also Helga Finter, "Antonin Artaud and the Impossible Theare: The Legacy of the Theatre of Cruelty," in *Antonin Artaud: A Critical Reader*, edited by Edward Scheer (London and New York: Routledge, 2004), 54.

144. On the "grain of the voice" (*grain de la voix*), see Roland Barthes, "The Grain of the Voice," in *Image, Music, Text*, translated by Stephen Heath (London: Fontana, 1977), 179–189.

145. "*Tsurai*" could also be translated as "painful," "heart-breaking," "bitter," "difficult," "tough," "cruel," "harsh," or "cold."

146. Richard Corliss, "The Movie that Motivated Cho?" *Time*, April 19, 2007, http://content.time.com/time/arts/article/0,8599,1612724,00.html (accessed February 23, 2016).

147. Ibid.

148. Jinhee Choi and Mitsuyo Wada-Marciano, eds., *Horror to the Extreme: Changing Boundaries in Asian Cinema* (Hong Kong: Hong Kong University Press, 2009).

149. Park Chan-wook quoted in Kim Young-jin, *Korean Film Directors: Park Chan-wook*, translated by Colin A. Mouat (Seoul: Seoul Selection, 2007), 107.

150. Choi Aryong, "Sympathy for the Old Boy: An Interview with Park Chan Wook," http://www.ikonenmagazin.de/interview/Park.htm (accessed April 27, 2016). Also cf. Kim Sung-Hee, "Family Seen Through Greek Tragedy and Korean Film: *Oedipus the King* and *Old Boy*," *The Journal of Drama* no. 30 (June 2009): 151–184.

151. Choi Aryong, op. cit.

152. Artaud, "No More Masterpieces," 74–75.

153. Artaud, "The Theater and the Plague," 30.

154. Artaud, "The Theater and Cruelty," 85.

155. Artaud, "The Theater of Cruelty (First Manifesto)," 92–93.

156. Artaud, "The Theater and Cruelty," 85.

157. Artaud, "The Theater and the Plague," 31.

158. Park Chan-wook quoted in Kim Young-jin, 107.

159. Kim Young-jin, 49.

160. Gilles Deleuze and Félix Guattari, *A Thousand Plateaus: Capitalism and Schizophrenia*, translated by Brian Massumi (Minneapolis: University of Minnesota Press, 1987), 167–91.

161. Artaud, "The Theater of Cruelty (First Manifesto)," 89, 91.

162. Hollier, 163; Weiss, 157; also cf. Finter, 54.

163. Julia Kristeva, *Powers of Horror: An Essay on Abjection*, translated by Leon S. Roudiez (New York: Columbia University Press, 1982).

164. Brigid Cherry, *Horror* (London; New York: Routledge, 2009), 112.

165. Kristeva, 4.

166. One of the most controversial scenes in *Oldboy* occurs after Oh Dae-su has been released from captivity and enters a restaurant where Mi-do is working as a sushi chef. The scene in question shows Oh Dae-su consume a live octopus whole. Although devouring an octopus whole while it is still alive may seem abject in the West, it is considered a perfectly normal, even mundane, part of Korean cuisine, especially at seaside restaurants located in coastal towns. Nevertheless, it is also considered potentially dangerous if the tentacles get stuck in one's throat, causing suffocation. In a Korean context, Oh Dae-su's act of devouring live octopus is not evidence of how dehumanized (or animalized) he has become, but rather a reaffirmation of his newfound freedom to eat something other than the Chinese dumplings he had been served throughout his captivity. On the other hand, the fact that it was auto-suggestion that prompted Oh Dae-su to enter the sushi restaurant in the first place may be construed as implying that such "freedom" is ultimately illusory. While filming this scene, the actor who plays Oh

Dae-su (Min-sik Choi) actually devoured four live octopi on set. Since live animals were killed on film, this particular scene has caused quite a bit of controversy outside of South Korea. Perhaps it is for this reason that when *Oldboy* received the Grand Prix Award at Cannes, Director Park Chan-wook made a point of expressing gratitude to the sacrificed octopi during his acceptance speech!

167. Dino Franco Felluga, *Critical Theory: The Key Concepts* (New York: Routledge, 2015), 5.

168. Barbara Creed, *The Monstrous-Feminine: Film, Feminism, Psychoanalysis* (London: Routledge, 1993), 71–72; Cherry, 115–16.

169. Creed, 14.

170. Later, Mi-do hallucinates a giant ant sitting in a subway car, which she tells Oh Dae-su is symptomatic of loneliness.

171. I have made extensive use of Flux Sound & Picture Development's *Pure Analyzer System* software for the analysis of surround sound elements in *Oldboy* and other films included in this study.

172. When considering the role of sound design in *Oldboy*, mention must also be made of the sound reproduction equipment (in the form of reel-to-reel tape and cassette players) that occasionally appears in close-up. Such sound reproduction devices appear at pivotal moments in the narrative as if to underscore that some of Oh Dae-su's most traumatic memories are on tape loop. The only way to overcome the trauma is to change or destroy the tape.

173. Gilles Deleuze, *Cinema 1: The Movement-Image*, translated by Hugh Tomlinson and Barbara Habberjam (Minneapolis: University of Minnesota Press, 1986), 87.

174. Ibid., 110.

175. Herwig Todts, *James Ensor: Paintings and Drawings from the Collection of the Royal Museum of Fine Arts in Antwerp* (Schoten, Belgium: BAI, 2008), 109.

176. Ibid., 109.

177. Ella Wheeler Wilcox, *Poems of Passion* (Los Angeles: Indo-European Publishing, 2010), 83. "Solitude" was first published in *The New York Sun* on February 25, 1883.

178. Ibid., 83.

179. Dawn Ades, *Dali* (London: Thames and Hudson, 1982), 145.

180. Artaud, "Letters on Cruelty," 103.

181. Manohla Dargis, "Sometimes Blood Really Isn't Indelible," *New York Times*, March 3, 2005, http://www.nytimes.com/2005/03/03/movies/sometimes-blood-really-isnt-indelible.html (accessed June 12, 2017).

182. Ibid.

183. Alexander Walker, "The Cutting Edge of Censorship," *Evening Standard*, March 15, 2001, 29.

184. Martin, 58. Although Martin also employs the term "cinema of cruelty" in a chapter title devoted to Miike's *Audition*, he does not offer any sort of sustained engagement with its characteristics or derivation from Artaud's Theater of Cruelty. In fact, no mention is made of Artaud at all in Martin's study, which focuses far more attention on the reception of *Audition* than on the film itself.

185. Artaud, "The Theater and Cruelty," 85, 87.

186. Ibid., 86; Artaud, "No More Masterpieces," 82–83.

187. Artaud, "The Theater and Cruelty," 85.

188. Artaud, "No More Masterpieces," 83.

189. Artaud, "The Theater and Cruelty," 84.

190. Denis Hollier, "The Death of Paper, Part Two: Artaud's Sound System," in *Antonin Artaud: A Critical Reader*, edited by Edward Scheer (London and New York: Routledge, 2004), 159.

191. Deleuze, *Cinema 2*, 166.

192. Artaud, "The Theater and the Plague," 31.

6

Conclusion: Envelopes of Fear—The Temporality of Japanese Horror

Japanese ghosts are slower, they take their time.
—Kurosawa Kiyoshi[1]

After seeing the movie and going home—being alone in one's room and becoming scared—there's a sensation of dread that stays with one. To create an encroaching sensation of dread through a movie—that was the objective.
—Takahashi Hiroshi[2]

J-Horror Assemblages

In this study, I have analyzed contemporary Japanese horror cinema from a number of different angles: (1) resituating how we conceive of Japanese horror by attending to its intermediality and transnational hybridity in relation to world horror cinema; (2) studying the techniques by which Japanese horror develops a cinema of sensations that resonates with viewers by filling them with atmospherically enhanced dread and other intensities along the continuum of horror affects; and (3) analyzing the gender politics, sociopolitical issues, and problems of modernity that

© The Author(s) 2018
S. T. Brown, *Japanese Horror and the Transnational Cinema of Sensations*,
East Asian Popular Culture, https://doi.org/10.1007/978-3-319-70629-0_6

infuse it. I have approached J-horror not simply as a "genre" but as a cinematic "assemblage" in the sense that philosophers Gilles Deleuze and Félix Guattari have given that term in *A Thousand Plateaus* (*Mille plateaux*, 1980) and that Deleuze follows in his *Cinema* books.[3] It is in this sense that, as David Deamer notes, "A film is machinic. Cinema is composed of little machines, that compose slightly bigger machines, and bigger machines still. And little film machines can be joined with other little machines … for productive readings."[4]

In previous chapters, I have considered the complex assemblages formed by selected examples of J-horror cinema, analyzing their audiovisual relations in a manner that brings forth their complexity as sound-image machines that produce blocs of sensations entailing transnational links with other films and other assemblages. Insofar as every filmic assemblage is defined not by constants and homogeneity but by variants and heterogeneity, rather than extracting generic "invariants" from the films analyzed, I have sought to create a space for the "continuous variation of variables"[5] that they offer—paying particularly close attention to their microconnections with other films and assemblages in the transnational space of global cinema, their lines of continuous variation, and the splicing of different genre conventions across a range of films. If Deleuze and Guattari are correct in asserting that constants do not exist in themselves but are always reductions or extractions of variables,[6] then applying such an approach to individual case studies exemplifying the genre of Japanese horror helps move us away from monolithic conceptions of "J-horror" as national cinema and towards a more finely tuned understanding of the granular multiplicities and transcultural microflows circulating through the cinematic assemblages of Japanese horror in relation to world cinema, as evoked by Takahashi Hiroshi's direct questioning of the "Japaneseness" of "J-horror" that I considered in the Introduction.

Sensations of Horror

In my investigations into J-horror cinema, I have paid particularly close attention to the materialities of sensation that are produced by a wide range of cinematic techniques, both visual and sonic, in an effort to draw out the percepts and affects associated with Japanese horror's audiovisual bloc of sensations and aesthetics of resonance. If one conceives of J-horror as a sound-image machine that generates a compound of sensations, then given this study's emphasis on "resonance," it should come as no surprise that significant attention has been devoted to the role played by sound design in the production of sonic sensations—an area of study that has received relatively scant attention in the scholarship on J-horror. Of particular interest has been how the sonics of Japanese horror position the body of the spectator as a sort of resonance chamber for haptic sonority, in which the goal is not simply to decipher sonic noise into meaning but rather to have an encounter with the timbrality of sound, to feel the vibrations of sound at the molecular level, thereby making inaudible forces audible. In this way, horror approaches the "cinema of sensations" that philosopher Gilles Deleuze thought film could attain.

The sound design of Japanese horror cinema privileges unsettling background noises and ambiences, such as subtly ominous rumbling sounds, low-frequency electromechanical noises, and high-pitched buzzing (perhaps the screeches of modernity itself), which elicit a vague sense of foreboding or dread. Equally important is the omission of sound and the dynamic manipulation of silence. In Japanese horror, one frequently encounters an oscillation between silence and ambient noise that creates a profound sense of unease. Availing myself of spectrogram and surround sound analysis software in Chaps. 2 and 5, I have also considered how the positioning of audio in the surround sound space is manipulated to elicit specific responses from the audience.

Just as important as sound design to Japanese horror cinema is the cinematography that visualizes horror. One encounters a wide range of camera moves and techniques employed to underscore particular moments of horror and their associated percepts and affects, including extreme close-ups, low-angle and overhead shots, tilted horizon (or Dutch angle) shots, as well as upside-down and off-axis shots. By deviating from the normal vertical and horizontal axes of the image, extreme states of mind are conveyed and sensations of uneasiness and disequilibrium evoked. Such shot selections also underscore the importance of framing techniques to Japanese horror, whose complexities I discussed in relation to doppelgänger films in Chap. 3 vis-à-vis the numerous permutations that are played out across the divided surface of the framed screen. Other cinematographic choices, such as breaking the 180-degree rule to throw the audience off balance, have also been considered.

Also noteworthy is the role played by lighting in Japanese horror, especially the play of light and shadow and what Isabel Pinedo has called "the prominence of blind space in the horror film," in terms of which "what lurks outside the frame or unclearly within it generates uncertainty about what one is seeing."[7] Insofar as the problem of light is inseparable from the problem of color, I have also considered the expressive role played by colored lighting effects and the psychological and affective associations of different colors within a film.[8] Cinematography and lighting are, of course, essential elements in the construction of mise-en-scène along with set design, props, costumes, composition, and actor blocking. Enormously important for any consideration of the formal aspects of Japanese horror is an engagement with mise-en-scène, especially the architectural settings (dilapidated hospitals, rundown apartment buildings, abandoned factories, and desolate warehouses) that are used as the spaces in which Japanese horror unfolds. In most cases, buildings that have fallen into disrepair or ruin serve as architectural metaphors for the decaying state of modernity and the disintegration of the nuclear family and a traditional sense of community.

Affective Envelopes

What the J-horror assemblage offers is not simply an ensemble of genre conventions, but, more importantly, a compound of sensations with distinctive intensities, rhythms, and durations. In *What is Philosophy?* Deleuze and Guattari discuss how various artistic assemblages modulate sensations so that they "vibrate, couple, or split apart,"[9] but also of interest are the modes of temporality that are specific to the bloc of sensations produced. Relevant to any such consideration is the issue of timing. In a fascinating essay on "Time and Timing" in cinema, Susan Feagin delineates the key characteristics of timing in film. Feagin uses the term "timing" to describe both "the duration of an image, that is, the length of time an image persists" and "the durational relationships between and among images in a film."[10] Timing in both senses of the word affects an audiovisual spectator's responses to a horror film, not only modulating the dynamics of tension and relaxation but also eliciting quite specific affects, moods, and feelings, such as fear, dread, terror, suspense, shock, disgust, and so forth. Although the sequence of images is another aspect of a film's temporal dimension, Feagin restricts timing to the durational aspects of a film.[11] "Simply put," writes Feagin, "sequencing concerns what came before and what came after; timing concerns how long, how long before, and how long after, and how these interactions affect audience response. Timing presupposes sequencing, since the duration and durational relations of the presentation of actions and events are dependent on the images of a film appearing in a certain sequence. Sequencing does not, however, presuppose timing; rather, it makes timing possible."[12] Timing in the sense of "durational relationships" includes "the relative duration of images earlier in the movie, the length of time elapsed between or among them, and the length of time elapsed between them and the present image, which may itself have a significant duration."[13] The interval between and among images—i.e., the relative duration of the durational relationships and whether they expand or contract in relation to what precedes or follows—is what is crucial.[14] Whether one is watching horror or comedy, melodrama or thriller, the effectiveness of timing is essential to a film's success at eliciting the desired emotional responses from an audience.[15]

Here it is important to recognize that, although sound does not enter into Feagin's account, timing applies not only to the durational aspects of individual images and the durational relationships between images, but also extends to the sonic dimensions of film and the sound-image relationships at play. As suggested by my extensive discussion of sound design in Chap. 2 and intermittently throughout other chapters, the timing of sound edits, sound effects, music, and dialogue is just as important to an audience's response to a film as the timing of images per se. Another way to conceive of timing that is quite relevant to Japanese horror and underscores the importance of its sonic dimension is in terms of "envelopes."

In the history of musical instruments, the concept of sound envelopes developed as a way to describe the time-based emergence, development, and release of a given sound: i.e., how the amplitude (or loudness) and harmonic content of a sound changes over time. For example, in the development of musical synthesis, the "envelope generator" was introduced by electronic music composer Vladimir Ussachevsky (1911–1990) in conjunction with his student Robert Moog (1934–2005), the inventor of the famed Minimoog Model D synthesizer, as a circuit to control such time-based dynamics. In 1965, Ussachevsky described the main functions of the envelope generator in terms of "T1 (attack time), T2 (initial decay time), ESUS (sustain level), and T3 (final decay time)."[16] Not long after, the four stages of an envelope became codified as "attack," "decay," "sustain," and "release" (ADSR). This standardized terminology remains in use today on most hardware and software synthesizers:

> Envelopes are the contours that shape the sound coming from the Oscillators and the Filters. A basic ADSR-style envelope determines how quickly a sound will begin, its initial decay, what level it sustains at, and how long it will fade out after the note has been released. These different elements of the envelope are called stages. Most synthesizers have 4-stage envelopes, often called ADSR envelopes, which stands for Attack, Decay, Sustain and Release. Complex envelopes contain contours with more than four stages. Complex envelopes allow a much greater degree of control in shaping the sound, and offer tremendous flexibility when shaping sounds and can be very useful in creating rhythmic shapes.... Each Layer has a dedicated AMP (Amplitude) envelope and a dedicated FILTER envelope, while there are four Modulation envelopes that are common to both Layers.[17]

Such sonorous envelopes, whether simple or complex, greatly impact the dynamic shape and timbre of electronic sounds and apply equally to our perception of sounds produced by acoustic instruments as well. For example, what distinguishes the timbre of a piano from a saxophone or a violin has as much to do with the respective temporal envelopes and distinctive attacks of the sounds produced by each instrument as it does with the particular harmonic spectrum (fundamental frequency and overtones) associated with them. As demonstrated in Chaps. 2 and 5 by means of the spectrograms that were applied to specific examples of horror sound design, which provided a visualization of temporal envelopes in relation to the spectral harmonics of sound in a given scene, such concepts are not limited to musical instruments. Indeed, envelopes are an essential aspect of the acoustic signature of any given sound, providing the dynamic shape of a sound—its amplitude container.

In closing, I would like to propose the concept of envelopes as an alternative way to conceive of the particular timing associated with the affective dynamics that are at work in the audience's reception of Japanese horror.[18] One of the most persistent variables, if not constants, of Japanese horror is its mode of temporality. J-horror has long been associated with "slow-burn" cinema—what one critic describes as J-horror's characteristic "slow-burn, creeping atmosphere of anxiety."[19] As Kurosawa Kiyoshi observes, "Japanese ghosts are slower, they take their time."[20] Coral Castillo summarizes the slow-burn effect as follows: "The slow burn horror movie makes you relive it over and over again. Think about the what ifs. It grows on you like a deadly plague. It makes you triple check that you are awake and your imagination is making you believe that the shadow in the corner is not just a shadow in the corner."[21]

If the slow-burn style has become one of the signature traits of J-horror cinema in films ranging from *Ringu* to *Audition*, from *Kairo* to *Bilocation*, then I would suggest that its effectiveness is largely dependent upon the distinctive contours of the affective envelopes constituting the "slow-burn" effect. Although it goes beyond the scope of this study, the attack-decay-sustain-release stages of such envelopes may be found not only in the overall arc of a given film, but also in individual acts within a film, individual scenes within an act, individual sequences within a scene, and individual shots within a sequence. Largely avoiding the rapid cuts so prevalent in Hollywood horror, the persistence of dread touted by *Ringu* screenwriter Takahashi Hiroshi as one of the distinguishing traits of J-horror cinema is frequently modulated by affective envelopes that are animated by slow attack and long release times. In the end, J-horror's aesthetics of dread, which creates a sense of anticipatory fear that causes viewers to experience duration as "thick, enveloping, [and] saturating,"[22] has just as much to do with the particular timing and duration of such affective envelopes as it does with the compound of sensations associated with it. It is through the resonant contours of such affective envelopes and a mode of temporality that is characterized by slow attack and long release times that invisible forces are rendered visible and inaudible forces audible in J-horror's dread-filled cinema of sensations, sending a chill up one's spine that persists long after a movie has faded to black.

Notes

1. Kurosawa Kiyoshi, "Broken Circuits," *Kairo*, directed by Kurosawa Kiyoshi (2001), translated as *Pulse*, subtitled Blu-Ray (London, England: Arrow Video, 2017).
2. Takahashi Hiroshi, "Interview with Producer Hiroshi Takahashi," *Marebito*, directed by Shimizu Takashi (2004), subtitled DVD (Los Angeles, CA: Tartan Video, 2006) (translation modified).
3. Gilles Deleuze and Félix Guattari, *A Thousand Plateaus: Capitalism and Schizophrenia*, translated by Brian Massumi (Minneapolis: University of Minnesota Press, 1987); Gilles Deleuze, *Cinema 1: The Movement-Image*, translated by Hugh Tomlinson and Barbara Habberjam (Minneapolis: University of Minnesota Press, 1986); Gilles Deleuze, *Cinema 2: The Time-Image*, translated by Hugh Tomlinson and Robert Galeta (Minneapolis: University of Minnesota Press, 1989). Deleuze conceives of cinema as the machinic assemblage of "matter-images [*images-matière*]," which has "as its correlate a collective assemblage of enunciation"(*Cinema 1*, 82, 85).
4. David Deamer, *Deleuze, Japanese Cinema, and the Atom Bomb: The Spectre of Impossibility* (New York: Bloomsbury, 2014), 25.
5. *Thousand Plateaus*, 94–99.
6. Ibid., 103.
7. Isabel Pinedo, *Recreational Terror: Women and the Pleasures of Horror Film Viewing* (Albany, N.Y.: State University of New York Press, 1997), 53.
8. See my analysis in Chap. 4 of the important role played by color in Miike Takashi's notorious *Audition* (*Ōdishon*, 1999, Japan).
9. Gilles Deleuze and Félix Guattari, *What is Philosophy?*, translated by Hugh Tomlinson and Graham Burchell (New York: Columbia University Press, 1994), 175, 168.
10. Susan L. Feagin, "Time and Timing," in *Passionate Views: Film, Cognition, and Emotion*, edited by Carl R. Plantinga and Greg M. Smith (Baltimore: Johns Hopkins University Press, 1999), 168–169.
11. Ibid., 173–174.
12. Ibid., 174.
13. Ibid., 169.
14. See also David Bordwell, *Narration in the Fiction Film* (Madison, Wis.: University of Wisconsin Press, 1985), 74–98.

15. Feagin, 168–170.

16. Trevor Pinch and Frank Trocco, *Analog Days: The Invention and Impact of the Moog Synthesizer* (Cambridge, MA: Harvard University Press, 2002), 59.

17. *Omnisphere 2 Reference Guide*, https://support.spectrasonics.net/manual/Omnisphere2/layer_page/envelopes/index.html (accessed July 2, 2017).

18. For a discussion of the concept of "sonorous envelopes" in a psychoanalytic context, see Didier Anzieu, "L'enveloppe sonore du Soi," *Nouvelle Revue de Psychanalyse* no. 13 (1976): 161–179; Edith Lecourt, "The Musical Envelope," in *Psychic Envelopes*, edited by D. Anzieu and translated by Daphne Briggs (London: Karnac, 1990), 211–235.

19. Kyu Hyun Kim, "*Kyōfu*," in *The Encyclopedia of Japanese Horror Films*, edited by Salvador Murguia (Lanham, Maryland: Rowman & Littlefield, 2016), 187.

20. Kurosawa Kiyoshi, "Broken Circuits," *Kairo*, directed by Kurosawa Kiyoshi (2001), translated as *Pulse*, subtitled Blu-Ray (London, England: Arrow Video, 2017).

21. Coral Castillo, "A Slow Burn Into Your Soul: 13 Slow Burn Horror Movies," *The Lazy Audience*, February 24, 2016, https://thelazyaudience.wordpress.com/2016/02/24/a-slow-burn-into-your-soul-13-slow-burn-horror-movies/ (accessed July 6, 2017). Needless to say, slow-burn horror also shares traits with "slow cinema." On "slow cinema," see Tiago De Luca and Nuno Barradas Jorge, eds., *Slow Cinema* (Edinburgh: Edinburgh University Press, 2016); Justin Remes, *Motion(less) Pictures: The Cinema of Stasis* (New York: Columbia University Press, 2015); and Ira Jaffe, *Slow Movies: Countering the Cinema of Action* (New York: Columbia University Press, 2014).

22. Robert Spadoni, "Carl Dreyer's Corpse: Horror Film Atmosphere and Narrative," in *A Companion to the Horror Film*, edited by Harry M. Benshoff (Chichester, West Sussex, UK; Malden, MA, USA: Wiley Blackwell, 2014), 157–159.

Bibliography

Abe Kōbō. 2003. *The Face of Another*. Trans. E. Dale Saunders. New York: Vintage.

Abel, Richard. 1984. *French Cinema: The First Wave, 1915–1929*. Princeton: Princeton University Press.

Adamowicz, Elza. 1998. *Surrealist Collage in Text and Image: Dissecting the Exquisite Corpse*. Cambridge/New York: Cambridge University Press.

Ades, Dawn. 1982. *Dalí*. London: Thames and Hudson.

Adorno, Theodor. 2009. *In Search of Wagner*. Trans. Rodney Livingstone. London: Verso.

Adorno, Theodor, and Hanns Eisler. 2010. *Composing for the Films*. New York: Continuum.

Altman, Rick, ed. 1992. *Sound Theory/Sound Practice*. New York: Routledge.

Antonioni, Michelangelo. 1964. *Il deserto rosso* (*Red Desert*). Rome: Film Duemila.

Anzieu, Didier. 1976. "L'enveloppe sonore du Soi." *Nouvelle Revue de Psychanalyse* 13: 161–179.

Artaud, Antonin. 1958. *The Theater and Its Double*. Trans. Mary Caroline Richards. New York: Grove Press.

———. 1970. *Œuvres complètes*. Paris: Gallimard.

Aspley, Keith. 2010. *Historical Dictionary of Surrealism*. Lanham: Scarecrow Press.

© The Author(s) 2018
S. T. Brown, *Japanese Horror and the Transnational Cinema of Sensations*,
East Asian Popular Culture, https://doi.org/10.1007/978-3-319-70629-0

Augoyard, Jean-François, and Henry Torgue. 2005. *Sonic Experience: A Guide to Everyday Sounds*. Trans. Andra McCartney and David Paquette. Montreal: McGill-Queen's University Press.

Bachnik, Jane M. 1998. "Time, Space and Person in Japanese Relationships." In *Interpreting Japanese Society: Anthropological Approaches*, ed. Joy Hendry, 91–116. London/New York: Routledge.

Baird, Robert. 2000. "The Startle Effect: Implications for Spectator Cognition and Media Theory." *Film Quarterly* 53 (3): 12–24.

Balmain, Colette. 2008. *Introduction to Japanese Horror Film*. Edinburgh: Edinburgh University Press.

———. 2009. "Oriental Nightmares: The 'Demonic' Other in Contemporary American Adaptations of Japanese Horror Film." In *Something Wicked This Way Comes: Essays on Evil and Human Wickedness*, ed. Colette Balmain and Lois Drawmer, 25–38. Amsterdam: Editions Rodopi.

Barthes, Roland. 1977. *Image, Music, Text*. Trans. Stephen Heath. London: Fontana.

Bataille, Georges. 1985. "Eye." In *Visions of Excess: Selected Writings, 1927–1939*, ed. Allan Stoekl, 17–19. Minneapolis: University of Minnesota Press.

Bazin, André. 2013. *The Cinema of Cruelty: From Buñuel to Hitchcock*. Ed. François Truffaut. Trans. Sabine d' Estrée. New York: Arcade Publishing.

Beck, Jay. 2016. *Designing Sound: Audiovisual Aesthetics in 1970s American Cinema*. New Brunswick: Rutgers University Press.

Beck, Jay, and Tony Grajeda, eds. 2008. *Lowering the Boom: Critical Studies in Film Sound*. Urbana: University of Illinois Press.

Bellmer, Hans. 2005. *The Doll*. Trans. Malcolm Green. London: Atlas Press.

Belton, Robert J. 1991. "Androgyny: Interview with Meret Oppenheim." In *Surrealism and Women*, ed. Mary Ann Caws, Rudolf E. Kuenzli, and Gloria Gwen Raaberg, 63–75. Cambridge, MA: MIT Press.

Birtwistle, Andy. 2010. *Cinesonica: Sounding Film and Video*. Manchester: Manchester University Press.

Blanchot, Maurice. 1969. *L'entretien infini*. Paris: Gallimard.

———. 1993. *The Infinite Conversation*. Trans. Susan Hanson. Minneapolis: University of Minnesota Press.

Blum, William. 1971. "Toward a Cinema of Cruelty." *Cinema Journal* 10 (2): 19–33.

Blumstein, Daniel T., Richard Davitian, and Peter D. Kaye. 2010. "Do Film Soundtracks Contain Nonlinear Analogues to Influence Emotion?" *Biology Letters* 6: 751–754.

Bonitzer, Pascal. 1985. *Peinture et cinéma: Décadrages*. Paris: Editions de l'Etoile.

Bordwell, David. 1985. *Narration in the Fiction Film*. Madison: University of Wisconsin Press.

Brejzek, Thea, and Lawrence Wallen. 2015. "Derealisation, Perception and Site: Some Notes on the Doppelgänger Space." In *Perception in Architecture: Here and Now*, ed. Claudia Perren and Miriam Mlecek, 2–10. Newcastle upon Tyne: Cambridge Scholars Publishing.

Breton, André. 1969. "Second Manifesto of Surrealism." In *Manifestoes of Surrealism*, 117–194. Trans. Richard Seaver and Helen R. Lane. Ann Arbor: University of Michigan Press.

———. 1997. *Anthology of Black Humor*. Trans. Mark Polizzotti. San Francisco: City Lights Books.

———. 2002. *Surrealism and Painting*. Trans. Simon Watson Taylor. Boston: MFA Publications.

Brown, Steven T. 2001. *Theatricalities of Power: The Cultural Politics of Noh*. Stanford: Stanford University Press.

———. 2010. *Tokyo Cyberpunk: Posthumanism in Japanese Visual Culture*. Basingstoke: Palgrave Macmillan.

Buñuel, Luis. 1985. *My Last Breath*. London: Flamingo.

———. 2003. *My Last Sigh*. Trans. Abigail Israel. Minneapolis: University of Minnesota Press.

Burlingame, Jon. 2012. "John Williams Recalls *Jaws*." *The Film Music Society*, August 14. http://www.filmmusicsociety.org/news_events/features/2012/081412.html?isArchive=081412. Accessed 4 Apr 2017.

Buse, Peter, and Andrew Scott. 1999. "Introduction: A Future for Haunting." In *Ghosts: Deconstruction, Psychoanalysis, History*, ed. Peter Buse and Andrew Scott, 1–20. New York: St. Martin's Press.

Carroll, Noël. 1990. *The Philosophy of Horror, or, Paradoxes of the Heart*. New York: Routledge.

Cartwright, Lisa. 1995. *Screening the Body: Tracing Medicine's Visual Culture*. Minneapolis: University of Minnesota Press.

Castillo, Coral. 2016. "A Slow Burn into Your Soul: 13 Slow Burn Horror Movies." *The Lazy Audience*, February 24. https://thelazyaudience.wordpress.com/2016/02/24/a-slow-burn-into-your-soul-13-slow-burn-horror-movies/. Accessed 6 July 2017.

Cherry, Brigid. 2009. *Horror*. London/New York: Routledge.

Chion, Michel. 1994. *Audio-Vision: Sound on Screen*. Trans. Claudia Gorbman. New York: Columbia University Press.

———. 1999. *The Voice in Cinema*. Trans. Claudia Gorbman. New York: Columbia University Press.

————. 2003. "The Silence of the Loudspeakers, or Why with Dolby Sound It Is the Film that Listens to Us." In *Soundscape: The School of Sound Lectures, 1998–2001*, ed. Larry Sider, Jerry Sider, and Diane Freeman, 150–154. London/New York: Wallflower Press.

————. 2009. *Film, A Sound Art*. Trans. Claudia Gorbman. New York: Columbia University Press.

Choi Aryong. "Sympathy for the Old Boy: An Interview with Park Chan Wook." http://www.ikonenmagazin.de/interview/Park.htm. Accessed 27 Apr 2016.

Choi Jinhee, and Mitsuyo Wada-Marciano, eds. 2009. *Horror to the Extreme: Changing Boundaries in Asian Cinema*. Hong Kong: Hong Kong University Press.

Chong Doryun. 2012. "Tokyo 1955–1970: A New Avant-Garde." In *Tokyo 1955–1970: A New Avant-Garde*, ed. Doryun Chong, 26–93. New York: Museum of Modern Art.

Chris, D. 2005. *Outlaw Masters of Japanese Film*. London/New York: I.B. Tauris.

Cooke, Mervyn. 2010. *A History of Film Music*. Cambridge: Cambridge University Press.

Cord, William. 1995. *An Introduction to Richard Wagner's Der Ring des Nibelungen: A Handbook*. Athens: Ohio University Press.

Corliss, Richard. 2007. "The Movie That Motivated Cho?" *Time*, April 19. http://content.time.com/time/arts/article/0,8599,1612724,00.html. Accessed 23 Feb 2016.

Cottenet-Hage, Madeleine. 1991. "The Body Subversive: Corporeal Imagery in Carrington, Prassinos and Mansour." In *Surrealism and Women*, ed. Mary Ann Caws, Rudolf E. Kuenzli, and Gloria Gwen Raaberg, 76–95. Cambridge, MA: MIT Press.

Coulthard, Lisa. 2012. "Haptic Aurality: Resonance, Listening and Michael Haneke." *Film-Philosophy* 16 (1): 16–29.

————. 2013. "Dirty Sound: Haptic Noise in New Extremism." In *The Oxford Handbook of Sound and Image in Digital Media*, ed. Carol Vernallis, Amy Herzog, and John Richardson, 115–126. New York: Oxford University Press.

Creed, Barbara. 1993. *The Monstrous-Feminine: Film, Feminism, Psychoanalysis*. London: Routledge.

da Silva, Jorge Bastos. 2005. "A Lusitanian Dish: Swift to Portuguese Taste." In *The Reception of Jonathan Swift in Europe*, ed. Hermann Josef Real, 79–92. London: Thoemmes.

da Silva, Joaquín. 2016. "J-Horror and Toshi Densetsu Revisited," January 4. http://eiga9.altervista.org/articulos/jhorrorandurbanlegendsrevisited.html. Accessed 5 May 2017.

Dalmais, Jean. 2005. "Resonance." In *Sonic Experience: A Guide to Everyday Sounds*, Eds. Jean-François Augoyard and Henry Torgue. Trans. Andra McCartney and David Paquette. Montreal: McGill-Queen's University Press.

Dargis, Manohla. 2005. "Sometimes Blood Really Isn't Indelible." *New York Times*, March 3. http://www.nytimes.com/2005/03/03/movies/sometimes-blood-really-isnt-indelible.html. Accessed 12 June 2017.

Davis, Nick. 2013. *The Desiring-Image: Gilles Deleuze and Contemporary Queer Cinema*. Oxford/New York: Oxford University Press.

Deamer, David. 2014. *Deleuze, Japanese Cinema, and the Atom Bomb: The Spectre of Impossibility*. New York: Bloomsbury.

Deleuze, Gilles. 1986. *Cinema 1: The Movement-Image*. Trans. Hugh Tomlinson and Barbara Habberjam. Minneapolis: University of Minnesota Press.

———. 1989. *Cinema 2: The Time-Image*. Trans. Hugh Tomlinson and Robert Galeta. Minneapolis: University of Minnesota Press.

———. 2004. *Francis Bacon: The Logic of Sensation*. Minneapolis: University of Minnesota Press.

Deleuze, Gilles, and Félix Guattari. 1980. *Mille plateaux*. Paris: Éditions de Minuit.

———. 1987. *A Thousand Plateaus: Capitalism and Schizophrenia*. Trans. Brian Massumi. Minneapolis: University of Minnesota Press.

———. 1994. *What Is Philosophy?* Trans. Hugh Tomlinson and Graham Burchell. New York: Columbia University Press.

Deleuze, Gilles, and Timothy S. Murphy. 1998. "Vincennes Seminar Session, May 3, 1977: On Music." *Discourse* 20 (3/Fall), *Gilles Deleuze: A Reason to Believe in This World*: 205–218.

Deleuze, Gilles, and Claire Parnet. 1977. *Dialogues*. Paris: Flammarion.

———. 2007. *Dialogues II*. Rev. ed. Trans. Hugh Tomlinson and Barbara Habberjam. New York: Columbia University Press.

Derrida, Jacques. 2001. *Writing and Difference*. Trans. Alan Bass. London: Routledge.

Dietrichson, Lorentz. 1870–79. *Det skönas värld: Estetik och konsthistoria med specielt afseende på den bildande konsten. Populärt framställda*. Stockholm: Oscar L. Lamms förlag.

Dixon, Wheeler W. 2015. *Black & White Cinema: A Short History*. New Brunswick: Rutgers University Press.

Doi Takeo. 1986. *The Anatomy of Self: The Individual Versus Society*. Tokyo/New York: Kodansha International.

Donnelly, Kevin. 2005. *Film and Television Music: The Spectre of Sound*. London: British Film Institute.

Dorman, Andrew. 2016. *Paradoxical Japaneseness: Cultural Representation in 21st Century Japanese Cinema*. London: Palgrave Macmillan.

Dostoyevsky, Fyodor. 1950. *Crime and Punishment*. Trans. Constance Garnett. New York: Vintage Books.

———. 2007. *The Double and The Gambler*. Trans. Richard Pevear and Larissa Volokhonsky. New York: Vintage.

"Double Feature: Kiyoshi Kurosawa." *Entrevues Belfort International Film Festival*. http://www.festival-entrevues.com/fr/retrospectives/2014/double-feature-kiyoshi-kurosawa. Accessed 29 Oct 2015.

Dreger, Alice Domurat. 1998. "The Limits of Individuality: Ritual and Sacrifice in the Lives and Medical Treatment of Conjoined Twins." *Studies in History, Philosophy, Biology and Biomedical Science* 29 (1): 1–29.

———. 2004. *One of Us: Conjoined Twins and the Future of Normal*. Cambridge, MA: Harvard University Press.

Drummond, Phillip. 1977. "Textual Space in *Un Chien Andalou*." *Screen* 18 (3): 55–119.

Durgnat, Raymond. 1968. *Franju*. Berkeley: University of California Press.

Edelstein, David. 2006. "Now Playing at Your Local Multiplex: Torture Porn." *New York Magazine*, February 6. http://nymag.com/movies/features/15622/#. Accessed 9 Feb 2016.

Eggum, Arne. 2000. *Edvard Munch: The Frieze of Life from Painting to Graphic Art*. Oslo: Stenersen.

Eisenstein, Sergei. 2006. "On Colour." In *Color: The Film Reader*, ed. Angela Dalle Vacche and Brian Price, 105–117. New York/London: Routledge.

———. 2010. "From Lectures on Music and Colour in *Ivan the Terrible*." In *Sergei Eisenstein: Selected Works: Volume III: Writings, 1934–1947*, ed. Richard Taylor, 317–338. London/New York: I.B. Tauris.

Eisner, Lotte. 1973. *The Haunted Screen*. London: Secker & Warburg.

Eisner, Ken. 1999. "Review of *Audition*." *Variety*, October 31. http://variety.com/1999/film/reviews/audition-1200459973/. Accessed 27 July 2016.

Elsaesser, Thomas, and Malte Hagener. 2015. *Film Theory: An Introduction Through the Senses*. Florence: Taylor and Francis.

Erlmann, Veit. 2010. *Reason and Resonance: A History of Modern Aurality*. New York: Zone Books.

———. 2011. "Descartes's Resonant Subject." *differences: A Journal of Feminist Cultural Studies* 22 (2–3): 10–30.

———. 2015. "Resonance." In *Keywords in Sound*, ed. David Novak and Matt Sakakeeny, 175–182. Durham/London: Duke University Press.

"Etiäinen." *Wikipedia*. https://en.wikipedia.org/wiki/Etiäinen. Accessed 7 Oct 2016.

Euripides. 1981. *Helen*. Trans. James Michie and Colin Leach. New York: Oxford University Press.

Evans, Dylan. 1996. *An Introductory Dictionary of Lacanian Psychoanalysis*. London/New York: Routledge.

Evans, Guy. 2007a. *Dirty Dalí: A Private View*. DVD. London: Channel 4.

Evans, Peter William. 2007b. "An *Amour* still *fou*: Late Buñuel." In *The Unsilvered Screen: Surrealism on Film*, ed. Graeme Harper and Rob Stone, 38–47. London: Wallflower.

Feagin, Susan L. 1999. "Time and Timing." In *Passionate Views: Film, Cognition, and Emotion*, ed. Carl R. Plantinga and Greg M. Smith, 168–179. Baltimore: Johns Hopkins University Press.

Felluga, Dino Franco. 2015. *Critical Theory: The Key Concepts*. New York: Routledge.

Finter, Helga. 2004. "Antonin Artaud and the Impossible Theare: The Legacy of the Theatre of Cruelty." In *Antonin Artaud: A Critical Reader*, ed. Edward Scheer, 47–58. London/New York: Routledge.

"FIPRESCI Prize." http://www.fipresci.org/festival-reports/2001/cannes-film-festival. Accessed 15 Jan 2016.

Fitch, Tecumseh, Jürgen Neubauer, and Hanspeter Herzel. 2002. "Calls Out of Chaos: The Adaptive Significance of Nonlinear Phenomena in Mammalian Vocal Production." *Animal Behaviour* 63 (3): 407–418.

Folkerth, Wes. 2002. *The Sound of Shakespeare*. London/New York: Routledge.

Forgacs, David. 2010. "Commentary." *Il deserto rosso*. Translated as *Red Desert*. Subtitled DVD. Directed by Michelangelo Antonioni. Irvington: Criterion Collection.

Foster, Hal. 2001. "Violation and Veiling in Surrealist Photography: Woman as Fetish, as Shattered Object, as Phallus." In *Surrealism: Desire Unbound*, ed. Jennifer Mundy, 203–226. Princeton: Princeton University Press.

Foster, David William. 2004. *Queer Issues in Contemporary Latin American Cinema*. Austin: University of Texas Press.

Foster, Michael Dylan. 2015. *The Book of Yōkai: Mysterious Creatures of Japanese Folklore*. Oakland: University of California Press.

Foucault, Michel. 1983. *This Is Not a Pipe*. Berkeley: University of California Press.

———. 1989. *The Order of Things: An Archaeology of the Human Sciences*. London/New York: Routledge.

————. 2003. *Abnormal: Lectures at the Collège de France 1974–1975*. Trans. Graham Burchell. London: Verso.

Frank, Alison. 2013. *Reframing Reality: The Aesthetics of the Surrealist Object in French and Czech Cinema*. Bristol: Intellect.

Freeland, Cynthia. 2004. "Horror and Art-Dread." In *The Horror Film*, ed. Stephen Prince, 189–205. New Brunswick: Rutgers University Press.

Freud, Sigmund. 1955. "The 'Uncanny.'" In *The Standard Edition of the Complete Psychological Works of Sigmund Freud*, trans. and ed. James Strachey, vol. XVII, 217–256. London: Hogarth Press.

————. 2003. *The Uncanny*. Trans. David McLintock, 123–159. New York: Penguin Books.

Gauthier, Xavière. 1971. *Surréalisme et sexualité*. Paris: Gallimard.

Genette, Gérard. 1997. *Palimpsests: Literature in the Second Degree*. Lincoln: University of Nebraska Press.

Gengaro, Christine Lee. 2013. *Listening to Stanley Kubrick: The Music in His Films*. Lanham: Scarecrow Press.

Glee, Felicity. 2013. "Surrealist Legacies: The Influence of Luis Buñuel's 'Irrationality' on Hiroshi Teshigahara's 'Documentary-Fantasy.'" In *A Companion to Luis Buñuel*, ed. Rob Stone and Julián Daniel Gutiérrez-Albilla, 572–589. Malden: Wiley-Blackwell.

Golman, Harry. 2005. *Kenneth Strickfaden, Dr. Frankenstein's Electrician*. Jefferson: McFarland & Company.

Goodman, Steve. 2009. *Sonic Warfare: Sound, Affect, and the Ecology of Fear*. Cambridge, MA: MIT Press.

Gorbman, Claudia. 1987. *Unheard Melodies: Narrative Film Music*. Bloomington: Indiana University Press.

Grilli, Peter. 2007. "The Spectral Landscape of Teshigahara, Abe, and Takemitsu." *The Criterion Collection*, July 9. https://www.criterion.com/current/posts/607-the-spectral-landscape-of-teshigahara-abe-and-takemitsu. Accessed 19 Nov 2015.

Grimm, Jacob, and Wilhelm Grimm. 1860. *Deutsches Wörterbuch von Jacob Grimm und Wilhelm Grimm*. Leipzig: S. Hirzel.

Guattari, Félix. 1977. *La Révolution moléculaire*. Fontenay-sous-Bois: Recherches.

————. 2009. *Chaosophy: Texts and Interviews 1972–1977*. Ed. Sylvère Lotringer. Los Angeles: Semiotexte.

Gunning, Tom. 1990. "The Cinema of Attractions: Early Film, Its Spectator and the Avant-Garde." In *Early Cinema: Space, Frame, Narrative*, ed. Thomas Elsaesser and Adam Barker, 56–62. London: British Film Institute.

Hanich, Julian. 2010. *Cinematic Emotion in Horror Films and Thrillers: The Aesthetic Paradox of Pleasurable Fear*. New York: Routledge.

Hanssen, Eirik Frisvold. 2004. "Eisenstein in Colour." *Konsthistorisk tidskrift/ Journal of Art History* 73 (4): 212–227.

Hantke, Steffen. 2005. "Japanese Horror Under Western Eyes: Social Class and Global Culture in Miike Takashi's *Audition*." In *Japanese Horror Cinema*, ed. Jay McRoy, 54–65. Honolulu: University of Hawai'i Press.

Harper, Jim. 2008. *Flowers from Hell: The Modern Japanese Horror Film*. Hereford: Noir Publishing.

Heidegger, Martin. 2012. *Contributions to Philosophy (Of the Event)*. Trans. Richard Rojcewicz and Daniela Vallega-Neu. Bloomington: Indiana University Press.

Herbert, Daniel. 2009. "Trading Spaces: Transnational Dislocations in *Insomnia/Insomnia* and *Ju-on/The Grudge*." In *Fear, Cultural Anxiety, and Transformation: Horror, Science Fiction, and Fantasy Films Remade*, ed. Scott A. Lukas and John Marmysz, 143–164. Lanham: Lexington Books.

Hill, Matt. 2011. "Cutting into Concepts of 'Reflectionist' Cinema? The *Saw* Franchise and Puzzles of Post-9/11 Horror." In *Horror After 9/11: World of Fear, Cinema of Terror*, ed. Aviva Briefel and Sam J. Miller, 107–123. Austin: University of Texas Press.

Hoffmann, Sheila Weller. 2013. "What Should Edward 'I'm a Brave Martyr but I Wanna Go Home' Snowden Do Now?" *The Washington Post*, July 15. https://www.washingtonpost.com/blogs/she-the-people/wp/2013/07/15/ what-should-edward-im-a-brave-martyr-but-i-wanna-go-home-snowden- do-now/. Accessed 25 Jan 2016.

Holland, Norman N. "The Trouble(s) with Lacan." http://users.clas.ufl.edu/ nholland/lacan.htm. Accessed 21 Oct 2015.

Hollier, Denis. 2004. "The Death of Paper, Part Two: Artaud's Sound System." In *Antonin Artaud: A Critical Reader*, ed. Edward Scheer, 159–168. London/ New York: Routledge.

Honisch, Stefan Sunandan. 2016. "Music, Sound, and Noise as Bodily Disorders: Disabling the Filmic Diegesis in Hideo Nakata's *Ringu* and Gore Verbinski's *The Ring*." In *Transnational Horror Cinema: Bodies of Excess and the Global Grotesque*, ed. Sophia Siddique and Raphael Raphael, 113–132. New York: Palgrave Macmillan.

Hubert, Renée Riese. 1991. "From *Déjeuner en fourrure* to *Caroline*: Meret Oppenheim's Chronicle of Surrealism." In *Surrealism and Women*, ed. Mary Ann Caws, Rudolf E. Kuenzli, and Gloria Gwen Raaberg, 37–49. Cambridge, MA: MIT Press.

Hunt, Leon. 1990. "The Student of Prague." In *Early Cinema: Space, Frame, Narrative*, ed. Thomas Elsaesser and Adam Barker, 389–401. London: BFI Publishing.

Hurlbert, Anya C., and Yazhu Ling. 2007. "Biological Components of Sex Differences in Color Preference." *Current Biology* 17 (16): 623–625.

Hurlbert, Anya, and Angela Owen. 2015. "Biological, Cultural, and Developmental Influences on Color Preferences." In *Handbook of Color Psychology*, ed. Andrew J. Elliot, Mark D. Fairchild, and Anna Franklin, 454–477. Cambridge: Cambridge University Press.

Hutchings, Peter. 2004. *The Horror Film*. Harlow/New York: Pearson Longman.

Hyland, Robert. 2009. "A Politics of Excess: Violence and Violation in Miike Takashi's *Audition*." In *Horror to the Extreme: Changing Boundaries in Asian Cinema*, ed. Jinhee Choi and Mitsuyo Wada-Marciano, 199–218. Hong Kong: Hong Kong University Press.

Ince, Kate. 2005. *Georges Franju*. Manchester: Manchester University Press.

"Interview with Ishibashi Renji." 2016. *Ōdishon*. Translated as *Audition*. Subtitled Blu-Ray. Directed by Miike Takashi. Shenley, England: Arrow Video.

Iwasaka Michiko, and Barre Toelken. 1994. *Ghosts and the Japanese: Cultural Experience in Japanese Death Legends*. Logan: Utah State University Press.

Jones, Steve. 2013. *Torture Porn: Popular Horror After Saw*. New York: Palgrave Macmillan.

Jones, Emma. 2014. "Why Are There So Many Doppelgangers in Films Right Now?" *BBC Culture*, April 10. http://www.bbc.com/culture/story/20140410-why-so-many-doppelgangers. Accessed 19 Jan 2015.

Kalat, David. 2007. *J-Horror: The Definitive Guide to The Ring, The Grudge and Beyond*. New York: Vertical.

Kassabian, Anahid. 2001. *Hearing Film: Tracking Identifications in Contemporary Hollywood Film Music*. New York: Routledge.

Kennedy, Barbara M. 2000. *Deleuze and Cinema: The Aesthetics of Sensation*. Edinburgh: Edinburgh University Press.

Kerner, Aaron. 2015. *Torture Porn in the Wake of 9/11: Horror, Exploitation, and the Cinema of Sensation*. New Brunswick: Rutgers University Press.

Kihara Hirokatsu, and Nakayama Ichirō. 1990. *Shin mimibukuro: Anata no tonari no kowai hanashi*. Tokyo: Fusōsha.

Kim Young-jin. 2007. *Korean Film Directors: Park Chan-wook*. Trans. Colin A. Mouat. Seoul: Seoul Selection.

Kim Sung-Hee. 2009. "Family Seen Through Greek Tragedy and Korean Film: *Oedipus the King* and *Old Boy.*" *The Journal of Drama* 30: 151–184.

Kim Kyu Hyun. 2016. "*Kyōfu*." In *The Encyclopedia of Japanese Horror Films*, ed. Salvador Murguia, 186–187. Lanham: Rowman & Littlefield.

Kinoshita Chika. 2009. "The Mummy Complex: Kurosawa Kiyoshi's *Loft* and J-horror." In *Horror to the Extreme: Changing Boundaries in Asian Cinema*, ed. Jinhee Choi and Mitsuyo Wada-Marciano, 103–122. Hong Kong: Hong Kong University Press.

Kirihira, Donald. 1996. "Reconstructing Japanese Film." In *Post-Theory: Reconstructing Film Studies*, ed. David Bordwell, 501–519. Madison: University of Wisconsin Press.

Kittler, Friedrich. 1997. "Romanticism—Psychoanalysis—Film: A History of the Double." In *Literature, Media, Information Systems*, ed. John Johnston, 85–100. New York: Routledge.

Knee, Adam. 2009. "The Pan-Asian Outlook of *The Eye*." In *Horror to the Extreme: Changing Boundaries in Asian Cinema*, ed. Jinhee Choi and Mitsuyo Wada-Marciano, 69–84. Hong Kong: Hong Kong University Press.

Komparu Kunio. 1983. *The Noh Theater: Principles and Perspectives*. Trans. Jane Corddry. NewYork: Walker/Weatherhill.

Konaka Chiaki. 2003. *Horā eiga no miryoku: Fandamentaru horā sengen*. Tokyo: Iwanami Shoten.

Konno Ensuke. 2004. *Nihon kaidanshū: Yūrei hen*. Tokyo: Chūō Kōron Shinsha.

Kristeva, Julia. 1982. *Powers of Horror: An Essay on Abjection*. Trans. Leon S. Roudiez. New York: Columbia University Press.

Kurosawa Kiyoshi. 1997a. *Cure (Kyua)*. Tokyo: Kadokawa Shoten.

———. 1997b. *Kyua (Cure)*. Tokyo: Daiei.

———. 1999. *Kōrei (Séance)*. Osaka: Kansai TV.

———. 2001a. *Eiga wa osoroshii*. Tokyo: Seidosha.

———. 2001b. *Kairo (Pulse)*. Tokyo: Daiei.

———. 2003. "Interview." *Kyua*. Translated as *Cure*. Subtitled DVD. Directed by Kurosawa Kiyoshi. Chicago: Home Vision Entertainment.

———. 2006a. *Eizō no karisuma*. Tokyo: Ekusu Narejji.

———. 2006b. *Sakebi (Retribution)*. Tokyo: Tokyo Broadcasting System.

———. 2014. "Interview with Kiyoshi Kurosawa about His Double Feature Choices." Interview by Diane Arnaud and Lili Hinstin. Entrevues Belfort International Film Festival, October 9. http://www.festival-entrevues.com/sites/default/files/images/archives/interview_kurosawa_hd.pdf. Accessed 13 Nov 2015.

———. 2017. "Broken Circuits." *Kairo*. Translated as *Pulse*. Subtitled Blu-Ray. Directed by Kurosawa Kiyoshi. London: Arrow Video.

Kurosawa Kiyoshi, and Shinozaki Makoto. 2003. *Kurosawa Kiyoshi no kyōfu no eigashi*. Tokyo: Seidosha.

Kvideland, Reimund, and Henning K. Sehmsdorf, eds. 1988. *Scandinavian Folk Belief and Legend*. Minneapolis: University of Minnesota Press.

"*La condition humaine*, 1933." National Gallery of Art. http://www.nga.gov/content/ngaweb/Collection/art-object-page.70170.html. Accessed 12 Dec 2015.

Lacan, Jacques. 1953. "Some Reflections on the Ego." *The International Journal of Psycho-Analysis* 34 (1): 11–17.

———. 1993. *The Seminar of Jacques Lacan: Book III. The Psychoses, 1955–1956*. Trans. Russell Grigg. London: Routledge.

———. 2006. "The Mirror Stage as Formative of the *I* Function as Revealed in Psychoanalytic Experience." In *Écrits: The First Complete Edition in English*, 75–81. Trans. Bruce Fink. New York: W.W. Norton & Co.

Lang, Fritz. 1927. *Metropolis*. Berlin: Universum Film.

Lecourt, Edith. 1990. "The Musical Envelope." In *Psychic Envelopes*, ed. D. Anzieu, 211–235. Trans. Daphne Briggs. London: Karnac.

Lee, Nikki J.Y. 2011. "'Asia' as Regional Signifier and Transnational Genre-Branding: The Asian Horror Omnibus Movies *Three* and *Three … Extremes*." In *East Asian Cinemas: Regional Flows and Global Transformations*, ed. Vivian P.Y. Lee, 103–117. New York: Palgrave Macmillan.

Lessing, Gotthold Ephraim. 1910. *Laocoon: An Essay upon the Limits of Painting and Poetry*. Trans. Ellen Frothingham. Boston: Little, Brown and Co.

Leyda, Jay. 1960. *Kino: A History of the Russian and Soviet Film*. London: Allen & Unwin.

Lippit, Akira. 2005. *Atomic Light (Shadow Optics)*. Minneapolis: University of Minnesota Press.

LoBrutto, Vincent. 1999. *Stanley Kubrick: A Biography*. New York: Da Capo Press.

Lowenstein, Adam. 2005. *Shocking Representation: Historical trauma, National Cinema, and the Modern Horror Film*. New York: Columbia University Press.

———. 2011. "Spectacle Horror and *Hostel*: Why 'Torture Porn' Does Not Exist." *Critical Quarterly* 53 (1): 42–60.

———. 2015. *Dreaming of Cinema: Spectatorship, Surrealism, and the Age of Digital Media*. New York: Columbia University Press.

Macias, Patrick. 2001. *Tokyoscope: The Japanese Cult Film Companion*. San Francisco: Cadence Books.

Malkiewicz, Kris. 2012. *Film Lighting: Talks with Hollywood's Cinematographers and Gaffers*. 2nd ed. New York: Simon & Schuster.

Manders, Stanley. 2010. "Terror in Technicolor." *American Cinematographer* 91 (2): 68–76.

Marks, Laura U. 2000. *The Skin of the Film: Intercultural Cinema, Embodiment, and the Senses*. Durham/London: Duke UP.

Markus, Andrew L. 1985. "The Carnival of Edo: *Misemono* Spectacles From Contemporary Accounts." *Harvard Journal of Asiatic Studies* 45 (2): 499–541.

Martin, Daniel. 2015. *Extreme Asia: The Rise of Cult Cinema from the Far East*. Edinburgh: Edinburgh University Press.

"Mating Film with Video for 'One from the Heart.'" 1982. *American Cinematographer* 63 (1): 22–24, 92–93.

Matsutani Miyoko. 1986. *Gendai minwa ko*, 5 vols. Tokyo: Tachikaze Shobō.

McDonald, Keiko I. 2000. "Stylistic Experiment: Teshigahara's *The Face of Another*." In *From Book to Screen: Modern Japanese Literature in Films*, 269–286. Armonk: M.E. Sharpe.

McRoy, Jay. 2005a. "Case Study: Cinematic Hybridity in Shimizu Takashi's *Ju-on: The Grudge*." In *Japanese Horror Cinema*, ed. Jay McRoy, 175–183. Honolulu: University of Hawai'i Press.

———, ed. 2005b. *Japanese Horror Cinema*. Honolulu: University of Hawai'i Press.

———. 2008. *Nightmare Japan: Contemporary Japanese Horror Cinema*. Amsterdam/New York: Rodopi.

Mes, Tom. 2001a. "Interview with Kiyoshi Kurosawa." *Midnight Eye*, March 20. http://www.midnighteye.com/interviews/kiyoshi-kurosawa. Accessed 17 Sep 2015.

———. 2001b. "Interview with Takashi Miike." *Midnight Eye*, May 1. http://www.midnighteye.com/interviews/takashi-miike/. Accessed 14 Aug 2016.

———. 2003a. *Agitator: The Cinema of Takashi Miike*. Surrey: FAB Press.

———. 2003b. "Review of *Gozu*." *Midnight Eye*, May 21. http://www.midnighteye.com/reviews/gozu/. Accessed 14 Dec 2015.

———. 2013. *Re-Agitator: A Decade of Writing on Takashi Miike*. Surrey: FAB Press.

———. 2016. "Audio Commentary." *Ōdishon*. Translated as *Audition*. Subtitled Blu-Ray. Directed by Miike Takashi. Shenley: Arrow Video.

Messer, Thomas M. 1971. *Edvard Munch*. New York: H.N. Abrams.

Metropolitan Museum of Art. 1987. *The Renaissance in Italy and Spain*. New York: Metropolitan Museum of Art.

Meuris, Jacques. 2007. *René Magritte: 1898–1967*. Los Angeles: Taschen.

Miike Takashi. 2006. "Audio Commentary for *Box* by Director Takashi Miike." *Three … Extremes*. Subtitled DVD. Directed by Miike Takashi, Park Chanwook, and Fruit Chan. Santa Monica: Lions Gate Entertainment.

———. 2009. "Interview by Film Critic Wade Major." *Gokudō kyōfu daigekijō: Gozu.* Translated as *Gozu.* Subtitled DVD. Directed by Miike Takashi. Burbank: Cinema Epoch.

Mirka, Danuta. 1997. *The Sonoristic Structuralism of Krzysztof Penderecki.* Katowice: Music Academy in Katowice.

———. 2000. "Texture in Penderecki's Sonoristic Style." *Music Theory Online* 6 (1), January. http://www.mtosmt.org/issues/mto.00.6.1/mto.00.6.1.mirka. html. Accessed 7 May 2015.

———. 2001. "To Cut the Gordian Knot: The Timbre System of Krzystof Penderecki." *Journal of Music Theory* 45 (2): 435–456.

Monastra, Peggy. 2000. "Krzysztof Penderecki's *Polymorphia* and *Fluorescences.*" In *The Rosaleen Moldenhauer Memorial: Music History from Primary Sources: A Guide to the Moldenhauer Archives*, ed. Jon Newsom and Alfred Mann, 350–357. Washington, DC: Library of Congress.

Munch, Edvard. *Edvard Munch's Writings.* Digital archive, published by the Munch Museum, MM T 2785-077-080, Dated 1909–1911, Sketchbook. http://emunch.no/TRANS_HYBRIDMM_T2785.xhtml. Accessed 13 Nov 2015.

Munroe, Alexandra. 1994. *Japanese Art After 1945: Scream Against the Sky.* New York: H. N. Abrams.

Nagib, Lúcia. 2006. "Towards a Positive Definition of World Cinema." In *Remapping World Cinema: Identity, Culture and Politics in Film*, ed. Stephanie Dennison and Song Hwee Lim, 30–37. London/New York: Wallflower Press.

Nakamura Yasuo. 1971. *Noh: The Classical Theatre.* Trans. Don Kenny. New York: Walker/Weatherhill.

Nakata Hideo. 1998. *Ringu (Ring).* Tokyo: Tōei.

Nancy, Jean-Luc. 2002. *À l'écoute.* Paris: Galilée.

———. 2007. *Listening.* Trans. Charlotte Mandell. New York: Fordham University Press.

Nietzsche, Friedrich. 2002. *Beyond Good and Evil: Prelude to a Philosophy of the Future.* Trans. Judith Norman. Cambridge/New York: Cambridge University Press.

Nochlin, Linda. 1995. *The Body in Pieces: The Fragment as a Metaphor of Modernity.* New York: Thames and Hudson.

Nussbaum, Martha C. 1995. "Objectification." *Philosophy & Public Affairs* 24 (4): 249–291.

Olson, Donald W., Russell L. Doescher, and Marilynn S. Olson. 2004. "When the Sky Ran Red: The Story Behind *The Scream.*" *Sky & Telescope*, February, 20–35.

Omnisphere 2 Reference Guide. https://support.spectrasonics.net/manual/ Omnisphere2/layer_page/envelopes/index.html. Accessed 2 July 2017.

Oppenheim, Meret. *X-ray of My Skull.* https://www.sfmoma.org/artwork/96.188. Accessed 22 Nov 2015.

Ōshima Kiyoaki. 2010. *J-horā no yūrei kenkyū.* Musashino: Akiyama Shoten.

"Outrage." *Oxford English Dictionary Online.* Oxford University Press. http:// www.oed.com.libproxy.uoregon.edu/view/Entry/133856?result=1&rskey= xKx1ma&. Accessed 9 Mar 2016.

Partridge, Loren W. 2015. *Art of Renaissance Venice 1400–1600.* Oakland: University of California Press.

Paul, Jean. 1960. In *Sämtliche Werke*, ed. Norbert Miller. Munich: Hanser Verlag.

Peirse, Alison, and Daniel Martin, eds. 2013. *Korean Horror Cinema.* Edinburgh: Edinburgh University Press.

Pethő, Ágnes, ed. 2015. *The Cinema of Sensations.* Newcastle upon Tyne: Cambridge Scholars Publishing.

Philips, John. 2006. "*Agencement*/Assemblage." *Theory, Culture & Society* 23 (2–3): 108–109.

Pinch, Trevor, and Frank Trocco. 2002. *Analog Days: The Invention and Impact of the Moog Synthesizer.* Cambridge, MA: Harvard University Press.

Pinedo, Isabel C. 1997. *Recreational Terror: Women and the Pleasures of Horror Film Viewing.* Albany: State University of New York Press.

———. 2014. "Torture Porn: 21st Century Horror." In *A Companion to the Horror Film*, ed. Harry M. Benshoff, 345–362. Chichester/Malden: Wiley Blackwell.

Poe, Edgar Allan. 1982. "William Wilson." In *The Complete Poems and Stories of Edgar Allan Poe, with Selections from His Critical Writings*, 277–292. New York: A. A. Knopf.

Prideaux, Sue. 2005. *Edvard Munch: Behind the Scream.* New Haven: Yale University Press.

Quandt, James. 2007. "Video Essay." *Tanin no kao.* Translated as *Face of Another.* Subtitled DVD. Directed by Teshigahara Hiroshi. Irvington: The Criterion Collection.

———. "*The Face of Another*: Double Vision." *The Criterion Collection.* https:// www.criterion.com/current/posts/592-the-face-of-another-double-vision. Accessed 15 Nov 2016.

Ramirez-Christensen, Esperanza. 2012. "Japanese Poetics." In *The Princeton Encyclopedia of Poetry and Poetics*, ed. Roland Greene et al., 757–760. Princeton: Princeton University Press.

Rank, Otto. 1914. "*Der Doppelgänger.*" In *Imago: Zeitschrift für Anwendung der Psychoanalyse auf die Geisteswissenschaften*, ed. Sigmund Freud, vol. III, 97–164. Leipzig/Vienna/Zürich: Internationaler Psychoanalytischer Verlag.

———. 1971. *The Double: A Psychoanalytic Study*. Trans. Harry Tucker Jr. Chapel Hill: University of North Carolina Press.

Ravetto, Kriss. 2001. *The Unmaking of Fascist Aesthetics*. Minneapolis: University of Minnesota Press.

Rayns, Tony. 2004. "Review of *Gozu.*" *Sight & Sound* 14 (9): 64.

———. 2016. "Damaged Romance: An Appreciation by Tony Rayns." *Ôdishon*. Translated as *Audition*. Subtitled Blu-Ray. Directed by Miike Takashi. Shenley, England: Arrow Video.

Reiser, Stanley Joel. 1978. *Medicine and the Reign of Technology*. Cambridge/ New York: Cambridge University Press.

"Resonance." *Oxford English Dictionary Online*. Oxford University Press. http:// www.oed.com.libproxy.uoregon.edu/view/Entry/163743?redirectedFrom=re sonance&. Accessed 12 Dec 2016.

Richardson, Michael. 2006. *Surrealism and Cinema. Oxford*. New York: Berg.

Richie, Donald. 2005. *A Hundred Years of Japanese Film*. Tokyo: Kodansha International.

Richter, Hans. 1997. *Dada, Art and Anti-Art*. Trans. David Britt. New York: Thames and Hudson.

Riley, Philip J., ed. 1989. *MagicImage Filmbooks Presents Frankenstein*. Absecon: MagicImage Filmbooks.

———. 2010. *Robert Florey's Frankenstein Starring Bela Lugosi*. Albany: BearManor Media.

Roquet, Paul. 2016. *Ambient Media: Japanese Atmospheres of Self*. Minneapolis: University of Minnesota Press.

Rosemont, Penelope. 1998. "Introduction: All My Names Know Your Leap: Surrealist Women and Their Challenge." In *Surrealist Women: An International Anthology*, ed. Penelope Rosemont, xxix–lviii. Austin: University of Texas Press.

Royle, Nicholas. 2003. *The Uncanny*. New York: Routledge.

Rucka, Nicholas. 2005. "The Death of J-Horror?" *Midnight Eye*, December 22. http://www.midnighteye.com/features/the-death-of-j-horror/. Accessed 14 Mar 2017.

Ruddell, Caroline. 2013. *The Besieged Ego: Doppelgangers and Split Identity Onscreen*. Edinburgh: Edinburgh University Press.

Sandro, Paul. 1979. "The Space of Desire in *An Andalusian Dog.*" *1978 Film Studies Annual*, 57–63.

Scahill, Andrew. 2010. "Happy, Empty: On Authorship and Influence in the Horror Cinema of Kiyoshi Kurosawa." *Asian Journal of Literature, Culture and Society* 4 (2): 54–72.

Schaeffer, Pierre. 1966. *Traité des objets musicaux*. Paris: Seuil.

———. 2004. "Acousmatics." In *Audio Culture: Readings in Modern Music*, ed. Christoph Cox and Daniel Warner, 76–81. New York: Continuum.

Scheib, Richard. "Review of the Face of Another." *Moria: Science Fiction, Horror and Fantasy Film Review*. http://moria.co.nz/sciencefiction/face-of-another-1966-tanin-no-kao.htm. Accessed 3 Dec 2015.

Schloss, Karen B., and Stephen E. Palmer. 2015. "Ecological Aspects of Color Preference." In *Handbook of Color Psychology*, ed. Andrew J. Elliot, Mark D. Fairchild, and Anna Franklin, 435–453. Cambridge: Cambridge University Press.

Schneider, Steven Jay. 2004a. "Manifestations of the Literary Double in Modern Horror Cinema." In *Horror Film and Psychoanalysis: Freud's Worst Nightmare*, ed. Steven Jay Schneider, 106–121. Cambridge: Cambridge University Press.

———. 2004b. "Toward and Aesthetics of Cinematic Horror." In *The Horror Film*, ed. Stephen Prince, 131–149. New Brunswick: Rutgers University Press.

Schopenhauer, Arthur. 1988. *Die Welt als Wille und Vorstellung*. Zürich: Haffmans Verlag.

———. 2010. *The World as Will and Representation*. Trans. Judith Norman, Alistair Welchman, and Christopher Janaway. Cambridge/New York: Cambridge University Press.

Schwinger, Wolfram. 1989. *Krzysztof Penderecki: His Life and Work*. Trans. William Mann. London: Schott.

Screech, Tim. 1994. "Japanese Ghosts." *Mangajin*, 40. http://www.mangajin.com/mangajin/samplemj/ghosts/ghosts.htm. Accessed 27 Sep 2014.

Sebald, Hans. 1990. "Review of Norbert Krapf, *Beneath the Cherry Sapling: Legends from Franconia*." *German Studies Review* 13 (2): 312–313.

Semff, Michael, and Anthony Spira. 2006. "Introduction." In *Hans Bellmer*, ed. Michael Semff and Anthony Spira, 9–13. Ostfildern: Hatje Cantz Publishers.

Service, Tom. 2011. "Krzysztof Penderecki: Horror Film Directors' Favourite Composer." *The Guardian*, November 3. http://www.guardian.co.uk/film/2011/nov/03/krzysztof-pendercki-horror-soundtracks-david-lynch/print. Accessed 29 Apr 2015.

Sharp, Jasper. 2009. "Review of *Introduction to Japanese Film*." *Midnight Eye*, March 9. http://www.midnighteye.com/books/introduction-to-japanese-horror-film/. Accessed 14 Apr 2017.

Sharpe, Andrew N. 2010. *Foucault's Monsters and the Challenge of Law.* New York: Routledge.

Shildrick, Margrit. 2002. *Embodying the Monster: Encounters with the Vulnerable Self.* London: Sage.

Short, Robert. 2003. "Un Chien Andalou." In *The Age of Gold: Surrealist Cinema*, ed. Robert Short, 51–101. London: Creation Books.

Spadoni, Robert. 2007. *Uncanny Bodies: The Coming of Sound Film and the Origins of the Horror Genre.* Berkeley: University of California Press.

———. 2014. "Carl Dreyer's Corpse: Horror Film Atmosphere and Narrative." In *A Companion to the Horror Film*, ed. Harry M. Benshoff, 151–167. Chichester/Malden: Wiley Blackwell.

Spence-Jones, H.D.M., ed. 189-?. *The Pulpit Commentary.* New York: Funk & Wagnalls Co.

Stainforth, Gordon. 2015. "The Shining Music—Introductory Note," July. http:// www.gordonstainforth.co.uk/shining-music-intro. Accessed 2 Aug 2017.

———. "*Shining Music Charts.*" http://www.drummerman.net/shining/charts. html. Accessed 23 Aug 2015.

Stewart, Susan. 1993. *On Longing: Narratives of the Miniature, the Gigantic, the Souvenir, the Collection.* Durham/London: Duke University Press.

Stich, Sidra. 1990. *Anxious Visions: Surrealist Art.* Berkeley: University Art Museum.

Stilwell, Robynn J. 2007. "The Fantastical Gap Between Diegetic and Nondiegetic." In *Beyond the Soundtrack: Representing Music in Cinema*, ed. Daniel Goldmark, Lawrence Kramer, and Richard Leppert, 184–202. Berkeley: University of California Press.

Stivale, Charles J. "*Summary of 'Gilles Deleuze's ABC Primer' (L'Abécédaire de Gilles Deleuze, 1988/1995)*," *Part I.* http://www.langlab.wayne.edu/cstivale/d-g/ABC1.html. Accessed 24 Mar 2016.

Storaro, Vittorio. 2013. "The Author of Cinematography; or Rather: The Right to Consider Ourselves Co-Authors of the Cinematographic Image." In *L'arte della cinematografia*, ed. Vittorio Storaro, Bob Fisher, and Lorenzo Codelli, 8–9. Milano: Skira.

Strang, Brent. 2008. "Beyond Genre and Logos: A Cinema of Cruelty in Dodes'ka-den and Titus." *Cinephile: The University of British Columbia's Film Journal* 4: 29–35.

Suarez, Jillian. 2014. "Minotaure: Surrealist Magazine from the 1930s." *Guggenheim.org*, September 25. http://blogs.guggenheim.org/findings/minotaure-surrealist-magazine-1930s/. Accessed 23 Dec 2015.

Sugimoto Yoshio. 2010. *An Introduction to Japanese Society*. 3rd ed. Cambridge: Cambridge University Press.

Sutcliffe, James Helme. 1969. "Devil's Advocate." *Opera News* 33 (27): 15.

Sylvester, David. 1987. *The Brutality of Fact: Interviews with Francis Bacon*. London: Thames & Hudson.

———. 2009. *Magritte*. Brussels: Mercatorfonds.

Takahashi Hiroshi. 2006. "Interview with Producer Hiroshi Takahashi." *Marebito*. Subtitled DVD. Directed by Shimizu Takashi. Los Angeles: Tartan Video.

Teibel, Amy. 2005. "Israel May Use Sound Weapon on Settlers." *USA Today*, June 6. http://usatoday30.usatoday.com/news/world/2005-06-10-israel-soundweapon_x.htm#. Accessed 18 Sep 2015.

"The 25 Best Horror Films of All Time." 2010. *The Guardian*, October 22. http://www.guardian.co.uk/film/2010/oct/22/audition-miike-odishon-horror. Accessed 22 July 2016.

"The Conversation." 1974. *Internet Movie Database*. http://www.imdb.com/title/tt0071360/?ref_=nv_sr_1. Accessed 7 Sep 2015.

Théberge, Paul. 2008. "Almost Silent: The Interplay of Sound and Silence in Contemporary Cinema and Television." In *Lowering the Boom: Critical Studies in Film Sound*, ed. Jay Beck and Tony Grajeda, 51–67. Urbana: University of Illinois Press.

Todts, Herwig. 2008. *James Ensor: Paintings and Drawings from the Collection of the Royal Museum of Fine Arts in Antwerp*. Schoten: BAI.

Tomaszewski, Mieczyslaw. "Orchestral Works Vol. 1 Liner Notes." In Krzysztof Penderecki, *Penderecki: Orchestral Works, Vol. 1/Symphony No. 3/Threnody*, with Antoni Wit and Polish National Radio Symphony, Naxos, 2000, compact disc, liner notes.

Tomoda Yoshiyuki. 2012. *Sengo zen'ei eiga to bungaku: Abe Kōbō x Teshigahara Hiroshi*. Kyoto: Jinbun Shoin.

Tompkins, Joe. 2014. "Mellifluous Terror: The Discourse of Music and Horror Films." In *A Companion to the Horror Film*, ed. Harry M. Benshoff, 186–204. Malden: Wiley Blackwell.

Tsunemitsu Tōru. 1993. *Gakkō no kaidan: Kōshō bungei no tenkai to shosō*. Kyoto: Mineruva Shobō.

Uchiyama Kazuki, ed. 2008. *Kaiki to gensō e no kairo: Kaidan kara J-horā e*. Tokyo: Shinwasha.

Vail, Mark. 2014. *The Synthesizer: A Comprehensive Guide to Understanding, Programming, Playing, and Recording the Ultimate Electronic Music Instrument*. Oxford: Oxford University Press.

Vanoye, Francis. 2004. "Cinemas of Cruelty?" In *Antonin Artaud: A Critical Reader*, ed. Edward Scheer, 178–183. London/New York: Routledge.

Vonnegut, Kurt. *Conversations with Kurt Vonnegut*, Ed. William Rodney Allen. Jackson: University Press of Mississippi, 1988.

Waldby, Catherine. 2000. *The Visible Human Project: Informatic Bodies and Post-Human Medicin*. London: Routledge.

Walker, Alexander. 2001. "The Cutting Edge of Censorship." *Evening Standard*, March 15, 29.

Wallace, Irving, and Amy Wallace. 1978. *The Two*. New York: Simon & Schuster.

Ward, Donald, ed. and trans. 1981. *The German Legends of the Brothers Grimm*, 2 vols. Philadelphia: Institute for the Study of Human Issues.

Washitani Hana. 2008. "*Ringu* sanbusaku to onnatachi no media kūkan: Kaibutsu kasuru 'onna,' muku no 'chichi.'" In *Kaiki to gensō e no kairo: Kaidan kara J-horā e*, ed. Uchiyama Kazuki, 195–223. Tokyo: Shinwasha.

Webber, Andrew J. 1996. *The Doppelgänger: Double Visions in German Literature*. New York: Oxford University Press.

Wee, Valerie. 2014. *Japanese Horror Films and Their American Remakes*. New York: Routledge/Taylor & Francis Group.

Weis, Elisabeth. 1982. *The Silent Scream: Alfred Hitchcock's Sound Track*. Rutherford: Fairleigh Dickinson University Press.

Weis, Elisabeth, and John Belton, eds. 1985. *Film Sound: Theory and Practice*. New York: Columbia University Press.

Weiser-Aall, Lily. 1965. "En studie om vardøger." *Norveg* 12: 73–112.

Weiss, Allen S. 2004. "K." In *Antonin Artaud: A Critical Reader*, ed. Edward Scheer, 151–158. London/New York: Routledge.

Wetmore, Kevin J. 2012. "'Torture Porn' and What It Means to Be American." In *Post-9/11 Horror in American Cinema*, 95–115. New York: Continuum Publishing.

Whale, James. 1931. *Frankenstein*. Universal City: Universal Pictures.

Whittington, William. 2007. *Sound Design & Science Fiction*. Austin: University of Texas Press.

———. 2010. "Acoustic Infidelities: Sounding the Exchanges Between J-Horror and H-Horror Remakes." *Cinephile* 6 (1): 11–19.

Wilcox, Ella Wheeler. 2010. *Poems of Passion*. Los Angeles: Indo-European Publishing.

Wilkinson, Alissa. 2014. "What's With All the Movies About Doppelgängers?" *The Atlantic*, March 14. http://www.theatlantic.com/entertainment/archive/2014/03/whats-with-all-the-movies-about-doppelg-ngers/284413/. Accessed 19 Jan 2015.

Williams, Linda. 1991. "Film Bodies: Gender, Genre, and Excess." *Film Quarterly* 44 (4): 2–13.

Williams, Tony. 2004. "Takashi Miike's Cinema of Outrage." *Cineaction* 64: 54–62.

Winckelmann, Johann Joachim. 2006. *History of the Art of Antiquity*. Trans. Harry Francis Mallgrave. Los Angeles: Getty Research Institute.

Wood, Ghislaine. 2007. *The Surreal Body: Fetish and Fashion*. London: V & A Publications.

WWWJDIC Japanese Dictionary Server, s.v. "*bakeru*." http://nihongo.monash. edu/cgi-bin/wwwjdic?1F. Accessed 3 Dec 2015.

Yokosawa Kazuhiko, Karen B. Schloss, Michiko Asano, and Stephen E. Palmer. 2015. "Ecological Effects in Cross-Cultural Differences Between U.S. and Japanese Color Preferences." *Cognitive Science*, 1–27.

Yoshimoto Mitsuhiro. 1993. "Melodrama, Postmodernism, and Japanese Cinema." In *Melodrama and Asian Cinema*, ed. Wimal Dissanayake, 101–126. Cambridge: Cambridge University Press.

Zimmer, Catherine. 2011. "Caught on Tape? The Politics of Video in the New Torture Film." In *Horror after 9/11: World of Fear, Cinema of Terror*, ed. Aviva Briefel and Sam J. Miller, 83–106. Austin: University of Texas Press.

Index[1]

---

[1] Note: Page numbers followed by 'n' refer to notes.

© The Author(s) 2018

S. T. Brown, *Japanese Horror and the Transnational Cinema of Sensations*, East Asian Popular Culture, https://doi.org/10.1007/978-3-319-70629-0

CPSIA information can be obtained
at www.ICGtesting.com
Printed in the USA
BVHW011847241119
564636BV00006BA/169/P